Complete Handbook of Winning Football Drills

Complete Handbook of Winning Football Drills

DONALD E. FUOSS
California State University, Sacramento

ALLYN AND BACON, INC.
Boston • London • Sydney • Toronto

Library of Congress Cataloging in Publication Data

Fuoss, Donald E.
Complete handbook of winning football drills.

1. Football—Coaching. I. Title.
GV956.6.F85 1984 796.332′07′7 83-15706
ISBN 0-205-08071-5

Printed in the United States of America

10 9 8 7 6 5 4 3 2 1 87 86 85 84 83

to Christopher Brett
and Kimberly Kyle

Contents

Foreword *xxiii*
Preface *xxv*
Legend *xxxi*

PART I Practice Drill Planning and Organization for Effective Teaching–Coaching 1

Chapter 1 The Importance and Purpose of Drill 3
Purpose and Objective of Drill 3
Types of Drills 4
Selection of Drills 6

Chapter 2 Drill Guides and Suggestions for Effective Teaching-Coaching and Player Learning-Performance 9
Accomplish the Objective of the Drill 9
Keep the Drill Simple 9
Select Drills with More Than a Single Reaction 10
Give the Progressive Points of Concentration 10
Inform Your Players of the Purpose of the Drill 10

Limit the Duration of Repetitions of the Drill 11
Present the Drill with a Positive Approach 11
Emphasize Running Drills 11
Use a Variety of Drills 12
Work with a Few Players 12
Do Not Coach Both Offense and Defense at the Same Time 12
Demonstrate the Drill Properly 13
Arrange the Demonstration Advantageously 13
Commence the Drill with One Word—Eliminate Verbosity 14
Insist on a "Good Football Position" at All Times 14
Habitize by Using a Starting Count and a Whistle 14
Use the "Buddy" System for Teaching 14
Select Competitive Game-like Drills 15
Use Drills to Build Morale, Pride, and Enthusiasm 15
Use Names to Identify Drills 15
Use a Marked-off Area for Drills 15
Use Drills as a Means to an End 16
Give Adequate Consideration to All of the Fundamentals 16
You Must Know and Teach Adherence to the Rules 16
Adhere to the Laws of Learning and to Educationally Sound Principles of Teaching-Coaching 17

Chapter 3 Practice Schedule Organization Guides and Suggestions, Including Warm-Up Drills and Exercises 19

Plan and Organize Your Time and Practice Program 19
Practice Schedule Breakdown 20
A Detailed Breakdown of the Warm-up and Individual Periods 22

1. Stationary Running Drill 24
2. Stomach-Chest Puffing Drill 24
3. Hamstring Stretching Drill 24
4. Front Stretching Drill 24

5. Knee Stretching Drill 25
6. Hip Stretching Drill 25
7. Bouncing Drill 25
8. Hip Whipping Drill 26
9–10. Working the Knees Drills (progressive) 26
11. All-Over Stretching Drill 26
12. Neck Stretching Drill 27
13. Shoulder Stretching Drill 27
14. Rotating Stretching Drill 27
15. Opposite Hand-Opposite Foot Drill 28
16. Push-ups Drill 28
17. Bouncing Drill 28
18. Bicycle Drill 29
19. Abdominal Tenser Drill 29
20. Knee Raise Drill 29
21. Wrestler's Bridge Drill 30
22. Hill Climb Drill 30
23. Reach Way Back Drill 30
24. Toe Raisers and Quarter-Knee Bends Drill 31
25. Jumping Jacks Drill 31

Organizing the Four-Stations Drills 32
Individual-Group or Combination-Team Periods 40

PART II Drills for Teaching-Coaching Proper Running Form Basics, Agility, and Reaction 43

Chapter 4 Teaching-Coaching Proper Running Form and "Good" Football Position Basics and Principles 45

Body Control 46
Proper Running Form Basics 46
The Basics of a "Good" Football Position 49

Chapter 5 Agility and Reaction Drills 51

1. High Stepper or Toe Dance Drill 52
2. Carioca or Grapevine Drill 53
3. Straddle Drill 54
4. Cross-Over Drill 54
5. Turn Around and Sprint Drill 55

6. Spot Running or Footfire Drill 55
7. Stationary High-Knee Running Drill 56
8. Forward High-Knee Running Drill 56
9. Forward-Backward-Sprint Drill 56
10. Running Backward Drill 57
11. Grab Grass or Scoop Drill 57
12. Forward Rolls (Somersault) Drill 58
13. Broadjumping-Somersault-Sprint Drill 58
14. Broadjump-Somersault-Wave Drill 59
15. Somersault-Shed-Wave Drill 59
16. Somersault and Tackle Drill 60
17. Follow-the-Leader Drill No. 1 60
18. Follow-the-Leader Drill No. 2 61
19. Lateral Wave Drill 61
20. Crab or Scramble Drill 62
21. Shoulder Rolls Drill 62
22. Seat Rolls and Crab Drill 63
23–26. Log Roll or Figure 8 Drills 63
    23. Three-Man Log Roll Drill 63
    24. Log Roll and Shed Drill 63
    25. Log Roll and Tackle Drill 63
    26. Double Log Roll, Shed, Pursue, and Tackle Drill 63
27. Spinning Drill 64
28. Quarter-Circle-Crab Drill 65
29. Quarter-Eagle, Sprint-Wave Drill 65
30. Down-Up or Quick Grass Drill 66
31. Forward Run-Somersault-Wave Drill 66
32. Cover Ball-Fumble Drill 67
33–35. Running Ropes or Rope Maze Drills 68
    33. Single Stepping Rope Drills 68
    34. Two Feet Together Rope Drills 68
    35. Two Feet Together Lateral Hop Drill 68
36. Softball Drill 70
37. Hip Opener Drill 70
38. Flash Drill 71
39–40. Footwork Rope Jumping Drills 71
    39. Jump Rope Drill 71
    40. Jump Rope 100 or 440 Yards Drill 72
41. Over and Back Bag Jumping Drill 72
42. Step Up-Down Drill 72
43. Hopscotch Drills 73

44. Squirm or Circling Drill 74
45. Crab-Straddle Bag Drill 75
46. Four Corners-Cover Ball Drill 76
47–48. Jingle Jangle Drills 77
47. Lateral Jingle Jangle Drill 77
48. Jingle Jangle Conditioning Drill 77
49. Agility and/or Reaction Drills 79

PART III Drills for Teaching-Coaching Offensive Fundamentals and Techniques 81

Chapter 6 Offensive Line Drills 83
1. Stance and Starts Board Drill 84
2. One-on-One Board Drills 85
3–7. Two-Man Sled Drills 86
3–4. Six-Point and Four-Point Explosion or Shoulder Shoot Drills 86
5. Drive-Up Drill 87
6. Drive Block Sled Drill 87
7. Belly Slammer Drill 87
8. Four Positions Bag Drill 88
9. One-on-One Shoulder Block Drills 88
10–11. Board and Sled Trap Drills 89
10. Board Trap Drill 89
11. Sled Trap Drill 89
12–14. Pulling Drills 90
12. Short and Long Trap Drills 90
13. Sealing Inside Drill 90
14. Downfield Blocking Drill 90
15. One-on-One Air Bag Drill 91
16. Balance or Belt Buckle Drill 91
17. Pass Rusher-in-the-Middle Drill 92
18. Blocker-in-the-Middle Drill 93
19. Burma Road Blocking Drill 94
20. Mass Blocking Drill 95
21. Around-and-Through Downfield Blocking Drill 95
22. Three-S or Splits-Stance-Starts Drill 96
23. One-on-One (Three-on-Three) Challenge or All-Purpose Drill 98
24–27. Segmented Offensive Line Drills 99
24. Center and One Guard Drills 99

25. Center and Both Guards Drills 99
26. Guard and Tackle, and Tackle and End Drills 99
27. Guard, Tackle, and End Drills 99
28. Inside (Offensive) Drill 101
29. Offensive Half-Line Drill 103
30. Offensive Line Blocking Drill 104
31. Offensive Scrimmage Drills 104
32. Pass Protection Versus Defensive Stunts Drill 106
33. Pass Protection and Coverage Drill 108
34–37. Seven-Man Sled Drills 109
34. Seven-Man Explosion Drill 109
35. Team Starts or Take-Off Drill 109
36. In-and-Out Shoulder Block Drill 109
37. Repeat Drill 110
38. Bag-Circle Shoulder Block Drill 110
39. Big Bag Drill 111
40. Monster or Chute Drills 112
41. Huddle and Alignment Drill 114

Chapter 7 Center Play Drills 117
1. On-the-Line Drill 118
2. One-on-One Rotation Drill 119
3. Reverse (Unwinding) Technique Drill 119
4. Weighted Football Drill 120
5. Extra Flip Drill 120
6. Center's Loosening and Stretching Drill 121
7. Hand-Slap Drill 121
8. Overhead Passing Drill 121
9. Underhand Passing Drill 122
10. Bull's-Eye Drill 122
11. Center's Semi-Spread Punt Bag Drill 122
12. Hustle Drill 124
13. Center Drills 126

Chapter 8 Passing and Receiving Drills 127
1. Passer's Wrist Drill 128
2. Parallel Passing Drill 129
3. Passer's Circle Drill 130
4. Quick Pass Drill 130

5. Passer's Clock Drill 131
6. In-the-Cup and Scramble Drills 132
7. Passer's Bull's-Eye Drill 132
8. Canvas-Net Passing Drill 133
9–10. Quick Pass-Receiver Drills 134
   9. Passer's Quick Pass Drill 134
   10. Receiver's Quick Pass or Nuisance Drill 134
11. Passer's Decision Drills 135
12. Receiver's Circle Drill 136
13. Receiver's Quick Hands Drill 137
14. Receiver's Figure 8 Drill 137
15. Receiver's Bad Pass Drill 138
16. Receiver's (Defender's) Three-Man Square Drill 139
17. Receiver's Dog-Fight Drill 140
18. Outmaneuver-the-Defender Drill 140
19. Pass Cuts Drill 141
20. Sideline Cut or Square Out Drills 142
21. Receiver's Releasing Drill 143
22–23. Skeleton Pass Offense Versus Pass Defense Drills 144
   22. Pass Offense Versus Three-Deep Secondary with Linebackers (4–4, 6–2, Split 6, 5–3) 144
   23. Pass Offense Versus Box-Wing Secondary with Linebackers (5–2, 4–3, 3–4, 6–1) 144
24. Running Pass or Option Run-Pass Drill 145
25. No. 1 Versus No. 2 Skeleton Pass Offense-Defense Drill 145
26. Roll-out (Sprint-out)/Throwback Pass Drill 147
27. One-Handed Catch Circle Drill 148
28. Receiver's (Defender's) Crossbar Drill 148
29. Receiving and Downfield Blocking Drill 149
30. Short and Long Arch Passing Drills 150
31. Pitch-Catch Drill 150
32. Passer's Warm-up Drill 151
33. Scramble or "May Day" Drill 152
34. Passer's Reaction Drill 153
35. Passer's Off-Balance Drill 153

36. Receiver's Off-Balance Drill 154
37. Passer-Receiver Pitch-Catch Drill 154
38. Wide-outs (Flankers) Alignment Drills 155
39. The "Passing Tree" (Routes-Patterns) Drills 157
40. Globetrotter or Quick Fingers Drills 160
41. Offensive Scrimmage (Passing) Drills 160

Chapter 9 Offensive Backfield Drills 161

1. Chain Ball Handling Drill 162
2. Circle Ball Handling Drill 163
3. Back's Blocking Drill 163
4. Controlled Pass Protection Blocking Drill 165
5. Back's Pass Protection Blocking Drill 165
6. Mend-the-Cup Drill 167
7. Shake-the-Tackler or Evasive Running Drill 167
8. Evasive Running Circle Drill 168
9. Running-the-Square Drill 169
10. Zig-Zag Running Drill 169
11. Ball Carrier's Sideline Drill 170
12. Gauntlet Drill 171
13. Circle Gauntlet Drill 172
14. Obstacle Course Drills 172
15. Two-Man Sled Shoulder Drive And Pivot Drill 174
16. One-on-One Challenge Drill 175
17. Hare-and-Hound Drill 176
18. Roll or Sprint-Out and Run Drill 176
19. Follow Your Blocker Drill 177

20–21. Skeleton Offense Drills 178
- 20. Ball Handling Drill 178
- 21. Skeleton Versus Live Perimeter or Outside Drill 178

22. Follow-the-Ball Drill 178
23. Ten (Twenty or Thirty) Yards-and-In Drill 180
24. Up, Over, and In, or TD Drill 181
25. Running Back (Tailback) Bag Drill 181

26. Running Ropes and Hand-Off Drill 183
27. Offensive Scrimmage Drills 185

PART IV Drills for Teaching-Coaching Defensive Fundamentals and Techniques 187

Chapter 10 Defensive Line Drills 189
1–4. One-Versus-One Drills 190
1. Stance and Alignment Drill 190
2. Block Protection Drills 191
3. Forearm or Shoulder Lift Drill 191
4. Reaction Drill 192
5–7. Two-Man Sled Drills 192
5. Forearm Left and Reaction Drill 192
6. Hand or Forearm Shiver and Reaction Drill 192
7. Hit and Reaction Drill 193
8. Explosion or One-Versus-Two Drills 194
9. Around-the-Circle Hitting Drill 195
10. One-Versus-Three Drills 195
11. Defensive Reaction Machine Drills 196
12. Two-Versus-Three Drills 197
13–15. Defensive Line Drills 198
13. Three-Versus-Five Drills 198
14. Five-Versus-Seven Drills 198
15. Six-Versus-Seven Drills 198
16. Inside (Defensive) Drill 199
17. Defensive Half-Line Drill 200
18–19. Defensive Line Drills 201
18. Seven-Versus-Seven Drill 201
19. Seven-Versus-Eight Drill 201
20. Jumping Defensive Alignments Drill 202
21. Pursuit Drill 203
22. Sideline Pursuit Drill 203
23. Pass Rush-and-Peel Drill 204
24. Pass Rush Deflection Drill 206
25. Leverage Drill 207
26. Three-on-Three (One-on-One) Challenge Drill 207

27–29. Defensive Scrimmage Drills 209
27. Goal Line (6–5) Defense Drill 209
28. Slow Whistle Drill 209
29. Special or Critical Situations and "Fringe" Drills 209
30–33. Seven-Man Sled Drills 210
30. Forearm or Hand Shiver Drill 210
31. Forearm Lift or Flipper Drill 210
31. Roll-Out or Spin-Out Drill 210
33. Team Reaction Drill 211
34. Defensive Bucker Board Drill 212
35. Gap Charge-Bag Drill 213
36. Defensive Line Drills 213

Chapter 11 Linebacking Drills 215
1. Lateral Run Bag Drill 216
2. Backward and Forward Zig-Zag Bag Drill 217
3. Square Bag Drill 218
4. Combo Zig-Zag and Lateral Run Bag Drill 219
5. Combo Lateral Over and Around Run Bag Drill 219
6. Bag Wave Drill 220
7. Key-Reaction Drills 221
8. Show Head-Maintain Alignment Drill 222
9–11. Progressive Hitting Drills 222
9. Hit-Hit-Hit Drill 222
10. Hit-Shuffle-Hit Drill 223
11. Ricochet and Triangle Drills 224
12. Key-React-Tackle Drill 224
13. Wham or Divide Drill 225
14. Bull-in-the-Ring Shed Drill 226
15. Knight-the-Linebacker Drill 227
16. Ward-Off Leverage or Outside Shed Drill 228
17. Inside Shed Drill 229
18. Eye-Opener or Outside Shed Drill 230
19–28. Pass Defense Drills 230
19. Going-for-the-Ball Drill 230
20. Back-Up and Going-for-the-Ball Drill 231
21. Going-to-the-Spot Drill 232

22. Five Spots Drill 233
23. Fight-Back Drill 234
24. Fight-Up Drill 234
25. Chugging Receivers Drill 235
26. Man-for-Man Coverage Drill 236
27. Defender's Quick Hands Drill 237
28. Defender's Net Drill 239
29. Up, Over, but Not In, or No TD, Drill 239
30. Linebacking Drills 240

Chapter 12 Defensive Secondary Drills 241

1. Defensive Wave Drill 242
2. Run-the-Line Drill 243
3. Mirror Quickness Drill 244
4. Sprint-Back Interception Drill 245
5. Forward-Backward-Diagonal Drill 246
6. Straight-Ahead Interception Drill 246
7. Aggressive Interception Drill 247
8. Aggressive Live Interception Drill 245
9. Break-Off Interception Drill 249
10. Angle Interception Drill 250
11–14. Tip Interception Drills 251
    11. Straight-Ahead Tip Drill 251
    12. Stationary (Manager) Tip Drill 251
    13. Criss-Cross Tip Drill 251
    14. Side Tip Drill 251
15. Combat Tip Drill 252
16. Defender's (Receiver's) Crossbar Drill 253
17. Defender's (Receiver's) Square Drill 253
18. Figure 8 Interception Drill 254
19. Hash Mark Drill 256
20. Roll-Back Drill 257
21. Secondary's Back-Up Drill 257
22. Deep-Middle-Shallow Drill 258
23. Dog Fight or Position-on-Receiver Drill 260
24. Overlap Drill 261
25. Reaction and Rotation Drill 261
26. Big Tip Drill 263
27. Team Reaction Drill 263

28. Two-on-One or Release Drill 264
29. Stretch or Three-Deep Zone Drill 266
30–31. Defensive Perimeter Versus Skeleton Offense Drills 267
30. Skeleton Pass Defense-Offense Drill 267
31. Outside (Defensive) Drill 267
32. Defensive Secondary Drills 269

Chapter 13 Tackling Drills 271
1. Straight-On Form Tackling Drill 272
2. Sprint Tackling Drill 273
3. Angle Form Tackling Drill 274
4. Back-to-Back Form Tackling Drill 275
5. Supine Tackling Drill 276
6. Shoulder Roll Tackling Drill 276
7. Somersault Tackling Drill 277
8. Wave-Shed-Tackle Drill 278
9. Leader Wave-Tackle Drill 279
10. Circle-Escape Tackling Drill 280
11–12. In-the-Hole Tackling Drills 280
11. One-Versus-One Tackling Drill 280
12. Two-Versus-Two Tackling Drill 280
13. Open-Field Tackling Drill 1 281
14. Open-Field Tackling Drill 2 282
15–16. Sideline Tackling Drills 282
15. Tackler Versus Ball Carrier 282
16. Tackler Versus Blocker and Ball Carrier Drill 282
17. Lateral Fill Tackling Drill 284
18. Ward-Off Leverage Tackling Drills 284
19. Three-on-Three (One-on-One) Challenge Drill 285
20. Across-the-Square Tackling Drill 286
21. Bag Tackling Drill 287
22. Tipper-Tackler Drill 288
23–25. Two-Man Sled Tackling Drills 289
23. Close-Up Tackling Drill 289
24. Sprint Tackling Drill 289
25. Sled-Bags Tackling Drill 290
26. "Bounce" Form Tackling Drill 291
27. Tackling Drills 292

PART V Offensive and Defensive Drills for Teaching-Coaching the Signal Callers, and the Kicking Game 293

Chapter 14 Drills for Teaching-Training Offensive and Defensive Signal Callers 295
Training the Signal Callers 297
Methods and Drills for Training the Signal Callers 298
1. Starting Count-Hand Clap Drill 299
2. Slides or Tranparencies Drill 300
3. Film-Loops Drills 300
4. Flash Cards Drill 300
5. Defensive and Offensive Testing Drills 301
6. Skeleton Drills 310
7. Paper-and-Pencil and Blackboard Drills 311
8. Film Study and Analysis Drill 311
9. Game Study and Analysis Drill 314
10. Offensive and Defensive Game Plan Drills 318
11. Offensive and Defensive Check Drills 318
12. Scrimmage-Scoring Zone Offense Drill 319
13. Scrimmage-Danger Zone Offense Drill 319
14. Scrimmage-Touchdown Sequence or Clutch Offense Drill 320
15. Scrimmage-Stop (Kill-the-Clock) Drill 321
16. Scrimmage-Delay Offense or Run-out-the-Clock Drill 321
17. Scrimmage-Racehorse or Go-Go-Go Offense Drill 322
18. Scrimmage-Giving-Up-a-Safety Drill 323
19. Third-Down Calls Drill 323
20. Waste Down Drill 324

Chapter 15 Offensive and Defensive Kicking Game Drills 325
Drills for the Punter 326
1. Punter's Loosening and Stretching Drill 326
2. Stance and Balance Drill 326
3. Quarter-and-Half-Turn Balancing Drills 327
4. Kicking-Balancing Drill 329
5. Catch and Position the Ball Drill 330
6. Hold and Drop the Ball Drill 330
7. Ball on the Foot Drill 330
8. Walk-Through Drill 331
9. Control Drill 332
10. Self-Retrieving Punting Drill 332
11. Towel or Flag Drill 333
12. Pressure Drills 333
13. Wet Football Drill 335
Offensive and Defensive Kicking Game Drills 336
14–15. Tight Punt Alignment and Protection (Blocking Rules) Drills 336
14. Tight Punt Alignment and Protection Drills 336
15. Spread Punt Alignment and Protection Drills 336
16–17. Punt Alignment, Protection, and Coverage Drills 338
16. Tight Punt Coverage Drill 338
17. Spread Punt Coverage Drill 338
18. Down 10-and-In Punt Coverage Drill 339
19. Punt Return-Upright Dummies Drill 341
20. Punt Return Drills 341
21. Twin Safeties Punt Return Drill 343
22. Combination Punt Coverage-Return-Pass Receiving Drill 344
23. Punting-Conditioning Squad Drill 345
24. Punt Coverage-Return-Tackle Drill 346
25–26. Individually Blocking the Kick Drills 347
25. Blocking the Punt Drill 347
26. Blocking the Placement Attempt Drill 347

27–28. Team Schemes Blocking the Kick Drills 349
27. Schemes for Blocking the Punt Drill 349
28. Schemes for Blocking the Placement Attempt Drill 349
29–31. Kick-Off Alignment and Coverage Drills 351
29. Regular Kick-Off Alignment and Coverage Drills 351
30. Kicking-Off from the Hash Mark Drill 351
31. Recovering the Short (On-Side) Kick Drill 351
32–34. Kick-Off Alignments and Return Drills 354
32. Wedge (Middle) Return Drill 354
33. Middle (Cross-Block) and Sideline Return Drills 354
34. Defensing the Short (On-Side) Kick Drill 354
Drills for the Place Kicker 359
35. Place Kicking Drills 359
36. Alignment, Protection and Coverage Place Kick Drill 360
Additional Situational Kicking Game Drills 361

Foreword

I am pleased to have the opportunity to review and comment on *The Complete Handbook of Winning Football Drills* by Dr. Donald E. Fuoss. Some years ago, Don Fuoss and I were assistant coaches together at a major college that had a nationally ranked winning football program, before our career paths parted and each moved on respectively to head collegiate football coaching positions at other institutions. Therefore, I've known Don and have been aware of his coaching and writing credits for a number of years.

Owing to his background, Don is well qualified to author football books. He has been a winning head football coach with undefeated seasons at both the high school and collegiate levels. He has lectured at approximately eighty clinics throughout the United States and Canada, and has authored more than eighty articles for the professional journals and magazines, mostly on technical aspects of football. All of his previously authored books have been well received and widely read by coaches. This book, Don's tenth to date, is likely to have even greater acceptance and appeal because football coaches at all levels are always interested in acquiring good drills for teaching-training purposes. The author is highly knowledgeable, articulate, and he writes well. Coaches understand Don because he writes and talks in the language of football coaches.

This book fills a need. Several hundred drills are categorized according to the *purpose* of each under various offensive and defensive phases, so that it is extremely easy to locate numerous drills for teaching-coaching pass offense, pass defense, offensive line play, etc. The *procedure* for each drill follows, so the drill will be properly conducted. Each drill concludes with important *coaching points*, and often illustrative diagrams, so that football coaches will get the most out of utilizing the drill properly. Each phase of the game of football is covered in depth.

It would not be inaccurate or a misnomer to refer to this book as a complete *encyclopedia* of football drills. It's an excellent reference source; a comprehensive and detailed collection of good football drills in a single volume.

Similarly, it would not be inappropriate for the publisher to include "The Best" . . . *Winning Football Drills* in the title. All of the drills, even the old standby ones, are the best that are used presently by high school, college, and professional football coaches. It is obvious the drills have been collected from different sources, including many from winning football programs and coaching staffs.

This book is a single source of collated football drills well written by a longtime "student" of the game who has an analytical mind and a good technical knowledge of football. Any coach would do well to read and study Fuoss' material, and should find this book a beneficial teaching aid. It is a welcome addition to the football coach's library.

Probably few people in or outside of the coaching profession have published as much about the game of football as Dr. Don Fuoss. It is a genuine pleasure for me to endorse and praise both the author and his latest publication, *The Complete Handbook of Winning Football Drills*. Both are winners!

Ron Meyer
Head Football Coach
New England Patriots

Preface

While football may be thought of as a game of strategy and tactics, reduced to its basic components it is a game of movement and the execution of the fundamental skills of running, blocking, tackling, passing, receiving and kicking. Other things being equal, proficiency in the fundamentals of the game is the winning edge in athletics. The successful coach teaches sound fundamentals, and the successful team is one that is well grounded in sound offensive and defensive fundamentals of the game. Probably the most important basic element in coaching, however, is one's approach to teaching. Successful coaches are effective teachers. It is not necessarily *how much* you teach your players, but *how effectively* your players learn to perform what you have taught. According to psychologists, learning occurs when there is a relatively permanent change in behavior, which usually occurs as the result of experience or practice. Functional drills are an important part of the coaching-learning process.

The purpose and scope of this book is to present the most comprehensive single source available of accepted football drills for teaching and developing the skills and techniques of the game. If a player cannot execute the fundamental skills or cannot make them a spontaneous part of his play, he will never be an outstanding performer. The best players perform the proper fundamentals and techniques reflexively as the result of repetitive drill. Football is not just a matter of theory. Unless a technique works under game conditions, it does not add to successful team play.

The objective in coaching is to create in practice sessions the various situations your players will face in a game, and then to drill until your players can react reflexively and instinctively to the different situations.

Good game performance is likely to be the result of well-organized and frequently practiced drills. Since there are hundreds, possibly even a thousand or more drills available from which to choose, a coach's problem becomes one of selecting the proper drills to accomplish the desired objectives for effective teaching-learning.

Careful consideration should be given to your selection of drills. A drill may be a "good" one for a particular coach, but of limited or no value to another coach. Decide what your team needs, and drills will be more wisely selected. A drill must be viewed in relation to its proper context to the game of football. The type and selection of a particular drill, and the amount of time you devote to it in your practice schedule, may be objectively decided by perusing the *purpose* of the drill and then making the following determinations:

- *Are we going to use what this particular drill teaches?*
- *How much are we going to derive from this particular drill?*
- *How much are we going to use it in a game?*

Succinctly, a coach must drill for a purpose and select drills that meet that purpose.

The format of this book is to present numerous selected drills for teaching all of the fundamental skills and techniques of the game. After a brief introductory section at the beginning of the chapter, each drill is presented as follows: purpose, organizational procedure, coaching points. Many of the drills are illustrated by diagrams.

The book is divided into five sections. Part I consists of three chapters on the importance and purpose of drills. Several dozen drill and practice guides and suggestions are presented. If adhered to, they will result in more effective teaching-coaching and player learning-performance.

Given that a player who does not move well most likely will be ineffective in the other basic skills, especially blocking and tackling, running or movement might well be considered the most important of the basic skills. Every athlete should learn how to run correctly. Most anyone can be taught to run at least a little faster if he has the desire to do so. Therefore, Part II consists of two chapters dealing with drills for teaching proper running techniques and for developing agility and reaction. Football quickness is very important and can be taught.

Part III, consisting of four chapters, deals with drills for teaching-coaching offensive line and backfield techniques and the fundamentals of blocking, passing and receiving, and running with the football.

Part IV, also consisting of four chapters, is a compilation of drills for teaching-coaching the defensive fundamentals and techniques of line play, linebacking, secondary play, and tackling.

Since most games are won by well-planned, well-practiced reactions to tactical and situational variables, and numerous games are lost as the result of improper responses to the same situations, in Part V a separate chapter is included for teaching-coaching the offensive and defensive signal callers. Similarly, the concluding chapter deals with drills for teaching-coaching offensive and defensive kicking game fundamentals and techniques.

At no time in the compilation of material for this book was the objective to acquire a specified number of drills such as 350, 450, 700, or whatever, although many more could have been included merely by modifying and varying drills, or by including drills of lesser value. Some drills are obviously better than others. No attempt has been made to present the drills in a progressive order of importance, as this would be an impossible task. The *purpose of the drill* is the determining factor in its placement in the book, although the same drill might well be employed to teach different fundamentals, techniques, or a segment of the game of football. Drill and practice guides and suggestions are offered in Chapter 2.

The material presented in this book has been derived from literally hundreds of sources. No effort has been made to identify specific drills as "belonging to" or "invented by" or "used by" a particular "name" coach, team, or institution, since affixing rightful ownership and proper credit would be an impossibility. Also, it would be a waste of time from the author's viewpoint since the focus is on functional drills for effective teaching-coaching, not on "name dropping" which teams or coaches utilize specific drills. Practically *all* well-coached football teams utilize many of the drills included in this book because the drills incorporate the fundamental skills, techniques, and segments of the game of football that coaches wish to have their teams perform effectively and efficiently.

Information and materials have been derived from all levels of competition, including some from "name" coaches with outstanding football reputations. However, as explained, "names" are not utilized. Affix your own "names" or coin your own terms to identify specific drills as "yours." Some coaches undoubtedly have done this, merely changing the name of particular drills to their own choosing. Only the name has changed; the purpose of the drill remains the same.

From a personal standpoint, the materials presented herein are the result of having been a member of the coaching profession for thirty years, more than twenty of which were as an active head or assistant football coach at the university, college, and high school levels of competition; having attended to date approximately 150 football clinics, including having lectured at approximately 80 clinics and football seminars throughout the United States and Canada; having sat through an undetermined number of staff meetings and football "bull" sessions where techniques, skills, plays, segments of the game, and other aspects of football have been analyzed and discussed in minute detail; having contributed approximately 80 technical articles to professional journals and magazines in the field of football coaching; having authored six books and co-authored three others, plus studying and analyzing the contributions of numerous other author-coaches; and having been a "student" of the fascinating game of football for three and a half decades.

Older, experienced football coaches, with longevity in the profession undoubtedly will recognize the drill format in this book as the same as the one I authored some years ago while an assistant coach on a major university football staff in the Big Ten. That particular drills book was extremely popular, remaining as one of the top five all-time bestsellers in the Coaches' Book Club for almost fifteen years before it went out of print. The popular format of purpose, procedures, and coaching points has been retained in this enlarged, updated book of drills, as it cannot be improved upon. The assumption is that coaches want a quick, ready reference for teaching-coaching so their players do not become bored and unmotivated as the result of engaging in the same drills daily. This book should accomplish that purpose.

It has been stated, "Football is a game of many skills put together successfully. . . ." This book presents drills for teaching-coaching those fundamental skills, techniques, and segments of the game that are an inherent, integral part of sound, basic, winning football. It is applicable to *all* levels of football competition and will be useful to the experienced and the novice coach and player.

ACKNOWLEDGMENTS

Grateful appreciation is herewith expressed to all persons who shared in the preparation of this book. No claim of originality is made for much of the material contained in the book, garnered from coaching experience, sources, football friends, colleagues and acquaintances over the past thirty-five years, as explained in the Preface. The interpretations and applications, however, are my responsibility.

While the author of a book may be accorded the recognition and credit, usually the publication is the result of a team effort since the process is extended and all aspects must be coordinated. While a grateful "thank you" is inadequate, it is expressed with genuine sincerity and heartfelt appreciation to each member of the "team" with whom I have worked. Melissa O'Meara typed the manuscript, and this was not an easy task since she had to decipher my handwritten scribbled materials and then try to interpret unfamiliar football terminology so all of it made sense. Jim Montich assisted in the preparation of the numerous diagrams utilized herein. Superscript Associates "polished" and edited the final manuscript for publication. Hiram Howard and Jack Stone of Allyn and Bacon not only recruited me to author this and other books, but their encouragement and patience are most appreciated because this project was not a small undertaking.

To achieve any degree of success, a coach's family must be team members, too. Loving appreciation is expressed to my wife, Fran, who for thirty-five years always has encouraged me to strive for excellence in pursuing anything I have ever undertaken, and to our daughter, Donna, mother of the two youngsters to whom this book is dedicated, for their continued love, assistance, and unfailing support.

Donald E. Fuoss

LEGEND

○ Offensive Player
● Ball Carrier
⊕ Center
⊘ Pulling Lineman (or Key Blocker)
Ⓟ Passer
Ⓧ Split or Flexed End (wide-out)
Ⓨ Tight End
Ⓩ Flanker Back (wide-out)
Ⓡ Running Back or Tailback
Ⓕ Fullback
Ⓚ Kicker (punter or place kicker)
Ⓒ Coach
Ⓜ Manager

| E | T | G | ⊕ | G | T | E | "On Lines"

——————→
— — — — — —→ Path of Player
———‖———→ Backfield Fake
∿∿∿∿∿∿→ Backfield Motion
- - - - - - - - - - - -→ Forward Pass

▽ Defensive Lineman
▽(E) Defensive End
▽(T) Defensive Tackle
▽(N) Defensive Noseman
▽ Linebacker (strong, middle, weak)
X Secondary Defender (safety, cornerback, halfback)
□ Large Upright Dummy
■ ▬ Vertical or Horizontal Dummy (placed on side on the ground)
• Rubber Cones

XXXXXBBBBB—Kick-off/Kick Return Symbols

PART I

Practice Drill Planning and Organization for Effective Teaching-Coaching

1

The Importance and Purpose of Drill

While football may be thought of as a game of strategy and tactics, reduced to its basic components it is a game of movement and the execution of the fundamental skills of running, blocking, tackling, passing, receiving, and kicking. Other things being equal, proficiency in fundamentals is the winning edge in athletics. Winning teams are made up of players well versed in the fundamental skills. These skills are developed through constant repetitive practice or drill of the various offensive and defensive fundamentals and techniques through which desired habits are formed. Performing skills correctly as the result of effective teaching-coaching, or performing them *almost* correctly as the result of ineffective learning, usually means the difference between success and failure in athletic competition. Learning how to perform correctly the fundamental skills and techniques of the game is one of several reasons for the necessity of drill, since they are usually taught most effectively through drills.

PURPOSE AND OBJECTIVE OF DRILL

Since the situation changes every second the football is in play, an objective of drill is to develop the coordination of the athlete's eye, mind, and body so he can react reflexively without delay or conscious thought to each situation that arises. The athlete who is successfully drilled to react in this manner acquires "football sense" and usually optimizes his potential. Not infrequently he becomes an outstanding performer.

Drills will aid in developing and reinforcing a player's confidence and poise. The more often a skill is performed correctly, the more positive and confident a player becomes in his performance under competent coaching. Many players do not have a great deal of ability, but develop into competent performers through repetitive drills. In time they learn to perform skills and techniques more naturally. Confidence is developed through steady, concentrated effort to perform correctly. The athlete who does not believe in himself will never rise above mediocrity in his performance. Personnel is molded into a competently performing football team only through constant practice, drill, and diligence until the fundamentals of the game become second nature. A team well grounded in sound fundamentals is difficult to defeat and will consistently prove to be in the thick of any game.

No phase of coaching is more important or more difficult than slotting players in their proper position. Through drills you can more accurately evaluate a player's ability, coordination, reaction, agility, and coachability. At the same time a player is more likely to recognize his own weaknesses and is thereby in a better position to evaluate himself and his ability. Under such conditions a player is more apt to accept the coach's selection and slotting of team personnel.

A football drill should not be an isolated entity, although at times both coaches and players fail to comprehend this. While a particular drill may be isolated from the overall game for the purpose of strengthening a particular phase of football, it is actually a segment of the game. A drill should be utilized to improve a particular fundamental or technique or segment of the game of football. Although this will be discussed in greater detail in Chapter 2, your football players must be able to comprehend and visualize the relationship between a drill and its application to a game situation.

TYPES OF DRILLS

All drills may be categorized broadly as agility, reaction, game situation, warm-up, and/or conditioning drills. These in turn may be divided into *contact* and *non-contact* types of drills, depending upon the particular purpose of the drill.

In some instances it is difficult to categorize a drill accurately since it depends upon the *purpose* of the particular drill. As an example, warm-up drills or exercises may be considered as a facet of the conditioning program, or as a separate category when wind sprints, running laps, relays, and similar activities are used to develop endurance. If the purpose of the drill is to develop endurance, stamina, and strength, then the resistance should be increased and the time of the activity prolonged. By going through certain agility and reaction drills (Chapter 3) at a slower pace, they might broadly be classified as warm-up drills. On the other hand, merely by extending the number of reactions to more than five, or by extending the duration of the same drill to approximately six seconds, it could be classified as a conditioning drill rather than an agility or a reaction drill. *You should always consider the purpose of the drill.* If the drill is to improve agility and reaction, it should *not* be prolonged so that fatigue becomes a deterring or influencing factor in the performance of the activity. Rather the duration of the drill, as well as the resistance the athlete must overcome, is limited as the player reacts to a stimulus of sight, sound, and touch. Agility and reaction are a vital part of game-situation drills.

In an attempt to categorize the drills, the purpose of the drill is the determining factor as to its placement in this book, although it is acknowledged that the same drill could be utilized to teach different fundamental skills, techniques, or segments of the game. As an example, particular drills may be used to teach both offensive *or* defensive fundamentals or segments of the game, but as is discussed in the next chapter, a basic principle is that you should *not* coach both the offense and defense at the same time. At the conclusion of each chapter in Parts II through V, additional drills are cross-referenced by *name and chapter only.* These may be utilized with the drills discussed within the chapter to teach-coach a specific fundamental or a segment of the game.

Identifying Drills by Definition

In order to differentiate and clarify, the following are defined as they relate to drills:

Agility is the quality or state of being agile; nimbleness.

Reaction is a response to a stimulus; a reciprocal or return action or influence.

(Game) Situation is the combination of circumstances existing at a moment of time (in a game or practice session).

Condition(ing) is something established or agreed upon as a requisite. It affects the ability to play, mental attitude, pride, morale, teamwork, spirit.

Warm-up is a process which elicits acute physiological (and psychological) changes that prepare an individual for strenuous physical performance.

(To) drill is to instruct thoroughly, to discipline. It includes any experience, physical or mental, enforced with regularity and constant repetition.

A *contact* drill is one in which the player hits or is hit by another player, or players aggressively hit each other. It may be a "thud" drill in which an offensive player hits out at the defensive player, but there is controlled reaction by the defender, who sort of "catches" rather than reacts aggressively. This is still classified as a contact drill. Hitting the ground or blocking a sled, dummy, or air bag are considered passive contact drills by some. Others consider these to be *non-contact* drills because a player does not make contact with another player aggressively. Even in non-contact drills a defensive player, with arm shields and/or an air dummy, may react to an offensive blocker aggressively, though the drill probably will focus on the offense and limited (controlled contact) by the defense.

Most of the drills in this book will deal with segments of the game of football and/or game situation drills. A selected number of warm-up drills will be included in Chapter 3 to illustrate how warm-up drills or exercises may be woven into the typical practice session. Most experienced coaches have their own warm-up regimen. Conditioning drills will not be included because they are practically a separate entity. There are numerous books available on conditioning athletes.

SELECTION OF DRILLS

One objective in coaching is to create in practice those situations players will face in a game and then to repeat these situations until players can react instinctively due to rapid recognition and familiarity. It is commonly accepted in coaching that only through purposeful and sufficient practice drills can a coach be reasonably certain of good game performance. Good game performance is the result of well-organized practice sessions where numerous drills have been utilized for teaching-coaching-learning purposes.

Since there are literally hundreds of drills from which to choose, some much better than others, a coach's problem is to select the drills needed to accomplish what he desires to achieve. The drills he selects should fit *his* philosophy of football, theory, objectives, and methods of coaching. A coach must devise ways of thoroughly covering the essentials of his system of football.

Careful consideration should be given to your selection of drills. A drill may be good for one coach but of limited or no value to another coach. Drills should be designed for a specific purpose. Decide what your team needs, and drills will be selected more wisely. In many cases the drills selected should comprise a part of your offense or defense. Line drills, as an example, should be closely related to the line fundamentals and techniques that you teach. At other times it is necessary to work on a specific fundamental simply to develop that fundamental rather than to develop a part of your offense or defense.

Practice Like You Expect to Play the Game

It is an accepted coaching premise that the way one practices is the way one performs in game competition. From a coaching standpoint, you should organize and conduct your practice sessions the way you *want* your players to perform in game competition. Since coaching football is always a race against time, a coach should not spend time practicing techniques, drills, strategy, or tactics that are not applicable to the way he wants his players to perform during the game. *Practice the way you are going to play.* The drills you select must present an actual rather than a hypothetical situation. A drill must be viewed in relation to its proper context to the game of football. Not all coaches remember these tenets when selecting drills.

How to Select Drills

The type and selection of a particular drill, and the amount of time you devote to it in your practice schedule, may be decided by looking at the *purpose* of the drill and answering the following questions:

- *Are we going to use what this particular drill teaches?*
- *How much are we going to derive from this particular drill?*
- *How much are we going to use it in a game?*

To answer these questions a coach must thoroughly analyze his own offense, defense, and kicking game. To illustrate with a discussion of offense only, you must determine the basic skills for *all* of your linemen and backs. You must then determine how much each fundamental skill and technique is used in the various positions of your offense. You accomplish this task by tabulating the assignments of *each* position on *every* play and analyzing, for example, the percentage of time an offensive guard will use a straight shoulder block, a reverse shoulder block, a combination block, a cut-off and a reach block, short and long trap blocks, pull out and lead, the various types of pass blocks, and *all* other fundamentals and techniques that he must perform in order to carry out his offensive assignments. Only after you have done this will you have a definite indication of how much time should be devoted in your practice schedule to teaching-coaching-drilling-practicing these offensive fundamentals and techniques, for you have determined what each player must do offensively and the number of times he must do it. You are then ready to select appropriate drills to teach these fundamental skills and techniques.

Once the season gets underway, you can tabulate how much you actually utilized segments of your offensive attack by analyzing your offensive drive chart after each game. As an example, if the drive chart for a particular game indicates that you ran the ball 60 percent of the time, passed 20 percent, and punted or attempted field goals 20 percent because you could not move the football otherwise, you then need to know *which* running and passing plays were specifically used. How many times, if any, did your offensive interior linemen trap block, man block, double-team, pull and lead? Did your 20 percent passing game consist of pocket, play action, sprint-outs, screens, or what types of passes? All of these plays require different player-performance techniques. Which were successful? Which were not? Some coaches install relatively simple offensive running and passing attacks. As an example, some coaches do not utilize a trapping game, or do not employ a drop-back cup protection passing attack. Therefore, in their practice sessions they never include drills for teaching-coaching these fundamentals and techniques. On the other hand, if the drive chart indicates a team ran 60 percent of the time, and three-quarters of those plays used one-on-one blocking, then approximately three-quarters of the practice time allotted for offensive linemen should be utilized coaching-performing man blocking.

Most coaches probably have too much offense. It is not unusual for a team to practice skills, techniques, and plays that they seldom or never use in a game. Conversely, a coach may not drill his team sufficiently in the fundamentals, techniques, or plays they actually use in a game. Only by tabulating and analyzing each player's assignment-task on every play, teaching-coaching these skills and techniques in practice, then matching up the number and percentage of time a player actually performs these in a game and placing the teaching-coaching emphasis on what each player is doing or has done to further perfect these fundamentals and techniques, can a coach be reasonably certain he is covering the right things adequately. The manner in which they are taught and how the practice schedule will be organized depends mostly on situational coaching variables, a detailed discussion of which is beyond the intent and scope of this book. Chapter 3, however, offers some suggestions and guides for practice organization.

The cardinal points to remember are that you drill for a purpose, and you select drills that meet that purpose. Additional guides and suggestions pertaining to drill selection, organization, and administration are discussed in the next chapter.

2

Drill Guides and Suggestions for Effective Teaching-Coaching and Player Learning-Performance

In order for your players to derive optimum learning-performance results from the coaching staff's teaching-coaching, it is necessary to adhere to a number of principles, guides, and suggestions in the selection, planning, organization, and administration of your football drills. Below are discussed a number of these principles, guides, and suggestions. No effort is made to prioritize them in their order of importance.

ACCOMPLISH THE OBJECTIVE OF THE DRILL

You should keep in mind the specific objective or purpose of the drill and direct it toward this end. You should expect the drill to accomplish the specific objective you had in mind when selecting the drill.

KEEP THE DRILL SIMPLE

The drill should not be too involved or complicated. Complex drills mean long explanations and clarifications. Talk only when necessary. Too much explanation can "kill" a good drill, and a coach can end up conducting an on-the-field "talk seminar" with the players listening rather than performing.

SELECT DRILLS WITH MORE THAN A SINGLE REACTION

A drill with more than a single reaction has more merit than a drill with only one reaction. Since coaching is always a race against time, do not select drills that teach only agility unless that particular agility is also a technique or fundamental. Check to see if drills have a secondary purpose. Accomplish the primary and secondary purpose.

GIVE THE PROGRESSIVE POINTS OF CONCENTRATION

Inform your players of the progressive points of concentration. When teaching-coaching fundamentals and techniques, you should commence at the first point of concentration and progress to the concluding point in the sequence. As an example, the progressive or sequential points in teaching-coaching-learning defensive line play would be:

- the proper stance;
- move on movement or charge on the snap of the football;
- deliver a blow to neutralize (control) the blocker, and protect your territory;
- locate the football or the ball carrier;
- pursue at the correct angle to the football or ball carrier;
- make the tackle!

You must be specific in explaining and demonstrating (or having players demonstrate) the drill and what you want in its execution.

INFORM YOUR PLAYERS OF THE PURPOSEOF THE DRILL

Players are likely to be more receptive, learn more quickly, and perform more efficiently and effectively if they know the *why* of the drill, as well as how to perform it. By acquainting your players with the objectives of the drill, they know what to look for. Numerous young and inexperienced players simply cannot visualize and comprehend the purpose of all drills and where some of the drills fit into the game situation. The *why* explains the carry-over from the drill to the game situation.

LIMIT THE DURATION OF REPETITIONS OF THE DRILL

You must be careful not to change inadvertently the purpose of the drill by extending its duration and/or the designated number of repetitions. To get a maximum effort or performance from your players, it is advisable that you inform them of the number of repetitions or the duration of the drill and what is expected of them in effort and performance. While you may inform them you expect an all-out effort in their performance in all drills, you are not likely to get it unless the players are aware of the duration or repetitions of the drill(s). Should you extend the drill and the players are not expecting it, in the future your players may hold back because they are expecting you to extend the drill again. Always keep in mind the purpose of the particular drill(s) you are utilizing. Some coaches have a tendency to extend drills, forgetting their purpose, and, as a result, turn an agility or reaction drill into a conditioning drill. After this occurs several times it is almost impossible to get players to react quickly or to display agility because they are expecting the drills to be extended. Under such conditions players tend to "hold back" and not give an all-out performance effort, which negates the purpose of the drill(s) and is a waste of time from a teaching-coaching-learning standpoint.

PRESENT THE DRILL WITH A POSITIVE APPROACH

Use a positive approach with the emphasis on the *correct,* not the incorrect, method of performing the drill. Since active participation is more effective than passive reception, do not expend valuable time explaining and demonstrating how *not* to perform the drill, technique, or fundamental. It is of questionable value when one uses a negative approach of explaining and pointing out the incorrect ways or how *not* to perform. This does not imply that incorrect or faulty methods of performance should be overlooked or remain uncorrected.

EMPHASIZE RUNNING DRILLS

Since football is a game of movement, a drill that includes a lot of running, especially if it is challenging and competitive, is better than one that does not include running. A player who does not move well is likely to be ineffective in the other basic skills, too. Consequently, players must be taught to run correctly, which will be discussed in detail in Chapter 4. Many coaches feel this is accomplished best by having drills in which running is the secondary purpose and not the primary one. The objective is to run the players without them realizing they are doing so much running, as is the case when drills are interesting and competitive. When a player runs "laps," he is very much aware of the amount of running he is doing.

USE A VARIETY OF DRILLS

A variety of drills and the element of change create greater interest. Vary your drills, but accomplish the same objectives. Try to eliminate the element of boredom and strive to retain the element of fun in practice. While this is not always possible, repetition of the same familiar drills leads to boredom. Variety of drills generally eliminates boredom and contributes to having fun.

WORK WITH A FEW PLAYERS

Work with a small group of players when possible, always stressing the fundamentals. In various coaching setups this is not possible, and by necessity a coach is compelled to work with a larger group of players than is desirable for effective teaching-coaching. Under such conditions many players must come along on their own, with the coach giving most of his attention to the more advanced "key" players on whom he is relying to play and to win.

DO NOT COACH BOTH OFFENSE AND DEFENSE AT THE SAME TIME[1]

Do *not* try to coach both the offensive and defensive players at the same time. If the purpose of the drill is to teach defensive techniques, then correct the defensive player's errors. Do not coach the offensive player's

[1]An important teaching-learning-coaching point for numerous drills that follow deals with the utilization of scout squad members for demonstration purposes in group and team drills, particularly those that are "live" or involve scrimmaging. Since you are attempting to teach your regulars the oppositions's tendencies, they need a "good picture" of what to expect. From your selection of game-simulated drills and situations, scout squad members must be taught-coached to emulate as best they can what the opposition is likely to do offensively and defensively.

A coach can only encourage scout squad members to do their best skillwise. To carry out specific assignments whether on offense or defense, however, large flash cards should be prepared by the coaching staff prior to practice illustrating what you want the scout squad members to do. These cards should be numbered consecutively matching up with a "grocery list" the offensive coordinator has set up versus the defensive scout squad and/or the defensive coordinator has set up versus the offensive scout squad. If another coach is available to run the scout squad, this would be best, but a manager or even another player who is not performance unless he fails to follow your instructions and the defensive player is unable to react correctly. For example, if you are teaching a defensive back to key and react to an offensive tight end's block, do not be concerned with the end's blocking technique. Coach the defensive back's proper reaction to the offensive block. If the tight end is instructed to block but instead he releases downfield, then correct the offensive end's faulty play because the defensive back is unable to react correctly in this situation.

DEMONSTRATE THE DRILL PROPERLY

A demonstration loses some of its effectiveness when the performer noticeably slows down or loses accuracy because of fatigue. It is debatable whether a coach should demonstrate unless he has more skill than his players and is in physical condition to complete the demonstration in a normal manner. Many successful coaches never attempt to demonstrate certain drills, techniques, and fundamentals, but do their best teaching-coaching by explaining the action as a more skilled member of the team performs. A drill properly performed often produces the desired results; improperly performed it is unlikely to have the desired result.

ARRANGE THE DEMONSTRATION ADVANTAGEOUSLY

Arrange the drill demonstration advantageously for both the demonstrator and the observers. If a player cannot see the demonstration or hear the explanation, he probably will not derive everything desired from the performance. Neither the coach nor the demonstrator will do his best if environmental conditions are unfavorable. When planning drills, take into consideration drill areas, facilities, and the equipment necessary.

---

involved in the drill may be utilized to hold up the flash cards in the huddle for each player to see his designated alignment/assignment. While the flash cards must be prepared in advance prior to practice, valuable time is not expended during practice explaining individually what each player is to do on every assignment. Time is better spent teaching-coaching your regulars, who are expected to recognize and react to your opposition's offensive and defensive tendencies during the game, than instructing your scout squad members how to perform. Then, too, with flash cards the drills will be run more quickly and more often, and your regulars are likely to get a better "picture" of your opposition's tendencies.

Probably the most important coaching point, however, deals with motivating your scout squad members, and their attitude toward performing as the upcoming opponents. If the coaching staff, particularly the head coach, is laudatory of the performance of the scout squad members, and they in turn recognize they are making a contribution to the success of the team, it is likely they will give their best. This is all a coach can ask of any squad member.

COMMENCE THE DRILL WITH ONE WORD—ELIMINATE VERBOSITY

After the players are familiar with the drill and it has been identified by name, one word, such as "*ready*" or "*position,*" should be sufficient to alert them that the drill is ready to commence. Use the practice time fully by eliminating verbosity and keeping in mind that active participation is more effective than passive reception. In most drills either a player does the hitting or he gets hit. When he hears the word "ready" or "position," he should immediately assume a good football position preparatory to commencing the drill and then hit or be hit.

INSIST ON A "GOOD FOOTBALL POSITION" AT ALL TIMES

Insist on a *good football position* both offensively and defensively at all times. Check the fundamental position, stance, and start in all drills. It is more important to perform a technique or fundamental correctly a few times than it is to perform it numerous times incorrectly. Players should not be permitted merely "to go through the motions," performing from an improper football position.

HABITIZE BY USING A STARTING COUNT AND A WHISTLE

When possible start the drill by using your regular starting count or cadence and terminate the drill with a whistle. While this may not be feasible at all times, you are trying to develop a conditioned reflex to your starting count and the whistle. It is desirable to commence the drill and to terminate it under game conditions when possible.

USE THE "BUDDY" SYSTEM FOR TEACHING

When possible use the "buddy" system, directed by a coach, where the players check each other for errors of technique. It is not possible, nor is it always desirable, to drill all of the players at the same time. Since some players generally must wait their turn, it is desirable to have them check the performing players for errors of technique. Some coaches refer to this as developing a *learning attitude.* The players not only learn what they must do correctly; they also correct the players who perform incorrectly.

SELECT COMPETITIVE GAME-LIKE DRILLS

A competitive, game-like drill is better than one where an individual does not compete against another player. Since football is a competitive game and competition is an important factor in our society, you get better results if the players compete against each other in drills.

USE DRILLS TO BUILD MORALE, PRIDE, AND ENTHUSIASM

A team must be prepared mentally as well as physically. It is impossible to develop outstanding teams without good morale and pride. Conversely, a squad with limited ability but with fine morale and pride can develop into a winner. If your team has morale and team pride, it can win or at least play as well as it is capable of playing. If a team lacks morale and pride, it cannot possibly reach its potential. Developing team pride and morale is very important. If a team does not have pride and morale, it will not be a winner. The outstanding characteristic always present in a winner is enthusiasm. It is one of the most compelling and powerful forces in life. It is the spirit of enthusiasm that often achieves the seemingly impossible. Winning spirit is primarily willingness to practice well. Winning comes second; wanting to be a winner comes first. Developing these intangibles—morale, pride, and enthusiasm—depends on many factors, one of which is to have interesting practice sessions.

USE NAMES TO IDENTIFY DRILLS

To identify drills, give them meaningful names or use descriptive words. This serves two purposes. It saves time. You merely call out the name of the drill and the players line up in position ready to commence. Because some drill names denote toughness, e.g., Bull-in-the-Ring, King of the Hill, and Clobber-the-Linebacker, it also develops intangible qualities of morale, pride, and enthusiasm. Most players want to be "The Bull" or "The King." It is a gimmick that appeals to a player's ego and helps to develop intangibles if the drills are interesting, motivating, challenging, and competitive.

USE A MARKED-OFF AREA FOR DRILLS

Areas along the sidelines marked off by three rows of five-yard squares will eliminate loss of practice time in setting up drills. These squares will enable a coach to have proper spacing, which is most important for specific drills. Note, for example, as you read drills in other sections of the book, the frequency of occasions when performing players are five yards apart or the restraining lines are five yards apart.

USE DRILLS AS A MEANS TO AN END

A drill is a means to an end, not the end in itself. Do not drill the initiative out of a player. Keep in mind the previously mentioned questions: "Are we going to use what this particular drill teaches? How much are we going to derive from this particular drill? How much are we going to use it in a game?"

GIVE ADEQUATE CONSIDERATION TO ALL OF THE FUNDAMENTALS

Give adequate consideration to all of the fundamentals of the game—running, blocking, tackling, passing, receiving, and kicking. A coach should analyze each player's job in the game and then see that the player spends a proportionate amount of time on each phase in practice. It is not systems or plays that win games, but players who execute the fundamentals better than the opposition. Sharpness in fundamentals is the winning edge in athletics. It is not necessarily *how much* you teach your players, but it is *how effectively* they perform what they have been taught. Select practical and effective drills that will develop individual and team fundamentals and techniques under game-simulated conditions. Develop agility and reaction by repeating the situations in your offense and defense where these skills are necessary.

YOU MUST KNOW AND TEACH ADHERENCE TO THE RULES

The rules governing scholastic, collegiate, and professional football are not identical. Some techniques, strategies, and tactics that are permitted in professional football, for example, are illegal and will sustain a penalty in collegiate and scholastic football; or some may be permissible in professional and collegiate football, but not in scholastic competition. While it is commendable for a coach to be familiar with the rules at all three levels of competition, it is imperative that he know thoroughly all of the rules at the level at which he coaches. Frequently many coaches are not thoroughly familiar with all of the rules at their own level of competition.

All television viewers are influenced considerably by a high saturation of collegiate and professional football games, and many, including scholastic coaches and players, are not aware of some of the subtle differences in a number of rules. Also, many high school coaches attend clinics where collegiate and professional coaches lecture on football techniques, tactics, and strategies. Frequently a number of the lecturers have never coached at the scholastic level, and they may not be aware of the differences between what they are discussing and what is permissible under scholastic rules. Scholastic coaches, in turn, may teach some of the techniques, tactics, and strategies advocated in clinics, unaware that what they are teaching-coaching is not permissible under scholastic rules. At whatever level one is coaching, he should know the rules so he does not inadvertently teach-coach something that is not permissible at his team's level of competition. Also, a coach must correct immediately in practice and during the game any illegal technique, tactic, or strategy that is likely to sustain a penalty and is not within the spirit of the rules of the game. Therefore, at the level of competition at which one coaches—scholastic, collegiate, or professional—one must know and teach adherence to the rules.

ADHERE TO THE LAWS OF LEARNING AND TO EDUCATIONALLY SOUND PRINCIPLES OF TEACHING–COACHING

Successful coaches employ many widely different procedures. No one system or method is correct for every coach. What proves to be successful for one coach may be unsuccessful when tried by another coach. There is no one winning system for all. However, a great majority of successful coaches adhere to certain basic principles. Probably the most important basic element in coaching is one's approach to teaching. Successful coaches are effective teachers. Therefore, a knowledge of the laws of learning and sound principles of teaching should prove beneficial in attaining desirable results. This applies not only to drills, but also to practice organization (Chapter 3), and to coaching football generally.[2]

[2]For additional information on the psychology of learning and teaching-coaching effectiveness, the reader is directed to pages 225–65 in Donald E. Fuoss and Robert J. Troppmann, *Effective Coaching: A Psychological Approach* (New York: John Wiley & Sons, Inc., 1981).

3

Practice Schedule Organization Guides and Suggestions, Including Warm-up Drills and Exercises

While the drill guides, suggestions, and principles in the previous chapter should be adhered to in order to derive optimal teaching-learning results, there must be an overall practice plan that gives adequate consideration to all of the basic individual and team fundamentals of the game: running, blocking, tackling, passing, receiving, and kicking. Briefly, a coach should select practical and effective drills that will develop individual and team fundamental skills and techniques under simulated game conditions. You develop agility and reaction by repeating the situations in your offense and defense where these skills are necessary.

PLAN AND ORGANIZE YOUR TIME AND PRACTICE PROGRAM

No phase of coaching is more important than organizing your time and practice program so all facets of the game receive adequate consideration and attention. A *general* plan is included below. Within this general plan, a coach must have a *specific* detailed, organized plan, including methods for developing his players and evaluating each player's performance and potential. For illustrative purposes, a detailed plan utilizing drills for developing and evaluating all *line* personnel also is included below. This plan can be modified easily to develop and evaluate all other player personnel, too. Since every coaching situation is different, the practice schedule and one's plan of organization must be "tailor made" to fit the particular coaching situation. Both the general overall practice schedule breakdown and the specific suggested plan that follow are adaptable to practically any coaching situation.

PRACTICE SCHEDULE BREAKDOWN

It is suggested as a *point of departure* to allot *approximately* 50 percent of the available practice time to offense and 50 percent to defense, with the various phases of the offensive and defensive kicking game receiving their apportionment. Another general type of breakdown is to allot *approximately* 50 percent of the practice time to defense (offense), 35 percent to offense (defense) and 15 percent to the kicking game, depending upon a coach's particular philosophy and the importance he attaches to the offensive, defensive, and kicking games. A further breakdown would be to allocate approximately 25 percent to Individual, 30 percent to Group or Combination, and 45 percent to Team work, if this particular plan of organization is employed. You analyze each player's job in the game and see that he spends a proportionate amount of time on each phase in practice.

A typical football practice schedule would be divided into four periods: Specialty, Individual, Combination or Group, and Team work. The drills a coach uses would be designed and selected to fit into this type of practice schedule organization. The typical small college and high school coaching staff, generally limited to only several assistants, could modify this practice plan according to its own circumstances. Each plan must be tailored to fit the situation.

Specialty Period (At the Beginning or Conclusion of Practice)

The specialty time segment is devoted to the development by each individual of his particular specialty. All passers work with their throwing, while punters and place kickers work on their kicking specialties. Safeties handle the punts, and the receivers practice catching the football. Offensive interior linemen work on pulling, trapping, or other phases of their game. The same specialty development applies to the defensive linemen, the secondary personnel and linebackers, the offensive backs, and to all other players.

Some coaches prefer to have their specialty work at the conclusion of practice after the termination of the team work. The punters, place kickers, passers, and receivers remain for their specialty work, and the other squad members go to the locker room. There are various reasons why some coaches prefer this procedure; one is to commence practice with a brief squad meeting and then have all players go on the field together.

Other coaches prefer to have the specialists report first and have the other players come to the field after they dress. While the punters, passers, place kickers, and receivers are working on their specialties, the remaining players report to their position coaches and commence working on their individual weaknesses or some other phase of their game that becomes a specialty to them.

Warm-up Period: Stretching and Flexibility

The Warm-up Period was not mentioned previously as a separate phase of the practice schedule organization because the warm-up routine can be handled in several different ways. Generally there is a pre-practice Warm-up Period prior to the work on individual weaknesses and specialties. In the pre-practice warm-up, a player loosens and stretches his muscles on his own, although he may be under the direction of a coach. A second method is for the position coach to direct and supervise the warm-up stretching and flexibility exercises as part of the work done in the Individual Period. A third method is for the Warm-up Period to be placed after the Specialty Period or the pre-practice work, but before the Individual Period. After the horn has sounded indicating the termination of the specialty work, the entire squad assembles together at one end of the field. An assistant coach or one of the players directs the warm-up exercises or drills, and other coaches station themselves between the rows of players and supervise them. The types of warm-up drills or exercises are presented later in this chapter.

Individual Period

Or the squad may be divided up by positions with each coach directing their warm-up work, then progressing to agility, reaction, and conditioning drills at his position station on the field. Emphasis is then placed on the development of the blocking, tackling, and running of each individual. Here the emphasis is on individual fundamentals and techniques, offensively and defensively.

Combination or Group Period

This segment of time in the practice schedule breakdown is devoted to small units or skeleton drills, both live and dummy. As an example, one combination group might be linebackers and defensive secondary versus the opposition's pass offense. Another combination might be the defensive line versus the opposition's offensive running game. Offensively another group of backs might be working on timing their plays and ball handling. A fourth group might be working on offensive line blocking versus the opposition's defensive alignments and stunts. Each group rotates and progresses so that the players are drilled both offensively and defensively, if necessary. Of course, the size of the squad and the number of assistant coaches available determine the number of work groups, progressions, and the rotation of personnel. This progression type of teaching gives the individual a better view of the overall picture and still permits the coaching staff to concentrate on coaching-teaching the individual in the group. Combination or group drills will be illustrated later in the book.

Team Period

The next progression is to the Team Period, where emphasis is placed on developing the team as a whole unit. This is necessary in order to polish the timing of plays, to check offensive and defensive alignments and assignments, and to put the individual into a simulated game situation. There are limitations on the progress a team can make in individual and group work because many players will react quite differently in a game situation. How well the fundamentals have been mastered will show up in team drills. The objective here is the development of the team in working together as a unit. The best athletes in the world will fail to win if they do not work together in a team sport. On the other hand, teamwork will often overcome definite limitations of individual players and develop the team into a winner. Appropriate team drills will be suggested in another section of the book.

A DETAILED BREAKDOWN OF THE WARM–UP AND INDIVIDUAL PERIODS

While the Individual Period is broken down here only for linemen, the warm-up regimen is for all players. It makes little difference whether it is the "quick-quick" routine or the more conventional warm-up exercises. All players should go through at least a five-minute organized warm-up routine in order to stretch and loosen the muscles in preparing for more strenuous activities that will follow. The entire warm-up routine should be done rapidly in order to complete it within the five-minute allotted time. By following the same warm-up routine daily, the players soon become familiar with the progression, and after several sessions it is not necessary to announce or explain the next exercise in the progression. At the conclusion of each exercise the "leader," who may be either a player or an assistant coach, may clap his hands several times and then immediately commence the next warm-up exercise in the routine. The squad members follow the leader's example, hand clap several times, then pick up the leader's exercise, generally "talking it up" throughout the exercises.

A Suggested Warm-up Regimen

Following is a suggested warm-up sequence, spread over a five-minute period, with each exercise being repeated quickly several times, before progressing to the next exercise:

1. Neck rotation—clockwise; counterclockwise.
2. Shoulder (arms) rotation—forward; backward.
3. Torso rotation—clockwise; counterclockwise.
4. Hamstring stretch—cross the left foot over the right foot, bend forward at the waist, and reach for the toes. Do not bounce; lock the knees.
5. Hamstring stretch—cross the right foot over the left foot and repeat as 4 above.
6. Stretch out—sit down on the right heel, extend the left leg forward, keep the left leg straight, and reach for the toes.
7. Stretch out—sit down on the left heel, extend the right leg forward and repeat as 6 above.
8. Hill climber—from a four-point stance with the left knee flexed up near the chin inside the arms, and the right leg extended to the rear, stretch pushing back the rear leg and down with the tail, elevate the chin and face upward, back swayed.
9. Hill climber—reverse the feet, flex the right knee up near the chin inside the arms, and repeat as 8 above.
10. Neck bridges—front and rear, flipping over on command, pivoting around on the head, keeping the shoulders off the ground; clockwise and counterclockwise.
11. Rapid bicycles—on the back, small circles with the feet.
12. Quick grass drills—"up," "down" very quickly, always coming up into a good football (breakdown) position.
13. "Quick-quick"—standing position (sight or sound) hands to helmet, thighs, chest, waist, etc.

Additional Football Warm-up Drills and Exercises

The following drills and exercises may be considered more suitable for the warm-up regimen. They probably should not exceed the time limitations of the specified five-minute period for warm-up.

1. STATIONARY RUNNING DRILL

Purpose: To get the heart and respiratory system "tuned-up." It aids the respiratory strength development, which helps in all forms of effort.

Procedure: The feet are lifted off the ground about six inches each time, just above a jog pace, keeping the body loose and easy. Run for ten seconds breathing normally, then hold the breath for ten seconds while running. Repeat this sequence throughout the duration of the drill.

Coaching Points: Stress jogging and loosening-up. The duration of the drill is two to three minutes.

2. STOMACH–CHEST PUFFING DRILL

Purpose: To warm the stomach muscles, stretch the chest structure and increase the circulation of blood throughout the body.

Procedure: The player lies on his back, takes a deep breath and holds it while alternating puffing stomach out, pulling it in, and puffing chest out (high).

Coaching Points: Do the drill to a count of ten, then rest a few seconds. Repeat.

3. HAMSTRING STRETCHING DRILL

Purpose: To stretch the hamstring muscles prior to participation.

Procedure: Stand with the feet comfortably apart. Bend the knees, reach forward, and place the palms of the hands flat on the ground about two inches in front of the feet. Slowly straighten the knees, with the heels of the feet retaining contact with the ground. After straightening the legs, the player should hold this position for two to three seconds.

Coaching Points: Repeat the exercise ten to twelve times slowly and hold the position for two to three seconds each time.

4. FRONT STRETCHING DRILL

Purpose: To stretch the muscles in the front of the thighs, stomach and chest and to aid in back and joint flexibility.

Procedure: With the knees together, kneel on the ground, insteps tucked under the buttocks and arch backward touching the back of the head to the ground.

Coaching Points: Do this exercise slowly. Repeat it six to eight times. Stress keeping the knees together and the back arched at all times. (See Chapter 15, (1) Punter's Loosening and Stretching Drill.)

5. KNEE STRETCHING DRILL

Purpose: To stretch the muscles and attachments of the knees.

Procedure: Sit on the ground with the feet extended forward. The left ankle is crossed over the right knee at the lower end of the thigh bone. With the right hand pull the left foot upward along the thigh, and at the same time press the left knee downward with the palm of the left hand (on the inside of the knee). Alternate.

Coaching Points: The pressure should be exerted for three to four seconds on one knee, then on the other knee. Repeat this procedure two to four times for each knee, alternating left and right.

6. HIP STRETCHING DRILL

Purpose: To stretch the large hip muscles.

Procedure: Sit with the feet well apart flat on the ground, the knees flexed so they are above the ankles. Support the body with the hands on the ground, fingers extended to the rear. Rotate the knees downward and inward, trying to touch the inside of the knees on the ground.

Coaching Points: Repeat this procedure five to six times, holding for three to four seconds duration each time.

7. BOUNCING DRILL

Purpose: To increase the heart beat, develop the lower leg and foot muscles, and to develop explosiveness.

Procedure: Spring upward into the air as high as possible off of both feet, bouncing up and down.

Coaching Points: The body should be relaxed and not tense. Continue this drill for thirty to forty seconds duration, spinning upward and as high as possible each time.

8. HIP WHIPPING DRILL

Purpose: To loosen and stretch the muscles of the hips and to give the feeling of hip movement.

Procedure: Stand in a comfortable spread position with the hands on the hips. Keeping the stomach in, the chest elevated, the upper body over the feet, move only the hips by whipping them laterally to the right as far as possible then to the left in a similar manner.

Coaching Points: Stress moving only the hips to the side. Repeat this exercise twenty times, alternating right and left.

9–10. WORKING THE KNEES DRILLS (PROGRESSIVE)

Purpose: To develop flexibility and strength.

Procedure: (9) Lie on the stomach. Raise the right foot directly over the knee. Rotate the foot and lower leg, clockwise and then counter-clockwise, in as large a circle as possible. Start slowly and increase the speed. Alternate the feet, proceeding twenty to thirty seconds each time. (10) (a) Stand with the feet comfortably spread, knees well bent, hands on the knees. Bend the knees approximately six inches, then straighten legs briskly. Repeat this routine eight to ten times in rapid succession. (b) Move the knees laterally from side to side as far as possible, rolling on the inward and outward edges of the sides of the feet. Repeat this eight to ten times, clockwise and counter-clockwise. (c) Rotate both knees together, clockwise and counterclockwise. The circles should be wide, and the knees should be well bent in the forward and side parts of the circle. Straighten the legs on the back part of the circle (rotation). Continue this drill for twenty to thirty seconds duration.

Coaching Points: (Included with the procedure for each drill above.)

11. ALL–OVER STRETCHING DRILL

Purpose: To loosen most of the muscles of the body, especially the back and shoulders.

Procedure: Assume a leaning-rest (push-up) position, arms extended, with the body straight. Elevate the buttocks as high as possible in the air. At the same time suck in the stomach as far as possible, while lowering the head (chin) toward the stomach as far as possible. The legs and arms should be straight at all times. Then dip the pelvic girdle forward to the ground, arching the back as much as possible, while elevating the chin upward as high as possible. Alternate raising the buttocks and arching the back.

Coaching Points: Start slowly and increase the speed for thirty to forty seconds duration.

12. NECK STRETCHING DRILL

Purpose: To loosen the muscles of the neck.

Procedure: From a straddle position, hands on the hips, rotate the head slowly on its axis clockwise, and then counterclockwise, stretching the neck muscles.

Coaching Points: Stress making wide circles, forcing the chin downward toward the breastbone, outward toward the points of the shoulders, and upward as far as possible. The duration of this drill should be ten seconds each way.

13. SHOULDER STRETCHING DRILL

Purpose: To loosen the shoulder muscles.

Procedure: Stand comfortably with the arms hanging loosely at the sides, and then rotate the points of the shoulders upward, backward, downward, forward in as large a circle as possible. Then reverse the procedure and rotate the shoulders in the opposite direction.

Coaching Points: The duration is ten seconds each way. Progress to making large circles with the hands and arms, flinging them outward and upward away from the body. Then reverse the procedure downward and inward, crossing the arms in front of the body.

14. ROTATING STRETCHING DRILL

Purpose: To stretch and loosen the trunk muscles.

Procedure: From a straddle position with the hands on hips or clasped behind the neck, rotate the trunk from the waist clockwise while stretching as far as possible. Then reverse and rotate the trunk counterclockwise.

Coaching Points: Progress to a four-count cadence: forward, sideward (right), backward, sideward (left), forward, etc.

15. OPPOSITE HAND—OPPOSITE FOOT DRILL

Purpose: To stretch and loosen the muscles of the trunk and back.

Procedure: From a straddle position with the arms and hands extended straight laterally from the shoulders, on a four-count cadence touch the fingers of the right hand to the toes of the left foot. Then straighten to the original position, touch the fingers of the left hand to the toes of the right foot, and return to original position. Repeat the progression ten times.

Coaching Points: Stress flinging the arms upward and outward and returning to the original straddle position after touching the toes of the opposite foot, rather than merely remaining bent over throughout the entire drill.

16. PUSH-UPS DRILL

Purpose: To loosen and strengthen the muscles of the arms and shoulders.

Procedure: From a leaning-rest (push-up) position, weight of the body balanced on the fingers and toes, body rigid, without raising the buttocks or permitting the stomach to sag, bend the elbows and touch the face bar on the helmet to the ground. Then return to the original leaning-rest position.

Coaching Points: The body should not rest on the ground. Keep the body rigid. This drill may be used as a conditioner by extending the number of repetitions. Limit the repetitions here since it is used as part of a warm-up regimen.

17. BOUNCING DRILL

Purpose: To loosen the muscles of the arms and shoulders.

Procedure: The same as (16) Push-ups Drill, only the body is lowered slightly before the arms are extended, causing the player to bounce up and down in a series of short upward springs. As a variation, clap the hands together while the body is in the air.

Coaching Points: Same as Drill 16.

18. BICYCLE DRILL

Purpose: To loosen and stretch the muscles of the hips and legs.

Procedure: From a prone position on the ground, facing skyward, elevate the hips and legs directly over the head by placing the hands under the hips with the elbows on the ground. With the feet make large and small circles, and "ride the bicycle."

Coaching Points: Finish by letting the toes touch the ground at the back of the head, and "walk around" back there. Lower the feet for (19) Abdominal Tenser Drill.

19. ABDOMINAL TENSER DRILL

Purpose: To strengthen the muscles of the abdomen.

Procedure: From a prone position on the ground, facing skyward, raise the feet and legs off the ground six inches and hold them there with the legs straight. On the coach's command open the legs, close them, open, close, down. The arms should be at the sides, *not* supporting the body or legs.

Coaching Points: Do not extend this drill or it becomes a conditioner instead of a warm-up exercise.

20. KNEE RAISE DRILL

Purpose: To strengthen the muscles of the abdomen.

Procedure: Same as (19) Abdominal Tenser Drill, only this is done on a four-count cadence: 1) the knees are brought upward as close as possible to the chest; 2) the legs are straightened and extended upward; 3) the knees are bent and lowered to the chest, as is the position on the count of "one"; and 4) the legs are extended forward to their original position.

Coaching Points: Same as Drill 19. This drill, too, may be used as a conditioner.

21. WRESTLER'S BRIDGE DRILL

Purpose: To stretch and strengthen the neck muscles.

Procedure: Take a wrestler's bridge (rear) with the weight supported only by the toes and the back of the head, and roll around on the head, pivot, and finally flop over into a front bridge, i.e., facing downward.

Coaching Points: Keep the shoulders and body off of the ground and try to touch the face bar on the helmet to the ground when in a rear bridge position.

22. HILL CLIMB DRILL

Purpose: To stretch and loosen the leg and trunk muscles.

Procedure: From a sprinter's stance, the hands on the ground pointing forward, the left leg is bent with the knee up under the chest, and the right leg is straight and extended toward the rear, quickly reverse the position of the feet.

Coaching Points: Stress quickness, keeping the knees inside of the elbows and the head up. Do not extend the repetitions or the drill becomes a conditioner.

23. REACH WAY BACK DRILL

Purpose: To stretch the hamstring muscles and those of the trunk.

Procedure: From a straddle position, feet as wide apart as the shoulders, hands on the hips, on the first three counts bend at the waist and drive the hands downward and backward between the legs trying to touch the ground behind the heels. Bounce between counts, looking backward between the legs, attempting to reach the maximum distance on "three." Withdraw the arms and return to the starting position on "four."

Coaching Points: The knees should bend. Other warm-up drills should precede this one so as not to pull a hamstring.

24. TOE RAISERS AND QUARTER-KNEE BENDS DRILL

Purpose: To stretch the muscles of the feet and legs.

Procedure: Stand erect with the hands on the hips. On toe raisers go up on the toes, bounce up and down quickly, catching the weight as the heels are about to touch the ground. After ten quick repetitions progress to quarter-knee bends. On "one" bend the knees slightly, raising the heels from the ground, keeping the body erect. On "two" straighten the knees and lower the heels to the ground.

Coaching Points: Get up on the toes in both parts of this drill.

25. JUMPING JACKS DRILL

Purpose: To loosen most of the muscles of the body.

Procedure: From an erect position on the count of "one" assume a straddle position with the feet apart, the hands together over the head. On the count of "two" return to the original military (erect) position.

Coaching Points: Jump to a straddle position flinging the arms and hands outward and upward. Extend the arms. Snap to military position on the second command.

The Objectives of the Warm-up Regimen

A number of other exercises could be included as warm-up drills, but these will suffice for illustrative purposes. The objectives of warming-up must be kept in mind. An effective and efficient warm-up regimen should accomplish the following objectives:

- To prepare the heart and lungs for vigorous physical activity so the discomfort of body adjustment can be eliminated.
- To get the blood circulating freely throughout the body.
- To stretch the muscles in order to prepare them for rapid and effective contraction, and to remove any "kinks" and muscle shortening due to sitting, fatigue, carry-over, etc.
- To prepare the athlete physiologically and psychologically so he feels loose and ready to participate in physical activity.

Other warm-up drills or exercise may be utilized as there are literally hundreds of suitable ones to choose from. Each coach probably has his own particular warm-up routine. One only need to remember the objectives of warming-up, and that the emphasis should *not* be on conditioning. Many of the same drills may be used for conditioning merely by extending the number of repetitions or the duration, as was pointed out in Chapter 1. Since this is not the purpose of warm-up drills or exercises, they should be done quickly with only several repetitions of a limited number of drills during the allotted time. Thus, several dozen drills are included to illustrate the variety from which a coach can select a number to be accomplished within a specified period of allotted time.

Individual Period: The ABCs of Football

Somewhere in a coach's daily practice plan he should include agility, blocking, and contact or tackling drills, the ABCs of football for linemen, in order to teach and develop these necessary game fundamentals and techniques. The four-station drills are *one* method of organizing a fifteen-minute segment of the practice schedule during the Individual Period in order to assess the agility-reaction of your players and to teach and evaluate certain basic fundamentals and techniques. These drills also aid the coaches in evaluating their own teaching methods.

During pre-season practice in the fall and until the first regular season game, these drills may be used daily *except* on the days that scrimmage is scheduled. During the regular season these drills may be used on Monday and Tuesday of every week in September through early October. Later some of the hitting drills may be eliminated, but it is suggested the players continue to do the warm-up, agility-reaction, and form tackling drills, along with selected sled drills throughout the entire football season.

While the four-station drills may also be used as a conditioner, their value lies in teaching and evaluating agility-reaction and specific basic skills of a segment of the game for the line personnel. It should also be kept in mind that while the linemen and line coaches are at one end of the field going through agility-reactions and the four-station drills for fifteen minutes, the flanker and backfield coaches are at the opposite end of the field running their personnel through a series of drills with similar objectives in mind. However, the example here is limited in scope to linemen.

ORGANIZING THE FOUR–STATIONS DRILLS

On the sound of an air horn in place of the usual whistle, the squad will break into designated groups. The linemen should sprint to designated areas where the four-station drills will be conducted, after three minutes of four agility-reaction drills, as indicated in Figure 3–1. Some coaches may prefer to do the warm-up exercises in these small groups at the various stations, although there is value in having the entire squad together initially in one large group before breaking into small groups.

Station 2 (Figure 3-4)
Coach: Defensive Line
Personnel: All Guards
Drill: Hit, Reaction, Form Tackle
Alternate: Bucker/Shiver Board Drill (Figure 3-5)

Station 3 (not illustrated)
Coach: Offensive Line
Personnel: All Tackles
Drill: 7-Man Sled
Alternate: 2-Man Sled

SPRINT

Organizational Sequence:

a. All Stations 3 minutes (4 agility-reaction drills)
b. Station Drill 3 minutes each (12 minutes players rotate every 3 minutes; coaches remain)
c. Every coach teaches a game skill, technique, or fundamental and evaluates all linemen

SPRINT

SPRINT

SPRINT

Station 1 (Figure 3-3)
Coach: Center/Linebacker
Personnel: All Cs/LBers
Drill: Ward-Off/Shed
Alternate: Running Ropes and/or Overhead Ladder Drills

Station 4 (Figure 3-6)
Coach: Defensive End
Personnel: All ends except Split Ends (Xs)
Drill: Form Tackling
Alternate: Tackling Drills

Figure 3–1 Organizing the Four Stations

Merely for the sake of organization and in order to divide the linemen into small groups, on the sound of the horn these players go to designated areas, where the appropriate coach will conduct first the agility-reactions and then a specific designated drill:

Station 1. All centers and linebackers to the center-linebacker coach.
Station 2. All guards to the defensive line coach.
Station 3. All tackles to the offensive line coach.
Station 4. All ends, excluding split ends, to the defensive end coach.

If the coaching staff has only two line coaches, the above plan could still be employed by combining line personnel for stations 1–2 with the defensive line coach handling these players, and the offensive line coach handling personnel for stations 3–4. The personnel would then merely rotate back and forth between the two line coaches with each coach conducting two drills instead of four coaches each conducting a single drill as illustrated in Figure 3–1.

It is not necessary to have four stations as this depends on the available player personnel and the number of coaches. Obviously the larger the coaching staff, the more stations you could have. Nor is it necessary to allot three minutes to the agility-reaction drills and a total of twelve minutes to the players rotating through the four stations. If the groups are relatively small in number (8–15), and each coach is "pushing" the participants as they execute the particular fundamental or technique at his station, three minutes duration will be sufficiently demanding and is most effective for deriving the desired results from the drill. A shorter period of time, when working with 8–15 prospects, is not sufficient; and a longer period will be too demanding if the drills are done properly.

Let us now examine the ABCs of football and determine what linemen should be taught or practice daily.

A: Agility-Reaction Drills (for Linemen)

Select approximately four agility-reaction drills for a period of three minutes (of the fifteen-minute plan suggested), which *all linemen* will perform at *all* (four) designated *stations* before going into the specific skill or technique drills. There are any number of worthwhile and beneficial agility-reaction drills, more than three dozen of which are discussed, with numerous ones illustrated, in Chapter 5. After the routine is established, it is suggested that one new agility-reaction drill be introduced and substituted each week for one of the "old" drills. A partial list of agility-reaction drills follows:

- Log Roll, Figure 8, or Special Name ("Tiger"?) Drill
- Carioca or Grapevine Drill
- Lateral Wave Drill
- Crab or Scramble Drill
- Somersault or Forward Rolls Drill
- Hip Opener Drill
- Flash Drill
- Quarter-Eagle Drill
- Seat Rolls and Crab Drill
- High Stepper Drill

These and numerous other worthwhile agility-reaction drills are discussed in Chapter 5, although the objective is *not* variety or numbers. Part of the value of doing the same drills is familiarity, which leads to proficiency in performing the game skill, technique, or fundamental that is being taught-learned. Reaction drills may be utilized to develop both agility and reaction. Simple agility drills are of more limited value unless a stimulus (sight or sound) is added, along with the teaching of mobility and nimbleness, in order to secure the desired reaction. Therefore, as a coaching point, you should seldom employ drills that teach *only* agility, unless that particular agility is also a football technique or fundamental.

Drill Organization

In order to achieve the objective or purpose of the drill, *the emphasis should be on maximum effort and correct performance.* For this reason, it is suggested a number of the drills be set up in three-man units, which of course will depend on the number of players and coaches involved in the drills. As illustrated in Figure 3–2, in most agility-reaction drills each coach can easily teach and observe twelve players without difficulty by putting three-man units around his central position. After working with a single three-

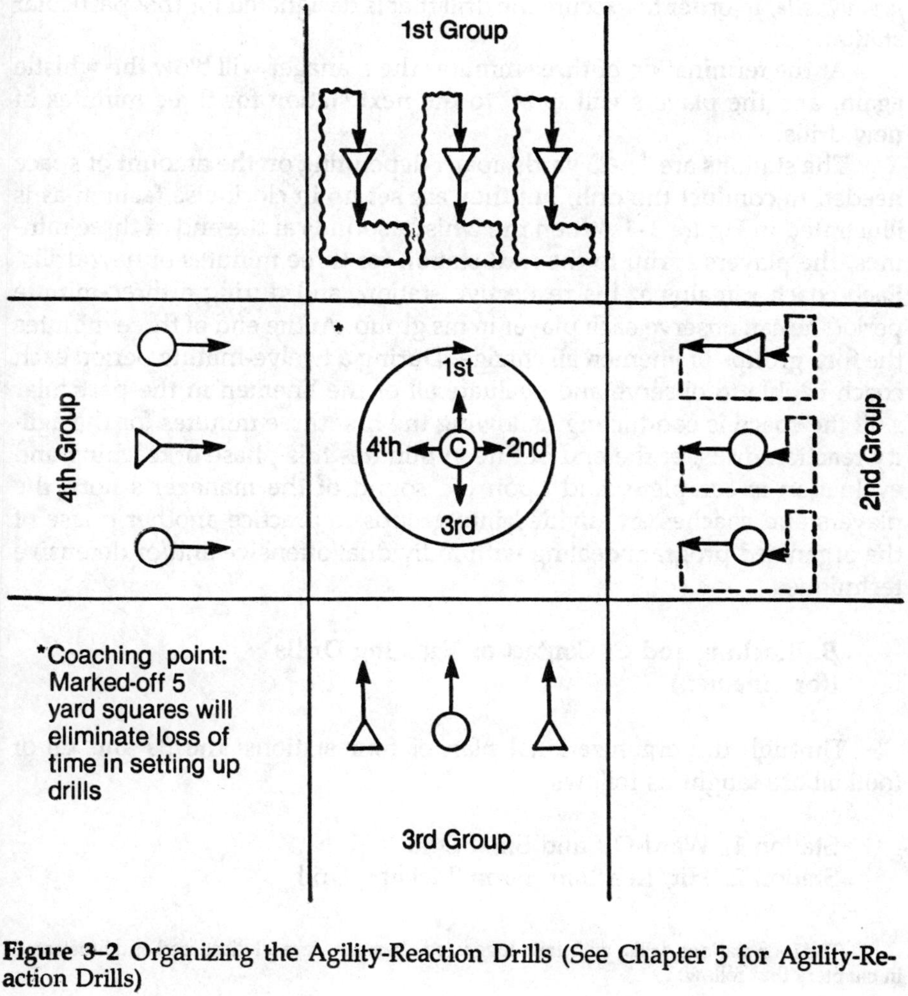

Figure 3–2 Organizing the Agility-Reaction Drills (See Chapter 5 for Agility-Reaction Drills)

man unit, all he need do is turn clockwise (or counter-clockwise) to the next three-man unit and repeat the procedure until he has drilled all four units involving twelve men. Therefore, it is possible for all players at each station to do all four of the selected agility-reaction drills in the specified three minutes of time allotted.

It will save considerable time if a coach will use a marked-off area for drills. Areas along the sidelines marked-off by rows of five-yard squares will eliminate loss of practice time in setting up drills. These squares will enable a coach to have proper spacing, which is most important in specific drills. Additional drill guides and suggestions were discussed in the previous chapter.

After three minutes the whistle will be blown by a manager who is keeping time, and the linemen will now execute the *B*s and *C*s of football. However, the players remain at the *same* stations and *do not rotate on the first whistle,* in order to execute the drill that is designated for that particular station.

At the termination of three minutes the manager will blow the whistle again, and the players will *sprint* to the next station for three minutes of new drills.

The stations are 15–25 yards apart, depending on the amount of space needed to conduct the drill, but they are set up in clockwise fashion as is illustrated in Figure 3–1. When the whistle sounds at the end of three minutes, the players sprint to the next station for three minutes of new drills. Each coach remains at his respective station, and during a three-minute period he can observe each player in his group. At the end of three minutes the four groups of linemen all change. During a twelve-minute period each coach is able to observe and evaluate all of the linemen in the particular skill the coach is conducting. Allowing the first three minutes for the agility-reaction drills, at the end of fifteen minutes this phase of teaching and evaluation is complete, and upon the sound of the manager's horn the players and coaches are divided into groups to practice another phase of the organized program dealing with individual offensive and/or defensive techniques.

B: Blocking and *C*: Contact or Tackling Drills (for Linemen)

Through the organizational plan of four stations[1] the *B*s and *C*s of football are taught as follows:

Station 1. Ward-Off and Shed Drill
Station 2. Hit, Reaction, Form Tackling Drill

[1]The four-stations drills, and their suggested alternates, are all discussed and illustrated in chapters that follow.

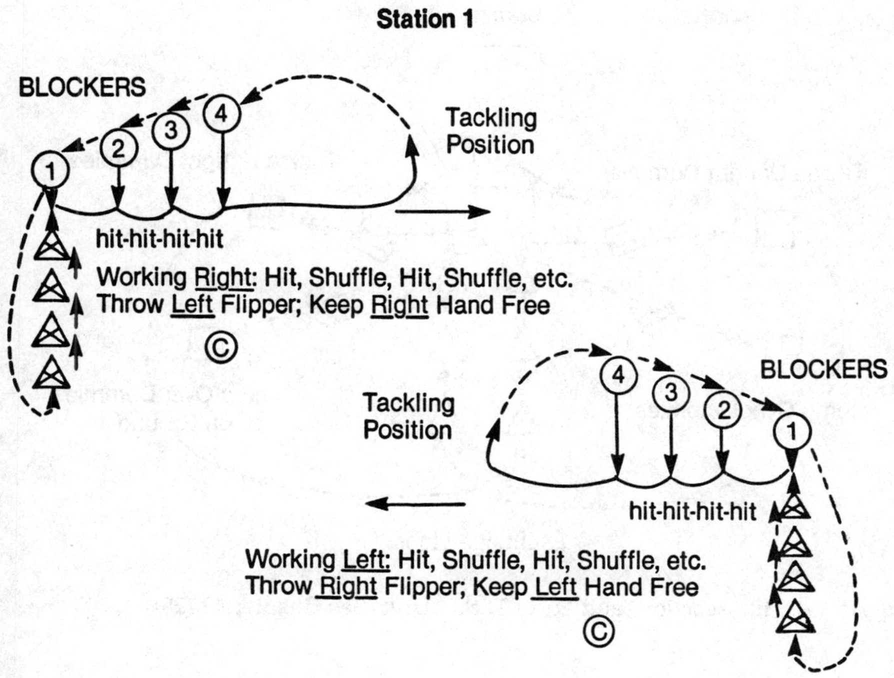

Figure 3–3 Ward-Off and Shed, Maintaining Leverage Drill (See Chapter 10 (25))

Station 3. Sled Drills
Station 4. Form Tackling Drill

Although the Ward-Off and Shed Drill (Figure 3–3) is excellent, physically it takes a great deal out of players. Therefore, if you intend to do rough work or scrimmage later in the practice session, it might be desirable to substitute another drill, such as Running Ropes and/or Overhead Ladder Drills, if such facilities are available. Or a coach may wish to include such drills as one of the four stations, although these do not fit the *B* or *C* categories above.

Since form tackling is taught and practiced at Station 4, the Bucker or Shiver Board Drill (Figure 3–5) may be substituted for the Hit, Reaction, and Form Tackling Drill (Figure 3–4) at Station 2, if such equipment is available.

At Station 3 it is probably most expedient to utilize the seven-man sled for this drill since only three minutes is allotted in the practice schedule. However, some coaches set aside at least five minutes daily in their practice schedule, apart from this particular fifteen-minute segment, for working on team starts and take-offs. If you adhere to this practice, then it would be better to utilize a two-man sled at Station 3 and not duplicate

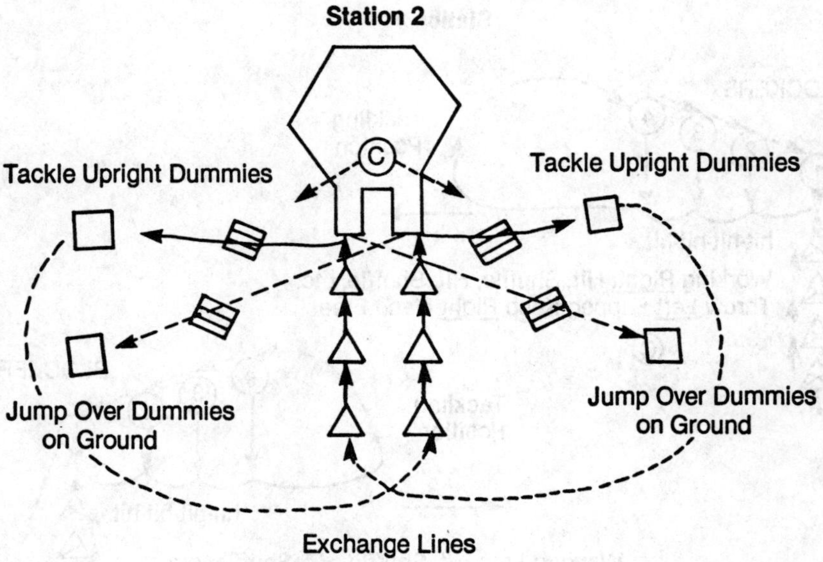

Figure 3–4 Hit, Reaction, and Form Tackle Drill (See Chapter 13 (25))

the take-off drill here or later in the practice schedule. Weather and field conditions dictate to some extent which piece of equipment to use as it may be difficult to move a seven-man sled if the footing and field conditions are poor due to inclement weather. If it appears your linemen's legs are getting "heavy" due to tiredness, especially late in the season, it would

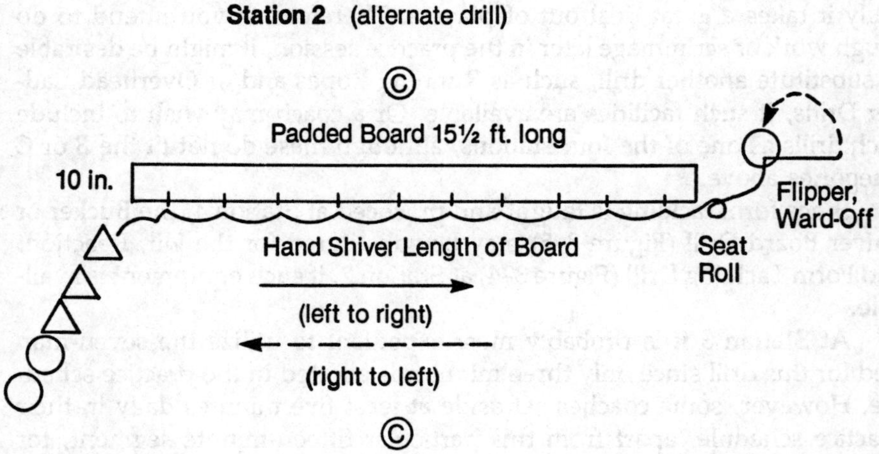

Figure 3–5 Bucker or Shiver Board Drill (See Chapter 10 (34))

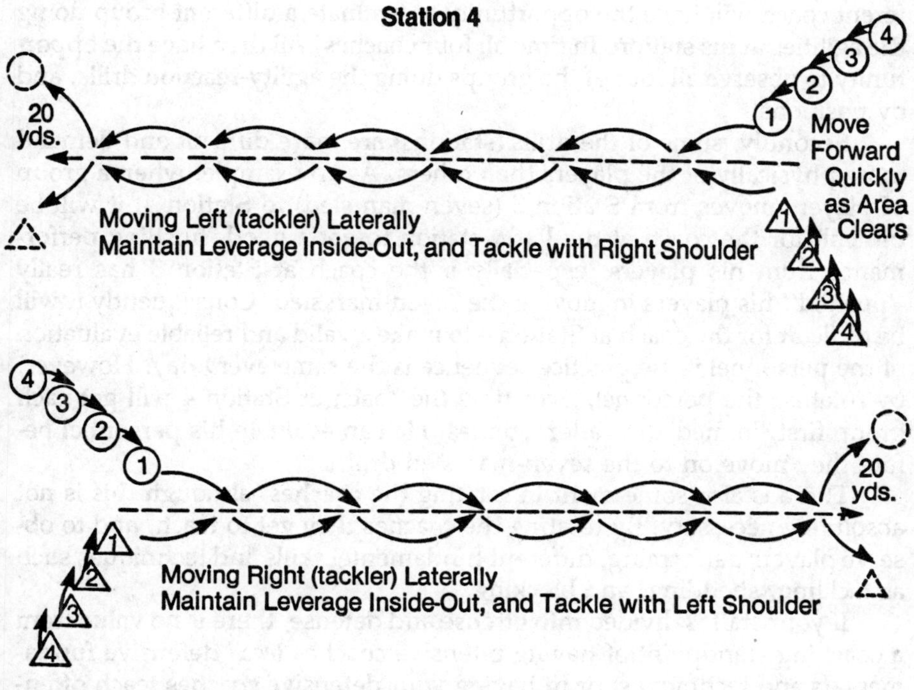

Figure 3–6 Form Tackling Drill (See Chapter 13 (26))

probably be better to substitute the two-man sled for the seven-man sled drill. However, at Station 3 it should be an offensive line drill.

Most any of the tackling drills in Chapter 13 may be substituted at Station 4 for the suggested form tackling drill (Figure 3–6). If a coach does not arrange his practice schedule carefully, his offensive linemen will have little opportunity to practice tackling techniques. On pass interceptions or when covering punts, the offensive linemen must be proficient tacklers and to do so they must be provided sufficient opportunities in practice to perfect tackling techniques and skills. The latter is why some coaches substitute defensive players to cover punts.

The suggested station drills above, their alternates and numerous other drills that may be utilized are presented in detail in other sections of this book. Many will be diagrammatically illustrated.

Organizational Coaching Points

When using the Four-Station Drills regularly, every couple of days it is advisable to rotate the groups of players so that each group is *not* always starting at the same station. As an example, instead of the centers and linebackers always commencing at Station 1, after a couple of days start them at Station 2. Several days later rotate them to Station 3, and later still they should commence at Station 4. This serves two purposes. First, a different coach will have the opportunity to evaluate a different group doing the agilities at his station. In time all four coaches will then have the opportunity to observe all four of the groups doing the agility-reaction drills, and by positions.

Secondly, some of the drills (stations) are more difficult and demand more physically of the players than others. As an example, when a group of players moves from Station 3 (seven-man sled) to Station 4, it will be difficult for the coach at the latter station to get a good, hustling performance from his players, especially if the coach at Station 3 has really "pushed" his players in moving the seven-man sled. Consequently it will be difficult for the coach at Station 4 to make a valid and reliable evaluation of the personnel if the practice sequence is the same every day. However, by rotating the personnel, over time the coach at Station 4 will get each group first, immediately after agilities. He can evaluate his personnel before they move on to the seven-man sled drill.

There is also some merit in rotating the coaches, although this is not absolutely necessary. By rotating the coaches they get to teach, and to observe players performing, different fundamental skills and techniques such as tackling, shedding, and blocking.

If your staff is divided into offense and defense, there is no value from a coaching standpoint of having offensive coaches *teach* defensive fundamentals and techniques, or in having your defensive coaches teach offensive fundamentals and techniques. However, there would be value in different coaches observing players performing different skills for the evaluation of player personnel.

INDIVIDUAL–GROUP OR COMBINATION–TEAM PERIODS

The above suggested practice plan will take twenty minutes, including five minutes for the suggested warm-up exercises or drills, three minutes for the suggested agility-reaction drills, and twelve minutes for the Four-Station Drills. By employing such a plan, a coach does not overlook the basic fundamentals and techniques of the game necessary to build a sound, winning football team. In brief the practice schedule is organized so the fundamentals, skills, and techniques are *taught* in the Individual Period; *practiced* in the Group or Combination Period; and then woven into an overall offensive and defensive *team effort* to be tested under simulated game conditions during the Team Period. Since the subject of Practice Organization merits book-length treatment, it is outside the scope of this book on drills. The reader's attention, however, is directed to the footnote below, which discusses the subject in detail.[2]

[2]Donald E. Fuoss and Rowland P. Smith, *Effective Football Coaching: Game-Winning Techniques for Preventing Mistakes and Errors* (Boston: Allyn and Bacon, 1981).

As noted in Chapter 1, the selection of a particular drill and the amount of time you devote to it in your practice schedule may be decided by looking at the *purpose* of the drill and answering the following questions:

- *Are we going to use what this particular drill teaches?*
- *How much are we going to derive from this particular drill?*
- *How much are we going to use it in a game?*

Before considering drills, however, let us analyze teaching-coaching proper running form basics, an area frequently overlooked by many football coaches.

PART II

Drills for Teaching-Coaching Proper Running Form Basics, Agility, and Reaction

4

Teaching-Coaching Proper Running Form and "Good" Football Position Basics and Principles

Despite the fact that this book is limited in scope to the presentation of football drills and excludes a detailed discussion of the overall execution and performance of the fundamentals and techniques of the game, it is imperative to include the basics and principles of proper running form and those of a "good" football position. In no other chapter will football techniques and fundamental skills be discussed in detail. However, coaching points frequently reiterated throughout will refer to the basics and principles discussed in this chapter.

The teaching-coaching of proper running form is frequently overlooked by many coaches as they rush immediately into conditioning their players and the teaching-coaching of their offensive and defensive systems of play, going on the erroneous assumption that all football prospects already adhere to proper running form and are knowledgeable about the basic principles of running. Since coaching is always a race against time, they presume it is unnecessary to waste valuable time reiterating the teaching-coaching basics of proper running form.

Instructing players to "maintain a 'good' football position" has to be one of the most common phrases uttered by coaches during practice sessions. However, it may well be the least explained, coached, and practiced phrases since the basics and principles of a "good" football position are violated frequently by many football players. Therefore, both the generalities and illustrated specifics of maintaining a "good" football position are discussed in this chapter as salient teaching-learning-coaching points.

BODY CONTROL

Considering the fact that a player who does not move well is likely to be ineffective in blocking and tackling and in executing the other fundamentals, running or movement might well be considered the most important of the basic skills. Of course a player can have good speed and mobility but lack the courage to block and tackle. Excluding this necessary ingredient of courage, running or movement must be considered one of the most important fundamentals because football is a game of movement.

To be successful, the offense must be able to cross the critical point-of-attack quickly. For the defenders to be successful, they must be able to react quickly and lend instantaneous support countering at the offensive point-of-attack. Since football is a game of movement with the situation changing every second the football is in play, one must maintain a good balanced position both offensively and defensively and always be ready to hit or be hit. Very few teams that can run, block, and tackle with good speed lose football games.

PROPER RUNNING FORM BASICS

Since proper running form is important, *every athlete should be taught how to run correctly.* Many coaches fail to teach-coach proper running form, going on the erroneous assumption that every football prospect already knows what constitutes good running form. Almost anyone can be taught to run at least a little faster if he has the desire to do so and adheres to proper body alignment and the other basic principles of running to be discussed. Since running is the oldest form of athletic conditioning, some phases applicable to running as conditioning will be included in this chapter.

In normal running, two distinct stepping actions may be identified: the lead step and the push-off step. The lead step involves moving the foot forward to contact the ground, and the push-off step uses the ground as a fixed point from which to propel the body forward. Three opposed muscle groups alternate actions in the lead and push-off steps. There is an opposed group for each of the three sections of the limb which act directly in running: the thigh, leg, and foot.

Basic Principles of Running

The basic principles of running correctly are as follows:

1. The body must be supple in order to attain the best results; therefore, *relax* when you run.
2. The toes should be pointed straight ahead, and you should run on the balls of the feet. A common mistake is for an athlete to run on his toes, the erroneous assumption being he can run faster and it will increase his endurance. It does neither. In fact it slows down the runner, and toe running tires him more quickly. Also, running on the toes increases the chance of foot and leg injuries by straining the runner's shin and calf muscles and the Achilles tendon.
3. One should run with the head up and the eyes open, with the ankles, hips, shoulders, and head in a relatively straight line. The running angle is important, and one should not bend too far backward or forward. Leaning forward shortens the runner's stride and expends his energy. Obviously one should lean forward when trying to "break" a tackle, block a defender, or tackle the ball carrier in order to meet force with force. Also, a defensive lineman will be in a more crouched position when sliding laterally to move to the offensive point-of-attack than one pursuing some distance to get to the ball carrier. For open-field running, however, the running angle is important in that the runner should not be bent over or bent too far backward.
4. Arm action is important with the opposite arm and leg moving in unison. Keep the arms relaxed and run with a "hand in pocket" motion. The hands should not be brought forward higher than the shoulders, back further than the crest of the hip, or beyond the median of the torso. Pump the arms and legs in a relaxed piston-like movement when sprinting.
5. Develop a comfortable stride, the proper stride being approximately the height of one's body. Other than in a short sprint, you should be in the proper running angle with the proper stride approximately twelve to fifteen yards from the starting point.

Variant Forms of Running

Variant forms of running are helpful in developing the strength and limberness of particular muscle groups, in building the endurance factor, and in the improvement of locomotor balance. Some of these forms will be included briefly below.

1. *Running backwards* involves, in the lead step, hyperextension, rather than the flexion of the thighs found in running forward. This tends to stretch the extensors of the thigh which act in the push-off step of forward running. Running backwards also fosters balance, as it introduces into the athlete's repertoire of skills a seldom experienced locomotor movement. Running backwards as a drill mixes well with alternate bursts of running forward and will be explained and illustrated shortly.
2. *Lunge running* is accomplished by taking as large steps as possible. This places a heavy load on the extensors of the legs and thighs, as they must pull the body a farther distance forward per step than in normal stride running. Lunge running is a very strenuous activity. The High Stepper or Toe Dance Drill (Chapter 5) is a form of lunge running.
3. *Accentuated foot running* can take place only at a reduced speed, as time must be allowed for a powerful plantar flexion of the ankle and foot against the resistance of the ground, followed by an increased dorsal flexion recovery. This exaggerated foot and ankle action strengthens the contractions of the gastrocnemius, soleus, and peroneous longus, so their contribution to the total propulsive action of the limb in normal running will be increased. Accentuated foot running is not suitable as a race type of activity since it must be practiced at the player's desired rate of speed. Therefore, it will not be included with the drills, although one may practice it on his own as a warm-up or conditioning drill.
4. *High-knee running* is intended chiefly to stretch the extensors of the thighs, as knees are brought as close to the chest as possible during forward locomotion, thus decreasing the angle between thigh and trunk much more than in a normal gait. Stationary high-knee running accomplishes somewhat the same objective, only the participant remains at a fixed spot or station and does not move forward. Both of these drills, and other running drills, will be included in Chapter 5.
5. *Spot running* is the opposite of high-knee running, as the objective is to run in place keeping the feet close to the ground (about two inches) in order to touch the feet on the ground as rapidly as possible. It will be further explained in Chapter 5.
6. *Running up hill* can be used very effectively to bring the over-load principle into running. The steeper the slope, the greater the resistance, especially in the push-off step. By increasing the degree of slope, distance, and speed, as an athlete rounds into condition, a coach can foster increase of the three important muscle quali-

ties—strength, endurance, and quickness of contraction. Running up hill is probably the best exercise for overall hip flexion and is also an excellent conditioner. In some coaching situations, running the stadium steps regularly from the bottom to the top a specified number of times is substituted for running up hill.

7. *Running in sand* is an old standby for conditioning because the "give" factor of the sandy ground forces the extensors to push harder to achieve the same speed as on a hard surface. Running in sand is excellent for race activities.
8. *Running in shallow water* is another means of applying the overload principle to running. This is accomplished by increasing the depth as one's condition improves. It also has the advantage of providing resistance for the flexing, or leading movements, as well as the extensing, or push-off steps.

Short sprints develop speed. Distance running develops endurance. Running in circles and figure 8s strengthens one's ankles, knees, hips, and back.

Obviously some of the suggested running activities do not lend themselves to the formalized practice program but are applicable to the off-season conditioning program.

THE BASICS OF A "GOOD" FOOTBALL POSITION

Whether the player is an offensive or defensive lineman or back, the basic premise of a "good" football position is the same in that he should always be in a "hitting" or ready position so as to dominate as the "hitter," whether he is doing the hitting or going to be hit. Generally it means maintaining proper body alignment throughout every play, whether on offense or defense, being on-balance, and having one's body under control at all times. To a tackler, for example, it means having a good solid base, feet apart approximately shoulder width, and moving with short choppy steps, being careful not to over-stride, weight low in the tail, and knees flexed in order to uncoil and deliver a blow into the ball carrier. Also, in this situation, the tackler's back should be relatively straight, head up, eyes on the football, hands away from the body, and his body under control as he prepares to *run through* the ball carrier. From this good *hitting* position the tackler is able to shift with the runner, and his solid base gives him a good foundation for a driving tackle to dominate the ball carrier rather than being dominated by him (Chapter 13). The ball carrier, for his part, must maintain a "good" football position in order to dominate the "hitter."

From the generalities of a "good" football position, a good coach teaches his players the specifics relevant to the proper execution of the fundamentals of the game, as illustrated above.

Chapter 5 deals with drills for teaching agility and reaction, since a player must develop the ability to move quickly in any direction, maintaining a "good" football position throughout.

5

Agility and Reaction Drills

The true measure of football speed is quickness in an immediate area, and not necessarily how fast a player can run 50–100 yards. Movement, in football, refers to speed, quickness, and agility. The latter two are more important than speed, although lacking any of the three assets will limit the progress of a player. Except in a few football positions, speed is not measured in "raw terms," that is, how fast a player can run 50 or 100 yards.

Think of *agility* as "nimbleness." *Reaction* is "a response to a stimulus," such as to the offensive starting count or from a defensive standpoint the reaction to an action. The development of body control, agility, and the ability to react quickly and correctly are as important as the proper development of offensive and defensive fundamentals. Without these skills, a player will not be able to execute the necessary fundamentals. If he is unable to control his own body, he will be unable to control his opponent.

Reaction drills may be used to develop both agility and reaction, whereas simple agility drills are limited in value unless a stimulus is added, along with the teaching of mobility and nimbleness, in order to secure a desired reaction. Therefore, as a coaching suggestion, seldom employ drills that teach only agility unless that particular agility is also a technique or a fundamental. More than four dozen agility and reaction drills are included in this chapter, some of which are superior for improving reaction time and developing coordination and agility.

No attempt will be made to present any of the drills in a progressive order of importance. Other agility and reaction drills that teach additional fundamentals and techniques will be included in other sections of the book under appropriate categories. Since it is difficult to determine in which category some of the drills belong, they will be placed categorically according to their primary purpose throughout the book.

Included in the agility-action drills are tumbling drills, which develop the ability to control one's body in flight, as well as teach a player how to fall and roll without being injured.

There are numerous agility and reaction drills, and each drill has variations. The objective is not to present an infinite number of drills, although many of these may be revised for additional drills. Simple agility drills will be presented first, then reaction drills. Several agility-reaction drills for teaching-coaching techniques or fundamentals will be included, although this category will be considered in greater numbers in other sections of the book. The following drills may be used to develop agility and/or reaction.

1. HIGH STEPPER OR TOE DANCE DRILL

Purpose: To develop body balance and agility and to stretch and loosen the muscles during warm-up.

Procedure: Straddling a line and facing the opposite side of the field, the players follow one another across the width of the field, jogging with high-knee action, stretching out the legs, crossing back and forth over the line. Players should land on the toes, getting torsion in the hips, and exaggerate the natural swing of the arms.

Coaching Points: Emphasize high-knee action and hip movement, not speed. When landing on the toes, the right foot should alight on the left side of the line and the left foot on the right side of the line. Follow up with the Carioca Drill.

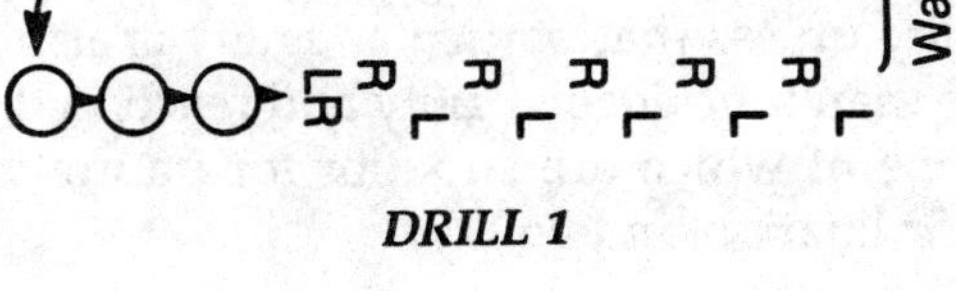

DRILL 1

2. CARIOCA OR GRAPEVINE DRILL

Purpose: To develop body balance, agility, coordination, quickness, and to stretch and loosen the muscles during warm-up.

Procedure: A single file of players standing on a line facing an end zone move laterally on the coach's starting command. When going to the left, each player steps laterally with his left foot first, crosses over with his right foot in front of his left. The player then steps laterally with his left foot, crosses with his right foot behind his left, repeating the procedure again and again for a specified distance (15 yards). Coming back on the line, the player working to his right, steps laterally with the right foot first,

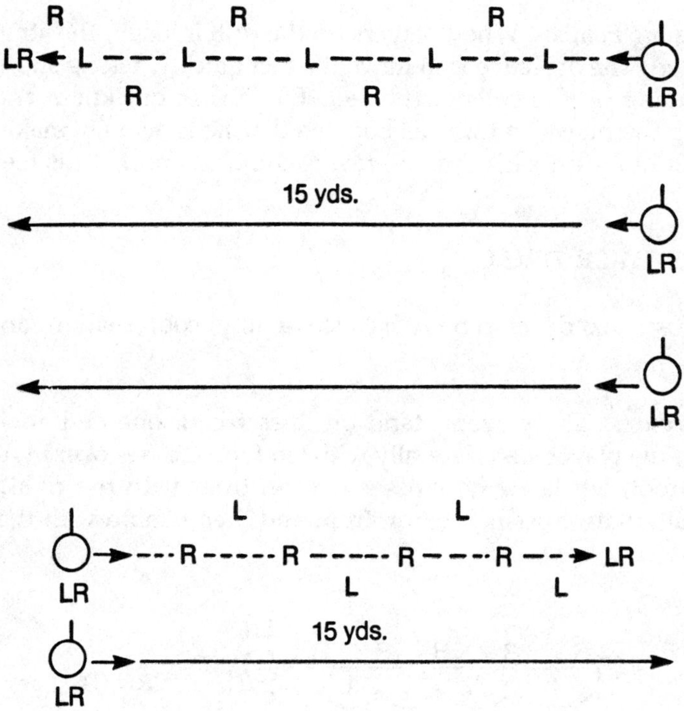

DRILL 2

crosses over with his left foot in front, steps laterally with his right foot crossing his left foot behind his right foot, etc.

Coaching Points: Stress maintaining a low center of gravity, opening the hips, short choppy steps, quick movement, rhythm, i.e., "carioca."

3. STRADDLE DRILL

Purpose: To develop body balance, agility, coordination, quickness, and to stretch and loosen the muscles during warm-up.

Procedure: Same as for (2) Carioca or Grapevine Drill. Players stand on lines facing one end zone, feet parallel but staggered so that heel of one foot (right) is in front of line, and toe of opposite foot (left) is behind the line. When going left, the player jumps laterally, just high enough to clear the ground, and reverses the position of his feet so that his left is forward and his right is behind the line, repeating the movement for the specified distance. When repeating the process moving down the line from the left, the player's first movement is laterally to his right, and reversing his feet in a straddle position each time he clears the ground.

Coaching Points: When players do the drill initially, the straddle will be extended. The objective is to move the feet quickly, taking short choppy steps, landing on the balls of the feet. Emphasize quickness and speed, permitting the player to turn his body so that he is actually making about one-eighth of a turn each time he reverses the position of his feet.

4. CROSS–OVER DRILL

Purpose: To develop body balance, agility, coordination, and quickness.

Procedure: The players stand on lines facing one end zone. When going left, the player steps laterally with left foot, crosses over in front with the right foot, left laterally, crosses over in front with the right, etc. He does *not* alternate crossing over in front and then behind with the off-foot

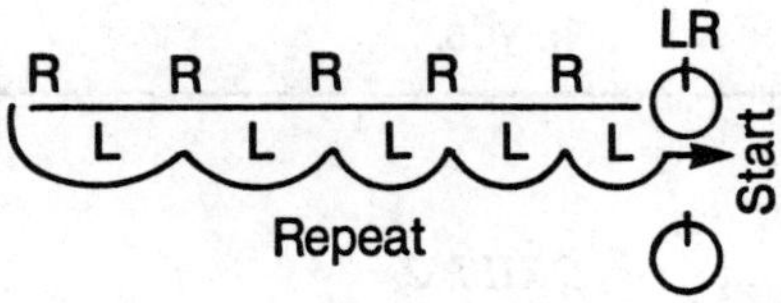

DRILL 4

as in the Carioca Drill. The shoulders are kept parallel with the line, and the arms and hands are extended away from the front of the body in a ward-off or shed position.

Coaching Points: Emphasize high-knee action when crossing over with the off-leg. Stress quickness and speed. Work both left and right. Since this drill is easier to perform than (2) Carioca or Grapevine Drill, it should be a lead-in drill to the Carioca.

5. TURN AROUND AND SPRINT DRILL

Purpose: To develop body balance, leg-arm action, and agility.

Procedure: On the coach's command the players start running in place using a high-knee action, pumping the arms vigorously, and turning slowly clockwise or counterclockwise. After one or two body revolutions, the coach gives a second command, "Go!" and the players whip around and sprint ten yards in the direction they faced initially.

Coaching Points: Warm up the players thoroughly before having them sprint and stress coordinated high-knee arm action.

DRILL 5

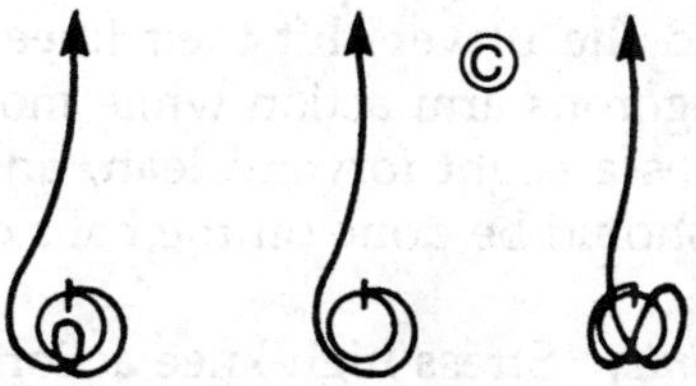

6. SPOT RUNNING OR FOOTFIRE DRILL

Purpose: To develop body balance, leg-arm action, and agility.

Procedure: Same as (5) Turn Around and Sprint Drill, only on command the players sprint in place as fast as they can, pounding their feet into the ground rapidly. Go five seconds of footfire, five seconds rest, five seconds of footfire, etc. Do not do more than five repetitions.

Coaching Points: Stress quickness and rapidity in moving the feet. Keep the feet about two inches from the ground in order that they touch the ground as rapidly as possible. Do not extend the drill unless conditioning is desired, instead of agility and reaction.

7. STATIONARY HIGH-KNEE RUNNING DRILL

Purpose: To develop body balance, quickness, and high-knee running action.

Procedure: Same as (6) Spot Running or Footfire Drill, only on the coach's command the players lift their knees high and pump their legs, rapidly sprinting in place. Touch the knees to the palms of the hands, which are held high above the waist parallel to the ground. Sprint rapidly for five seconds, rest for five seconds, sprint, rest, etc., for five repetitions.

Coaching Points: Stress the correct body alignment and good running form, running on the toes and the balls of the feet, not on the heels. Lift the knees to the palms of the hands; do not lower the palms to the knees. If the drill is used for conditioning, then sprint, jog, sprint, jog, instead of resting between the commands.

8. FORWARD HIGH-KNEE RUNNING DRILL

Purpose: To develop body balance, leg-arm action, and high-knee running action.

Procedure: Same as (6) Spot Running or Footfire Drill, only on the coach's command the players lift their knees high and pump their legs rapidly, using vigorous arm action while moving forward for five yards. The body assumes a slight forward lean, and the head is kept up at all times. The drill should be done on the balls of the feet and toes.

Coaching Points: Stress high-knee action, good body alignment, and correct running form. The emphasis is not on sprinting five yards, but on the vigorous running action causing the body to creep forward.

9. FORWARD-BACKWARD-SPRINT DRILL

Purpose: To develop body balance, leg-arm action, coordination, and agility.

Procedure: On the coach's command, the players creep forward using short choppy steps and a pumping arm action. On each succeeding command until they hear "Sprint!" the players whip themselves around 180° with the force of their shoulders and hips and continue creeping backward, turn and go forward, etc., until the final command, when they

DRILL 9

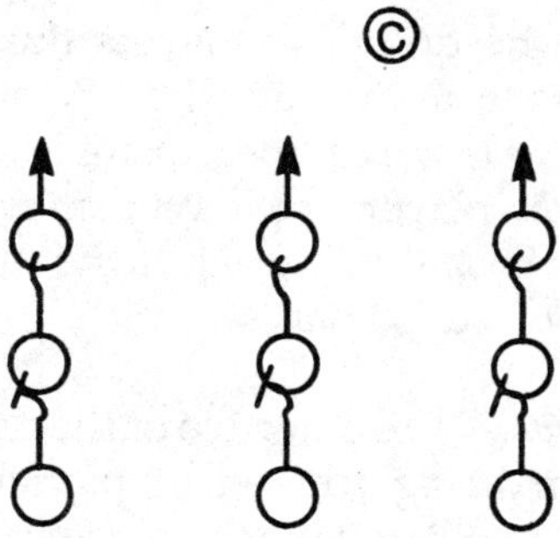

sprint ten yards. The line of direction remains the same throughout the drill, always moving away from the initial lineup position.

Coaching Points: Stress quickness, speed, good form and body alignment when running.

10. RUNNING BACKWARD DRILL

Purpose: To develop body balance and leg action.

Procedure: Same as (9) Forward-Backward-Sprint Drill, only the players line up facing away from the direction they intend to run backward. On the coach's command the players move backward, with a slight body lean forward, staying on their toes and the balls of their feet.

Coaching Points: Emphasize quickness and speed, *not* high-knee action. The latter action forces the torso up and the head back, which is not the desired body position.

11. GRAB GRASS OR SCOOP DRILL

Purpose: To develop body balance and recovery, coordination, reaction, and agility.

Procedure: This may be organized the same as (1) High Stepper Drill as the players follow each other across the width of the field at five-yard intervals, east and west. On the coach's command the first player sprints at top speed for five yards, bends over and tries to "scoop" or grab a handful of grass, regains his balance, sprints another five yards, bends to the opposite side and grabs grass with his near-hand, regains his balance, alternating from the right side to the left side, moving across the field. When the first player bends to scoop, the coach sends the second player after the lead player, and then continues at about five-yard intervals until all players are in the drill. The players then repeat the same procedure coming back across from the opposite side of the field. Or the drill may be set up with players in three lines, using the length (north/south) of the field. The first three players leave on command, and the coach continues to give commands each time he wants the players to bend and grab grass, for a specified distance (30 yards).

Coaching Points: The objective of the drill is to simulate body balance and recovery after being tripped or partially tripped. Therefore, stress speed, quickness, and reaction to the commands.

12. FORWARD ROLLS (SOMERSAULT) DRILL

Purpose: To develop body balance and agility and to teach a player how to fall and roll correctly on the ground, to regain his feet to an upright position, and to react quickly to (sight) movement.

Procedure: The players start from a low position, literally rolling into the drill rather than diving into it. The initial shock is taken up by the hands as the palms are placed on the ground. The chin is tucked forward on the breastbone as the player buckles his body and brings his knees into his chest. As the elbows bend, cushioning the impact with the ground, the player's weight is caught on his shoulder blades at the base of the neck and transferred downward to the buttocks as he rolls forward. He grasps both ankles and gives an additional tuck and pull to create the necessary momentum to elevate himself onto his feet and into a good football position. Repeat this procedure five or six times.

Coaching Points: Stress a low center of gravity and the proper method of landing on the ground. Do not permit the players to dive into the forward rolls. The roll is done diagonally, not laterally.

13. BROADJUMPING–SOMERSAULT–SPRINT DRILL

Purpose: To develop body balance and agility, and to teach players how to land correctly on the ground from an upright position.

Procedure: Starting from a good football position, the players broad-jump with both feet together twice, somersault once, and come up running for ten yards further.

Coaching Points: Stress quickness, bending the knees to get spring and leg snap when jumping, a low center of gravity, and the proper method of landing on the ground from an upright position.

DRILL 14

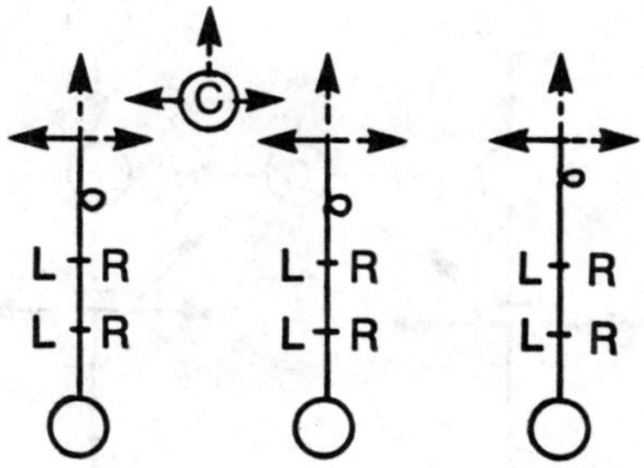

14. BROADJUMP–SOMERSAULT–WAVE DRILL

Purpose: To teach agility and reaction.

Procedure: The players broadjump twice with both feet together, somersault once, regain an upright "good" football position quickly, and react immediately to the coach's hand signal. If the coach raises his hand above his head, the players will regain their feet, sprint toward him, yell "Pass!" and raise their hands upward as they approach the coach who is simulating throwing a pass. If the coach makes a lateral movement with his hand, upon regaining their feet the players will plant their far-foot and break at a 90° angle from their original direction using a cross-over step on the correct angle of pursuit.

Coaching Points: Stress quickness, bending the knees to get spring and leg snap when jumping, a low center of gravity when somersaulting, and alertness for the coach's hand signal. Avoid false-stepping or running in an arc when reacting to the coach's lateral hand movement.

15. SOMERSAULT–SHED–WAVE DRILL

Purpose: To teach agility, shedding or warding off an opponent, and reaction.

Procedure: From a good football position each defensive player executes a somersault, comes to his feet in a good hitting position, and both offensive and defensive players execute forearm lifts, with the defender warding off or shedding the blocker and then reacting to the coach's hand signal, taking the proper angle of pursuit.

Coaching Points: Stress a low center of gravity for the defender as he executes his forward roll. The offensive player permits the defender to regain his feet before stepping forward and executing a shoulder lift or offensive block. Give the hand signal quickly so the defender can shed the

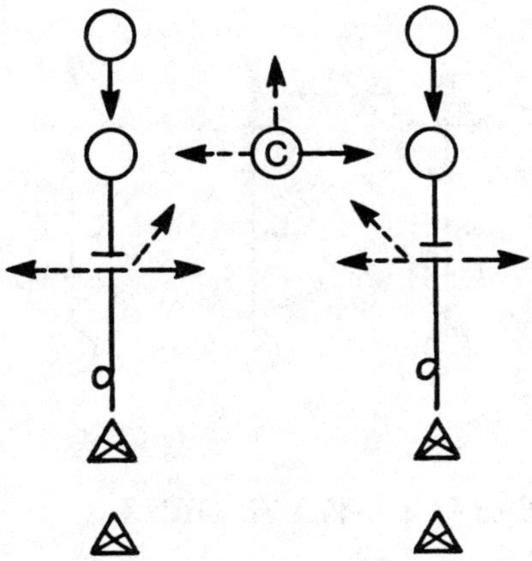

DRILL 15

blocker and react immediately. Alternate shoulders and the direction of pursuit, and stress no false-stepping, planting the far-foot and breaking at a 90° angle, using a cross-over step.

16. SOMERSAULT AND TACKLE DRILL

Purpose: To teach agility, reaction, and form tackling.

Procedure: From a good football position a defensive player executes a somersault and comes to his feet in a hitting position ready to form tackle the ball carrier who will step forward just as the defender regains his feet. The tackler carries the ball carrier backward five yards.

Coaching Points: Stress the proper techniques of good tackling. (See Chapter 13 for additional tackling drills.)

17. FOLLOW–THE–LEADER DRILL NO. 1

Purpose: To develop agility and quickness in reacting and changing direction.

Procedure: The leader is ten yards away from the followers who will "mirror" his movements—wave, somersault, crab, grass drill—until the leader raises his hand as if to pass. If defensive linemen are performing the drill, they terminate the drill by yelling "Pass!" and sprinting toward the leader with their hands raised upward. If secondary defenders are performing the drill, they, too, sound off when the leader raises his hand simulating a pass, but they drop back to cover their assigned zones.

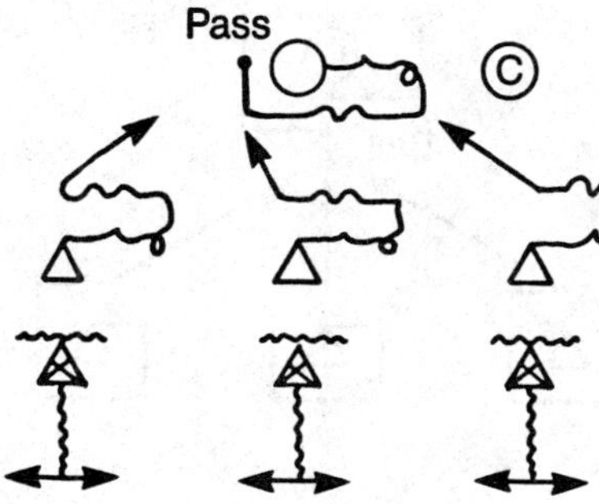

DRILL 17

Coaching Points: Stress quickness and do not permit the leader to extend the reactions beyond five, or the drill will be ineffective for developing agility and reaction. It will become a conditioning drill.

18. FOLLOW–THE–LEADER DRILL NO. 2

Purpose: To develop agility and reaction and to shed the blocker.

Procedure: Two lines face each other seven yards apart, so the defender can react to his offensive "buddy's" lateral movements, which will be flashed to him by the coach. The coach stands behind the defensive men and facing the offensive men, who watch his hand signals. After several hand signals, the coach will indicate the blockers should attack the defenders with a running shoulder block. The defenders will shed the blockers, and maintain a good football position throughout.

Coaching Points: Same as (15) Somersault-Wave-Shed Drill. If a ball carrier is added to the drill running behind his blockers, stress the proper fundamentals of good tackling.

19. LATERAL WAVE DRILL

Purpose: To develop quickness, agility, and reaction to movement.

Procedure: From a semi-upright stance, maintaining a good football position, the players watch the coach's hand signals, responding quickly to the direction designated, always moving at right angles when changing directions, and using a cross-over step when going laterally. If the players are linemen, the coach may conclude the drill by dropping a football to the ground simulating a fumble. The linemen must yell, "Ball!" and sprint to recover the fumble or "scoop" up to the football, depending on whether

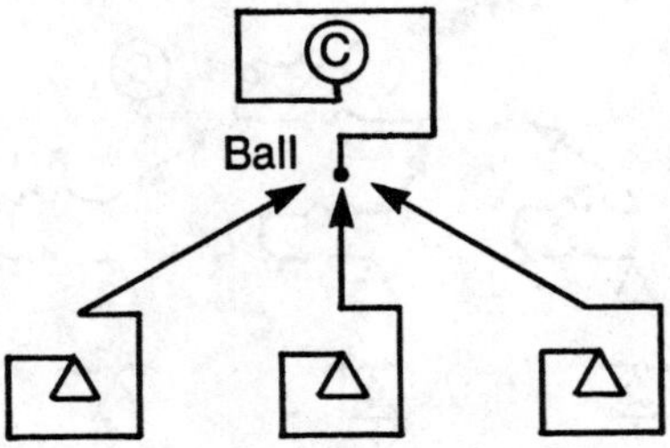

DRILL 19

or not rough work is desired and indicated by the coach. If defensive backs are doing the drill, when the coach raises the ball overhead the defenders yell, "Pass!" and simulate dropping backward or diagonally to cover their zones.

Coaching Points: Stress quickness, no false-stepping, and breaking at right angles instead of arcing or bowing when changing direction. Use no more than five reactions or the drill will become a conditioner instead of an agility-reaction drill.

20. CRAB OR SCRAMBLE DRILL

Purpose: To develop quickness, agility, and reaction to (sight or sound) movement.

Procedure: Same as (19) Lateral Wave Drill, only the players are down in a four-point stance, tail low, head up, back straight, weight evenly distributed on the fingertips and the toes, and reacting to hand signals by the coach. Bring the players up and running after the fifth reaction.

Coaching Points: Same as (19) Lateral Wave Drill, only the players use short, choppy steps, not crossing their feet when moving laterally, operating from a good balanced position and moving quickly, simulating defensive moves or pursuit after being knocked down by a blocker or continuing to scramble after slipping off a block. Bring the players up after the fifth reaction.

21. SHOULDER ROLLS DRILL

Purpose: To develop body balance and agility and to teach players how to land and roll on the ground correctly.

Procedure: As in (12) Forward Rolls (Somersault) Drill, the players start from a low position, literally rolling into the drill, rather than diving to the ground, in order to avoid injuries. Each player should fling his left hand and forearm between his legs, turn his head to the opposite side so his chin is against his collarbone, buckle his left leg and push off with his right foot, as his body weight and momentum will carry him forward into his roll. The point of the shoulder is downward and inward when the same hand is extended to the rear between the legs, and the impact is taken on the back of the shoulder blade and transferred diagonally down across the body to the buttocks and feet as the player completes his roll. He comes up into a good football position, flings the opposite hand and forearm (right) between his legs and rolls over the back of the right shoulder. Repeat.

Coaching Points: Stress flinging the arm and getting the point of the shoulder downward and inward. The roll is diagonally and not laterally. Stress the proper methods of landing and rolling.

22. SEAT ROLLS AND CRAB DRILL

Purpose: To teach agility and reaction to (sight) movement.

Procedure: The player crabs, then flips his body over rolling on his seat (butt) to the crab position, then crabs on all fours. Repeat the drill right and left. The player somersaults, regains his feet, then forearm lifts the man in front of him. Finally the player whirls around quickly to forearm lift the opponent coming from behind his position.

Coaching Points: Stress a low center of gravity, quickness, and operating from a good football position. You can use oral or hand signals for player reactions. Do not exceed more than five reactions, or the drill becomes a conditioner.

23–26. LOG ROLL OR FIGURE 8 DRILLS (FOUR PROGRESSIONS)

23. Three-Man Log Roll Drill

24. Log Roll and Shed Drill

25. Log Roll and Tackle Drill

26. Double Log Roll, Shed, Pursue and Tackle Drill

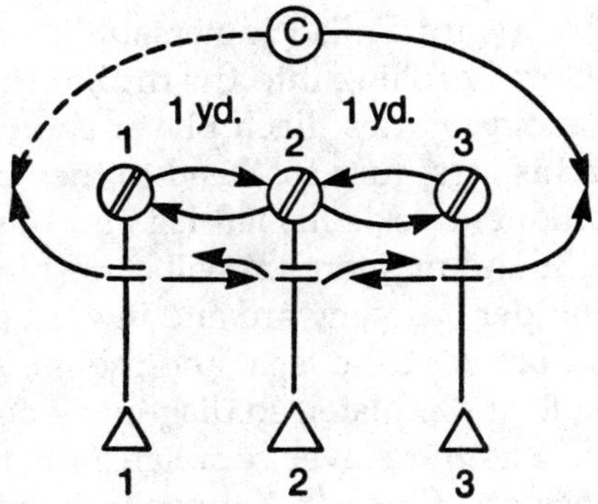

DRILL 26

Purpose: To develop agility and reaction in: (23) getting up from the ground; (24) shedding a blocker; (25) tackling; and (26) shedding, pursuing, and tackling.

Procedure: The players are on the ground on all fours on their fingertips and toes, five yards apart. On the coach's command player No. 1 springs upward and over No. 2, and the latter rolls to the outside; then player No. 3 goes over No. 1. The player coming from the outside position goes over the player in the middle, and rolls to the opposite side. The player in the middle stays low and rolls to the outside. The drill is continuous until the coach yells, "Up!" If both lines are log rolling at the same time, as in Drills 24, 25, and 26, when the command "Up" is given, the offensive players (24) try to block the defenders, who will shed them. In Drill 25 the offensive players move forward and are form tackled by the defensive men. In Drill 26 they block the defenders, who will shed them, pursue and tackle (tag) the ball carrier (coach), or react to the coach's hand signals.

Coaching Points: The drills are done in series of three-player units, and quickness should be stressed. In Drill 26 do not extend the log rolls, or the fundamentals are unlikely to be performed correctly since the drill will become a conditioner instead of an agility-reaction drill.

27. SPINNING DRILL

Purpose: To develop body balance and coordination.

Procedure: Any number of two-man "buddy" units can perform the drill at the same time. One player gets on the ground in a six-point stance, and a second player rests his chest on the back of the down player. The top player's feet are spread so that he has room to operate in a semi-circle arc from the head of the down player to either side, back to his hips. He may hold his hands and arms away from his body for balance, or place them behind his back. On the coach's commands of "Right," "Left," etc., the "spinner" moves in the specified direction as quickly as possible. He should stay on his toes and the balls of his feet.

Coaching Points: Stress quickness. If the top man is permitted to make a complete circle, caution must be exercised so he does *not* step on the down player's ankles or trip over the latter's extended feet. Also, instruct the down player not to extend his head upward, and to place his hands on the ground in a straight plane with his shoulders, keeping his weight on his knuckles—not on his extended fingers.

28. CRAB–CIRCLE–CRAB DRILL

Purpose: To develop agility and reaction.

Procedure: Operating from a four-point stance with the head up, tail down, back straight, good base, weight on the hands and the balls of the feet, each player responds to the hand and verbal signals of the coach—"Crab right (left)," "Circle left (right)," etc.

Coaching Points: Do not extend for too many reactions or the drill becomes a conditioner; stress quickness, including circling.

DRILL 28

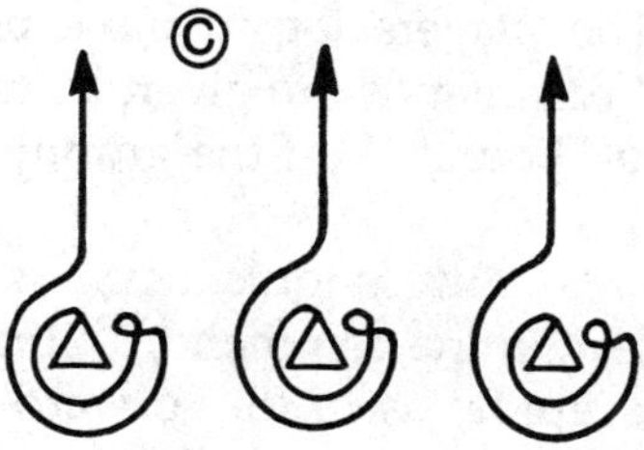

29. QUARTER–EAGLE, SPRINT–WAVE DRILL

Purpose: To develop body balance, agility, and reaction and to simulate moving to meet a blocker coming from any direction.

Procedure: The players are in a semi-upright stance with their knees partially flexed, the head up, tail down, hands and arms away from the body in a good defensive football position. On the command or starting count, the players start hopping in place, both feet together, somewhat

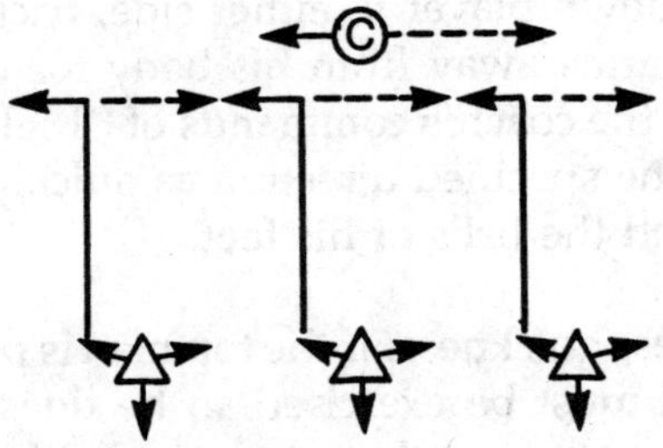

DRILL 29

similar to the rapidity of moving the feet in (6) Spot Running or Footfire Drill. On the coach's commands of "Right! Right!," "Left! Left!," etc., the players execute one-quarter turns on every command until the coach yells, "Sprint!" or "Go!" Then they whirl around, if facing away from the coach and their original position, and sprint toward him. As they approach the coach, he indicates by hand signal the direction of lateral movement they are to take.

Coaching Points: Stress quickness when hopping in place and turning. Do not give too many quarter turns (reactions), or the drill becomes a conditioner instead of an agility-reaction drill.

30. DOWN–UP OR QUICK GRASS DRILL

Purpose: To develop agility and reaction to verbal commands.

Procedure: The players jog in place until the "Down–Up, Down-Up," or "Sprint" commands are given by the coach. The players should attempt literally to "bounce" off the ground and come up running.

Coaching Points: Stress quickness, commanding "Down-Up" as quickly as possible. On the command, "Sprint," the players run in place moving their feet rapidly as in (8) Forward High-Knee Running Drill. It will become a conditioning grass drill if the reactions are extended to more than five.

31. FORWARD RUN–SOMERSAULT–WAVE DRILL

Purpose: To develop body balance, agility, coordination, physical toughness, and conditioning.

Procedure: A combination of Drills 12, 19, and 21, the players do a running forward roll or shoulder roll every time the coach yells, "Down," as they sprint thirty yards or more down the field. The players face the

DRILL 31

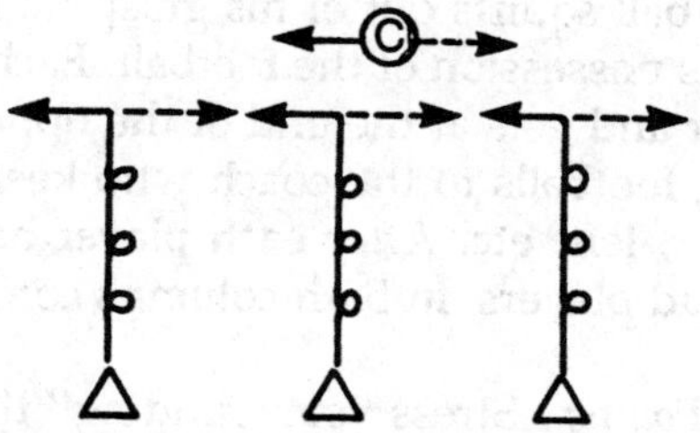

coach, who runs backward staying out in front of the players giving verbal commands to them. After several commands, the coach yells, "Right!" or "Left!" and the players move laterally as in the Wave Drill.

Coaching Points: Same as Drills 12, 19, and 21. The drill is demanding if the players run for a period of time and are ordered, "Down" a number of times. This drill is good for conditioning the players, especially linemen, if conditioning is what the coach wishes to accomplish.

32. COVER BALL–FUMBLE DRILL

Purpose: To develop quickness and reaction to a "loose" football and to compete for the possession of it.

Procedure: The coach stands with a manager between two columns of players and flips, tosses, bats, rolls, or bounces a football in front of the lead player in the right-hand column, and then in the left-hand column. Each player must yell, "Ball!" indicating a loose football, and sprint to

DRILL 32

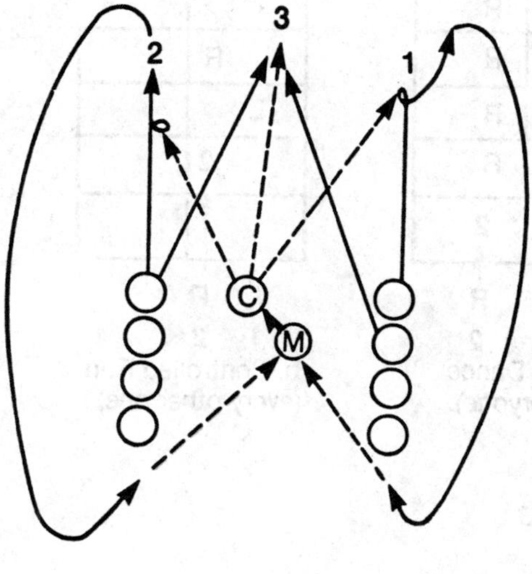

cover it. If the ball squirts out of his grasp he must get up and go after it until he secures possession of the football. Each player returns the football to the manager and gets at the end of the opposite column. The manager keeps handing footballs to the coach who keeps the drill moving rapidly right, left, right, left, etc. After each player has had a turn going after a football, the lead players in both columns compete for one football.

Coaching Points: Stress "surrounding" the football, bringing it up to the chest with the arms and hands encircling it, and tucking the chin, lowering the head and drawing the knees up to the chest for protection. Roll forward. Also stress not falling flat on the football. The drill is good for conditioning and developing physical toughness, if extended.

33–35. RUNNING ROPES OR ROPE MAZE DRILLS

33. Single Stepping Rope Drills

34. Two Feet Together Rope Drills

35. Two Feet Together Lateral Hop Drill

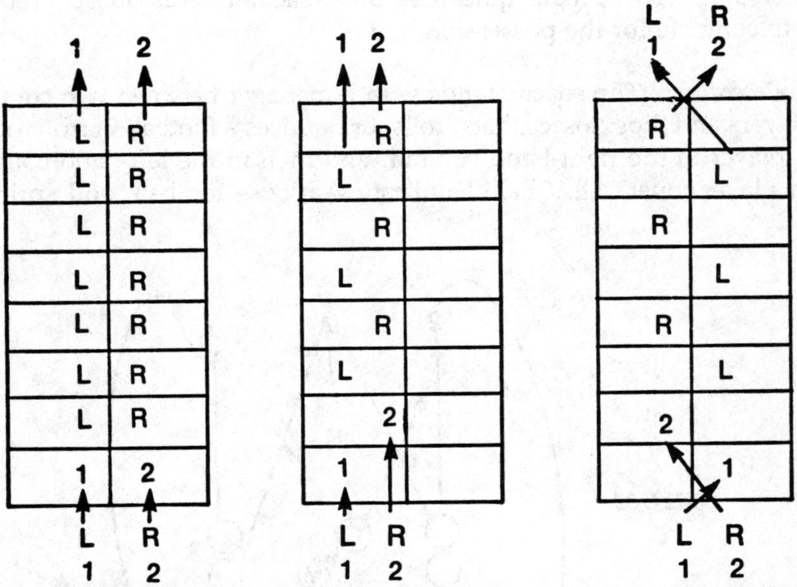

a. Toe Dance (everyone)

b. Controlled Run (every other one)

c. Controlled Run (crossover every other one)

DRILL 33

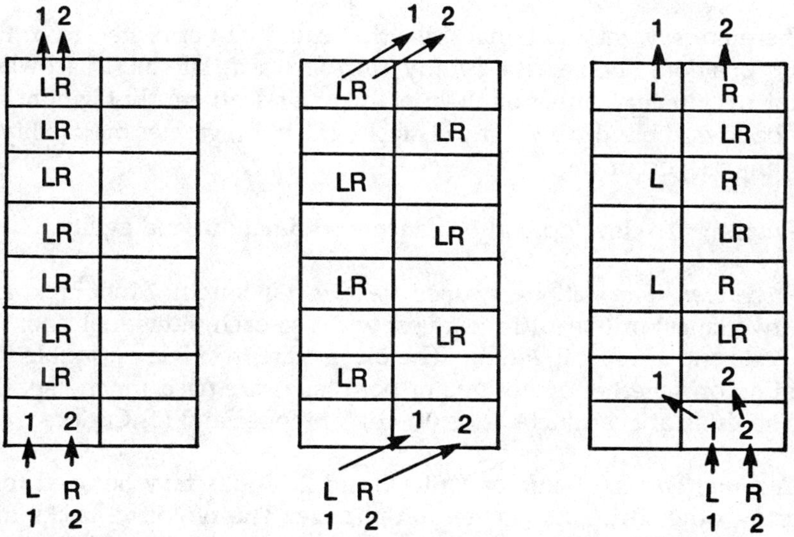

a. Bunny Hop (every one)

b. Controlled Hop (crossover every other one)

c. Hopscotch (feet together, then apart)

DRILL 34

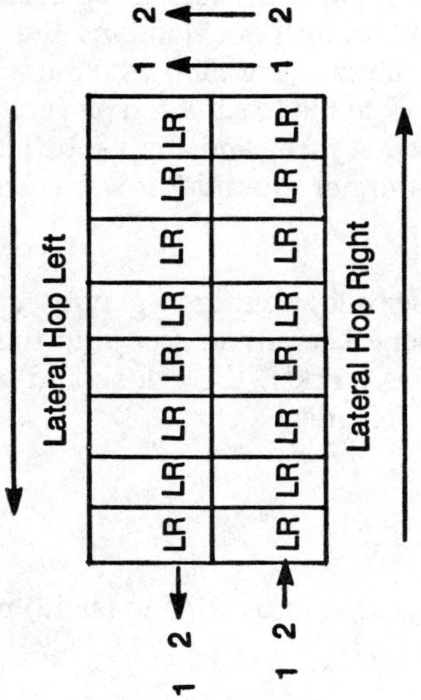

There are several additional drills that could be performed from this sideways position, such as the bunny hop forward, laterally, backward; crossing over (every other one); hopscotch; and others. But when one jumps backward blindly over an obstacle, there is a greater probability of injuries occurring.

DRILL 35

There are several additional drills that could be performed from this *sideways* position, such as the Bunny Hop forward, laterally, backward; crossing over (every other one); hopscotch; and others, but when one jumps backward blindly over any obstacle, there is a greater probability of (ankle) injuries occurring.

Purpose: To develop body balance, coordination, and agility.

Procedure: The stationary ropes are 60 feet in length, 1 foot high, and 4 feet (two lanes) or 6 feet (three lanes) wide, so each individual "box" is 2 feet wide and 1½ feet in length. The players are in single or double file, depending on whether or not one or both lanes are used for the specific drill. The drills are conducted like (1) High Stepper and (2) Carioca.

Coaching Points: Same as Drills 1 and 2. Ropes may be used for a number of other drills, too, where applicable. The offensive backs may carry a football and shift it from arm to arm. (See Chapter 9, (26) Running Ropes and Hand-Off Drill.)

36. SOFTBALL DRILL

Purpose: To develop agility and reaction.

Procedure: The players line up in a single file facing the coach 5–7 yards apart. A defender assumes a good football position, and the coach rolls a softball to the right or left of the player facing him, who must move laterally, scoop up the ball, and toss it back to the coach. Each player moves quickly to the end of the line to await his turn, and the next defender assumes his stance as the coach rolls another grounder toward the lead man in the column of players.

Coaching Points: Stress maintaining a low center of gravity, operating from a low base and stance, shuffling laterally to scoop up the ball, and quickness. Although the drill moves quickly, the ball should not be rolled with too much force toward the defender.

37. HIP OPENER DRILL

Purpose: To develop agility, quickness, and reaction to (sight) movement.

Procedure: Operating in three-man units one yard apart, the players are in a semi-upright stance facing the coach. The latter uses hand signals to indicate "Right" or "Left." The players turn (open) their hips, legs, and feet in the direction indicated by the coach, but *keep their shoulders square to him.* They quickly return to their original position after each hand signal by the coach.

Coaching Points: After 5–6 quick repetitions, the coach raises both hands, and the players pass rush him. Stress opening the hips, not merely stepping back with the foot in the direction the coach indicates. *Both* feet should be turned toward the sidelines when the coach indicates "Left" or "Right" by his hand signal, but the lineman will continue to face the coach. Stress quickness and quick feet.

38. FLASH DRILL

Purpose: To develop agility, quickness, and reaction to (sight) movement.

Procedure: Same as (37) Hip Opener Drill, only "Up" and "Down" directions are indicated by hand signal, in addition to "Right" and "Left" directions. On the "Up" signal the player "gathers" and leaps upward, hands and arms extended over his head. As he comes down in place, he immediately executes the next direction indicated by the coach. On the "Down" signal, the player quickly touches his right or left knee to the ground as indicated by the coach. He quickly springs to his feet and performs the next movement signaled by the coach. The drill is terminated by the coach raising both hands, indicating pass rush, as in (37) Hip Opener Drill.

Coaching Points: Stress quickness. The drill should not be extended beyond five quick repetitions, or it becomes a conditioner instead of an agility-reaction drill.

39–40. FOOTWORK ROPE JUMPING DRILLS

39. Jump Rope Drill: (individualized)

a. Both feet jumping as quickly as possible for one minute.
b. At a slower pace for two-and-one-half minutes, both feet, bicycle, right foot, left foot, repeat.
c. Same as above, adding movement to the right, left, forward, backward, after jumping off both feet, to the right and left. The coach may call out the direction for the player to move. Also, add double jumping one time after another for one minute.

40. Jump Rope 100 or 440 Yards Drill: (Individualized or Competitive)

a. Bicycle-style jump rope four times 100 yards dash.
b. Bicycle-style jump rope one time 440 yards dash.

Purpose: To develop quickness, agility, balance, and endurance.

Procedure: Starting from an upright erect position, feet together, holding the rope firmly in each hand, commence the progressive sequence listed above for the specified time/distance indicated.

Coaching Points: This is a good footwork drill, especially for quarterbacks and receivers, and may be done individually or in groups. In Drill 39(a) if a player misses three times during the one-minute jumping session, add one-half minute; in 39(b) during the two-and-one-half minute rope skipping if a player misses six times, add one additional minute of rope jumping; and in 39(c) for every miss beyond ten, add one minute. Work individually until each player masters the footwork. Drill 40 is for conditioning and endurance.

41. OVER AND BACK BAG JUMPING DRILL

Purpose: To develop agility, quickness, strength, and endurance.

Procedure: Blocking dummies are laid lengthwise on the ground, so that from a coiled position, feet together, each player jumps as quickly as possible back and forth over the dummies as many times as possible within thirty seconds. The feet should be kept together throughout the drill.

Coaching Points: Do not extend the drill beyond thirty seconds, or the drill becomes one of endurance. Stress quickness.

42. STEP UP–DOWN DRILL

Purpose: To develop foot strength, quickness, and endurance.

Procedure: Each player stands facing the bleachers, or bench, or a stool approximately twelve inches in height. On the coach's command of "Go," each player steps up with his left foot, and brings up his right foot in a 1–2 fashion, and then steps down with his left foot, followed by his right foot in a 3–4 fashion. The sequence is repeated as rapidly as possible for ten seconds.

Coaching Points: If the drill is extended beyond ten seconds, the emphasis is on endurance. The drill should be timed so improvement can be measured. Each player should count aloud the number of sequences he performs within the specified period of time.

43. HOPSCOTCH DRILLS

Purpose: To develop quickness of the feet and to improve reaction time.

Procedure: Standing with the feet together, each player leaps forward (backward) and lands with them apart and immediately gathers himself and leaps forward (backward) again landing with the feet together, repeating this procedure five times. Going forward or backward a player jumps vertically in the air after his fifth repetition and makes a complete about-face, turning 180° coming down with his feet together. Each player repeats the progressive sequence returning to where he commenced the drill. In another variation, if the player goes forward, he returns hopping backward, and vice versa.

DRILL 43

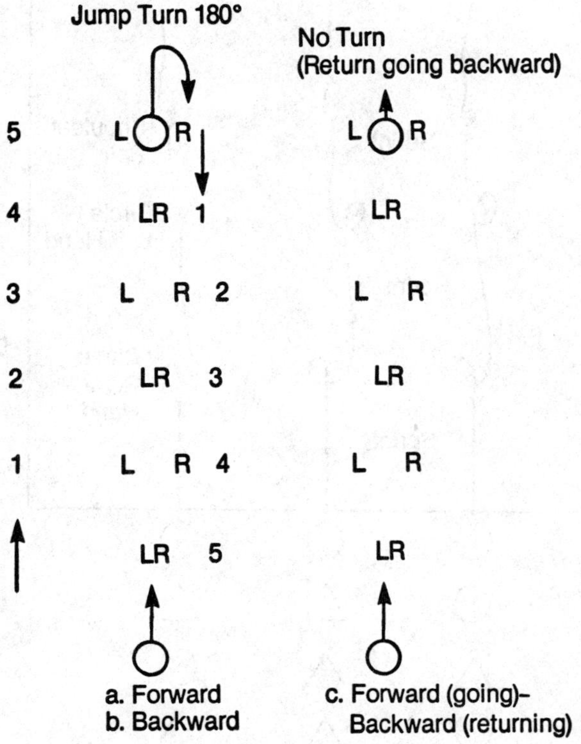

Coaching Points: Emphasize quickness, reaction, and improving individual reaction time.

44. SQUIRM OR CIRCLING DRILL

Purpose: To develop body control and to habituate getting up from the ground quickly.

Procedure: A twenty-yard marked-off area simplifies the procedures in this drill. Three lines of players line up in a three-point stance with their down hand on the first line. On the coach's command the player in each line sprints five yards to the next line, at which point all the individual's body weight is placed on the right hand and he pivots to his right a full circle around it. He gets up and sprints five yards more, this time dropping

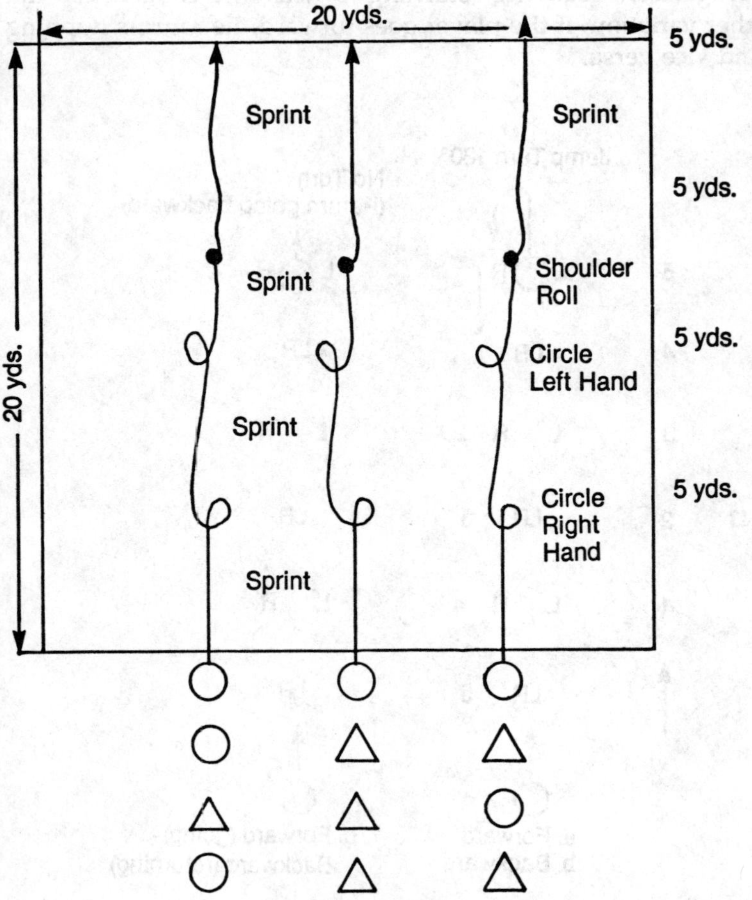

DRILL 44

his left hand to the ground supporting his full body weight as he circles 360° to his left. As he completes the circle he goes into a forward shoulder roll coming up to his feet and sprinting the remaining distance to the end of the twenty-yard area.

Coaching Points: Keeping the player's full body weight on his down hand when circling should be emphasized, along with shoulder rolling properly, as in Drill 21.

45. CRAB–STRADDLE BAG DRILL

Purpose: To teach players how to move quickly on all fours, and to develop quick feet.

Procedure: Four large blocking dummies are laid horizontally and vertically on the ground, almost butting up against each other in north, east, south, and west fashion. Columns of players align on the south and north dummies, and alternately one at a time crab-straddle the length of the bag until the player gets to the opening between the bags. Here he hand walks (spins on both hands counterclockwise (clockwise) stepping over two bags as he moves to his right (left) in order to crab-straddle back the length of the same bag but going in the opposite direction to his original starting position. He springs to his feet into a good football (ready) position.

Coaching Points: As soon as one player spins on his hands, hand walks, and steps over the bags and starts back to his original position, the coach should send the lead player in the opposite column crab-straddling down the length of his bag. At no time should two players be moving toward the center of the four bags at the same time, so as not to step on

DRILL 45

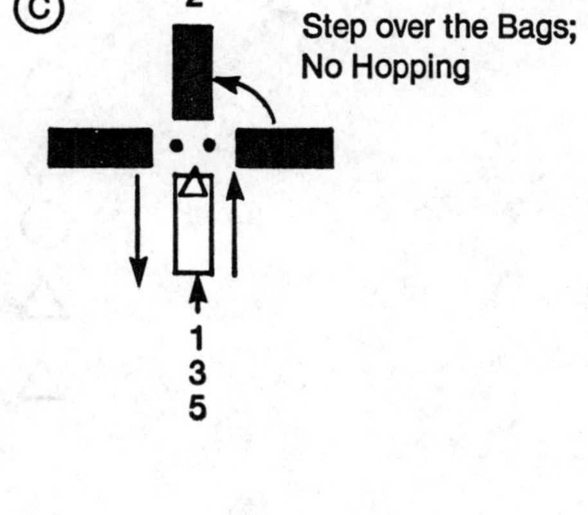

each other's hands or ankles. Emphasize quickness of movement, stepping (not hopping) over the bags, and ending up in a good ready position.

46. FOUR CORNERS–COVER BALL DRILL

Purpose: To improve the ability to change directions quickly, and to learn to cover a loose football.

Procedure: Four polyester cones are placed at the outside corners of a five-yard square. On the coach's command the lead player in the column near the first cone sprints to the second cone that is directly ahead and opposite his starting position, pivots around that cone, and sprints in a diagonal path to the third cone, pivots quickly around it and sprints to the fourth cone, pivots quickly around it and starts sprinting diagonally back toward his starting position. At some point, after he has pivoted around

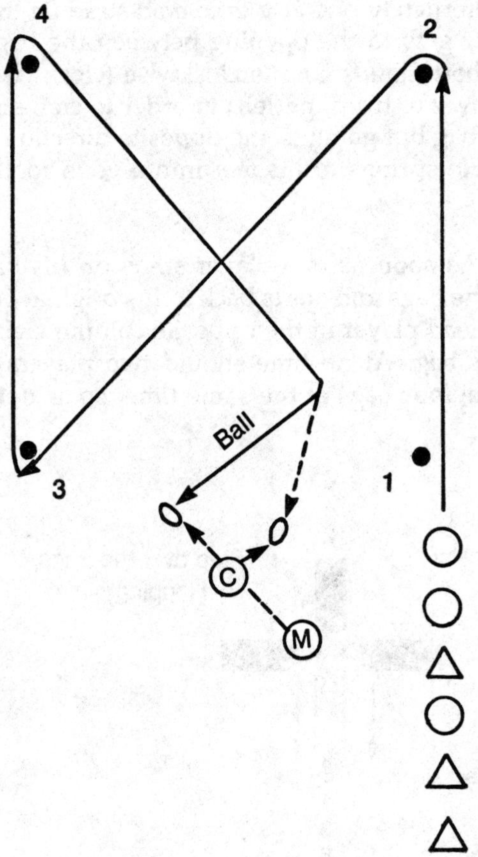

DRILL 46

the fourth cone and starts diagonally across the square toward the first cone, the coach flips, drops, places, bounces the football on the ground. The player yells, "Ball," and sprints to cover it quickly.

Coaching Points: Stress the importance of maintaining body position and control throughout, i.e., the player should try to maintain his body at the same plane without moving from one plane to another and then back again. Vary the point at which the football is "fumbled," i.e., drop it quickly just as the player pivots around the last cone or in the middle of his diagonal path or when he is almost back to his original position, etc. Also see (32) Cover Ball-Fumble Drill coaching points.

47–48. JINGLE JANGLE DRILLS

47. Lateral Jingle Jangle Drill

48. Jingle Jangle Conditioning Drill

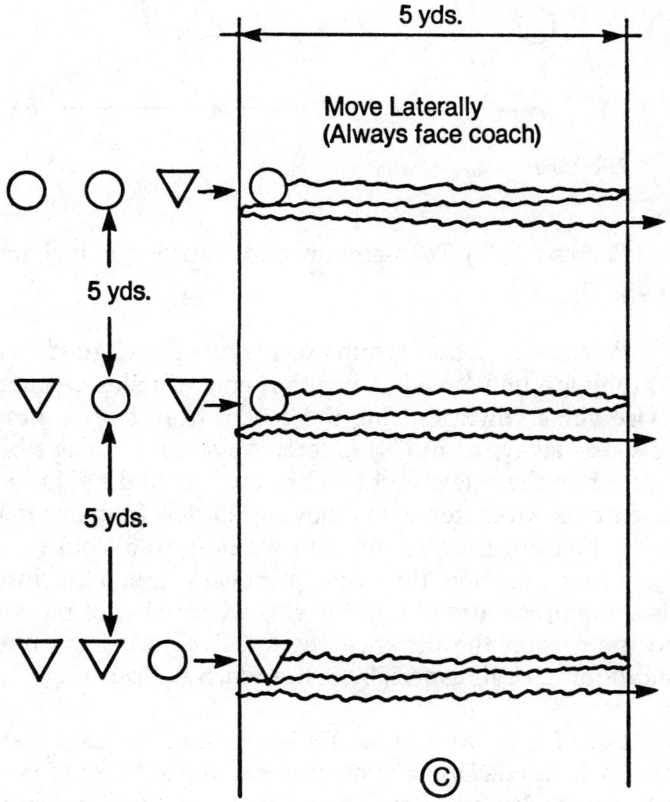

DRILL 47

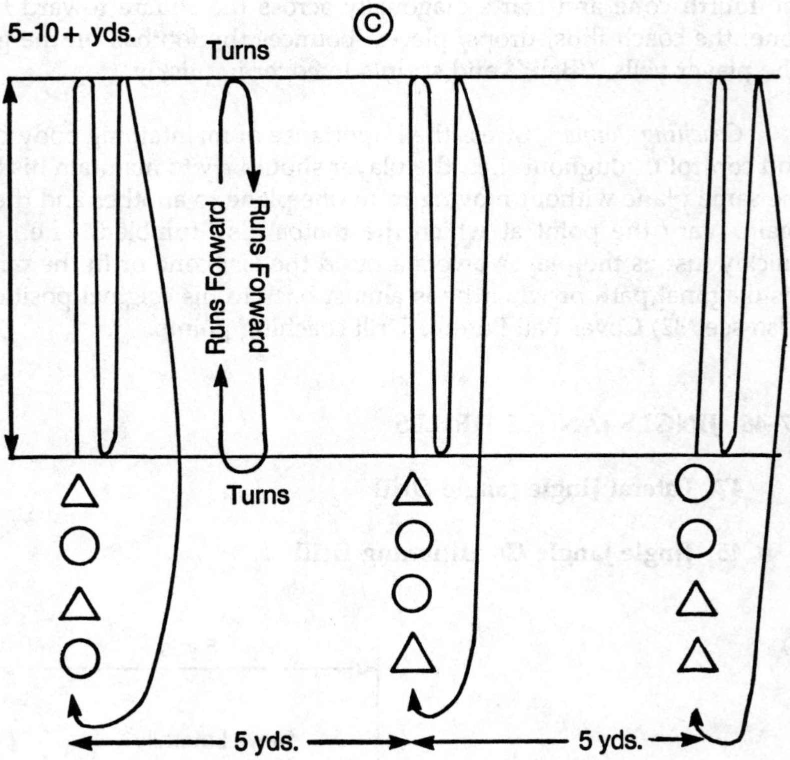

DRILL 48

Purpose: (47) To maintain and improve lateral movement; (48) to condition.

Procedure: Three groups of players are aligned five yards apart. In (47) they are in a "ready" position and will shuffle laterally east to west or vice versa, always facing the coach, from one line to an opposite line five yards away, as in (19) Lateral Wave Drill, always breaking at a right angle when their near foot touches the line to the side they are going, and using a cross-over step when moving laterally from line to line (three times). In (48) the three players sprint forward north to south or vice versa, stoop down, touch the line, turn and sprint back, touch the line, turn and repeat this same procedure ("X") times. (Any number of repetitions beyond six, and the greater the distance beyond five yards, the more strenuous the conditioning drill, especially if the coach is "pushing" the players.)

Coaching Points: Drill (47) is the same as (19) Lateral Wave Drill. In both Jingle Jangle Drills, stress maintaining a "flexed" position throughout and a quick change of direction without wasted movement.

49. AGILITY AND/OR REACTION DRILLS (ADDITIONAL)

The following drills are not included here but are explained in detail elsewhere.

See Chapter 6, (16) Balance or Belt Buckle Drill

See Chapter 11 (Bag Drills), (1) Lateral Run Bag Drill; (2) Backward and Forward Zig-Zag Drill; (3) Square Bag Drill; (4) Combo Zig-Zag and Lateral Run Bag Drill; (5) Combo Lateral Over and Around Run Bag Drill; (6) Bag Wave Drill.

See Chapter 12, (1) Defensive Wave Drill; (2) Run-the-Line Drill; (3) Mirror Quickness Drill.

There are other agility-reaction drills with numerous variations that may be substituted for the ones enumerated and discussed, but the objective is not variety or numbers. Part of the value of doing the same drills is familiarity, which leads to proficiency in doing the drill and developing competence in performing the fundamental skill or technique.

PART III

Drills for Teaching-Coaching Offensive Fundamentals and Techniques

6

Offensive Line Drills

Since its inception in 1869, much has changed in the way American football is played. There have been many key rule changes commencing in 1881, with upwards of 700 new rules since then. And although coaching is still an art, modern-day coaches are taking a more scientific approach to the game. This said, the basic precept remains the same: football games are won up front "in the trenches."

A backfield of outstanding players usually has little chance to display its ability behind a poor blocking line. Although there are additional ingredients necessary for a passing attack to be successful, if teammates cannot adequately protect their passer the other ingredients are ineffectual; and without effective blocking at the line of scrimmage, it is not possible to establish consistency in the offensive running game. A ball carrier can usually go only as far as effective blocking takes him. While it is unlikely a team can win consistently with an inadequate or an ineffective passing attack, it will *never* win regularly without an effective running attack—one that can consistently advance its ball carriers beyond the line of scrimmage. Regardless of the offense that a coach utilizes, the vital ingredient for success is effective blocking. This is a most important element in offensive football.

Offensive play is *assignment* football; defensive play is *reaction* football. Offensive line play is more difficult to teach-coach and for the player to master because after a player executes his assignment or applies his rule, he must then *react* to the reaction of the defender who is reacting to the blocker and the football. The successful blocker is the player who is taught and learns *whom* to block, and *how* to block effectively and efficiently.

Therefore, he must operate from a good, balanced, base position. Then he must get *off* with the starting count, and stay *on* his block until an official's whistle terminates the play. Teaching-coaching offensive line play entails considerable planning. Practice sessions must be organized so blocking fundamentals and techniques are *taught* in individual position work, *practiced* in group work, and then woven into the overall offensive effort to be tested under *scrimmage* conditions. The progress made in teaching offensive skills determines the speed at which a coach can install his offense. Time used to reduce the fundamental movements required to run an offense is time well spent. One should then allot practice time to teach, coach, and repeat these fundamentals in individual and group work before expecting a coordinated team effort.

The following drills may be used to teach offensive line fundamentals and techniques:

1. STANCE AND STARTS BOARD DRILL

(Boards are 10 feet long, 1 foot wide, 2 inches thick, with beveled edges on the top side. There are also available poly-covered-foam boards 2½ inches thick with beveled edges, 14 inches wide, and 8 feet long.)

Purpose: To teach proper stance, start or take-off, and how to run properly.

Procedure: Using the marked-off areas of five-yard squares, the boards are placed inside of the horizontal lines about 2½ feet, even and parallel with each other on and between the vertical lines so they are approximately 2½ yards apart. The players line up in columns, behind the horizontal line, covering each board lengthwise. On the coach's command the first player in each column moves forward and assumes a good offensive stance, and on the coach's starting count he charges down the length of the board, straddling it with his feet at hip width. He should retain the height of his stance the length of the board, and then level out, sprinting for five yards more. He returns to the rear of the column to wait his turn, while the commands are repeated for the next group of linemen who have already moved up to the forward horizontal line and have assumed their stance.

Coaching Points: Emphasize a good stance, an explosive start, and good form throughout. Specify which foot to step with first as a lineman must be able to take a six-inch step with the proper foot when he must cross charge. It is difficult to take only a six-inch step with the rear foot as one normally steps twelve to eighteen inches with the rear foot when he moves it first when charging. It is difficult to step with the front foot first since this is unnatural. By lining up with the front (or rear) foot approximately six inches from the horizontal line and indicating which foot to step with first, it is possible to check immediately as the player must touch the chalk line on his first step.

2. ONE–ON–ONE BOARD DRILLS (PROGRESSIVE)

Purpose: To teach the fundamentals of the straight shoulder block.

Procedure: A progressive drill where 1) a defensive player holds an upright dummy on the front edge of a board, and the blocker assumes a shoulder block position against the upright dummy. From the desired position the blocker meets limited resistance as he drives the dummy to the far end of the board. The holder now becomes the blocker and vice versa, and the dummy is driven back to its original position to the front edge of the board. If shoulder blocks are being taught, alternate the right and the left shoulder working for form. 2) The dummy is held in the middle of the board, and blocker fires-out on command, shoulder blocks the dummy, and drives it to the far end of the board. 3) The dummy is placed on the far end of the board, with the holder prepared to offer maximum resistance. The blocker attempts to drive the dummy and holder back five yards after turning them in the desired direction.

Coaching Points: Stress the proper fundamentals of shoulder blocking techniques.[1] Alternate left and right shoulder blocks. Use a whistle to

DRILL 2

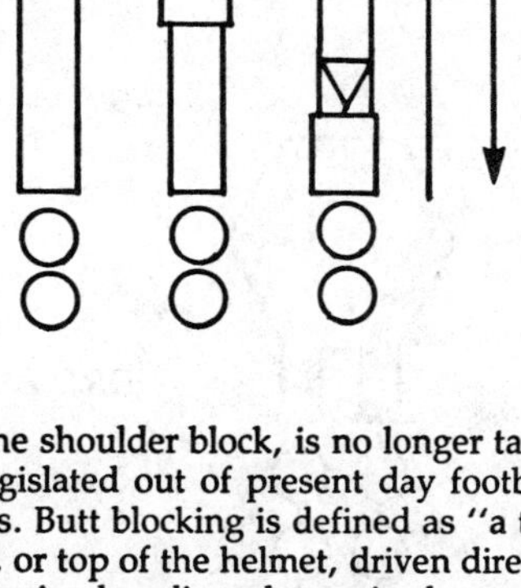

[1]"Butt" blocking, sliding into the shoulder block, is no longer taught or advocated by the prudent coach, as it has been legislated out of present day football by scholastic and collegiate regulatory governing bodies. Butt blocking is defined as "a technique involving a blow with the face mask, frontal area, or top of the helmet, driven directly into an opponent as the primary point of contact, either in close line play or in the open field." Both "butt blocking" and "face tackling" are personal fouls, each carrying a fifteen-yard penalty and ejection from the game for a flagrant violation.

terminate the drill. If the upright dummy is removed and the drill is done "live," it can be one of the toughest there is in football. The defender is stationed at the far end of the board and the blocker moves back proportionately to simulate various blocking situations. The boards are turned at slight angles inward and outward, simulating off-set blocking situations with the defender shading the blocker's left or right shoulder. (See Board Trap Drill (10) for teaching trap blocking with the boards.)

3–7. TWO–MAN SLED DRILLS

3–4. Six-Point and Four-Point Explosion or Shoulder Shoot Drills (Progressive)

Purpose: To develop power impact from the upper legs, buttocks, and back when coordinating shoulder and forearm lifting action, and to teach the shoulder block progressively.

Procedure: Add weight to the two-man sled (an extra three–four players or large weighted blocking dummies) or snug the sled against an object so it will not move. Two offensive blockers line up in a six-point stance (hands/knees/toes) opposite the blocking pads. On command both players extend fully, exploding into the pads with their inside shoulder and forearm. The head is up, back straight, body extended in a ramrod position, with the power impact delivered from the upper legs, buttocks, and back. Blockers should *not* follow-up with their feet. The blockers recoil to their original six-point position, and the drill is repeated three times on the coach's command in rapid succession. After the third blast both players seat roll to the outside, regain their feet, and move quickly to the ends of the opposite lines in order to repeat the drill with the opposite shoulder-forearm. Then you follow up with Four-Point Shoulder Shoot Drill in the same progression.

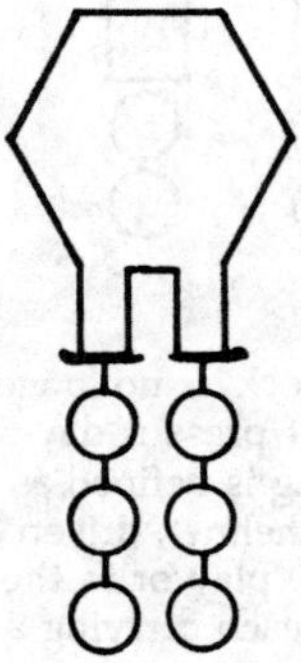

DRILLS 3 and 4

Coaching Points: Stress exploding into the machine with ramrod action. You should regulate and coordinate both players hitting the sled together.

5. Drive-Up Drill

Purpose: To teach the shoulder block and follow-through techniques.

Procedure: From a three-point stance two players both shoulder block a weighted two-man sled (as in the Explosion Drills) and drive-up to a standing position, moving their feet with short, choppy steps.

Coaching Points: Same as the Explosion Drills, plus following up with the feet. Stress the correct fundamentals of the shoulder block. Terminate the drill with a whistle.

6. Drive Block Sled Drill

Purpose: To develop shoulder blocking techniques, and to control an object that moves.

Procedure: Same as in the previous sled drills, only the machine is neither weighted nor scotched and is permitted to run free. The players shoulder block the machine for five yards. You should use your starting count and a whistle.

Coaching Points: Stress the correct blocking fundamentals, plus controlling the two-man sled.

7. Belly Slammer Drill

Purpose: To develop punch and to coordinate shoulder-forearm action.

DRILL 7

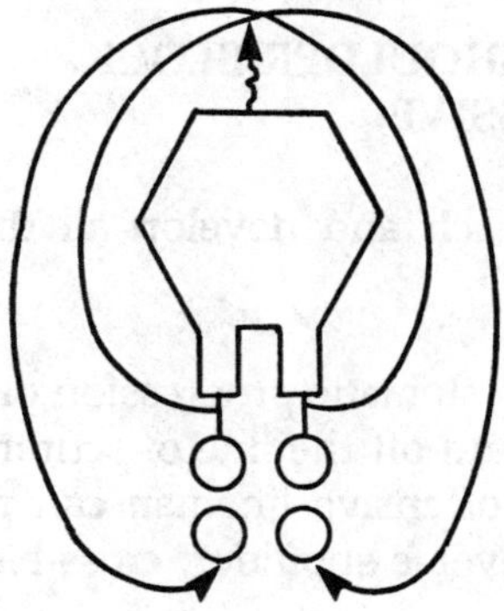

Procedure: Same as the previous sled drill (6), but the sled is permitted to run free. From their offensive stance on the starting count both players explode, lunging into the sled but not stepping forward. Since the machine is driven backward, the players will land fully extended on their stomachs. If they are taking only one blast, they jump up from their extended positions and sprint forward for five yards before returning to the ends of the opposite lines. If they are going to repeat the blast three times, after the first and second blasts they line up quickly in their offensive stance to fire-out again on the coach's command. After the third blast they get up and sprint forward as before, circling the sled and returning to the ends of the opposite lines.

Coaching Points: Expode into the pads on the sled. Do not move the feet. Regulate the second and third commands so the players will hit out together, if the drill is done more than once.

8. FOUR POSITIONS BAG DRILL

Purpose: To develop shoulder blocking techniques, including foot action.

Procedure: Same as (9) One-On-One Shoulder Block Drills (below), only the defensive player holds an upright dummy in one of four positions: nose-on, inside shoulder, outside shoulder, off the line. On the coach's command the offensive lineman executes the proper shoulder block (straight or reverse shoulder).

Coaching Points: Emphasize good stance and the proper shoulder-foot techniques, i.e., stepping with the correct foot first. You should sim ulate all situations, including cross-blocking and trapping. The bag holder should offer strong resistance. Use your starting count to commence the drill, and your whistle to terminate the activity.

9. ONE–ON–ONE SHOULDER BLOCK DRILLS (PROGRESSIVE)

Purpose: To teach and develop all the fundamentals of shoulder blocks.

Procedure: A systematic progression of shoulder blocks with the defender head-up on and off the line of scrimmage and off-set both on and off the line, so the offensive lineman can perfect the appropriate block straight shoulder, reverse shoulder, cross-block, pass block, et al.

DRILL 9

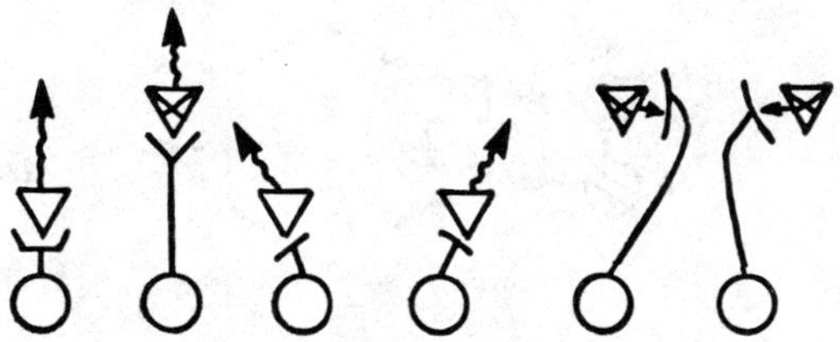

Coaching Points: Stress the correct blocking fundamentals. Employ the starting count and terminate the drill with a whistle.

10–11. BOARD AND SLED TRAP DRILLS

10. Board Trap Drill

11. Sled Trap Drill

Purpose: To teach pulling techniques and trap blocking.

Procedure: The blockers face straight ahead with (10) boards—(a) is a short trap, (b) is a long trap; or (11) a two-man sled at approximate right angles to the direction the offensive linemen are facing. The drill is done by the numbers. From their offensive stance, on the first count the offensive players apply all of the proper pulling techniques, with the main emphasis on the direction or position of the lead step, and then they stop. On the second command, the players continue with their movements and drive block the dummies on the boards as in (2) One-On-One Board Drills, or the sled as in (6) Drive Block Sled Drill.

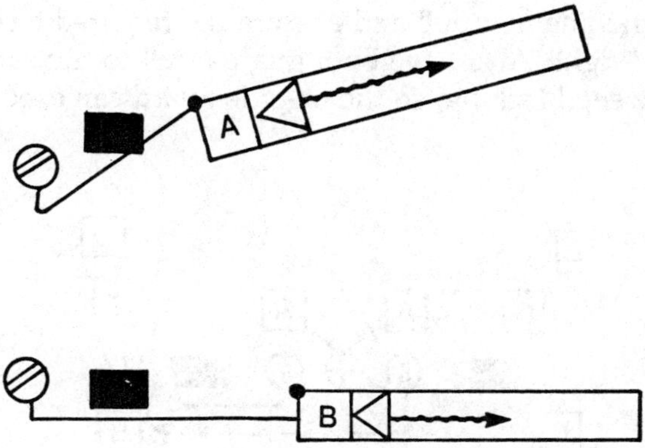

DRILL 10

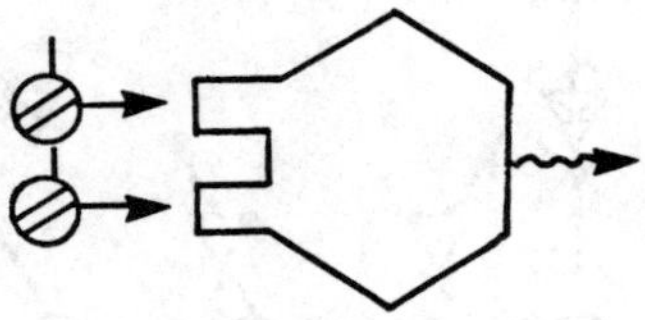

DRILL 11

Coaching Points: Stress the proper pulling and trap blocking techniques. In order for the sled to move freely and for the trappers to sustain their blocks, both men will have to block with their inside shoulder. Alternate the lines so the players are blocking with their right and left shoulder, and pulling left and right.

12–14. PULLING DRILLS (SEPARATE OR COMBINED)

12. Short and Long Trap Drills (A and B Illustration)

13. Sealing Inside Drill (C Illustration)

14. Downfield Blocking Drill (D Illustration)

Purpose: To teach interior linemen (guards illustrated) the proper fundamentals of pulling out of the line, and (A) executing the short trap, (B) the long trap, (C) sealing (blocking) inside and/or (D) downfield blocking.

Procedure: It may be set up separately so offensive linemen are working only on one or two phases of the drill, such as short and long trap blocking, or the four phases may be combined into one drill. The bag holders should set upright dummies in the illustrated positions. On the starting count the linemen pull and execute the required techniques. Run the drill left and right. Also have both guards pull to the same side (right or left), as in sweep blocking, so the on-side guard can execute the trap block and

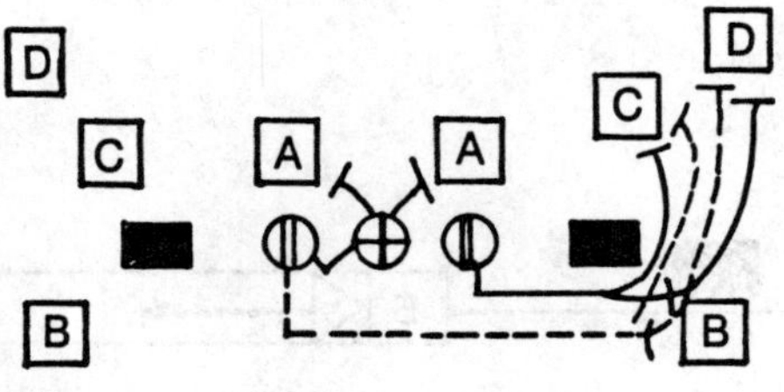

DRILLS 12–14

the off-side guard can go through and seal the inside or block the dummy downfield. Or the drill may be operated right and left at the same time with each lineman pulling to his side, and the offensive center blocking back either way.

Coaching Points: Stress the proper fundamentals and techniques of pulling out of the line and trapping, sealing inside, or blocking downfield.

15. ONE–ON–ONE AIR BAG DRILL

Purpose: To teach and develop all the fundamentals of shoulder blocks, especially against a slanting defender.

Procedure: This is the same as (9) One-On-One Shoulder Block Drills, only air bags are used. The defender holds an air bag against his chest firmly, from a half or three-quarters knee bend position, with his trunk upright, braced, and close to the offensive lineman's head. The various situations are set up for the blocker. When teaching the blocker to handle a veering, slanting defender, both men are given the starting count. The coach stands behind the offensive lineman and points in the direction the defender (facing him) should move with his air bag. The offensive blocker fires-out straight, and the air bag holder angle-charges from head up to the point of the shoulder indicated (no wider). The harder the defensive charge, the more suitable it is for the offensive blocker to use a reverse shoulder block to prevent penetration and to drive the defender in the desired direction. When practicing pass rush and pass protection, the rusher should stay low, hit and lift with the air bag, and *not* swat or jab the blocker with it. The blocker should unload, recoil, unload, etc., until the coach blows the whistle terminating the drill.

Coaching Positions: Stress getting off with the offensive starting count and taking the defender in the direction of his charge, not waiting until the defender charges and then trying to block him. For pass protection, stress maintaining a low center of gravity, a good football position, and not lunging at the rusher.

16. BALANCE OR BELT BUCKLE DRILL

Purpose: To develop body balance, coordination, agility, footwork, and to react to a one-on-one situation as in pocket pass protection.

Procedure: On the starting count the offensive lineman drop-steps and sets up as in pocket pass protection in a good fundamental position

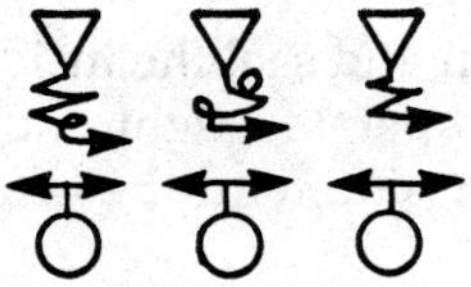

DRILL 16

with his head up, his tail down, back slightly arched, and his feet chugging. The defender is within one foot of the blocker, and moves laterally one to two yards in either direction, but makes no effort to get around or overpower the blocker. The protector should slide and shuffle, moving laterally with the rusher, staying in front of him and literally putting his chin on the defensive man's belt buckle. When the coach yells, ''Now!'' the blocker tries to unload on the rusher and stay with him until the whistle blows. The rusher also reacts when he hears the command, and tries to dispose of the blocker and get to the coach (passer).

Coaching Points: Stress the fundamentals for proper pass protection, including shuffling and sliding, and not jumping or lunging at the defensive man. The rusher (controlled) should twist, roll back, and head fake within his two to four yard lateral area, forcing the blocker to move laterally to stay in front of him.

17. PASS RUSHER–IN–THE–MIDDLE DRILL

Purpose: To develop the fundamentals of cup protection pass blocking, body balance, footwork, and coordination.

Procedure: Six players (blockers) line up on the inside of a five-yard square, and move in forming a circle so they are equidistant from each other. The rusher in the middle of the circle is the ''bull,'' and the rim men are the blockers. The rusher either runs directly at a blocker or tries to go between two blockers. The blocker accepts the challenge, unloads, recoils,

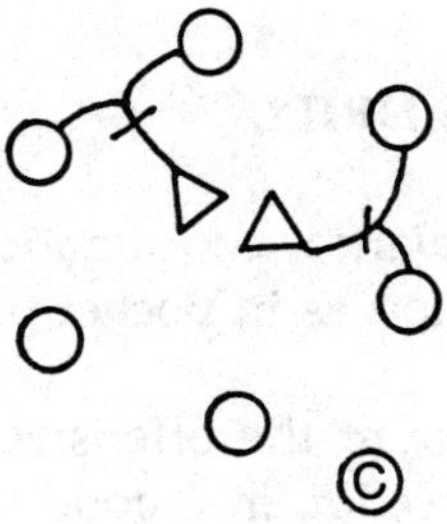

DRILL 17

and unloads again if the rusher comes directly at him. The man on each side of the blocker must shuffle and slide toward the blocker in the event the rusher veers to either gap or overpowers the blocker. If the rusher runs directly for a gap, the man on each side must close the gap and protect it. If the hub man (''bull'') breaks through a defender, he replaces the blocker and the latter now becomes the rusher. If the rusher does not get through after several tries, replace him with a man from the rim of the circle.

Coaching Points: Stress no illegal blocking. Everyone keeps his feet chugging throughout the drill. Put two rushers in the middle and let them stunt separately or come off of a stack alignment.

18. BLOCKER–IN–THE–MIDDLE DRILL

Purpose: To teach and practice the running shoulder block.

Procedure: Upright dummies are held on the outside of a ten-yard square, with the blocker in the middle. Upon the coach's command the blocker slams into the bag as hard as he can with a straight shoulder block and either pushes-off immediately or keeps chugging until the coach indicates the blocker should release from his block and sprint to the opposite side of the square, repeating the procedure three to four times until the whistle terminates the drill. The hub blocker is replaced by a bag holder, and the drill is repeated until each player has had his turn shoulder blocking.

Coaching Points: Stress quickness and speed so the drill moves at a fast pace. Stress the proper execution of fundamentals of the running shoulder block.

DRILL 18

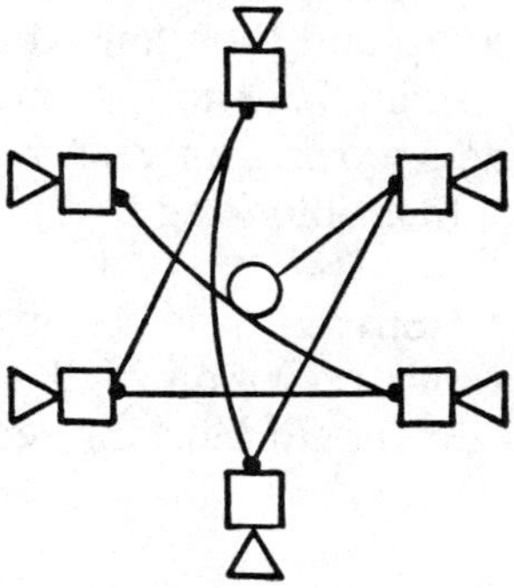

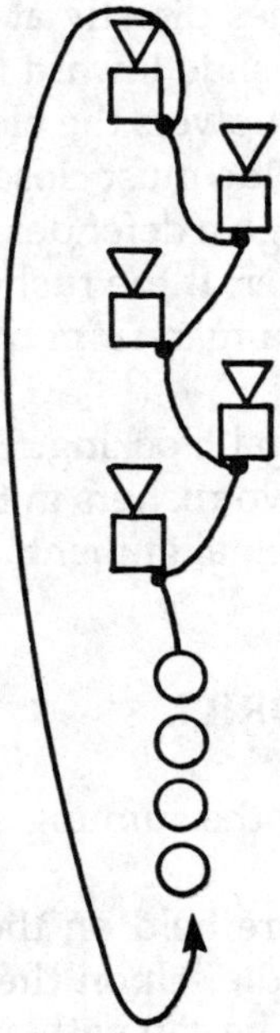

DRILL 19

19. BURMA ROAD BLOCKING DRILL

Purpose: To develop the running shoulder block and downfield blocking techniques.

Procedure: This is similar to (18) Blocker-in-the-Middle Drill, only the bags are ten yards apart in a zig-zag line. If the bags are held, the blocker does not leave his feet but slams into the dummy with a running shoulder block, pushes off and repeats the procedure as he sprints to the next bag. If bags are not held, after the blocker shoulder blocks through the top of the upright dummy, he regains his feet, sprints to the next dummy and repeats the procedure again. The bag holders should remain near the dummies and set them upright each time they have been knocked down. Or the blocker may pick up and then hold the last dummy after knocking it down, instead of sprinting back to the end of the blocking column (as illustrated), with holders moving forward and setting up the bags each time (as illustrated in (20) Mass Blocking Drill).

Coaching Points: Stress quickness and speed so the drill moves at a fast pace. Stress proper execution of the fundamentals of the running shoulder block and downfield blocking techniques. Emphasize no illegal blocking.

DRILL 20

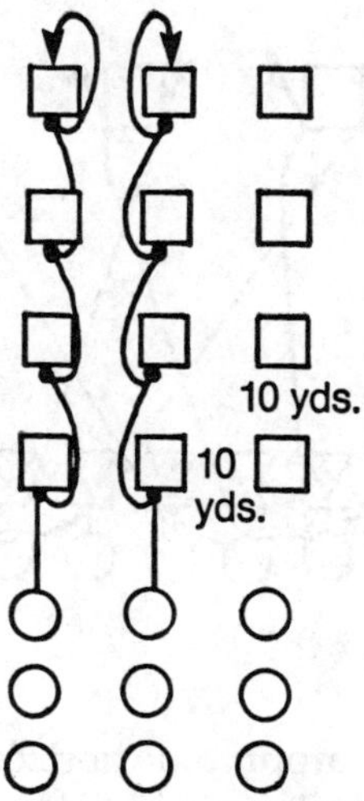

20. MASS BLOCKING DRILL

Purpose: To develop the running shoulder block and downfield blocking techniques. This drill may be used as a conditioner, too.

Procedure: This is similar to (19) Burma Road Blocking Drill, only the dummies are placed in straight lines ten yards apart. The blockers sprint forward, with the coach regulating the flow of blockers, toward the far end of the column of dummies. The holders must sprint forward toward the front end of the column of dummies, and after holding the front dummy the holder moves to the end of the line of blockers to await his turn. The coach gives the starting commands quickly so everyone must run to block or hold a dummy.

Coaching Points: Stress quickness, speed, and the proper execution of running and blocking fundamentals.

21. AROUND–AND–THROUGH DOWNFIELD BLOCKING DRILL

Purpose: To develop downfield blocking techniques, including releasing from the line of scrimmage.

Procedure: On the starting count, the on-side blockers (side designated by the coach) fire-out into the defenders holding the air bags, re-

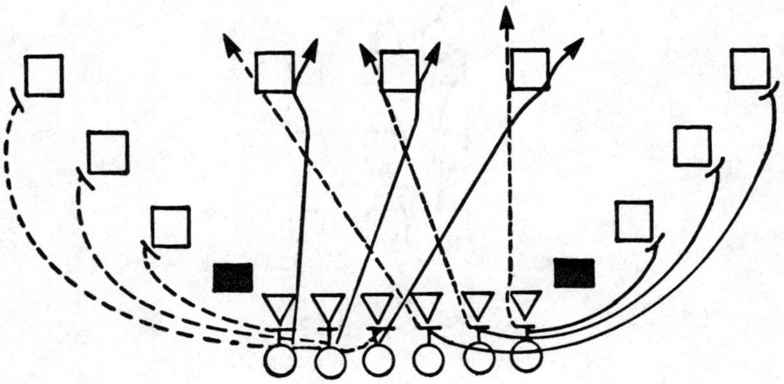

DRILL 21

lease, pull laterally around a horizontal dummy (black rectangle in illustration), and sprint downfield to block through upright dummies which are not held. The off-side blockers release inside of defenders, fight to get free if jammed at the line with the air bags, sprint downfield and block the dummies in the middle. After the blockers strike, roll, and regain their feet, they then set up the dummies, as the second group moves up into position and repeats the drill going to the opposite side. In the meantime the first group picks up the air bags which the holders have placed on the ground, as the latter have moved directly across the line to become the third group of blockers. When returning from blocking downfield, the players cross-over to the opposite side to become bag holders so when they become blockers they will be pulling and releasing through from both the right and left sides.

Coaching Points: Stress proper execution of pulling and releasing techniques, and the fundamentals of running and downfield blocking. Stress no clipping or illegal blocking.

22. THREE–S OR SPLITS–STANCE–STARTS DRILL

Purpose: To teach offensive linemen to take the proper line splits, stance and starts or team take-off.

Procedure: Vinyl-coated nylon, canvas, or fire hose is measured and marked off to illustrate your basic, wide, and tight offensive line splits, so the offensive players can visualize better the actual distances in the various offensive sets. While certain guides and principles (coaching points) will also be taught, in addition to running specific plays and passes from fixed line splits (basic, wide, tight) and in certain tactical situations, unless splits

Some "lines" include <u>hole numbering</u> in the spaces <u>between</u> the offensive linemen or <u>over</u> their positions (whichever is preferred).

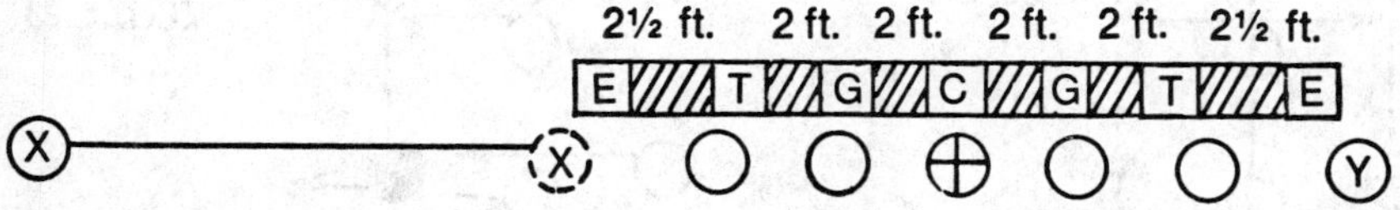

(See Chapter 8 (38) for split rules for flankers)

Vinyl-coated Nylon, Canvas, or Fire Basic Hose(sandweight "lines")

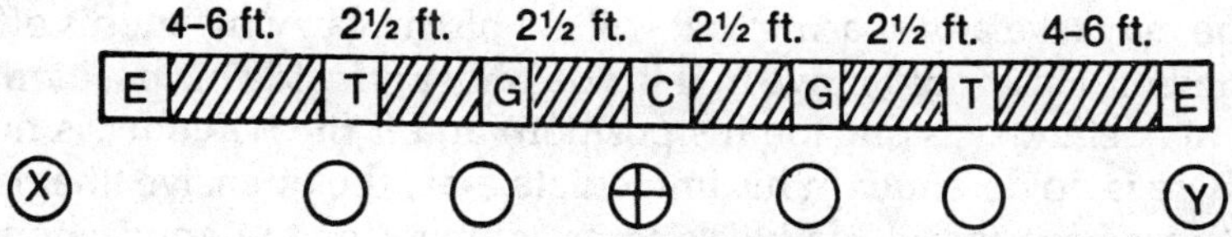

Vinyl-coated Nylon, Canvas, or Fire Hose Wide (for split back formation)

(Tighten to 6 in. between offensive linemen)

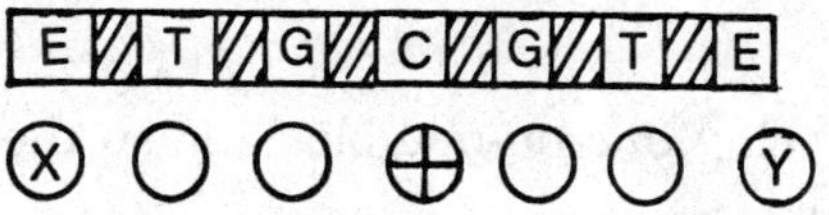

Vinyl-coated Nylon, Tight Canvas, or Fire Hose

DRILL 22

are coached and monitored offensive linemen will seldom vary their spacing and usually take static splits. Commence teaching offensive line splits on "lines," canvas or fire hose. Move the players away from the area, have them huddle, break, line up and check their splits for the set called in the huddle by the coach. After running the drill a number of times until the offensive linemen can conceptualize the purpose and difference in line splits, add defensive linemen and linebackers and then teach the application of the coaching points. Continue with teaching-coaching stance and starts.

Coaching Points: Stress that an offensive player should *never* split to a distance where a defender can beat him through the inside gap; other-

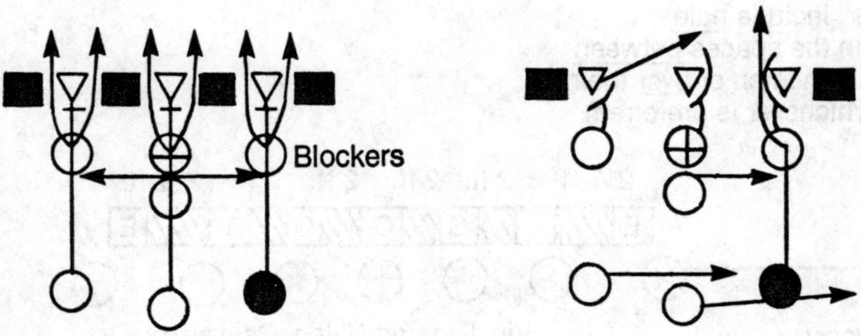

DRILL 23

wise he may take any spacing that will aid him in carrying out his offensive assignment. He should move in if his defender is inside his position; move out if his defender is outside his position; and if the defender is nose-on, or if there is no defender in his immediate area, the offensive lineman may adjust in or out to aid his blocking assignment or the application of his particular blocking rule.

23. ONE–ON–ONE (THREE–ON–THREE) CHALLENGE OR ALL–PURPOSE DRILL (OFFENSIVELY)

Purpose: To develop one-on-one blocking so the offensive lineman can defeat the defender.

Procedure: The offensive center, quarterback, ball carrier and offensive lineman versus a defensive lineman "live." The drill may be set up as three segments, although the principle is still one-on-one blocking. On the starting count the quarterback receives the ball from the center and executes a hand-off, and the ball carrier breaks off of his lineman's block between dummies that are placed two yards apart in horizontal positions on the ground.

Coaching Points: Stress offensive fundamentals and techniques, including getting off with the count. This is considered by many coaches as one of the best single drills in football since it incorporates ball handling, running, pursuing and tackling, and may be used offensively, as here and in Chapter 9, Drill 16, or defensively as in Chapter 10, Drill 26, and Chapter 13, Drill 19. It is referred to as the All-Purpose Drill for this reason. You should coach only one phase at a time. (As used here, you would coach only the offensive linemen.)

24–27. SEGMENTED OFFENSIVE LINE DRILLS

24. Center and One Guard Drills

25. Center and Both Guards Drills

26. Guard and Tackle, and Tackle and End Drills

27. Guard, Tackle, and End Drills

Purpose: To develop offensive line blocking fundamentals and techniques.

Procedure: Working separately with the two or three offensive linemen as indicated above, align one, two or three defenders in various positions and defensive sets so a systematic progression of offensive line fundamentals indigenous to that segment of offense can be taught, practiced, and coached. Although an offensive center is not absolutely necessary for those drills in which he is not directly involved, if possible a center

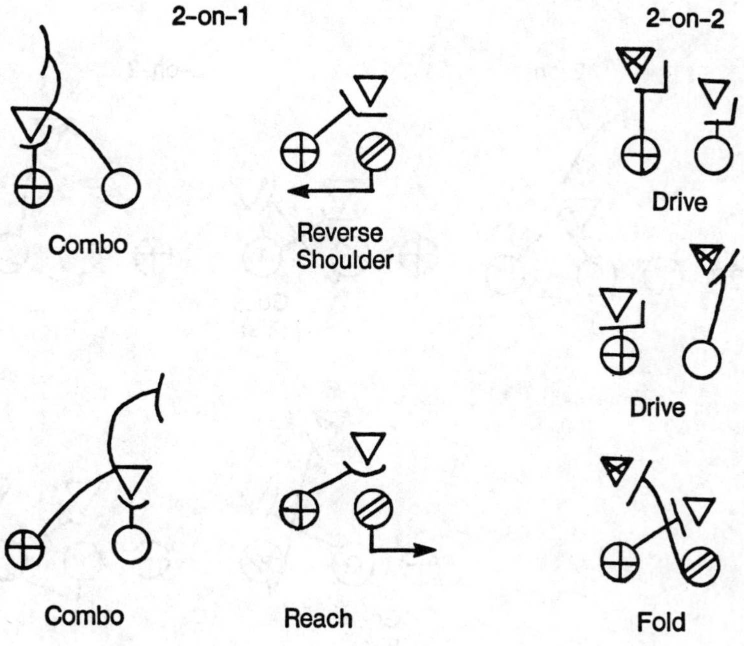

DRILL 24

Versus interior stunts 2-on-1 (not illustrated), but must be practiced, too).

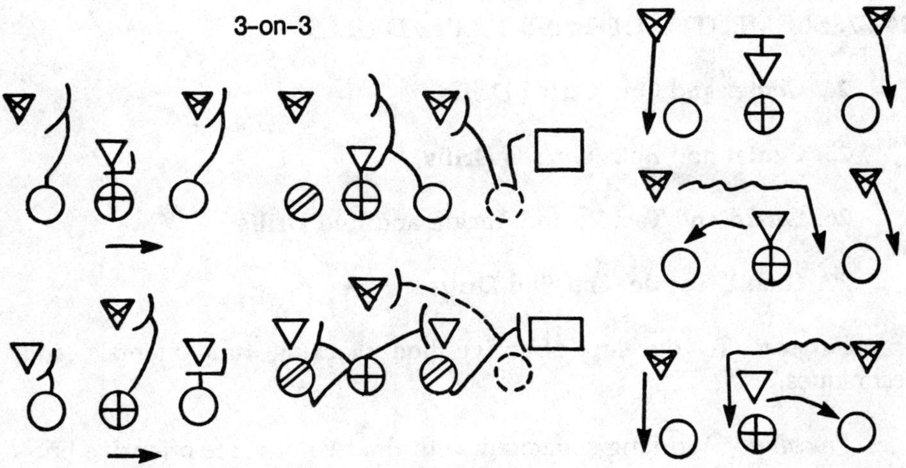

Versus interior line stunts must be practiced, too.

DRILL 25

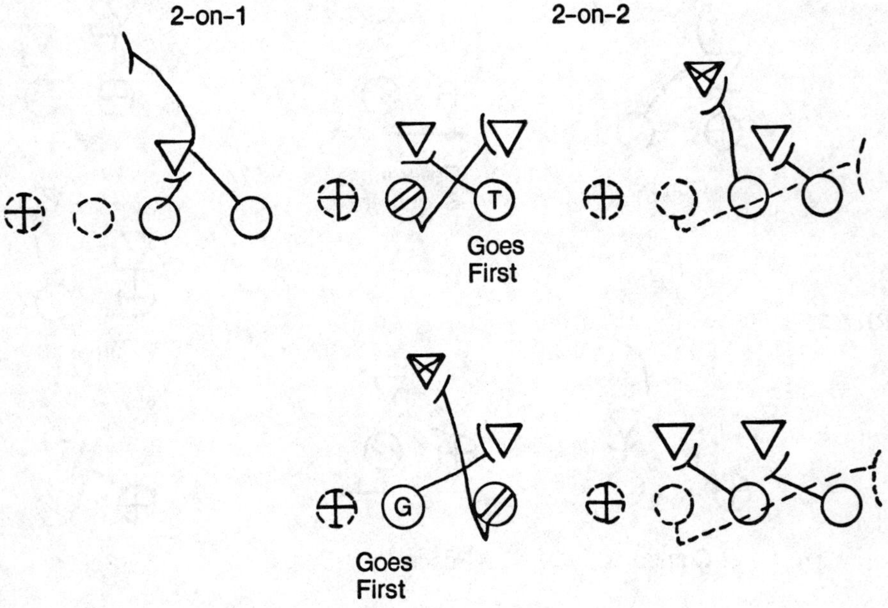

Versus stunts must be practiced, too.

DRILL 26

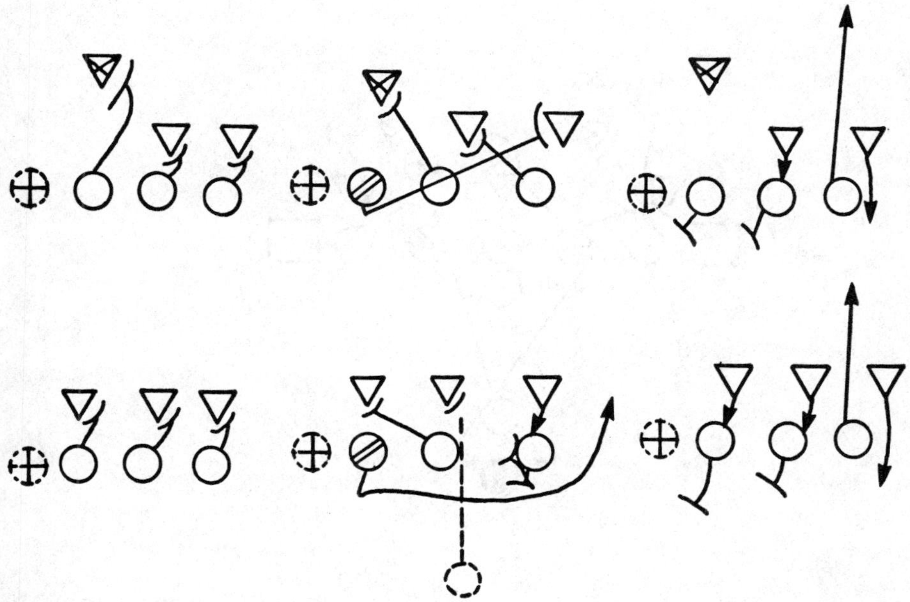

Versus stunts must be practiced, too.

DRILL 27

should be used with each unit. However, a manager or coach should act as the quarterback and use the offensive starting cadence and count.

Coaching Points: Place the defenders where they would be in odd and even alignments. Initially they should be instructed to read-react, and later to loop and veer as a *pattern* defensive charge (*not* solo charging of their own choosing). You should work on specific offensive fundamentals and techniques, and then the application of blocking rules on specific offensive plays in order to perfect line blocking and offensive assignments. A concerted effort should be made to have the players understand what the play is trying to accomplish, which is the rationale for the types of blocks being utilized. Frequently the latter is overlooked by the coach, and the players working in small segments cannot visualize the whole play.

28. INSIDE (OFFENSIVE) DRILL

Purpose: To teach and polish the inside running attack.

Procedure: The offensive team huddles, with the exception of the ends, while interior linemen, plus linebackers, deploy in the defensive

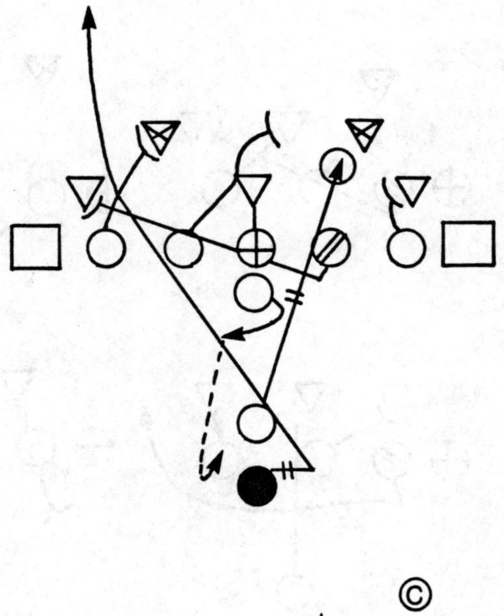

DRILL 28

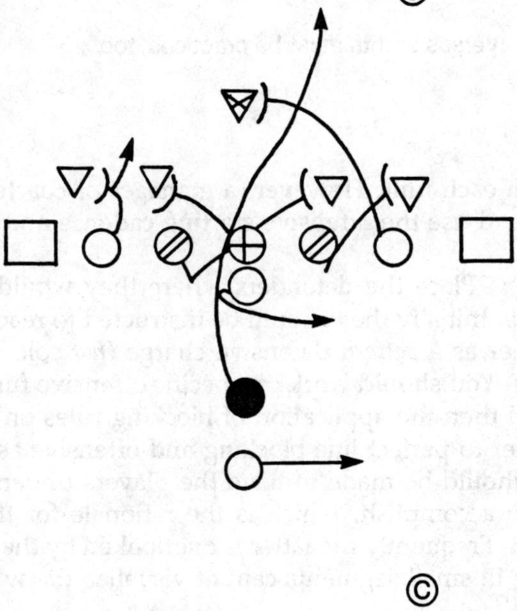

alignment specified by the coach. The offensive team breaks the huddle and runs the offensive play "live."

Coaching Points: Emphasize team take-off, application of blocking rules versus your opposition's defensive alignment, perfection of blocking assignments, and execution of inside running plays. See Chapter 9, (21) Outside (Offensive) Drill to teach and polish the outside running attack. See Chapter 2, note 1, on the use of flash cards to teach working against your opposition's alignments/tendencies.

29. OFFENSIVE HALF–LINE DRILL

Purpose: To teach and polish the offensive running attack, one side at a time.

Procedure: The same as (28) Inside (Offensive) Drill, only half of the offensive line is used. Work two offensive units separately at a time. Working on the left side attack, the No. 1 offensive unit's complete backfield, left side of the line and the center, and the No. 2 unit's right guard will be together. Working to the right will be the No. 2 unit's complete backfield, center and left guard, and the No. 1 unit's right side of the offensive line. Rotate backfields, centers and guards so they have the opportunity to practice on both the left and right side attacks. Change the defensive alignments, and then coordinate defensive stunts so the offensive linemen practice live blocking veering, slanting, looping defenders. You should then add the No. 2 offensive tackles and ends and repeat the drill.

Coaching Points: Emphasize team take-off, application of blocking rules, and perfecting blocking assignments and techniques. See Chapter 2, note 1, on the use of flash cards.

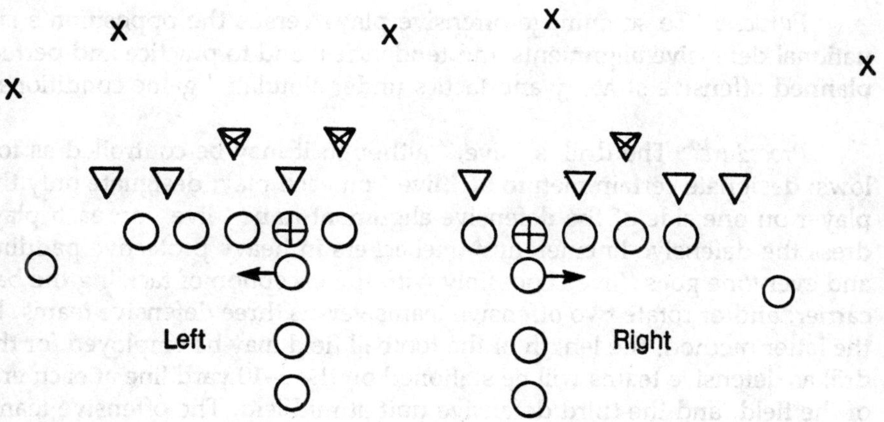

DRILL 29

30. OFFENSIVE LINE BLOCKING DRILL

(See Chapter 14, Drill 5 for numbering additional defensive alignments.)

Purpose: To polish offensive line blocking versus the opposition's defensive alignments.

Procedure: The emphasis is on perfecting offensive blocking assignments against your opposition's various situational defensive alignments. The defenders hold air bags, and the coach stands behind the offensive center to accept the snap-back (after calling out the offensive play and the snap count). Since backfield action is unnecessary, offensive backs are not utilized. The drill is dummy for the defenders as they accept the blocks with their air shields, but it is live for the offensive line as they polish their offensive attack and team take-off.

Coaching Points: Check the execution of proper offensive line fundamentals and techniques, and the proper application of blocking rules or assignments. The coach should change defensive alignments and call out the tendencies of your opposition. If defenders are not blocked, they call out "Here!" to check if an assignment has been busted. See Chapter 2, note 1, on the use of flash cards.

31. OFFENSIVE SCRIMMAGE DRILLS

(See Chapter 14 for specific team drills enumerated below under Coaching Points.)

Purpose: To scrimmage offensive plays versus the opposition's situational defensive alignments and tendencies, and to practice and perfect planned offensive strategy and tactics under simulated game conditions.

Procedure: The drill is "live," although it may be controlled as follows: designate certain men to be "live" on each play; designate only the player on one side of the defensive alignment to be "live" on each play; dress the defensive linemen and linebackers in heavy protective padding and everyone goes "live," possibly with the exception of tackling the ball carrier; and/or rotate two offensive teams versus three defensive teams. In the latter method, the length of the football field may be employed for the drill as defensive teams will be stationed on the 5–10 yard line at each end of the field, and the third defensive unit at midfield. The offensive teams work coming out of their Danger Zone, then in midfield, then going in for a score versus the opposition's goal line defense in the offensive Scoring

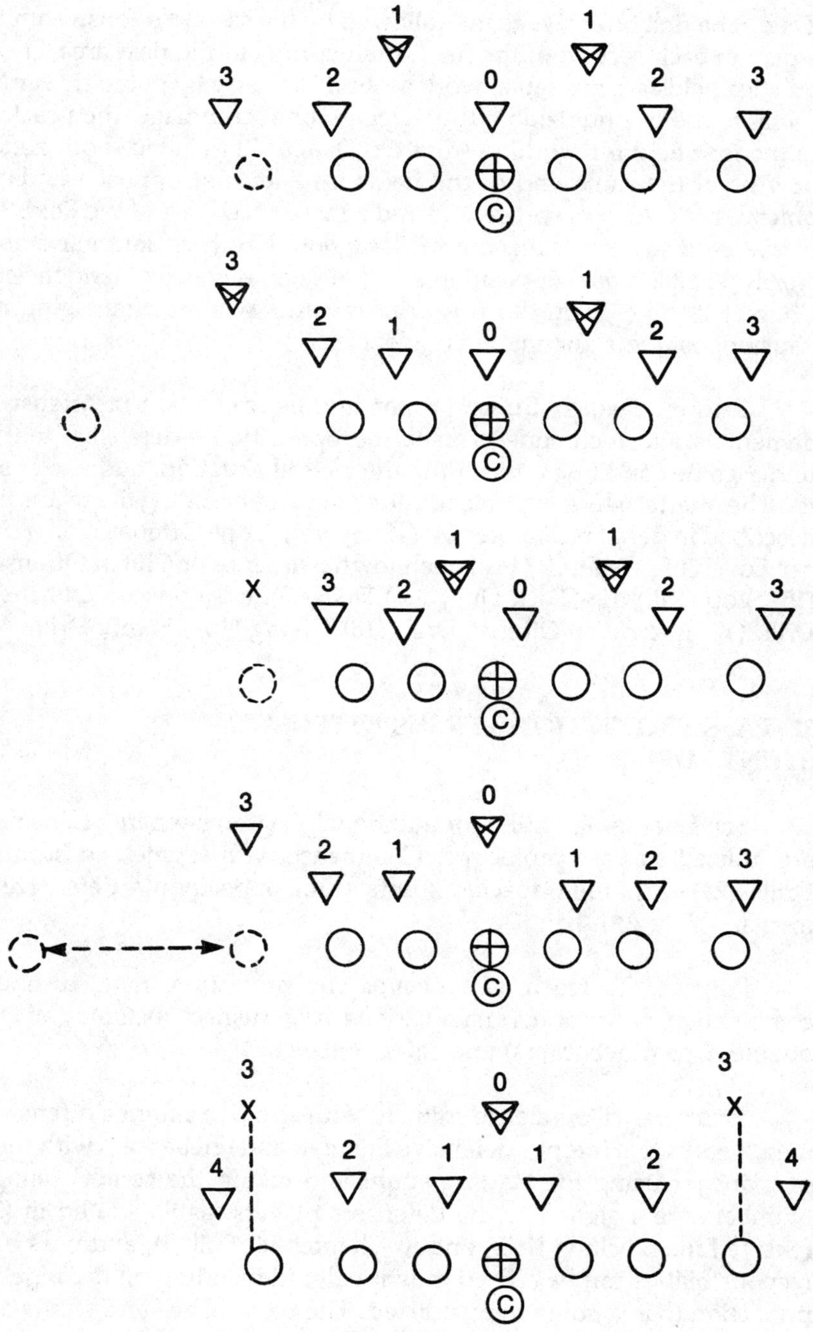

DRILL 30

Zone. The first offensive team, followed by the second offensive unit, runs a play in each section of the field, then sprints to the next area. If parallel practice fields are available, work around the circle by going from midfield across to the second field for the Scoring Zone scrimmage, then back across to the first field for working from the Danger Zone, since both zones will now be at the same end of the fields instead of at opposite ends of the practice area. Also the procedure and zones at each end of the fields should be reversed so your teams are working both North to South and South to North versus your opposition's situational defensive tendencies. See Chapter 2, note 1, on the use of flash cards when scrimmaging against your opposition's alignments/tendencies.

Coaching Points: Stress proper huddle, execution of offensive fundamentals and techniques versus the opposition's defensive tendencies under game conditions, including the tactical situation, and use of a whistle. The quarterbacks can practice directing and handling the teams in drills described in detail in Chapter 14: (12) Scoring Zone Offense Drill, (13) Danger Zone Offense Drill, (14) Touchdown Sequence or Clutch Offense Drill, (15) Stop (Kill)-the-Clock Drill, (16) Delay Offense or Run-Out-the-Clock Drill, (17) Racehorse Offense Drill, (18) Giving-Up-a-Safety Drill.

32. PASS PROTECTION VERSUS DEFENSIVE STUNTS DRILL

(See Chapter 9, Drill 6 for additional diagrams where offensive backs are utilized as pass protectors. Commence with segmented stunts as in Drills (24)–(27); then specific stunts from opposition's defensive alignments.)

Purpose: To teach zone or area cup protection, man, turnout, and combination protection versus various pass rushes, including single and double dogs (linebackers) and safety blitzes.

Procedure: Commence initially with the five interior offensive linemen, versus five interior defensive linemen and linebackers with the coach or manager using the starting count and taking the center's snap-back. Numbers are assigned to the defensive players (as illustrated in (30) Offensive Line Blocking Drill, and in Chapter 14, Drill 5), and pass blocking responsibilities can be affixed individually, depending on the type of pass protection that is going to be utilized. The pass rushes and stunts are controlled and regulated, progressing from straight rushes by the down linemen to single and double dogs (linebackers) strong and weak-side, with the safety blitz being added eventually. Later offensive backs (Chapter 9, Drill 6) may be added along with the tight end, plus the outside defensive rushers (ends or linebackers), as all of the offensive players must learn

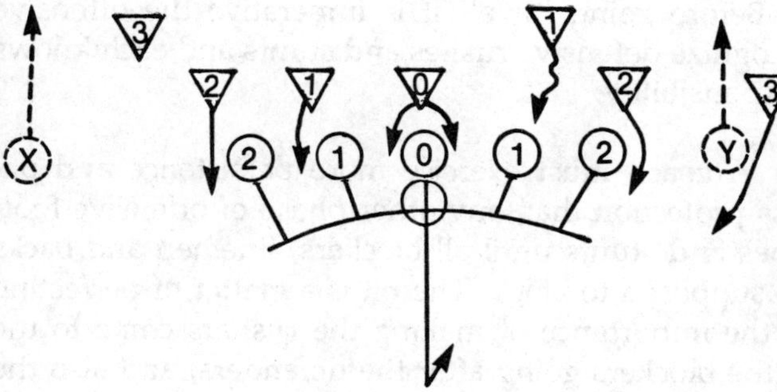

X, Y, and Z usually release as pass receivers, although on occasions Y (the tight end) may be instructed not to release but to stay in and protect the passer.

versus Oklahoma-Eagle adjustment pass rush

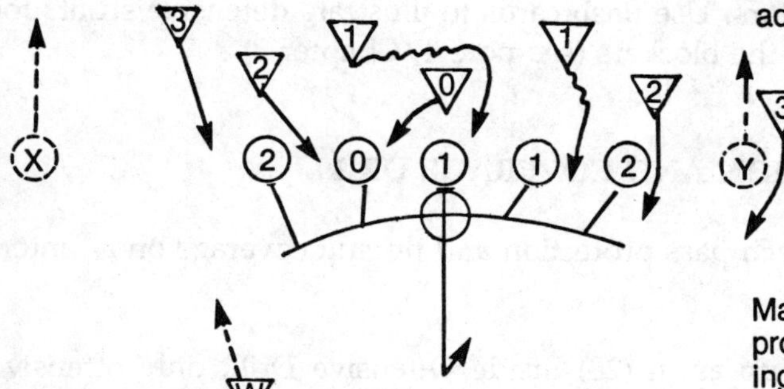

versus Oklahoma strong-side pass rush

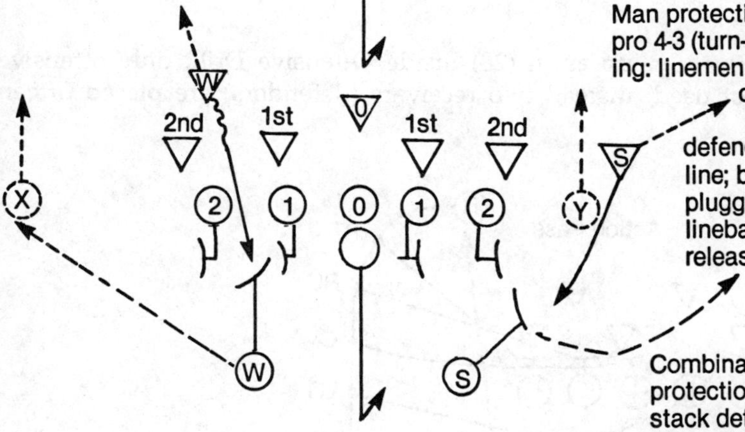

Man protection versus pro 4-3 (turn-out blocking: linemen block down linemen or standup defenders on the line; backs block the pluggers, i.e. linebackers; none, release.)

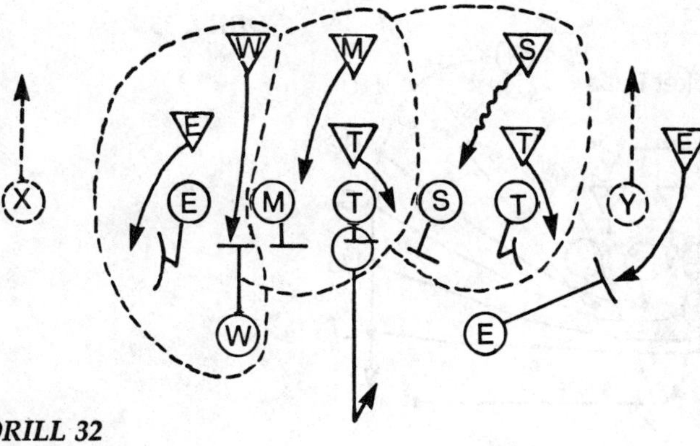

Combination ("combo") protection versus 4-3 stack defense; (weakside combo of tackle and back responsible for defensive end and WBer, weakside guard and center responsible for nose-tackle and MBer, strongside guard and tackle combo responsible for blocking SBer and tackle, and the strongside back blocks the outside rusher if he comes. If rushers drop-off, offensive backs protect inside or release in the flats.)

DRILL 32

their responsibilities. Before going "live" it is imperative the offensive linemen and backs recognize defensive rushes and stunts and each knows his pass protection responsibility.

Coaching Points: A coach must exercise more persistence and patience in teaching pass protection than any other phase of offensive football. Control the rushes and stunts until all blockers, linemen and backs know whom they are supposed to block. Then it is a matter of perfecting how to block. Stress the importance of making the rushers come to the blockers, rather than the blockers going after the defenders, and also the pass protectors adhering to all of the other proper fundamentals and principles of pass protectors. Use flash cards to illustrate defensive stunts for *both* the rushers and the blockers (see note 1, Chapter 2).

33. PASS PROTECTION AND COVERAGE DRILL

Purpose: To teach pass protection and pursuit coverage on an interception.

Procedure: Set up as in (28) Inside Offensive Drill, only offensive backs are not used; instead two receivers (defenders) are placed fifteen

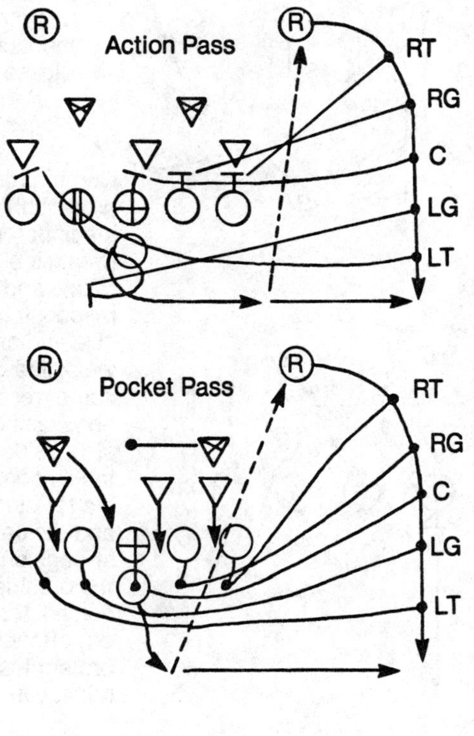

DRILL 33

yards downfield. The coach throws the football to one of the defenders, who "intercepts" the ball and returns it. The coach first calls out the type of pass so the offensive linemen will know from and to where the ball will be thrown. After carrying out their pass blocking assignments, the linemen must cover the pass and pursue the interceptor until every offensive player has tagged him.

Coaching Points: Stress the fundamentals of pass protection and the proper angles in pursuing the defender who has intercepted the pass.

34–37. SEVEN–MAN SLED DRILLS (OFFENSIVE)

34. Seven-Man Explosion Drill (Same as Drills 3–4 on Two-Man Sled)

35. Team Starts or Take-Off Drill

Purpose: To develop team starts or take-off.

Procedure: Each offensive lineman covers an arm (pad) on the seven-man sled. The quarterback calls out the play and starting count. The center snaps the ball and the linemen fire-out and block with the specified shoulder. A whistle terminates the drill. The second line moves forward immediately ready to drive block the seven-man sled.

Coaching Points: Look across the line to determine if all of the offensive blockers are up on the ball, if the line is straight, and if they are getting off together on the count. (See Chapter 9, (22) Follow-the-Ball Drill.)

DRILL 35

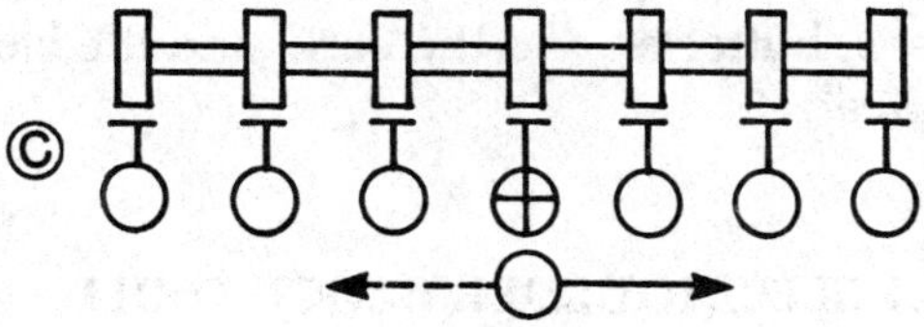

36. In-and-Out Shoulder Block Drill

Purpose: To develop the running shoulder block techniques.

Procedure: Starting from the left side of the sled and blocking with the right (or left) shoulder (or from the right side, blocking with the left (or right) shoulder), sprint forward and slam the designated forearm and shoulder into the first pad, back off two yards pumping the arms and legs, and then repeat the shoulder block on second through the seventh pad, to the far end of the sled.

Coaching Points: As soon as the first blocker bounces back from the first pad and moves forward to shoulder block the second one, the second blocker sprints forward to shoulder block the first pad, etc., following the first player down the line. Eventually seven men will be going in and out blocking the machine. Stress hitting the pads squarely with the designated shoulder and forearm, chugging the feet and pumping the arms each time.

37. Repeat Drill

Purpose: To develop power impact from upper legs, buttocks, and back when coordinating shoulder and forearm lifting action.

Procedure: Set up like (36) In-and-Out Shoulder Block Drill, only the blocker is in a six-point stance in front of the first pad on the seven-man sled. On the coach's command the player will slide to his right (or left), explode into the pad (as in the Explosion Drill), recoil and slide over in front of the next pad, uncoil, recoil and slide until he gets to the far end of the sled. Then he will roll to his outside, regain his feet, and get at the end of the line ready to come back in the opposite direction. Each time a player explodes, recoils and slides laterally, another player jumps into the lead position and replaces him. Eventually every pad is covered, and the players are all exploding, recoiling and sliding together in unison on the commands of the coach.

Coaching Points: Stress maintaining a straight back, head up, exploding into the pad like a ramrod. The power impact is delivered from the upper legs, buttocks, and the back, and the blocker should not follow up with his feet.

38. BAG–CIRCLE SHOULDER BLOCK DRILL

Purpose: To develop the fundamentals of the straight shoulder-scramble block against limited resistance.

Procedure: A large upright dummy is placed between two offensive linemen who are opposite each other in their offensive stance. Both players are given the starting count, and on the coach's command both right shoulder block the dummy from opposite sides. Working clockwise (counterclockwise when using a left shoulder block) both men maintain contact

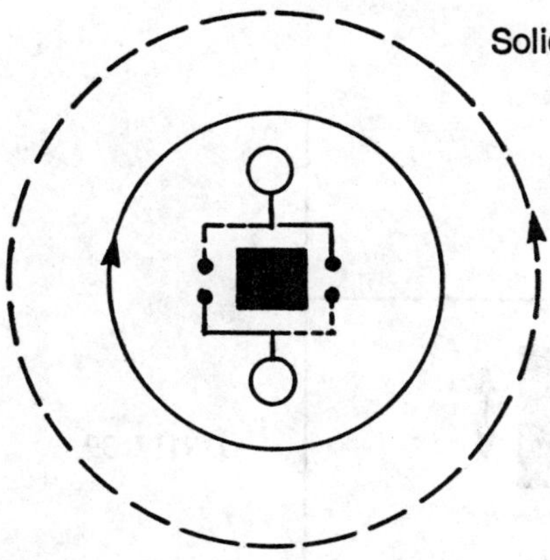

DRILL 38

with the shoulder, nape of the neck, and scramble block the dummy together from opposite sides.

Coaching Points: Stress the proper fundamentals of a shoulder block, including moving the feet. The objective is not for one blocker to overpower the other, but to get practice hitting and meeting resistance and limited rough work.

39. BIG BAG DRILL

(The bag is approximately 5 feet 9 inches in height, 4½ feet in circumference, and weighs 40 to 50 pounds.)

Purpose: To teach one-on-one pass blocking techniques, including agility and quickness.

Procedure: A large dummy constructed of heavy duck cloth (a gymnasium mat rolled tightly inside of a canvas bag may be utilized) is suspended by rope from an overhead support (such as the middle of the crossbar on the goal posts), so it can swing freely. The offensive lineman assumes his stance opposite the bag and the coach draws the bag back slightly and releases it. The lineman steps up and pops the bag, recoils and pops the bag again, trying to keep going for six consecutive hits. He should slide and shuffle, keeping his body in front of the swinging bag, and alternate shoulders in popping the dummy.

Coaching Points: Stress moving the feet, hitting and shuffling, maintaining proper alignment on the swinging bag, delivering a blow, using the hands legally (depending on scholastic or collegiate rules), operating

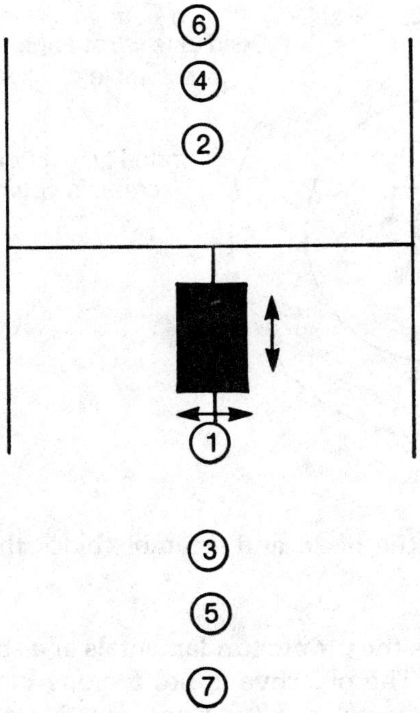

DRILL 39

from a good base with a low center of gravity, maintaining body balance at all times, and *not* lunging at the bag. The blocker should not hit, stop, and wait for the bag to come back to him again, but should pop the dummy, move his feet and align his body with the dummy for the next hit with the opposite shoulder.

40. MONSTER OR CHUTE DRILLS

(A contraption made of 1 inch pipe approximately 35 feet long, 4½ feet high, and 4½ feet in depth from front to back, braced across the top, and divided into seven chutes or stalls, which are 5 feet wide and are open front and back—"The Monster." There are also available commercially one-to-seven man chutes, plus those that may be installed on one-to-seven man blocking sleds that swing out of the way when not in use. A crossbar may be set at the desired height on support standards, or a rope may be stretched between the goal posts, if the teaching-coaching aids mentioned cannot be constructed or purchased.)

Purpose: To teach offensive linemen to stay low on their initial charge, and to take-off together with good form.

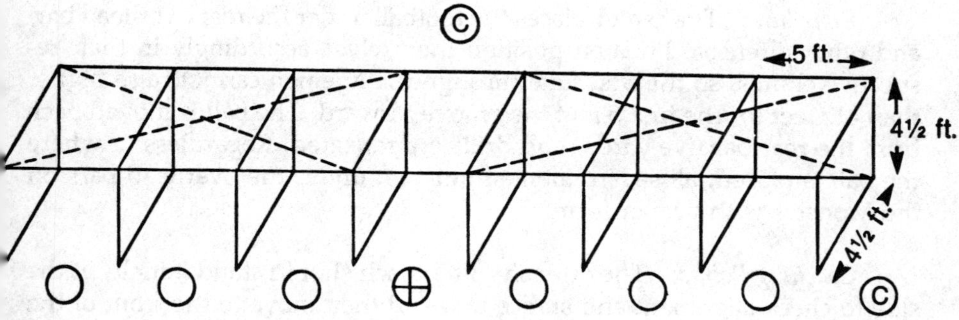
5 ft.
4½ ft.
4½ ft.

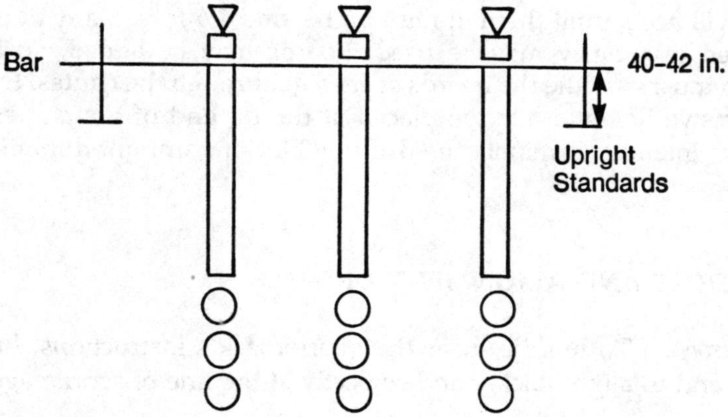
Bar
40–42 in.
Upright
Standards

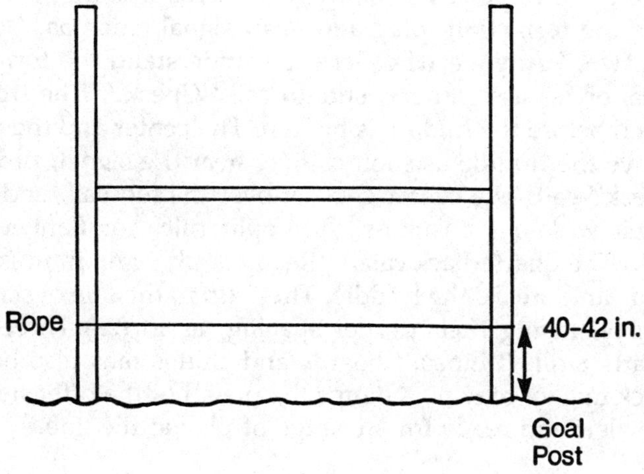
Rope
40–42 in.
Goal
Post

DRILL 40

Procedure: The center places the football under the rear overhead bar, and other offensive linemen position themselves accordingly in their respective chutes, so the first time through the linemen cannot raise higher than 4½ feet for the first 5 feet they move forward. The ball is moved back from the rear bar five yards, and drills are repeated. Regardless of where the ball is placed, all seven linemen must go under the overhead bars on the Monster with proper form.

Coaching Points: The offensive line coach should stand initially at the side to check alignment and stance first and then move to the front of the chutes or stalls to check proper stance, body alignment, proper arm-leg movement, team take-off, etc. It will not be necessary to admonish the charging linemen to stay low, as they are conscious of the overhead bars which will not permit them to raise up beyond 4½ feet. Many of the drills explained previously may be used. Boards may be added, so that the linemen must straddle the boards as they go through the chutes. Dummies or defensive linemen may be placed at the far end of the chutes so the offensive linemen terminate the drills by blocking upright dummies or go "live."

41. HUDDLE AND ALIGNMENT DRILL

Purpose: To huddle, hear the quarterback's instructions, break the huddle and to align quickly and correctly at the line of scrimmage.

Procedure: The center forms the huddle by quickly signalling with a raised hand his position approximately five yards behind where the football will be put into play. The quarterback steps into the huddle and generally calls the formation, play and snap signal, such as, " 'I' Right, 34 Power on two." Anyone who does not understand the formation, play, snap signal or his assignment, should call "Check." The trouble should be corrected before the huddle is broken. The center and the wide-outs (X and Z) leave the huddle as soon as they hear the signal, providing there is no "check" call. The center gets set over the football, and the flankers run to their wide-out positions. (See split rules for flankers, Drill (38), Chapter 8.) The quarterback calls, "Ready *break,*" and in unison everyone claps hands and breaks the huddle. They run to the line of scrimmage and align quickly, taking their proper spacing, as in (22) Three-S or Splits-Stance-Starts Drill. ("Lines," boards and chutes may also be used.) The quarterback may or may not change the play, but the offensive team must always be alert and ready for a change of play at the line.

Coaching Points: Huddle procedures: the center should form the huddle quickly not more than five yards from where the football will be

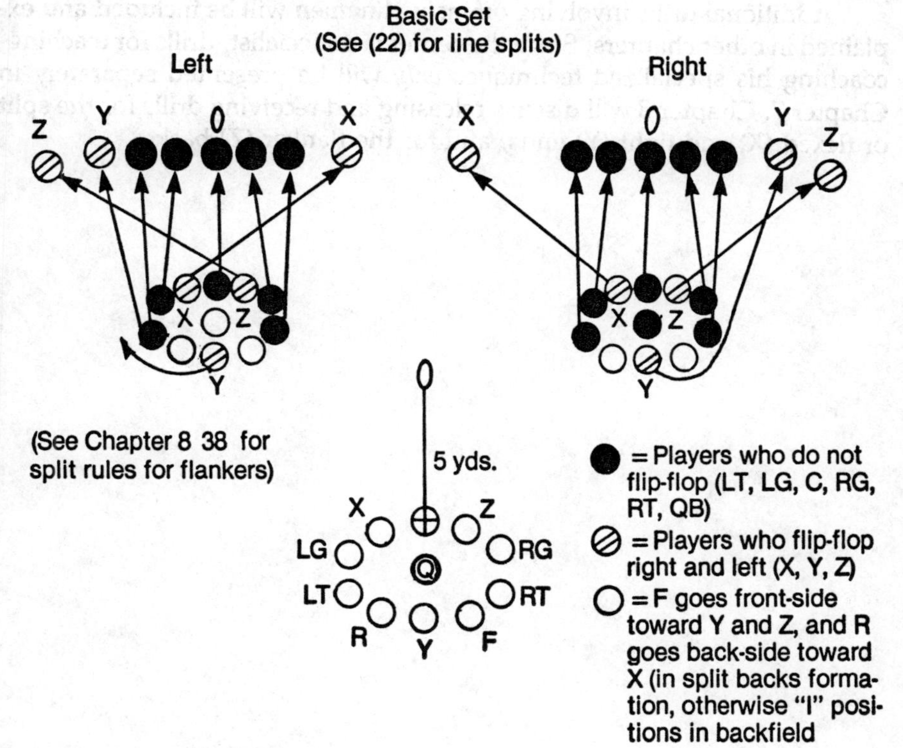

There are advantages and disadvantages both to flip-flopping the entire offensive line and backs, and to flip-flopping X, Y, and Z only and having the five interior linemen remain static in that their positions are the same in both right and left formations. (If flip-flopping the entire line, the huddle would have to be positioned and aligned differently in order to criss-cross or serpentine for a left formation, which is not illustrated above.)

DRILL 41

placed by the official; do not crowd or squeeze each other; absolutely no talking after the quarterback enters the huddle; look at the quarterback's face and *concentrate* on what he says; never lean on a teammate; maintain a compact and orderly huddle; call out "check" if a player wants the quarterback to repeat his instructions; the quarterback should call "time out" if any trouble is not resolved quickly in the huddle. Stress and check "break" procedures and how to align quickly on the football according to the formation called in the huddle; also check line positioning and spacing. Always be alert and ready for a change of play by the quarterback at the line of scrimmage. (See Chapter 14, (1) Starting Count-Hand Clap Drill.) Check position and alignment of wide-outs. (See Chapter 8, (38) Wide-outs (Flankers) Alignment Drill.)

Additional drills involving offensive linemen will be included and explained in other chapters. Since the center is a specialist, drills for teaching-coaching his specialized techniques *only* will be presented separately in Chapter 7. Chapter 8 will discuss releasing and receiving drills for the split or flexed (X) and tight (Y) ends, and for the flanker (Z) back.

7

Center Play Drills

The offensive center controls the timing of his team, and proper timing is the essence of any offense. The T-formation center snaps the football to his quarterback in a direct hand-to-hand exchange *approximately* seventy times in the typical collegiate game, *approximately* fifty-five times in the typical scholastic football game. If a team is pass-oriented, the number of offensive plays is likely to be greater; if run-oriented, the number of plays may be less. The number of offensive plays will depend also on your player personnel and their skills, and that of your opposition, as well as on situational variables. Regardless of the number of exchanges between a center and a quarterback, however, if any are improper or incorrect the center can cause his team's offense to falter through fumbles, miscues, and poorly timed plays. Therefore, the hand-back exchange of the football should be fast, accurate, and automatic.

The center, or some member on the football team, also must be able to make the long pass to the punter in punt formation, and to the holder's hands on placement and field goal attempts. If a team utilizes the "shotgun" formation, then the regular center must be able to make the medium (6–7 yard) "blind" pass to his quarterback, too, although this type of center pass is not recommended for the punting or placement aspects of the kicking game. In addition the center must be able to execute most of the same basic fundamentals and techniques as any other offensive lineman. The drills for teaching-coaching these skills are included in the preceding chapter. There are few other drills for the T-formation center. Drills for developing the center's ability to make the long pass to the punter are included below, and overall kicking game drills involving the center are in

Chapter 15. An excellent drill for the center and quarterback working together is included in Chapter 14, (1) Starting Count-Hand Clap Drill. Other drills for teaching-coaching center play fundamentals and techniques follow.

1. ON–THE–LINE DRILL

Purpose: To perfect the fundamentals of the automatic snap-back exchange between the centers and quarterbacks, and to get them ready for offensive practice.

Procedure: Each center puts the front tip of his football on a line, allowing about three yards between centers. A quarterback covers each center, and a defender holds an upright dummy or an air bag opposite each center. The coach calls out the cadence and snap count, and the exchange between the centers and quarterbacks is made on his command. Neither the centers nor the quarterbacks move their feet in an attempt to block or to pivot on the first three warm-up exchanges, as the emphasis is on perfecting the exchange. Upon receiving the snap-back, each quarterback immediately raises his football above his center's back so the coach can see the position of his hands on the football. Individual adjustment corrections should be made by the coach. The coach then designates the offensive play or the footwork for the quarterback, the starting count, and which of the quarterbacks is to call the cadence for everyone. The centers practice stepping with the proper foot and blocking the bags. The quarterbacks practice their pivots and play mechanics. The centers and quarterbacks practice the automatic exchange. After several exchanges, depending upon the number of centers, quarterbacks, and the time allotted in the practice schedule, the centers remain in their places and the quarterbacks rotate clockwise covering another center. The drill is repeated until every quarterback has worked with every center.

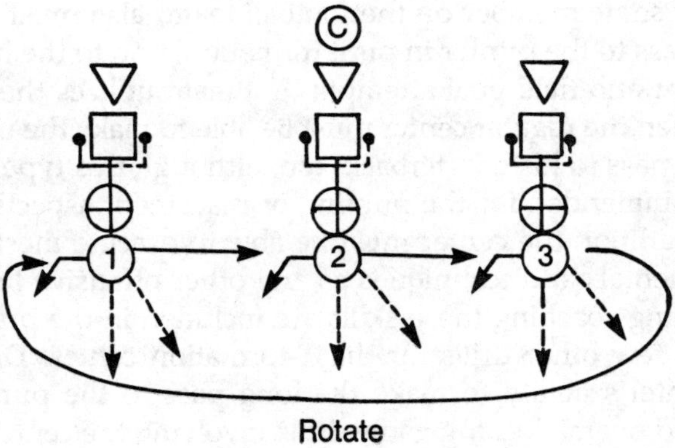

DRILL 1

Coaching Points: Stress the fundamentals of the automatic exchange and check the timing, exchange, stance, pivots, starting count cadence for the quarterbacks, and the blocking techniques of the centers.

2. ONE–ON–ONE ROTATION DRILL

Purpose: To teach and develop shoulder block techniques, and to practice the automatic center-quarterback snap-back exchange.

Procedure: Three centers work together so No. 1 assumes the offensive center's stance over the ball, No. 2 covers him as the quarterback, and No. 3 holds the bag for resistance. The coach works the three centers through a systematic progression of shoulder blocks versus the defender nose-up on and off the line, and off-set both on and off the line of scrimmage. The coach indicates the type of block and the starting count, and the center (quarterback) calls the snap count. Use a whistle to terminate the drill. Rotate the players after every block so No. 1 becomes the bag holder, No. 2 moves forward to snap the football, and No. 3 moves behind to become the quarterback. After each cycle a new defensive situation is set up for the rotating centers.

Coaching Points: Stress the correct blocking fundamentals and a perfect ball exchange. Show each quarterback (center) how and where to hold his hands to receive the snap-back. If only two centers are available for the Rotation Drill, the center and the bag holder rotate back and forth, and the coach acts as the quarterback.

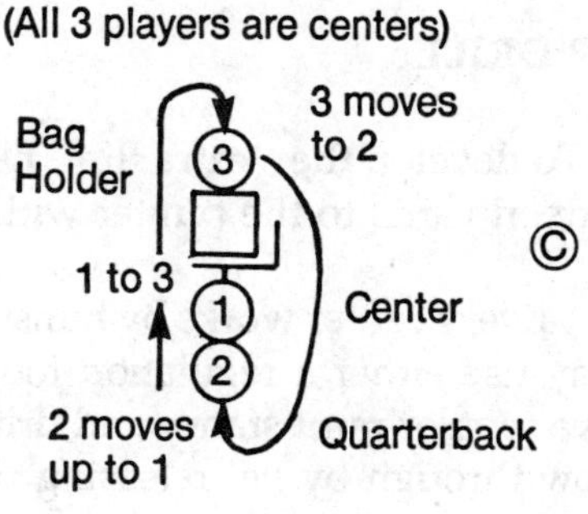

DRILL 2

3. REVERSE (UNWINDING) TECHNIQUE DRILL

Purpose: To teach the center where and how the quarterback wishes to receive the football on the snap-back exchange.

Procedure: The center and quarterback assume their stance, with the quarterback placing his hands in the center's crotch on the football, fingers on the lacing, in the manner he wishes to receive the ball from the center on the exchange. The center reaches back between his legs and takes the football from the hands of the quarterback, merely "unwinding," and places the ball on the ground at arm's length. They should continue practicing until the center gets the "feel" of it.

Coaching Points: No starting count is used; merely make individual corrections in the snap-back exchange mechanics.

4. WEIGHTED FOOTBALL DRILL

Purpose: To strengthen the center's arms and wrists by practicing with a weighted football.

Procedure: The centers *pair-off* and practice centering a weighted football (23 ounces) 5, 7, 10, 12 yards or more during the pre-practice period or during warm-up before working with the punters. (It is probably best to practice with weighted footballs during the off-season.)

Coaching Points: The training footballs are prominently labeled with white insert panels to identify them from the regulation footballs. Caution: the training (weighted) footballs should not be used for other than the purpose intended.

5. EXTRA FLIP DRILL

Purpose: To develop the "extra flip" necessary to get a football back thirteen or fourteen yards to the punter with speed and accuracy.

Procedure: Every center works by himself since he is *not* releasing the football. He may use either a regulation football or a weighted ball. The center assumes a regular punt stance and drives the ball back hard, but he checks his follow-through by *not* releasing the football. Six tries seem to give the center the "extra flip" necessary to make the long pass to the punter in deep punt formation with speed and accuracy.

Coaching Points: Stress the proper stance and hand position on the football.

6. CENTER'S LOOSENING AND STRETCHING DRILL

Purpose: To loosen and stretch the muscles prior to working with the punter or making the long pass.

Procedure: Every center works quickly by himself without a football. From a straddle position with his legs spread wide, the center reaches with both hands to his left ankle, forward, to his right ankle, and to the rear between his legs, as far as possible, in a four-count cadence. He should maintain body balance throughout the drill.

Coaching Points: Stress using this routine as one of the warm-up drills before centering the football for punting practice.

7. HAND-SLAP DRILL

Purpose: To develop hand quickness and follow-through with both hands.

Procedure: One center works with another center, but a football is *not* used. The center extends his hands forward on the ground, palms down, in his usual stance when centering for punts with his body weight in his tail. His buddy stands behind the center and puts his hands flush and under the center's tail. The center slaps his buddy's hands quickly, simulating the snap-back to the punter, maintaining good balance, following through, and snapping up his head upon contact of the hands. The procedure is reversed after two minutes of practice, with the buddy in the center's stance.

Coaching Points: Stress performing the mechanics quickly, but not too rapidly. Use as a warm-up drill for two minutes every practice session.

8. OVERHEAD PASSING DRILL

Purpose: To give the centers the proper feel of the football, and the proper placement of their hands when centering for punts.

Procedure: The centers pair off eight yards apart, using one football for two centers. The center grasps the football in the same manner as when passing it for a punt. *Standing* facing each other, the centers pass the football back and forth, with arms extended overhead. They observe their hand position on the football, and their follow-through motion.

Coaching Points: A warm-up drill for centers, about ten throws each, two minutes daily. Emphasize snapping the wrists and following through and *not* stepping forward in "whipping" the football back and forth.

9. UNDERHAND PASSING DRILL

Purpose: To build confidence as the centers get the feeling of their punting game stance and freedom in delivering the pass.

Procedure: One center assumes his punt stance seven yards from his buddy. The football is *not* placed on the ground but is whipped between his legs to the other center. Alternate the passing and receiving from one center to the other.

Coaching Points: Use as a warm-up drill prior to centering for punting in the pre-practice period.

10. BULL'S EYE DRILL

Purpose: To develop centering the ball with speed and accuracy for the punting game.

Procedure: A piece of canvas approximately five-feet square is stretched between the goal posts with a sixteen-inch hole in the middle of the canvas, with loose netting behind the hole forming an open drop pocket behind the canvas. An eight-inch red stripe and an eight-inch blue stripe are painted around the hole, so the target resembles a bull's-eye. The center is stationed fifteen yards from the canvas and makes fifteen passes as part of his pre-practice warm-up routine. Through diligent practice, most centers learn to pass the ball so it will hit inside the colored circles. A punter can normally handle any pass that strikes inside the circles.

Coaching Points: Use as a warm-up drill prior to centering for punting in the pre-practice period.

11. CENTER'S SEMI–SPREAD PUNT BAG DRILL

Purpose: To develop centering the ball with speed and accuracy *for those teams using the semi-spread punt formation.*

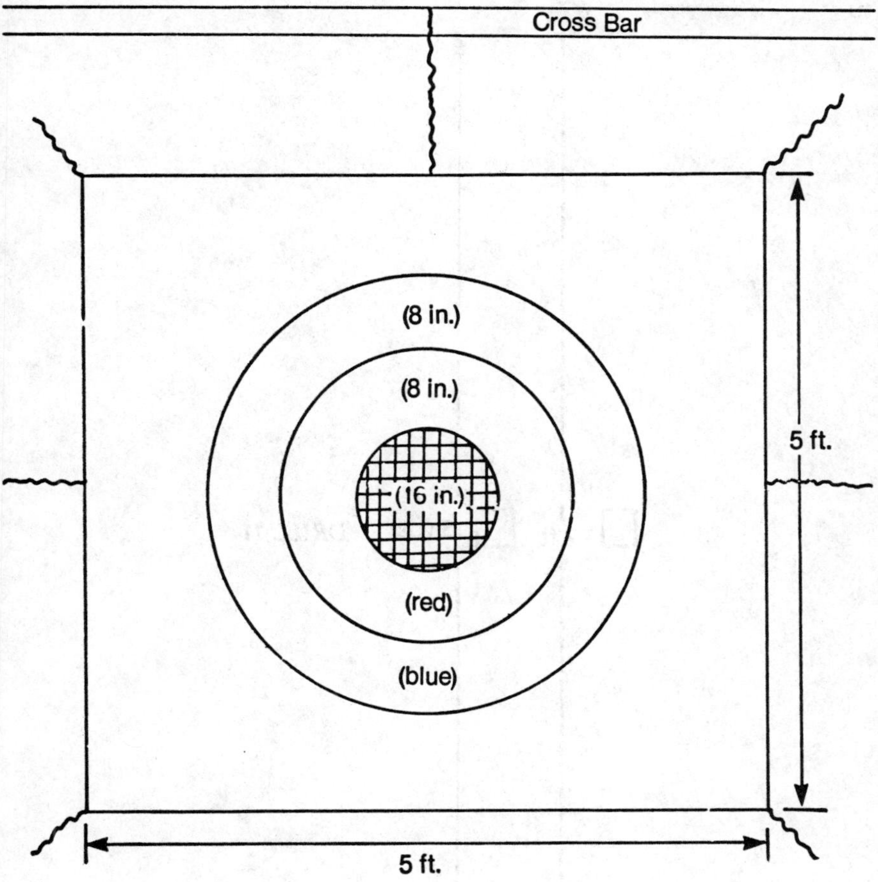

DRILL 10

Procedure: Two upright dummies are placed opposite each other about two feet apart at the top approximately 6½ yards from one center. Another center (punter) covers his partner 6½ yards directly behind the opening of the dummies, so they are approximately thirteen yards away from each other. Each center must pass the ball with speed and accuracy between the opening at the top of the upright dummies, which simulates the position and alignment of two of the offensive wedge men in the semi-spread punt formation.

Coaching Points: The punter (center) must give the center a target, with his kicking foot aligned splitting the bags. The punter should tell the center if he is not square with the line of scrimmage. Stress following through with both hands, instructing the center as a coaching point to try to "reach back and touch the fingertips" of the punter as he stands in position to receive the deep pass.

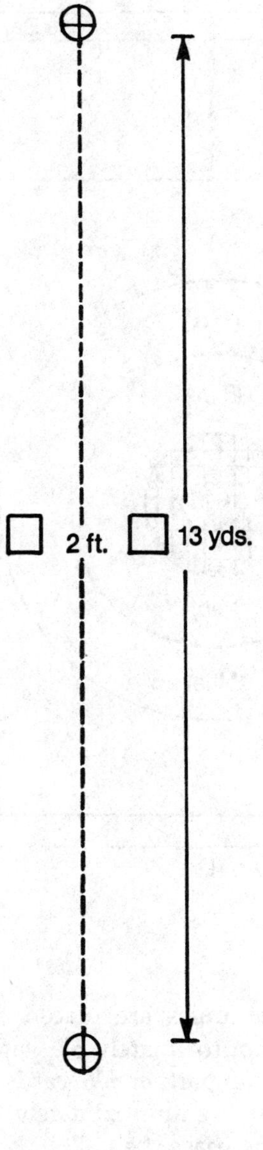

DRILL 11

12. HUSTLE DRILL

Purpose: To teach the centers to "hustle" breaking the huddle, getting over the ball, firing-out on the snap count, and then returning quickly to form the huddle again.

Procedure: Similar to (2) One-On-One Rotation Drill in that three centers will alternate on the center-quarterback exchange of the football. The football is placed on a line, and five yards downfield beyond the ball

DRILL 12

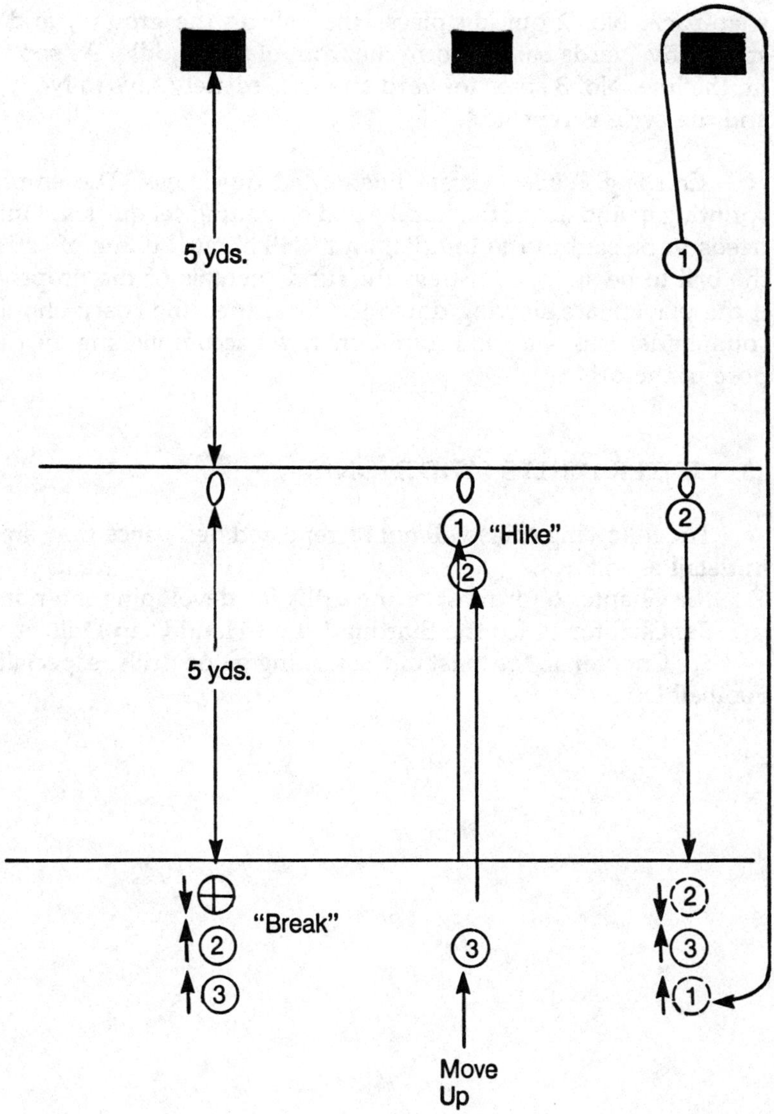

a dummy is placed on the ground. On this side of the football, five yards away, the three centers line up in a single column. The No. 1 center takes his regular position, back to the ball, forming the front of the huddle. The other two centers face the No. 1 center. Very quickly No. 2 says to No. 1, "Break" and they both sprint five yards forward with No. 1 getting over the football and No. 2 acting as the quarterback. Very quickly No. 2 says, "Hike" and the ball is snapped in a hand-back exchange. The No. 1 center sprints forward, circles the dummy downfield five yards away, and sprints ten yards back to the rear of the huddle behind No. 3. Upon receiving the snap-back, No. 2 quickly places the ball on the ground, and turns and sprints five yards back to form the front of the huddle. As soon as his feet hit the line, No. 3 steps forward and immediately says to No. 2, "Break," and the cycle is repeated.

Coaching Points: Stress hustle and quickness. The emphasis is on sprinting in and out of the huddle and on getting set quickly. Only "Break" needs to be said in the huddle, and "Hike" at the line of scrimmage for the ball to be snapped. Stress the fundamentals of the proper exchange. If the players are slowing down the drill, then the coach should give the commands. This is a good conditioner, yet accomplishing the desired purpose of the drill.

13. CENTER DRILLS (ADDITIONAL)

The following drills will not be repeated here since they are explained in detail as follows:

See Chapter 6 for most of the drills for developing interior linemen.

See Chapter 14 for the Starting Count-Hand Clap Drill.

See Chapter 15 for most of the kicking game drills, especially (13) Wet Football Drill.

8

Passing and Receiving Drills

The development of a successful passing attack depends on a competent passer, good receivers, adequate protection, and sound passing strategy. Many coaches maintain the passer must be better than average; others maintain he must be great. An effective passing game is much more than just "a couple of kids on the squad who seem to like to play pitch and catch."

Drills for passers and receivers are the content of this chapter. Drills for teaching-coaching offensive linemen to protect the passer are in Chapter 6, and those for offensive backs follow this particular chapter on passing and receiving drills. As for passing strategy, which includes well-conceived patterns and tactics to exploit the weaknesses of defensive coverages and personnel, there are some drills in Chapter 14 relating to passing and running strategy but for the most part this subject is beyond the scope of a drills text.

Before a coach considers which drills to utilize and to what extent, he must first consider philosophically how he is going to employ the passing game—as a basic offensive weapon? a supplementary attack? or as a complementary weapon? A coach who adopts the pass as his basic attack merely runs enough to keep the defense unsettled, but most of his offense is built around "putting the football in the air." Unless a coach has superior personnel and can "grind it out" consistently with his running game, he must consider the other two passing game alternatives. As a supplementary weapon the pass is utilized to "keep the defense honest," but it is much more than occasionally instructing your quarterback, "Throw a long incompleted pass anywhere downfield so they *think* we have a passing attack." The passing game must be practiced and perfected to the extent that it can be utilized with at least moderate success in certain situations when your running attack cannot garner the necessary yardage. Also, unless the pass is used to some extent and with some degree of success, it is fairly easy for the opposition to defense the team with an unbalanced running attack. Therefore, the forward pass is thought of by most football coaches as at least a supplementary weapon in relation to their running game.

The balanced attack is when a coach uses passing as a complementary weapon in relation to his running game. Each phase is equally dangerous, and the opposition must defend against both means of offensive attack. Such an offensive attack is ideal, but more often theorized than achieved. The reasons are beyond the scope of discussion, except to say that a coach cannot consider the forward pass as a separate entity involving *only* his passers and receivers, and unrelated to his running attack. A successful passing attack is a team effort, requiring the maximum performance of every team member. Then, too, the opposition and tactical situational factors can never be discounted, and have much to do with the success or failure of any attempted pass.

The inexperienced coach does not take into consideration that a successful passing attack generally takes a great deal more time and effort than that expended on developing an outstanding running game; and even experienced coaches do not always remember this fact. Yet both phases of the offense must be closely correlated and, unless done, the effectiveness of one phase will diminish in proportion to the ineffectiveness of the other phase of the offensive attack.

Most of the drills in this chapter are for developing individual skills in passing and/or receiving. A number of these drills may be performed in front of a net or canvas attached to the crossbar and goal posts. Several passers may work on passing drills at the same time throwing into the net or canvas, and receivers, linebackers (Chapter 11), and secondary defenders (Chapter 12) may use it as a backstop for their drills. The value of this suggested teaching aid is that individual performers have more opportunities to practice their skills in a shorter period of time, and it is easier to retrieve the footballs and to keep the drills moving at a more rapid pace.

Drills for teaching-coaching offensive passing game fundamentals and techniques follow.

1. PASSER'S WRIST DRILL

Purpose: To develop throwing a football with wrist and arm movement, and to eliminate winding-up and throwing sidearm.

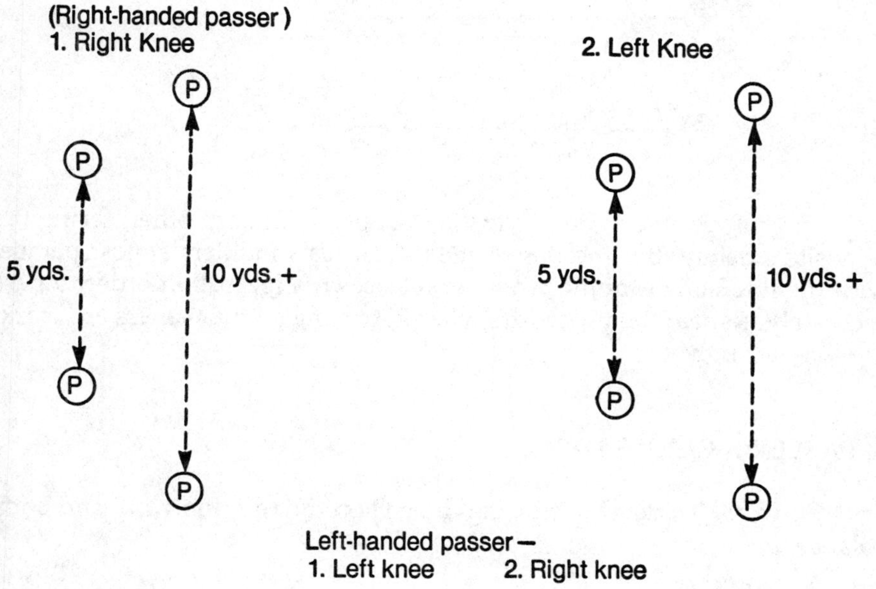

DRILL 1

Procedure: Facing each other and kneeling on the *right* knee (the left knee for a left-handed passer), one passer picks up the football from the ground and passes it to another passer, who is five yards away. The receiver (passer) makes a target for the passer. The receiver (passer) catches the ball and repeats the process. You increase the distance to ten yards plus, without undue strain or "muscling" the football in order to pass it the necessary distance. Repeat the drill kneeling on the *left* (opposite) knee.

Coaching Points: Stress the proper throwing fundamentals, and snappy wrist action for the passer. The receiver should make a target every time for the passer.

2. PARALLEL PASSING DRILL

Purpose: To develop passing the football on the run, footwork and body balance.

Procedure: Commencing at a distance of five yards apart from each other, the passers move laterally across the width of the field passing the ball back and forth to each other. The passer must lead the receiver with a soft pass. The distance is increased to ten yards plus.

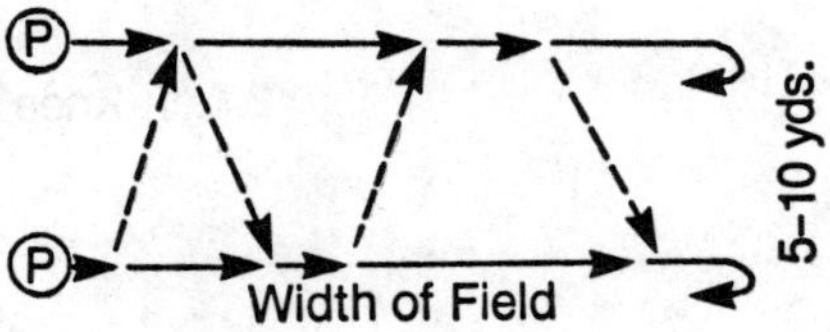

DRILL 2

Coaching Points: The players jog parallel with each other, facing the opposite sideline, but the passer must turn his shoulders almost parallel with the line he is running when he releases the football in order to pass accurately. Repeat the procedure when returning so the passers are working left and right.

3. PASSER'S CIRCLE DRILL

Purpose: To develop passing the ball on the run, footwork and body balance.

Procedure: The same principle as in (2) Parallel Passing Drill, only the passers work clockwise and counter-clockwise around an imaginary circle seven yards plus in diameter when commencing the drill.

Coaching Points: Stress squaring the shoulders, and leading the receiver with a soft pass. Stress the proper fundamentals of passing. The coach may blow his whistle to indicate a change of direction.

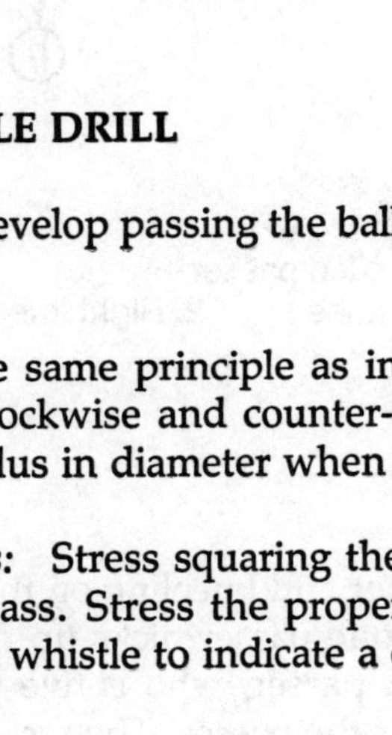

DRILL 3

4. QUICK PASS DRILL

Purpose: To get the "feel" of the football and to develop throwing with a wrist and arm movement and to eliminate winding-up and throwing sidearm.

Procedure: The passers face each other at five yards, then increase their distance to fifteen yards apart. One passer molds the ball and fires it quickly to his buddy, who catches it and fires it back quickly. The emphasis is on quickness and good passing fundamentals, except the feet are not positioned each time.

Coaching Points: The drill is similar to "playing catch" in baseball. Stress quickness and proper passing fundamentals, with the exception of toeing in and positioning the feet.

5. PASSER'S CLOCK DRILL

Purpose: To teach and develop proper footwork and passing fundamentals.

Procedure: A quarterback sets up in a passing position with the football cocked behind his right ear, his left hand over the front tip of the football, and his left foot in advance of his right foot. The coach will call aloud, "Ten o'clock!" "Twelve o'clock!" "Two o'clock!" and the passer must step in the proper direction (left oblique, straight, right oblique) with his lead (left) foot, pump the football in the direction called, check its forward progress with his left hand, and then "load" again by returning to his starting position with the ball cocked. Receivers are stationed at a distance of approximately fifteen yards in front of the passer at ten, twelve and two o'clock positions. After four or five commands, the coach yells, "Now, ten (twelve or two) o'clock," and the passer then steps and drills the ball to the receiver stationed at the position designated.

DRILL 5

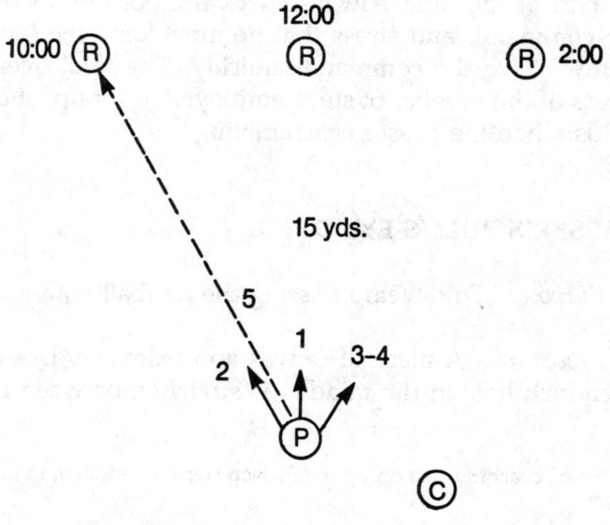

Coaching Points: The commands should be given quickly, The "Now" (or "Pass") command should be varied, i.e., second, third, sixth time, so the passer does not hold back early throwing motions waiting for the extended "Now" command. Stress the proper footwork, and quickness in "reloading" each time. The pass should be drilled, not lobbed.

6. IN-THE-CUP AND SCRAMBLE DRILLS (PROGRESSIVE)

Purpose: To develop the proper footwork (5, 7 and/or 9 steps) within the prescribed time (1.30, 1.75 and 1.95 seconds, respectively[1]) for drop-back passing from the cup; and to develop footwork (scramble) to evade simulated rushers.

Procedure: Using an offensive center and the starting count, the quarterback practices sprinting back the required number of steps (depth) within the prescribed time designated by the coach, who times the passer with a stopwatch. Progressing to the scramble drill, as the passer sets up, the coach indicates the direction the passer should move laterally or vertically by yelling, "Left!" "Right!" "Right!" "Up!" before yelling, "Now!" (or "Pass!"). The passer must shuffle in the direction indicated keeping his feet always in the correct relationship, and the football is cocked ready to throw, simulating moving around in the cup to evade rushers. A receiver is approximately fifteen yards from his passer, and he "mirrors" his passer's lateral movements so they are in the same plane.

Coaching Points: The passer must master getting set to throw from the desired depth within the prescribed time before moving to the scrambling part of the drill. Always check the position of the passer's feet on every command, and stress that he must keep the football cocked ready to throw. Give the commands quickly. The total overall time lapse, regardless of the number of steps employed to set up, should not exceed 5.0 seconds when the passer is scrambling.

7. PASSER'S BULL'S-EYE DRILL

Purpose: To develop passing the football with accuracy.

Procedure: A piece of canvas approximately five-feet square, with a sixteen-inch hole in the middle, is stretched between the goal posts with

[1]Some coaches teach only five or seven steps, in addition to the three-step drop in 0.9 seconds.

a net behind to stop the footballs. An eight-inch red stripe is painted first around the sixteen-inch hole in the middle, followed by an eight-inch blue stripe so the target resembles a bull's-eye. The passer lines up approximately ten yards away from the target, and continues to move back, until he can hit inside of the circles with a high degree of accuracy on the majority of his passes attempted.

Coaching Points: The passers should warm-up sufficiently prior to passing in the pre-practice period. The passers should not hold on to the ball and attempt to "guide" it through the hole. Have plenty of footballs available for the passers.

8. CANVAS-NET PASSING DRILL

Purpose: To develop passing the football with accuracy.

Procedure: The canvas, attached to the crossbar of the goal posts, with a net behind to stop the football, has five holes in it at various heights. The holes in the two upper corners (size of a receiver's open hands) sim-

DRILL 8

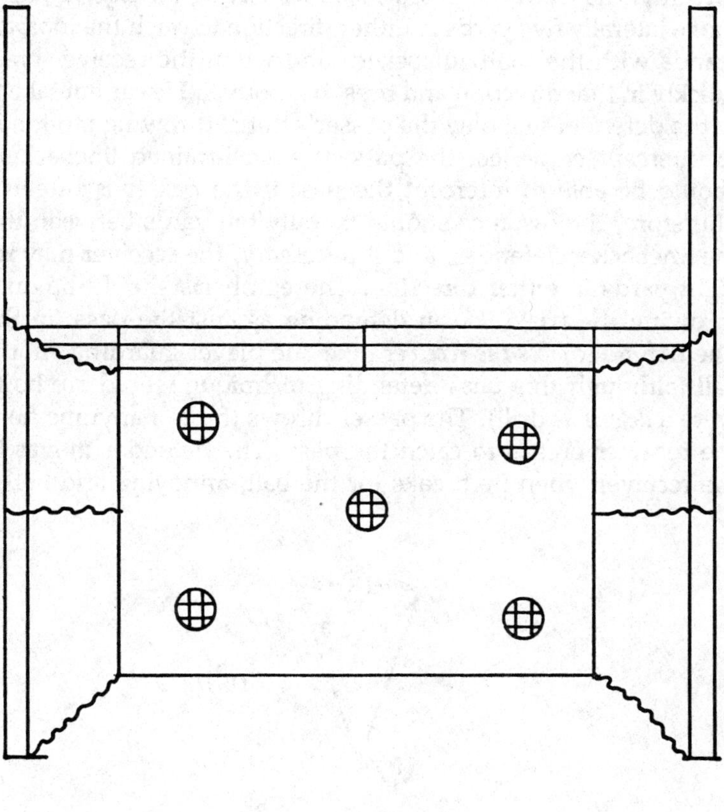

ulate the high pass. The hole in the middle of the canvas is for the jump pass. The holes in the lower two corners simulate the sideline pass. Working systematically the passer drills the football into the holes-pockets.

Coaching Points: The passers should warm-up sufficiently prior to passing in pre-practice period. Stress the proper fundamentals of passing. Have plenty of footballs available for the passers. They should not try to "guide" the football through the holes.

9–10. QUICK PASS–RECEIVER DRILLS

9. Passer's Quick Pass Drill

10. Receiver's Quick Pass or Nuisance Drill

Purpose: Passer (9) to develop quickness, accuracy, wrist action, and to anticipate when the receiver will be open. *Receiver* (10) to develop fighting for and concentrating on catching the football.

Procedure: (9) The defender sets up in front of the receiver ten to fifteen yards from the passer, *both men facing the passer.* The receiver may move laterally five yards in either direction to catch the football. The passer stands with the football cocked, and when the receiver breaks, he steps quickly in that direction and fires the football. He cannot fake the pass first, as the defender will play the passer's initial throwing motion in an attempt to intercept or deflect the pass. If a well-trained linebacker is used, he should be able to intercept the pass if the passer is fifteen yards away. Therefore, the distance should be only ten yards between the passer and the linebacker defender, and if necessary, the receiver may move laterally eight yards in either direction. The emphasis should be on quickness in throwing the pass, *not* on defending against the pass (in this drill). (10) The defender *faces the receiver,* like one player guarding another in basketball (although this pass defending technique would *not* be taught if this were a *defensive* drill). The passer throws the ball anytime he is ready, and the receiver breaks to catch the pass. The defender moves laterally with the receiver when he breaks for the ball, annoying and bothering him as

DRILL 9

the receiver attempts to catch it (which is the purpose of the drill, not teaching pass defense).

Coaching Points: Work separately with the passer (9) or the receiver (10), and do not attempt to coach both players at the same time. The receiver should attempt to catch every pass that is thrown.

11. PASSER'S DECISION DRILLS

Purpose: To teach and develop proper footwork and passing fundamentals.

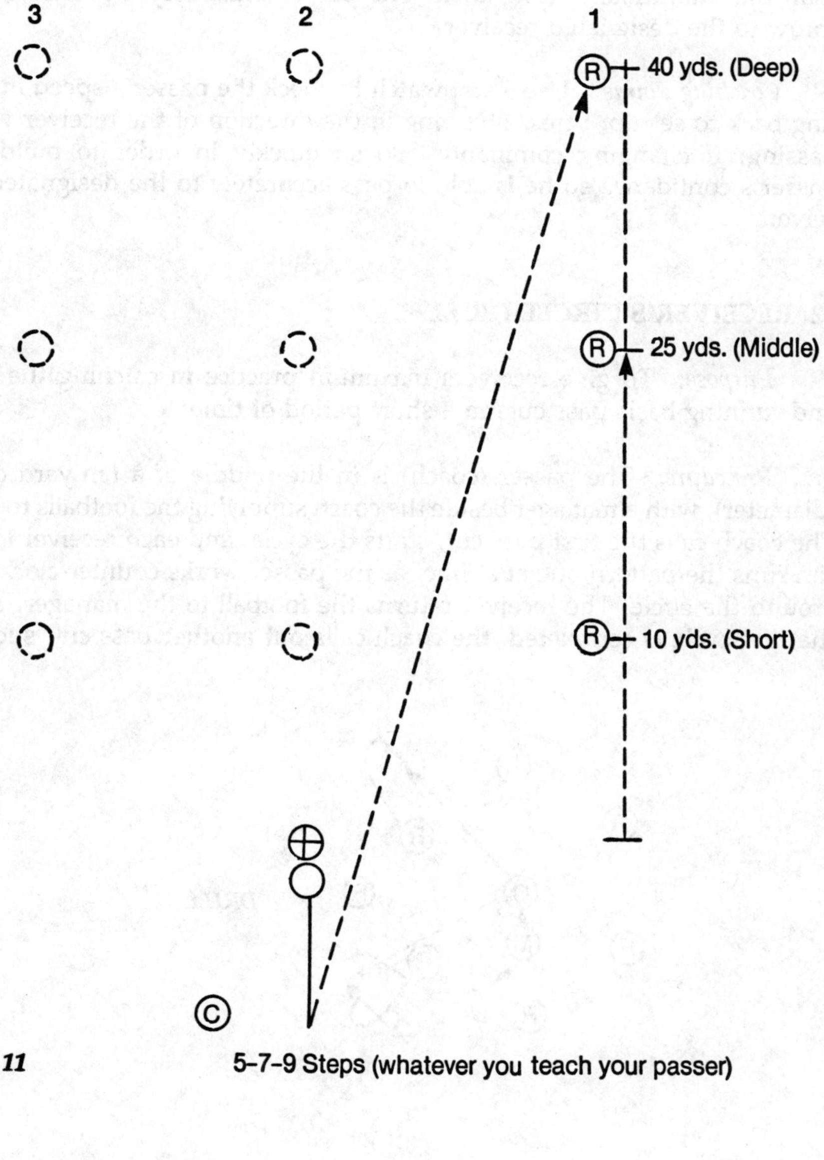

DRILL 11

Procedure: Receivers are stationed short (10 yards), middle (25 yards), and deep (40 yards) from the line of scrimmage facing the passer at a right oblique angle, in the middle, and then at a left oblique angle. Each of the three "cycles" consists of two parts: the passer works systematically warming up by receiving the snap-back, sprinting back to the prescribed depth (5, 7, or 9 steps, whatever you teach-coach), and passing right to his recievers short, middle, deep. In the second part of the first cycle, the coach designates whether the passer should throw short, middle, or deep, mixing up the commands. The second and third cycles follow, after the receivers move to the middle and left oblique, respectively, and are the same as the two-part first cycle. In the second part of the cycle, the coach may change his first command quickly and indicate a receiver other than the one initially designated. The passer must stay on-balance and throw to the designated receiver.

Coaching Points: Use a stopwatch to check the passer's speed in getting back to set up. Stress stepping in the direction of the receiver when passing. If changing commands, do so quickly in order to build the passer's confidence so he is able to pass accurately to the designated receiver.

12. RECEIVER'S CIRCLE DRILL

Purpose: To give receivers maximum practice in catching the ball, and running basic pass cuts in a short period of time.

Procedure: The passer (coach) is in the middle of a ten-yard circle (diameter), with a manager beside the coach supplying the footballs to him. The coach calls the first pass cut, starts the cycle, and each receiver in the rim runs the pattern one at a time, as the passer works counter-clockwise around the circle. The receiver returns the football to the manager. After the first cycle is completed, the coach calls out another pass cut, such as

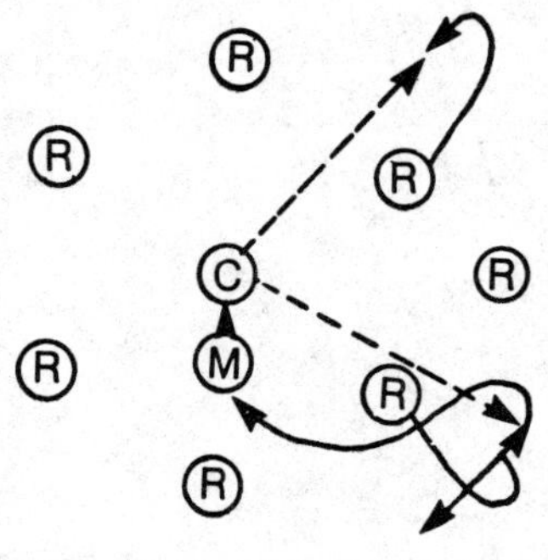

DRILL 12

hook, square-out left, square-out right, left-and-up, etc., and the drill is repeated until all of the basic pass cuts have been performed.

Coaching Points: Stress catching the football correctly, and not on running the pass cuts. Emphasize hustle and keeping the drill moving quickly.

13. RECEIVER'S QUICK HANDS DRILL

Purpose: To develop quickness in reacting to an oral command and in catching the football.

Procedure: A receiver is stationed directly in front of and facing a net (*with his back to the passer*), which serves as a backstop and hangs down from the crossbar between the goal posts. The passer (coach) is fifteen yards away with the football cocked ready to throw. As the coach says, "Now!" he fires the football at the back of the receiver, who whirls around and positions himself to catch the football.

Coaching Points: The coach throws the football when he says, "Now!" and does *not* wait until the receiver turns around. After the receiver becomes proficient, the passer (coach) should throw the football high or low, so the receiver has to slide and move to catch the pass. The passer can throw the football to any area inside the posts and under the crossbar. The drill may be used for all receiver and secondary pass defenders (Chapter 12), including linebackers (Chapter 11).

14. RECEIVER'S FIGURE 8 DRILL

Purpose: To develop catching the ball at various angles, and to give the receivers maximum practice in catching the ball in a short period of time.

Procedure: A receiver lines up ten yards away from the coach (passer), who has a manager on either side of him. A single receiver jogs through a figure 8 pattern, going back and forth toward each sideline, and crossing at a point ten yards directly in front of the coach each time. The passer throws the football anytime so the receiver is catching it over either shoulder, coming toward or going away from the passer, etc. The receiver catches the ball and tucks it away, before flipping it back to either manager. Or a manager retrieves the football if the receiver does not catch it. After half-a-dozen opportunities the coach calls for another receiver to replace

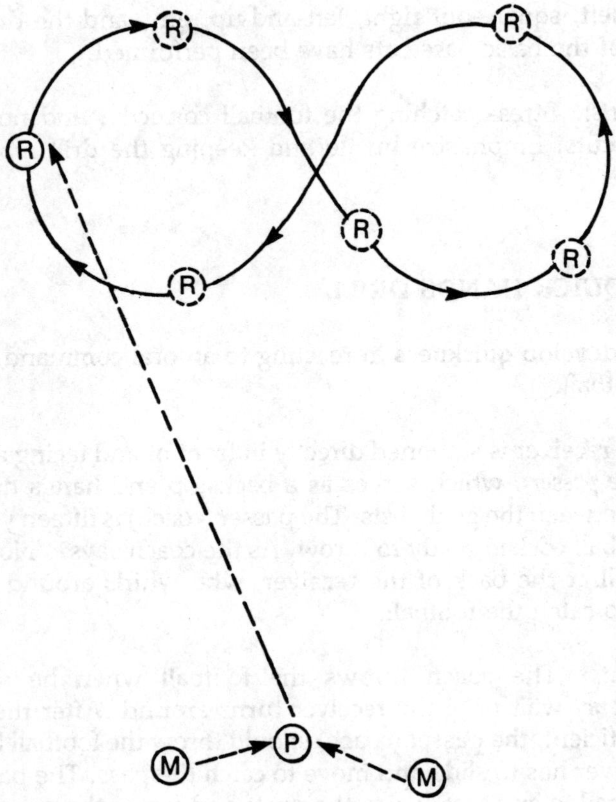

DRILL 14

the one who has been running the pattern, and the latter gets at the end of the line ready to take his turn again.

Coaching Points: Stress the correct fundamentals of catching the football. The emphasis is not on the distance the receiver runs, but on his catching the ball properly at various angles.

15. RECEIVER'S BAD PASS DRILL

Purpose: To develop catching the poorly thrown pass when the football is thrown behind the receiver's position.

Procedure: One at a time receivers come across the field at a slight angle or parallel with the line of scrimmage. The coach (passer) purposely throws the pass behind the receiver, who must plant, pivot, keep his eye on the football and catch it. The receiver puts the football away immediately, sprints five yards upfield, then circles back behind the passer, flip-

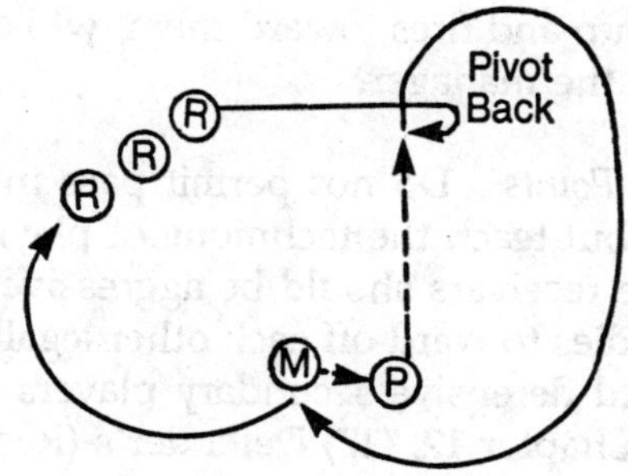

DRILL 15

ping the football to the manager as he goes to the end of the line ready to take his turn again.

Coaching Points: Stress pivoting properly, and *not* rolling back (turning away from the passer and taking his eyes off the football). Run the drill left and right. Stress the proper fundamentals of catching the football.

16. RECEIVER'S (DEFENDER'S) THREE–MAN SQUARE DRILL

Purpose: To develop receivers (defenders) in competing for the football when it is in the air, using their bodies to ward-off opponents.

Procedure: The passer (coach) stands in the middle of a twenty-yard square, and fires the football in the direction of a group of three receivers, who compete with each other to catch the pass. The coach turns quickly

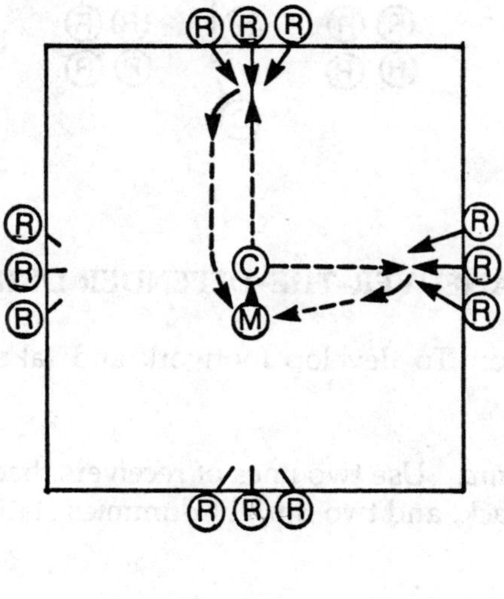

DRILL 16

to another group and fires toward them, while the first group is returning the football to the manager.

Coaching Points: Do not permit pass interference, such as holding and shoving, but teach the technique of playing the flight of the football in the air. The receivers should be aggressive and fight to catch the ball, using their bodies to ward-off each other legally. The drill may be used by linebackers and defensive secondary players as a pass defense drill. For variation see Chapter 12, (17) Defender's (Receiver's) Square Drill.

17. RECEIVER'S DOG–FIGHT DRILL

Purpose: To develop receivers competing for the football when it is in the air.

Procedure: The receivers line up in pairs, both running the same pass cut specified by coach (passer). He throws the football ahead, behind, favoring one man or the other, so that the receivers must compete with each other to catch the football. The objective is to catch the football, not to evade the other receiver. Alternate sides left and right, and also alternate the players in their inside and outside positions.

Coaching Points: Stress playing the football in the air, and not the man; no holding or shoving, but using the body to ward-off the opposition legally.

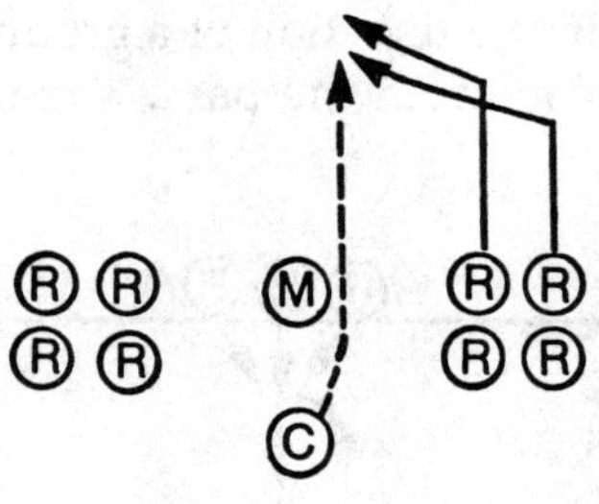

DRILL 17

18. OUTMANEUVER–THE–DEFENDER DRILL

Purpose: To develop footwork and fakes to outmaneuver the defender.

Procedure: Use two lines of receivers, backs and ends, but no center or quarterback, and two upright dummies stationed eight to ten yards up-

DRILL 18

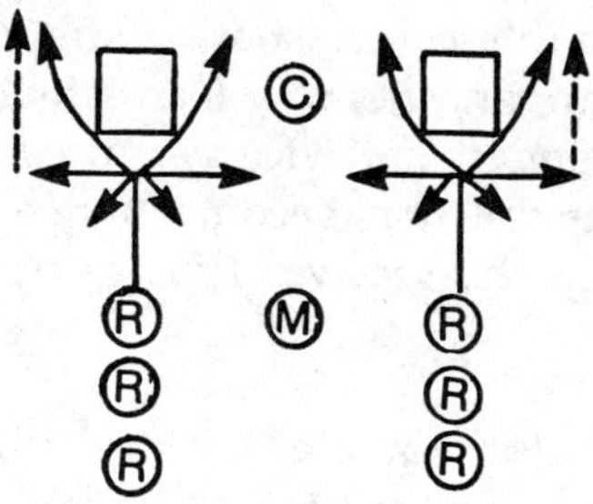

field, with the coach calling out the designated cut or maneuver. The receivers leave one at a time, alternating lines, with the manager calling the starting count, and the coach checking the footwork and fundamentals of the receiver. The receiver runs at about three-quarter's speed until he plants for his cut, then he increases his speed after breaking. The cuts or maneuvers that will be practiced are inside, outside, hook, hook and slide, hook and go, and others.

Coaching Points: Stress the proper planting procedure, and faking with the head, shoulders, facial expression, body, before cutting sharply. Check the initial speed in running the first leg of the pattern, then emphasize running full speed after planting and breaking. Stress the proper line-up, stance, and release on the starting count.

19. PASS CUTS DRILL

Purpose: To develop footwork and fakes to outmaneuver the defender.

Procedure: Same as (18) Outmaneuver-the-Defender Drill, only centers, quarterbacks and defenders are added. The coach indicates the cut or maneuver, and the receiver executes it. The defender does not try to break

DRILL 19

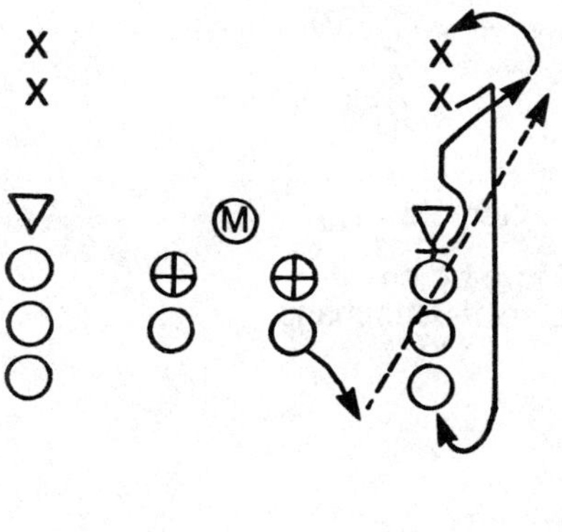

up the pass or to intercept it, but he studies the receiver's techniques so he can correct him, and he, too, learns by observation. The receiver then becomes the defender, and vice versa, each going to the end of the respective lines. The drill may become more aggressive after the players have warmed up. Then the receiver tries to outmaneuver and shake the defender.

Coaching Points: Same as for Drill 18. Check the proper line-up, release, initial speed, planting, faking, breaking, etc. Defenders with air bags may be placed on the inside shoulders of the receivers, so the receivers must employ releasing techniques in order to get off of the line of scrimmage and run the specified pass cut.

20. SIDELINE CUT OR SQUARE OUT DRILLS

Purpose: To teach receivers to run the sideline pattern properly and to improve the passer's timing and accuracy.

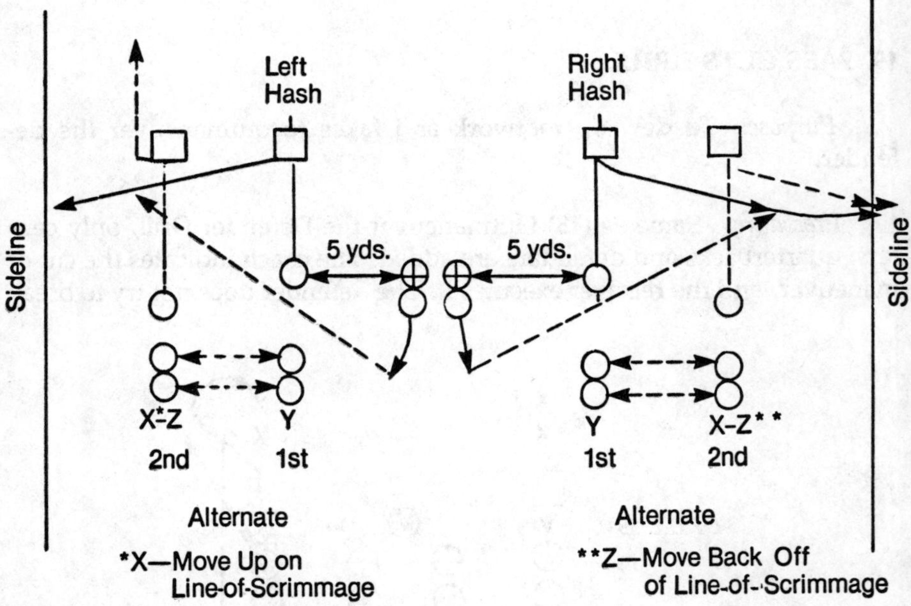

DRILL 20

Procedure: Half of your receivers are set up on the right hash mark, and half are set up on the left hash mark, with the centers and quarterbacks toward the middle of the field. Upright dummies (later replaced by defenders) are placed seven to eight yards upfield, head-on the receivers. The receivers and passers work together to complete the sideline pass before the receiver goes out-of-bounds. Extra receivers play pitch and catch while waiting their turn. If your tight ends and flankers flip-flop strong and weak side then you should rotate your personnel right and left side.

Coaching Points: Stress the proper stance, release, fake, cut and catching the football on the sideline before stepping out-of-bounds; also stress proper timing and fundamentals. The football should clear the sideline out-of-bounds if the pass is not completed. The quarterback should move to cover his pass every time. The quarterbacks and the receivers should rotate left and right. When the drill is live, have defenders play their position properly. In order to hold the defender in position, occasionally change up and run the sideline-and-up pattern, pumping the football toward the receiver just as he plants his foot as if to break to the sideline but then turns sharply upfield. The quarterback throws a long lead pass so the receiver can take it over his inside shoulder by running under the football on the sideline-and-up pattern.

21. RECEIVER'S RELEASING DRILL

Purpose: To teach receivers various techniques for releasing from the line of scrimmage for a pass.

Procedure: Tight ends and flankers assume their stance. Defenders with air bags are stationed head-on and/or on the inside and outside shoulders of the receivers. Starting from a one-on-one situation with a man head-on, and progressing to two-on-one, a receiver is taught to release by 1) using a quick head-and-shoulder fake in one direction before going the other way; 2) fake block or controlled block and slide out; and 3) crawl out on all fours.

Coaching Points: Remove the air bags and go live. Indicate which pattern the receiver should run after releasing. Use a stopwatch to determine the amount of time it is taking the receiver to release. Check the fundamentals of releasing, especially the position of the receiver's feet. Check the stance and the release route so the receiver is not throwing off the timing of the pass by releasing too wide and circling into the pattern.

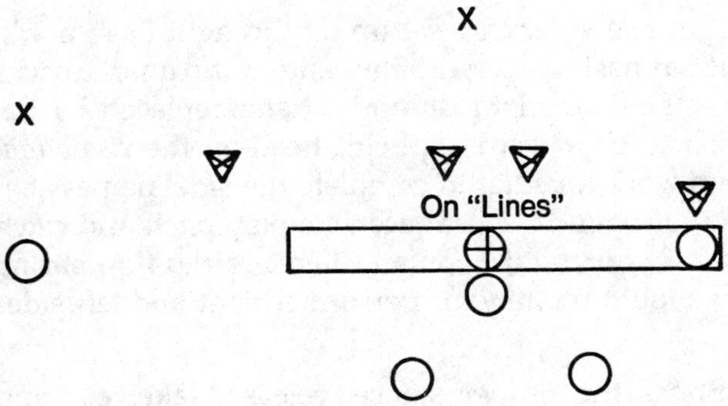

DRILL 22

22–23. SKELETON PASS OFFENSE VERSUS PASS DEFENSE DRILLS

22. Pass Offense Versus Three-Deep Secondary With Linebackers (4-4, 6-2, Split 6, 5-3)

23. Pass Offense Versus Box-Wing Secondary With Linebackers (5-2, 4-3, 3-4, 6-1)

Purpose: To teach your passer to recognize different secondary alignments and coverages, including underneath help and coverages by linebackers, and to polish your passing attack by exploiting weaknesses in coverages and defensive personnel.

Procedure: Set up a skeletal group of offensive backs, ends, flankers and the center versus (22) a three-deep defensive secondary with linebackers, such as in a 4-4, 6-2, Split 6, 5-3 alignment; and versus (23) a box-wing alignment with linebackers, such as in a 5-2, 4-3, 3-4, 6-1 defensive alignment. Illustrate basic secondary coverages, and where underneath linebacker help comes from in various pass coverages. Also illustrate where

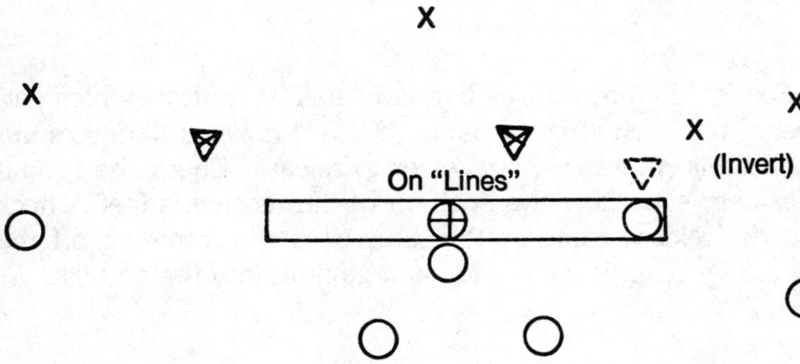

DRILL 23

there will be voids in the coverages if linebackers dog and/or a safety blitzes. Move linebackers around and off/on the line of scrimmage so the passer gets different "looks." The offense runs mostly drop-back passes, and the defense plays keys and reacts accordingly trying only to intercept the pass or deflect the football; no tackling. If linebackers rush, they should not tackle the passer but only tag him if he is unable to get his pass away within the specified amount of time.

Coaching Points: Do *not* coach both the offense and defense at the same time. When there is an incompletion or an interception, take time to explain why and illustrate what should have been done for a completion to have resulted. When the drill is dummy, run two offensive units versus one defensive unit. The second team should watch the defensive alignment and coverage, and then be set ready to run their pass play as quickly as the first unit completes their play. Move the drill from hash mark to hash mark, and call out the tactical situation so the quarterback can call the play in the huddle. Every so often run the drill live. Then check the passer throwing under pressure; the passer's protection (backs and tight end); and the patterns of the receivers. Occasionally call an outside running play so that the defensive players will not lay back for the pass all of the time.

24. RUNNING PASS OR OPTION RUN–PASS DRILL (See p. 146)

Purpose: To teach an offensive back to judge whether to run or pass on the option run-pass play.

Procedure: Same as for Drills 22 and 23, with the contain defender first coming across quickly forcing the pass, then laying back playing the zone forcing the back to run with the football. Then have the defender mix it up coming across or laying back. Work both to the left and right.

Coaching Points: Same as for Drills 22 and 23. Check the quarterback's pitch-back, the passer's steps, position, throwing mechanics and his ability to react correctly the run or pass situation. The passer should be moving toward the line with the football when he reacts to the defender he is cueing. Never use a player to pass if he is not a fairly good thrower.

25. NO. 1 VERSUS NO. 2 SKELETON PASS OFFENSE–DEFENSE DRILL

Purpose: To practice moving the offense via the passing game, and to build morale and have fun.

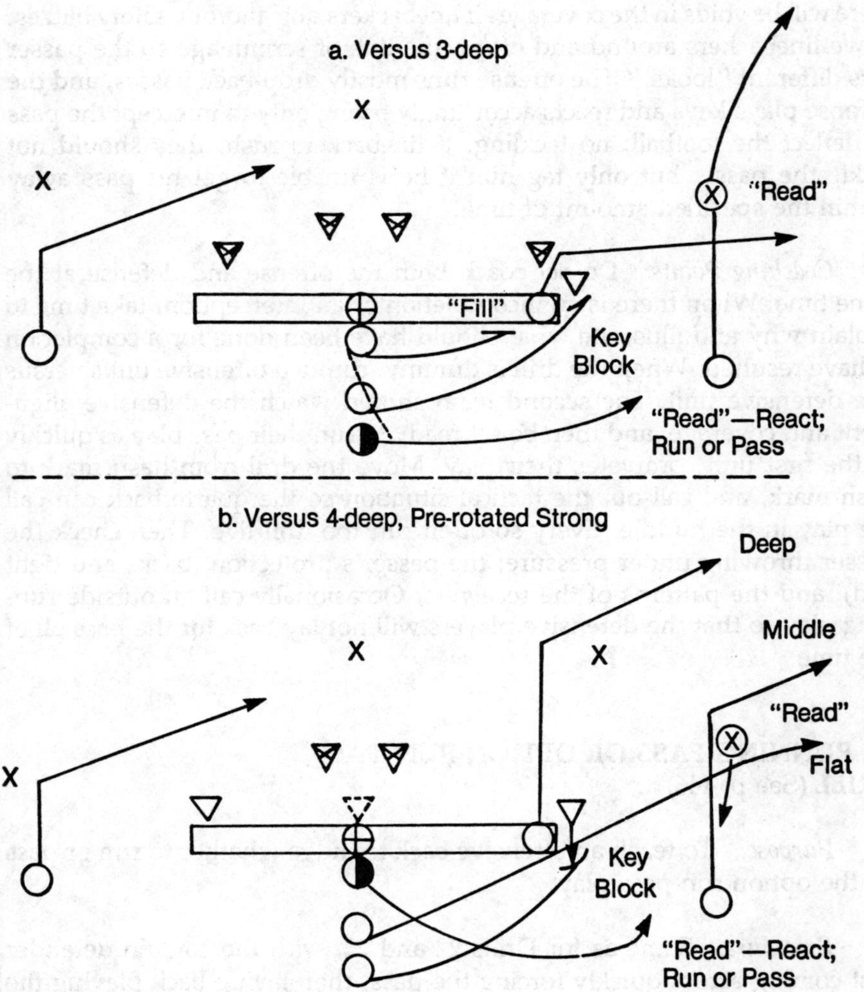

DRILL 24

Procedure: This is the same as Drills 22 and 23 in being a skeleton offense consisting of backs, ends (flankers) and a center versus defensive backs and linebackers, only the game is *tag*. The football is moved up and down the field as follows: The No. 1 offensive team is given the football on the 50-yard line versus the No. 2 defense. They huddle and run only pass plays, and they have four plays in which to score. If they fail to score within four plays, the football goes over to the No. 2 offensive team versus the No. 1 defensive team. *Offensive scoring* is one point for each yard gained on a completed pass-run (until tagged); 50 points for a touchdown. *Defensive scoring* is 25 points for every interception; 50 points for an interception returned for a touchdown; 5 points for breaking up a pass; 2 points for an incomplete pass not touched by the defense; and 2 points if the offense does not throw the football within three seconds (to compensate for linebackers not rushing the passer hard). The linebackers can blitz, but they must stop after penetrating three yards. The passer in turn must throw his pass within three seconds. Have one manager retrieve the football, another spot it, and the third manager keep score on a portable chalkboard following the ball up and down the field from his sideline position. The latter's word is final; no appeals. The team that intercepts the football takes possession where tagged. If the offense loses the ball in four downs and does not score, the other team takes possession on the 50-yard line, with the manager awarding points to the offense for the yards gained.

Coaching Points: The offense runs their own pass cuts and patterns, and the defense utilizes their secondary alignments and coverages. Set a time limit or the total number of points to be scored. Since the drill is competitive, it is *not* advisable to align your No. 1 offense versus your No. 1 defense, or you may "leave your game on the practice field." The "game" is fun, and is a good conditioner since it entails a lot of running. Keep the "game" moving. Announce in advance a "prize" or an award for the winning team. This "game" is not meant to be aggressive contact, so guard against injuries.

26. ROLL–OUT (SPRINT-OUT)/THROWBACK PASS DRILL

Purpose: To develop rolling-out (sprint-out) and throwing back passing techniques.

Procedure: Same as for Drills 22 and 23, only a second quarterback is added and stands to the left of the first quarterback and center. (A second center may be used, although he is unnecessary.) The second quarterback (the one on the left) simulates receiving the snap-back from the center and sprints-out to his right, along with the first quarterback who calls the snap count for both of them. The first quarterback (on the right) practices throwing the option run-pass to his flanker back or tight end, depending upon the reaction of the defenders on his side. The second quarterback practices throwing back either to his left flanker or left tight end, depending upon the reaction of the defenders on the backside. The pass pattern depends on whether secondary is in a diamond or box-wing alignment, and the positioning of the linebackers. The quarterbacks exchange places and repeat the drill, with the No. 2 quarterback now practicing the option run-pass to his right, and the No. 1 quarterback practicing the throwback to his left.

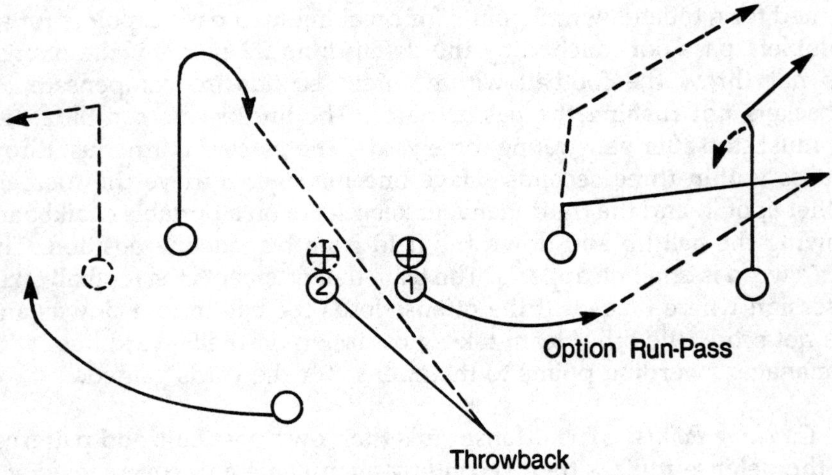

DRILL 26

Coaching Points: Turn backfield formation over and run the sprint-out left and then throwback to the right. Alternate quarterbacks.

27. ONE–HANDED CATCH CIRCLE DRILL

Purpose: To develop fingertip control in catching a football one-handed.

Procedure: Same as (3) Passer's Circle Drill, only two receivers work clockwise and counter-clockwise around a circle seven yards plus in diameter. One receiver throws a soft, high lead pass to the other, who attempts a one-hand catch or a tip back toward his body so he can catch the football with his other hand.

Coaching Points: Stress a high lead pass so the receiver has to tip the ball back toward his body off the fingertips of his outside (far) hand.

28. RECEIVER'S (DEFENDER'S) CROSSBAR DRILL

Purpose: To develop leaping into the air to catch the football.

Procedure: A single column of receivers (defenders) start on the five-yard line and sprint toward the goal posts. First time through, the receiver (defender) tries to touch the crossbar (10 feet from the ground) with his right hand; second time, left hand; and third time, both hands, simulating leaping into the air to catch (or defend against) the high pass.

Coaching Points: Stress gathering and leaping into the air without stopping, timing the take-off and touching the crossbar. The receiver (defender) should not grab the bar and/or attempt to swing on it. Also have players stand under the bar and attempt to jump vertically from a stationary position and touch the crossbar. This is a good pre-practice warm-up drill, after players are loose.

29. RECEIVING AND DOWNFIELD BLOCKING DRILL

Purpose: To develop catching the football, and blocking downfield after the reception.

Procedure: A center, quarterback, and two columns of receivers run pass cuts, using the offensive starting count. Three or four upright dum-

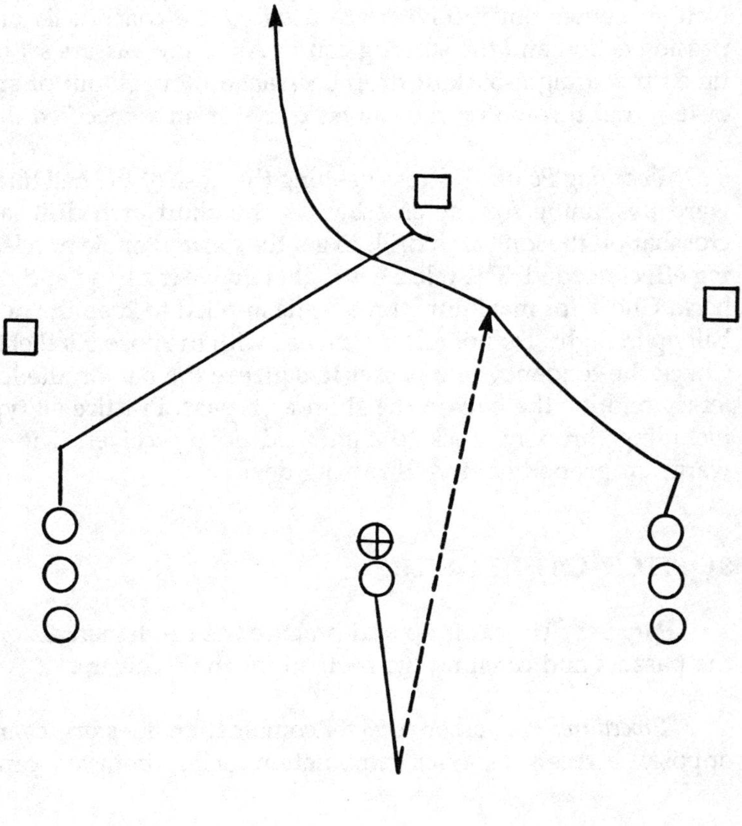

DRILL 29

mies are set up in the secondary simulating a diamond or box-wing alignment. The ball is thrown to either receiver, and the one who does not catch the football blocks downfield on the dummy nearest the player who makes the reception. The upright dummies are not held.

Coaching Points: Stress the proper fundamentals of passing, receiving and downfield blocking. If the pass is incomplete, the intended receiver retrieves the football and the other player still blocks through the nearest dummy. The blocker regains his feet and sets up the dummy as two more receivers release from the line of scrimmage for the pass.

30. SHORT AND LONG ARCH PASSING DRILLS

Purpose: To develop the proper angle of release for short and long passes, especially "hanging" the ball in the air for the deep receiver.

Procedure: One to three passers line up opposite the canvas or net attached to the goal posts, starting at a depth of fifteen yards and progressing backward to a depth of approximately thirty to thirty-five yards. Neither center nor receivers are used as the coach calls out the type of passing action and the starting count. All of the passers set up at the same time on a straight-back or drop-back action, or roll-out or sprint-out right or left, and throw into the canvas or net from a specified depth.

Coaching Points: Stress keeping the nose of the ball tilted slightly upward by aiming for the crossbar on the short arch drill, and above the crossbar on the long arch drill, to get the desired angle of release and hanging effect needed. The release is higher above the head and the ball is tilted back. Check for maximum force being applied to keep the nose of the football up in flight. Do not release the ball with the nose parallel to the ground. Check the tendency of a passer to squeeze the ball on the long arch pass; let up and lob the ball on the short arch pass. Practice all types of passes, including throwing back to simulated deep receiver. The passer should warm-up properly before throwing deep.

31. PITCH–CATCH DRILL

Purpose: To warm-up and practice the fundamentals of throwing for the passers and catching the football for the receivers.

Procedure: A passer-receiver combination lines up several yards apart opposite a receiver-passer combination facing them ten yards away. The

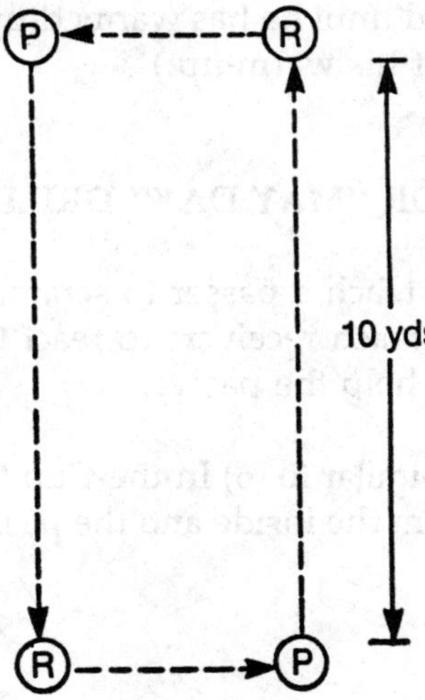

DRILL 31

quarterback throws the ball to the receiver opposite him, who catches the ball and flips it laterally to his quarterback who is beside him. The quarterbacks are passing the ball every time, but not catching it, and the receivers are catching the ball every time, but never passing it back to the quarterbacks.

Coaching Points: Stress the fundamentals of passing and receiving. Two balls may be used with their flights being parallel, since the passers are throwing only to the receivers. (The quarterbacks are diagonally opposite each other, as are the receivers.) This is a good warm-up drill.

32. PASSER'S WARM–UP DRILL (PROGRESSIVE)

Purpose: To practice warming-up, using the back-off and sprint-off techniques.

Procedure: Receivers are in two columns ten yards apart; they release one at a time straight up the field. The drill progresses as follows: The passer uses a step-back technique, left, right, etc., and throws left and right. The passer then uses a back-pedal or back-off technique and throws left and right. Finally, the passer uses a cross-over sprint-off technique, sets up the proper depth and throws left and right.

Coaching Points: Stress the proper techniques and the fundamentals of passing, including stepping in the direction the passer is throwing. The receivers do not sprint, but merely stride as a passer does not want to throw the ball hard until he has warmed-up properly. (The passer is using this drill as part of his warm-up.)

33. SCRAMBLE OR "MAY DAY" DRILL

Purpose: To teach a passer to scramble and throw when forced out of the pocket. To teach receivers to react to a "May Day" situation, i.e., to come back and help the passer.

Procedure: Similar to (6) In-the-Cup Drill, only you simulate that the rush is coming from the inside and the passer must run out of the cup and

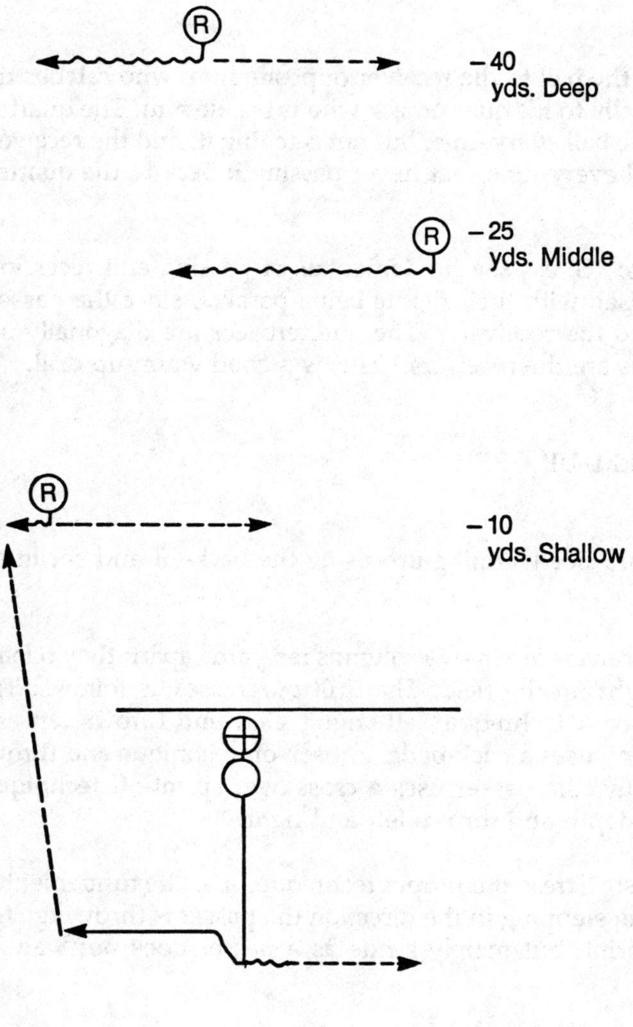

DRILL 33

scramble in order to pass the football. The passer sets-up in five or seven steps, but then breaks off at a 90° angle or an oblique angle right or left and throws to one of three receivers downfield, who are stationed shallow, middle, deep in zig-zag fashion. When the receivers see the passer scrambling they stay in their respective areas but move laterally with him in the same direction he is running. The passer now has receivers shallow, middle, and deep aligning with him in the direction he is running.

Coaching Points: Stress getting back quickly. Coach may yell, "Shallow!" "Middle!" "Deep!" or "Scramble!" If it is one of the first three commands, the quarterback throws immediately to the receiver indicated. If it is "Scramble!" the passer runs out of the pocket and the receivers start aligning themselves with the passer. Stress staying on balance, and the correct fundamentals of passing.

34. PASSER'S REACTION DRILL

Purpose: To teach a passer to react and throw immediately.

Procedure: The passer stands approximately six yards from the coach, facing him, simulating he has gone back to set-up to pass. His eyes are closed. The football is cocked in a ready position preparatory to throwing to a receiver downfield. With hand signals the coach moves the receiver around quickly. When the coach yells, "Now!" the passer opens his eyes, steps in the direction of the receiver and throws.

Coaching Points: Stress the proper fundamentals of passing. Work with the passer, not the receiver (who may be a manager).

35. PASSER'S OFF–BALANCE DRILL

Purpose: To teach the passer to regain his balance and pass the football quickly.

Procedure: The passer will work left and right, simulating rolling or sprinting-out. The receiver will align himself with the passer left and right. The ball is placed on the ground two yards from the passer either at a 90° angle or at a forward oblique angle. The passer must move either laterally or diagonally forward at an oblique angle, pick up the football, take several additional steps and pass the football quickly to his receiver. The passer may be off-balance, but he has a receiver open and tries to complete the pass, even while receiving a simulated rush.

Coaching Points: The passer should not merely throw the football. However, a roll or sprint pass is not difficult to throw since it is a soft, controlled pass. While the passer should throw on-balance, he should attempt to do so after only several steps and pass quickly after picking up the ball.

36. RECEIVER'S OFF–BALANCE DRILL

Purpose: To teach a receiver to regain his balance quickly and to catch the football.

Procedure: The receiver executes a somersault, crawls out on all fours (or another releasing technique) and the passer throws to him as he regains his feet.

Coaching Points: Stress using the hands to catch the ball. Even if he is off-balance, the receiver should make an effort to catch the football.

37. PASSER–RECEIVER PITCH–CATCH DRILL

Purpose: To practice passing and catching the football while warming-up.

Procedure: Two passers, approximately ten to eighteen yards apart, face each other, each with a column of receivers stationed five yards off to their left. The receivers will circle clockwise. When off to the passer's right, the receivers will circle counter-clockwise. Each passer has a manager by his side to hand footballs to him. Each passer calls ''Hike'' (or ''Go''), and the lead receiver in the column releases from the line of scrimmage. The passer molds the football quickly, steps and throws (lobs) the football to the receiver, who flips it to the manager near the other passer directing the other column of receivers. If the receiver misses catching the football, he retrieves it, flips it to the manager, and continues to the end of the other column of receivers coming from the opposite direction. Reverse the drill and run it counter-clockwise, so that passers and receivers practice going in both directions.

Coaching Points: Keep the drill moving, and try to have the passers establish a rhythm of passing-catching the football. The receivers jog, rather than run at full speed, and the passers lob rather than drill the football. It is a pitch and catch warm-up drill.

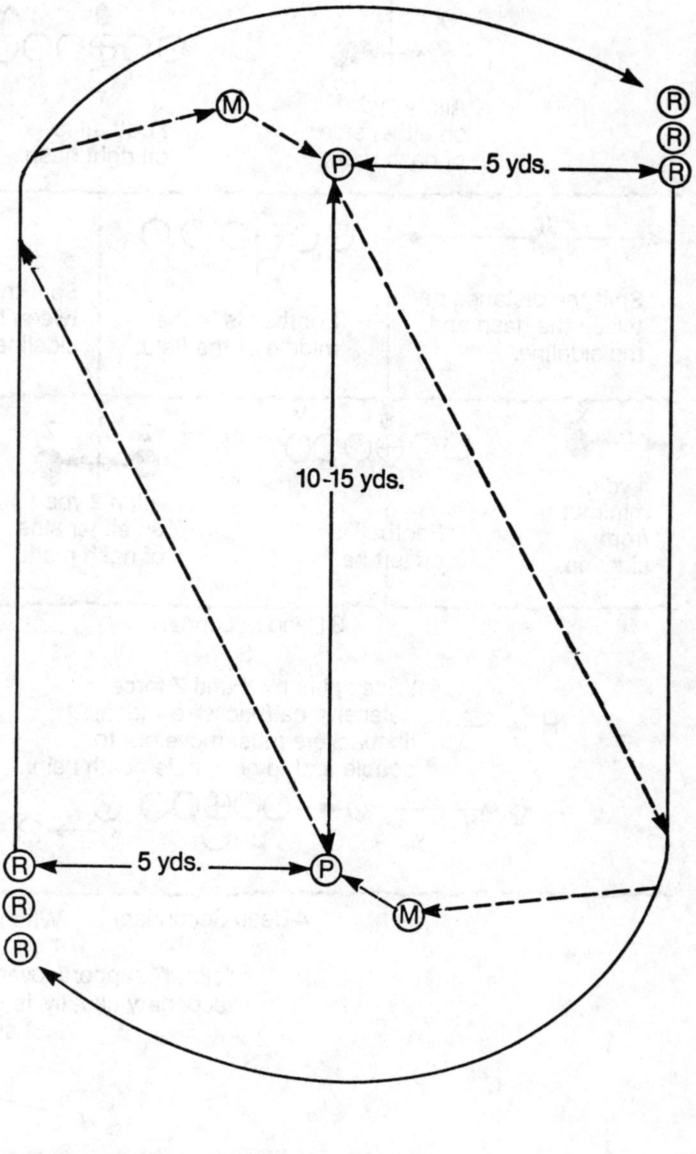

DRILL 37

38. WIDE–OUTS (FLANKERS) ALIGNMENT DRILL

Purpose: To teach flankers how and where to align horizontally in the *basic* offensive set. (See Chapter 6 (22) Three-S or Splits-Stance-Starts Drill.) To force defensive contain and coverage adjustments.

Procedure: Align the football on the right hash mark, in the middle of the field, and on the left hash mark, and send wide-outs left and right

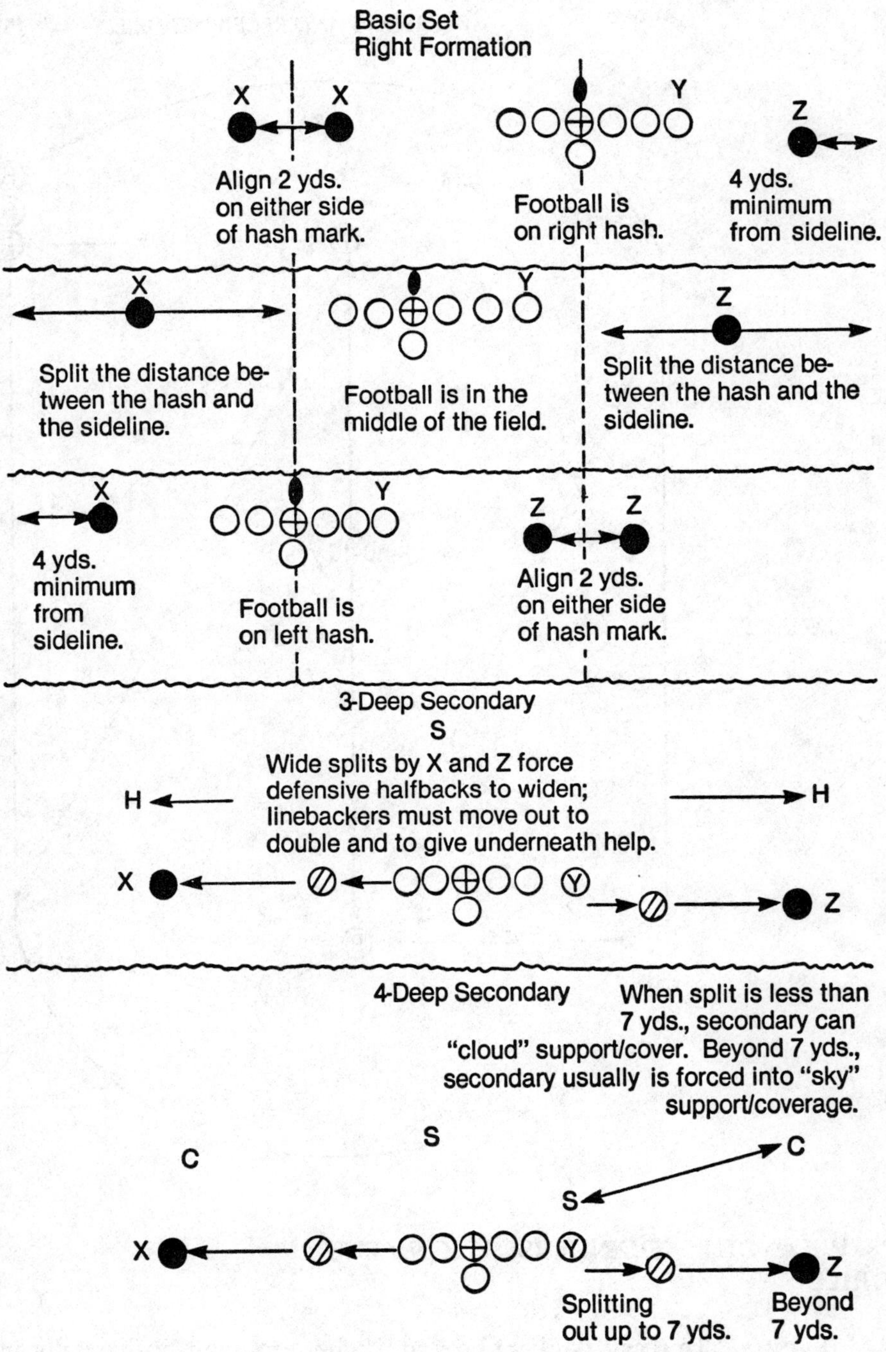

GENERAL GUIDES: Adjust splits to carry out your assignment; experiment with your splits to force defenders to make contain and coverage adjustments; do not tip off your intent when you split.

DRILL 38

depending on the strength of the offensive set. When the football is on the right hash, the flanker to the right should be no closer than four yards from that sideline, and the flanker to the left should align two yards on either side of the left hash. With the football on the left hash, the wide-outs rules for splitting are reversed from those indicated above. When the football is positioned in the middle of the field, each flanker splits the distance between the hash mark and sideline to his side of the field. Show how wide-outs can force different alignments and coverages versus three-deep and four-deep secondaries.

Coaching Points: Teach-coach the purpose of utilizing wide-outs. Encourage flankers to experiment with their splitting. They may adjust splits anytime to carry out their assignment or to make their job easier. Check to make certain they are not tipping-off their intent on plays to and away from their position, including when they are involved and not involved in the running play or pass.

39. THE "PASSING TREE" (ROUTES-PATTERNS) DRILL

Purpose: To teach receivers offensive passing terminology and individual pass routes, including which ones are short, medium and deep routes, and which specific individual routes are combined coordinated pass patterns.

Procedure: Working individually each receiver is taught-coached his "passing tree" routes so he comprehends passing terminology, such as "flat," "out and up," "hook," "post," "corner" (or "flag"), et al. Then, when teaching-coaching play action and drop-back passes, his assignment is the specific *pattern* (which is the individual route terminology specified in the coordinated pass play). Run all of your play action and drop-back passes as in (22)–(23) Skeleton Pass Offense-Defense Drills, and Chapter 9, (6) Mend-the-Cup Drill.

Coaching Points: Work individually and be certain receivers understand terminology and depth of routes before combining individual routes into specific coordinated pass patterns. Be certain receivers understand the theory and logic behind each pass pattern. Check routes versus coverages in (22)–(23) Skeleton Pass Offense-Defense Drills. Always check and correct breakdowns when scrimmaging live, such as in (6) Mend-the-Cup Drill, Chapter 9.

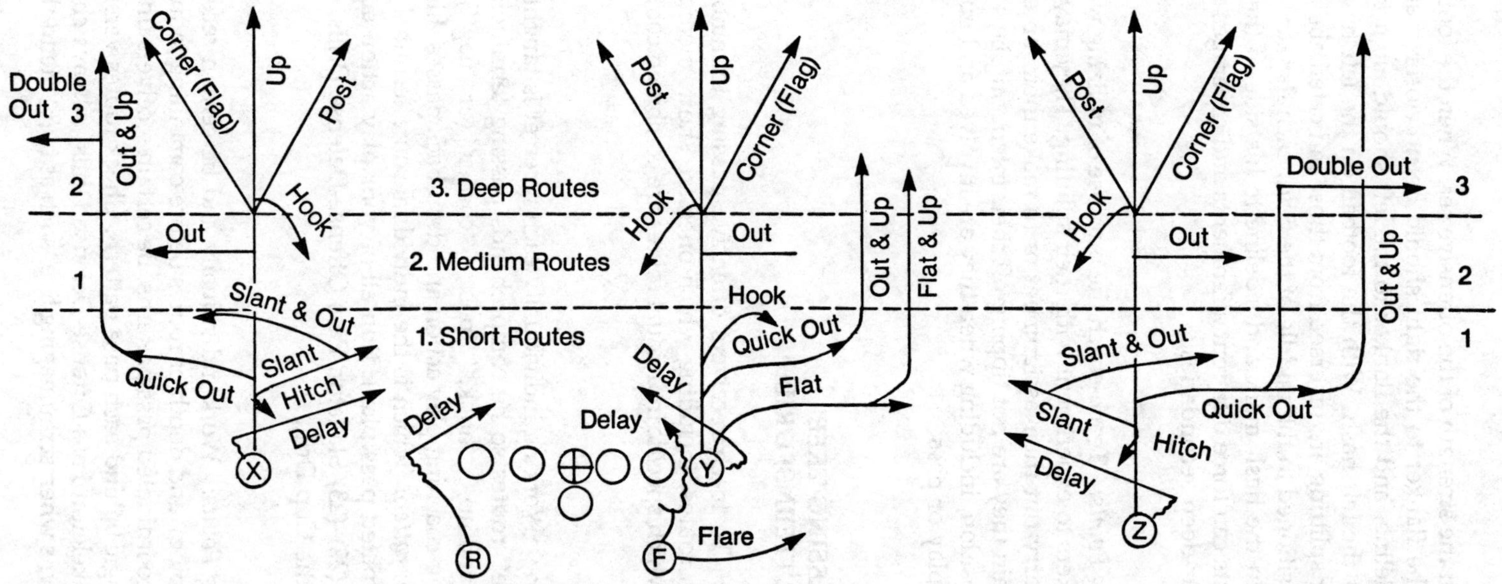
Double Out
3
2
1
Out & Up
Corner (Flag)
Up
Post
Hook
Out
Slant & Out
Slant
Quick Out
Hitch
Delay
X
3. Deep Routes
2. Medium Routes
1. Short Routes
Delay
R
Delay
F
Flare
Post
Up
Corner (Flag)
Hook
Out
Hook
Quick Out
Delay
Y
Flat
Out & Up
Flat & Up
Post
Up
Corner (Flag)
Hook
Out
Double Out
Out & Up
Slant & Out
Slant
Quick Out
Hitch
Delay
Z

DRILL 39

PLAY ACTION

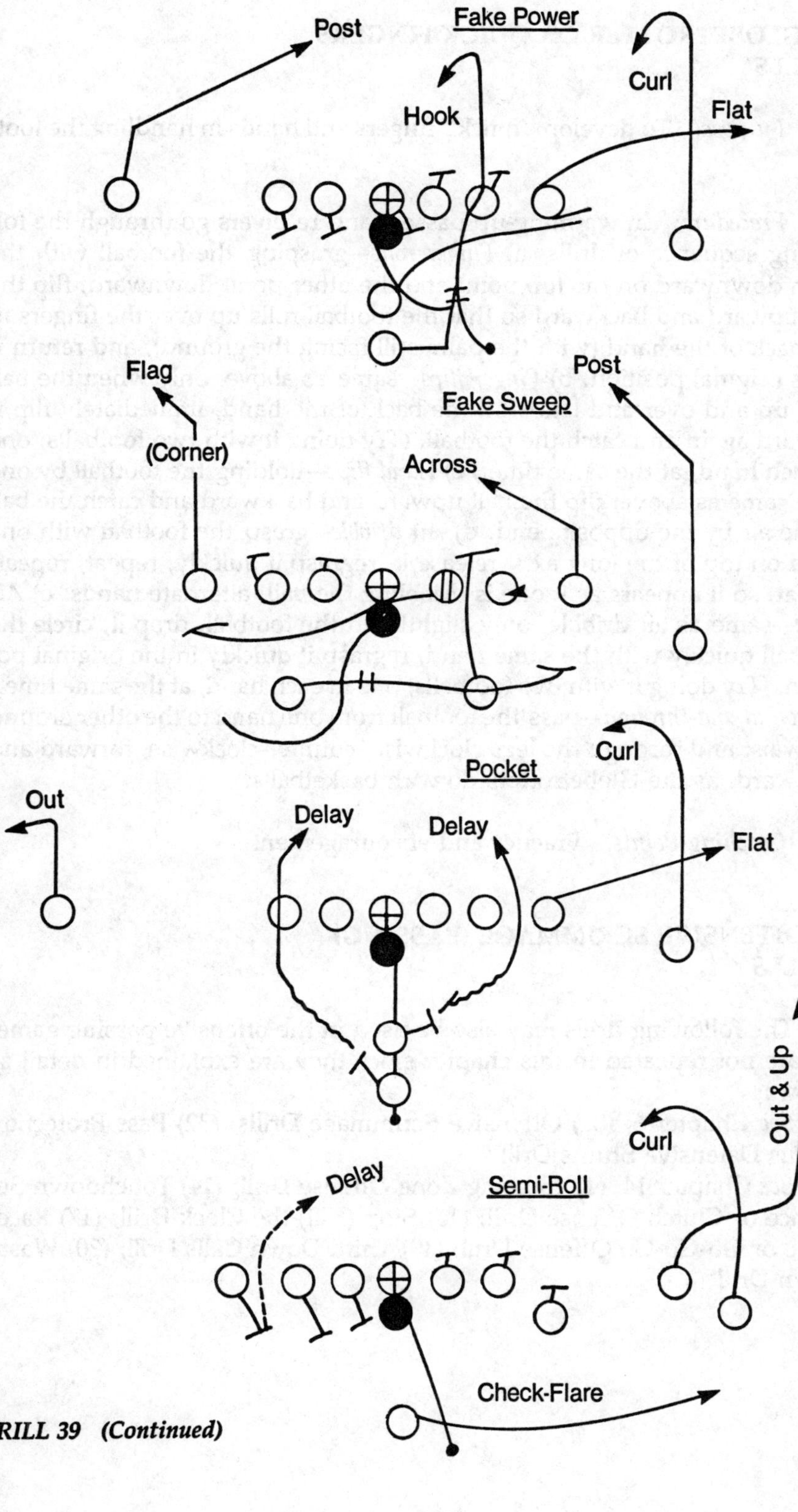

DRILL 39 (Continued)

40. GLOBETROTTER OR QUICK FINGERS DRILLS

Purpose: To develop "quick" fingers and hands in handling the football.

Procedure: In warming-up passers and receivers go through the following sequence of drills: a) *Finger rolls*—grasping the football with the palm downward on the top point and the other point downward, flip the ball upward and backward so that the football rolls up over the fingers to the back of the hand (with the palm still facing the ground), and return it to its original position. b) *Finger flips*—same as above, only when the ball flips up and over and lands on the back of the hand, immediately flip it forward again and catch the football. (Try doing it with two footballs, one in each hand, at the same time.) c) *Hand flips*—holding the football by one end, same as above, flip the ball upward and backward and catch the ball in the air by the opposite end. d) *Air dribble*—grasp the football with one hand on top of the long axis, release it, regrasp it quickly, repeat, repeat, repeat, so it appears as if one is dribbling the ball; alternate hands. e) *Air circle*—same as air dribble, only slightly lift the football, drop it, circle the football quickly with the same hand, regrasp it quickly in the original position. (Try doing it with two footballs, one in each hand, at the same time.) f) *Around-and-through*—pass the football from one hand to the other around the waist and through the legs clockwise, counter-clockwise, forward and backward, as the Globetrotters do with basketballs.

Coaching Points: Practice and encouragement.

41. OFFENSIVE SCRIMMAGE (PASSING) DRILLS

The following drills may also be used in the offensive passing game, but are not repeated in this chapter since they are explained in detail as follows:

See Chapter 6, (31) Offensive Scrimmage Drills; (32) Pass Protection Versus Defensive Stunts Drill.

See Chapter 14, (12) Scoring Zone Offense Drill; (14) Touchdown Sequence or Clutch Offense Drill; (15) Stop (Kill)-the-Clock Drill; (17) Racehorse or Go-Go-Go Offense Drill; (19) Third Down Calls Drill; (20) Waste Down Drill.

9

Offensive Backfield Drills

The majority of drills in this chapter are for developing individual skills and techniques of ball handling, ball carrying, and blocking, which are applicable not only to offensive backs but to receivers, too. Passing and receiving drills were presented in the preceding chapter, with the exception of pass protection drills for the offensive backs, which are included in this chapter. Few team drills are included here; the majority are presented in the last section of the book. Chapter 14 includes team drills involving offensive strategy and tactics. Those dealing with the offensive and defensive kicking game are presented in Chapter 15. No attempt is made to discuss the various "systems" of football, or any of the quarterback's mechanics, since these are beyond the scope of a book on drills and each is a book-length subject itself.

Just as a coach must adopt a philosophy as to how he intends to utilize the passing game (Chapter 8), he must also adopt a basic philosophy as to his utilization of the running game. A strong running attack should be an integral part of every team's offensive game. The ideal offense, of course, consists of a balance between the running and passing games. However, the time element generally does *not* permit most coaches to develop both phases equally well. A team must have some passing attack, however, since it is much easier to defense a team with only one type of offensive attack if it is reasonably well established that the offensive team cannot revert successfully to the other. When the passing game is strengthened, the running game is automatically strengthened, and vice versa.

The running techniques presented in Chapter 4 dealt with the basic principles and variant forms of running. While the principles of running are applicable to the discussion in this chapter, drills for teaching-coaching running techniques here have reference to the evasive or elusive maneuvers a ball carrier may use for in-close and open-field running to get by defenders. Also, while ball carrying in this chapter has reference to an offensive back taking the football behind his side of the line of scrimmage and running with it, the drills for teaching-coaching these techniques are applicable to any player gaining possession of the football, whether it is a pass receiver (Chapter 8), punt receiver, kick-off return specialist (Chapter 15), or somebody else.

The following drills may be used to teach-coach fundamentals and techniques to offensive backs and others.

1. CHAIN BALL HANDLING DRILL

Purpose: To teach, develop, and standardize the techniques of ball handling on the exchange in order to eliminate fumbling.

Procedure: Two columns of backs ten yards apart facing each other. The first player in line A moves forward and hands off the football to the first player in line B, who in turn hands the football to the second player in line A, repeating the exchange back and forth, as each continues to the end of the opposite line after making the exchange. The player receiving the football must make the proper pocket and reception in the prescribed manner. The player handing off has the responsibility of placing the football in the pocket in the prescribed manner. The second player in line A should not start moving forward until the first player in line B, who has received the hand-off, has complete control of the football and can hand off the exchange properly.

Coaching Points: Stress the fundamentals of handing off and receiving the football properly. Do not sprint and rush through the drill doing it incorrectly. The player receiving the hand-off should keep his shoulders square, form a pocket, and *not* turn his body to receive the football. By working left and right the players practice the exchange from both sides.

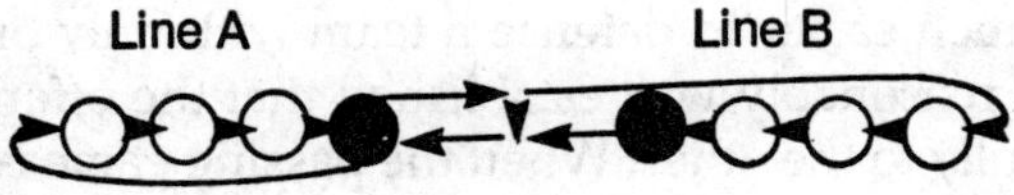

DRILL 1

DRILL 2

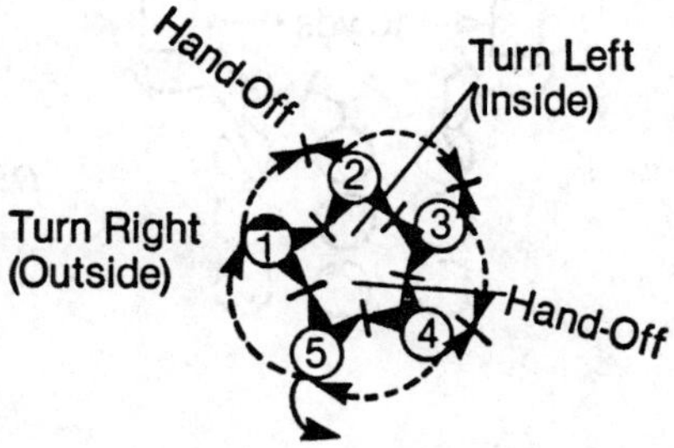

©

2. CIRCLE BALL HANDLING DRILL

Purpose: To teach, develop, and standardize the techniques of ball handling on the exchange in order to eliminate fumbling.

Procedure: Backs form a tight circle within an arm's length of each other, and the coach observes from outside their circle. The first player turns back to his left (inside), then on the second cycle he turns to his right (outside), and places the football in the pocket formed by the next back, using the prescribed exchange. The player receiving the football does not turn his head or body as the football is placed in the pocket. After receiving the football he turns and places it into the pocket formed by the player in the circle behind him.

Coaching Points: Stress the fundamentals of a proper exchange. Check the pocket and body alignment of the player receiving the football. The football should *not* be slammed upward into the stomach.

3. BACK'S BLOCKING DRILL

Purpose: To teach and develop blocking fundamentals and techniques.

Procedure: Two upright dummies are held on a line ten yards apart. (A third upright dummy may be placed between the two outside dummies in order to practice inside power blocking on the defenders, as illustrated in (13) Wham or Divide Drill, Chapter 11.) Three columns of backs align at their proper depth, but are practically side-by-side except when power blocking. The backs on the left work left, those on the right work right,

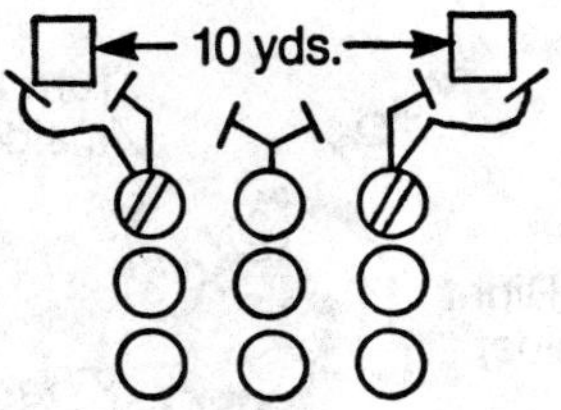

DRILL 3

and the fullbacks work both ways by themselves, and/or with their other backs. When blocking the defender (bag), the backs must take an inside-out position. When hooking an end defender, the back runs toward the dummy but slides his head and body beyond it to the outside above the waist, and keeps pressure outside-in on the bag. When power or isolation blocking, the fullback and another offensive back go shoulder-to-shoulder blocking the dummy.

Coaching Points: Stress the proper blocking techniques, and legally blocking the defensive end. Use your offensive starting count, and a whistle to terminate the drill.

4. CONTROLLED PASS PROTECTION BLOCKING DRILL

Purpose: To teach the proper fundamentals and techniques of pass protection.

Procedure: Four dummies are placed horizontally on the ground, each five yards apart, with defensive rushers two yards from the offensive backs. The rusher is instructed to come from the left, right or straight at the blocker, so the latter can practice blocking from inside-out on the rusher firing from the outside, and pick up any lineman or blitzing linebackers who comes through from the inside, using the proper pass blocking techniques.

Coaching Points: The drill is controlled. Check the proper blocking techniques and stress quickness for the offensive backs setting up imme-

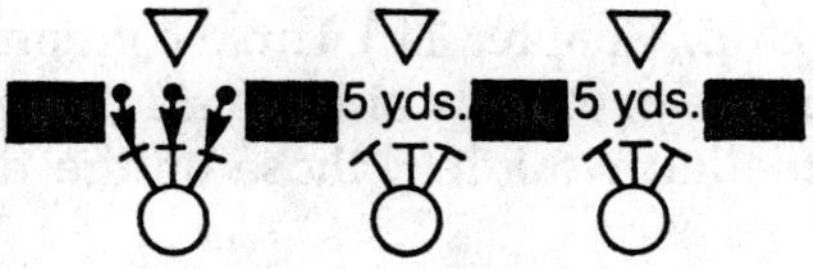

DRILL 4

diately. In all pass protection drills the backs should remember to cover to the side toward which they are blocking. The coach or passer yells, "Cover" and the offensive backs (and linemen) release from their blocks.

5. BACK'S PASS PROTECTION BLOCKING DRILL

Purpose: To develop the proper fundamentals and techniques of pass protection.

Procedure: An offensive backfield and center versus defenders, first controlled ("thud") and then "live." From the various backfield sets, the quarterback runs all of his pass plays where he sets up directly behind the center to throw the football. He works on driving back and setting up for the pass. The other backs execute the various types of pass protection techniques and fundamentals. The defenders rush hard, and the backs turn out to their side or block inside pluggers, depending on the specific blocking rules illustrated in Chapter 6 (32), Pass Protection Versus Defensive Stunts Drill, and in Drill 6 of this chapter.

Coaching Points: Stress the proper pass protection techniques and fundamentals. Use a stopwatch to check the quarterback getting back and setting up, and time his protection. Use a starting count and a whistle. Use the "lines" to insure aligning correctly, and to get the proper timing.

DRILL 5

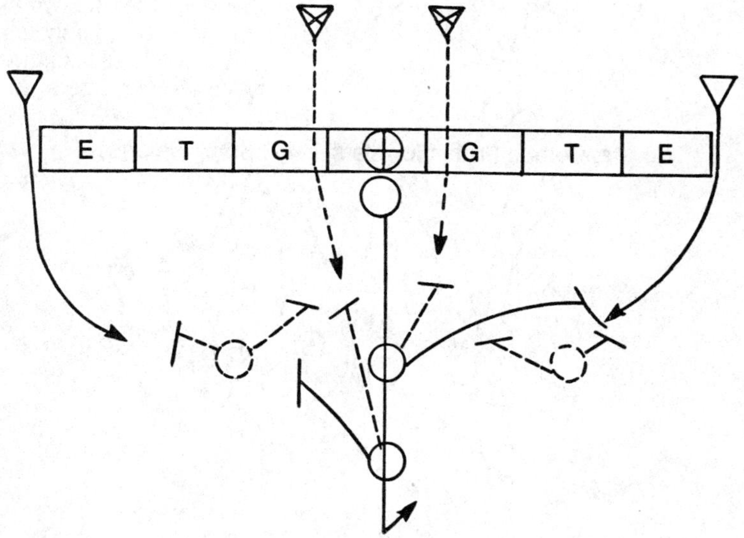

a. Zone or Cup Protection Versus Oklahoma Strong-side Rush

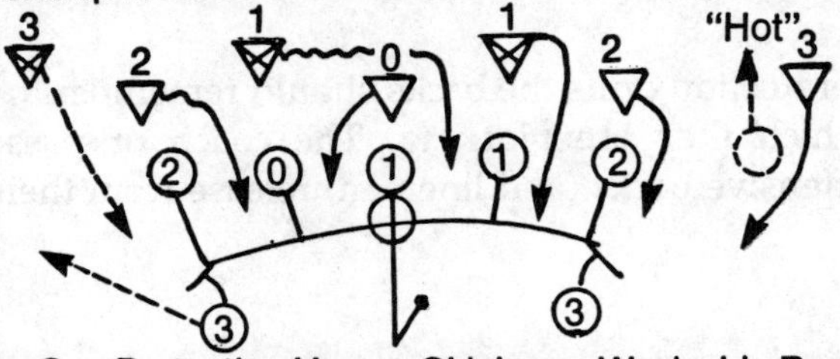

b. Zone or Cup Protection Versus Oklahoma Weak-side Rush

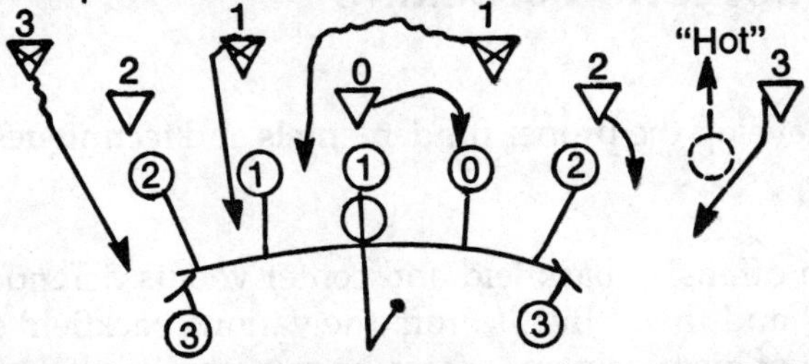

c. Man Protection Versus Rush 8 from Split 6 or 4–4 Defense

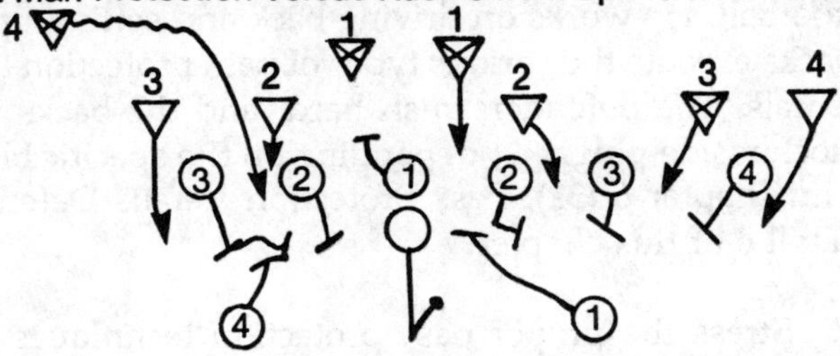

d. Man Protection Versus Pro 4–3

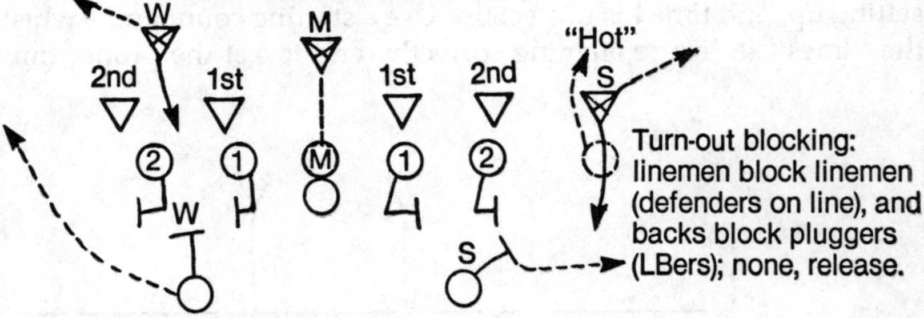

e. Combo Protection Versus 4–3 Stack Defense

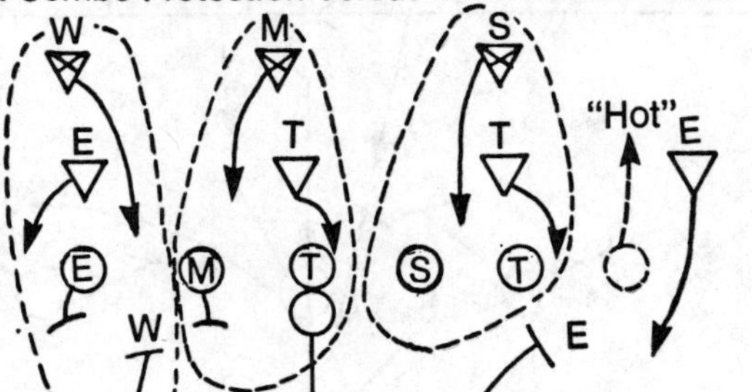

DRILL 6

6. MEND–THE–CUP (PASS BLOCKERS VERSUS PASS RUSHERS) DRILL

Purpose: To teach coordinated teamwork in blocking defensive stunts and "shooters" when protecting the quarterback passing from the pocket.

Procedure: Similar to (32) Pass Protection Versus Defensive Stunts Drill (Chapter 6), only the quarterback and offensive backs are added with offensive linemen. Using a huddle and the starting count, the offensive linemen and backs set up quickly in blocking the rushers, including blitzing linebackers. Defensive outside rushers are not used initially, as the objective is to teach the offensive backs to pick up any lineman breaking through, and to mend-the-cup, when pressure is not exerted from the outside.

Coaching Points: Use a stopwatch and a whistle. Stress protecting the passer and mending-the-cup, not chasing the shooters. Use flash cards, as described in note 1, Chapter 2, so rushers and blockers are familiar with stunts.

7. SHAKE–THE–TACKLER OR EVASIVE RUNNING DRILL (PROGRESSIVE)

Purpose: To develop agility, body balance, evasive running techniques.

Procedure: Upright dummies are placed five yards apart, not held, in a vertical line. A manager stands in front of the first dummy and as the runner approaches, he signals by hand right or left, after the coach has specified which evasive technique is to be used. The ball carrier weaves in and out quickly between the dummies, sprints to circle the last dummy, and returns to the end of the column of ball carriers in order to execute a different running technique. As soon as the first runner breaks and goes by the manager, the second runs directly toward him and the column of upright dummies before breaking in the specified direction using the prescribed running technique. A variation of this drill is for a manager to hold the first upright dummy by the side straps and move it left or right, simulating a defender attempting to make a tackle. The ball carrier breaks *opposite* the direction the manager moves the dummy. If the coach positions himself five yards beyond the last upright dummy he can better observe the ball carrier's evasive tactics.

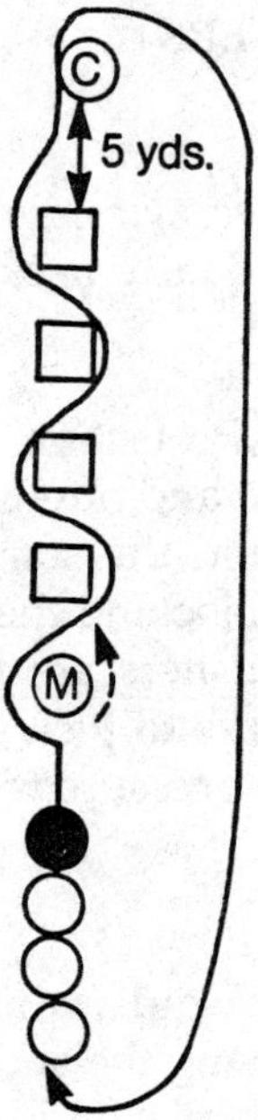

DRILL 7

After each technique has been practiced several times, the manager moves out of the way and the ball carrier uses the specified technique on each and every dummy in the column. When he gets to the last dummy he sprints for five yards more, then circles back to the end of the column of ball carriers.

Coaching Points: Stress running with the body under control. Always run directly toward the middle of each dummy, then break right or left, rather than angling from the outside of one dummy to the opposite side of the next one. The ball carrier should practice shifting the football in the prescribed manner, and may simulate straight-arming a tackler.

8. EVASIVE RUNNING CIRCLE DRILL

Purpose: To develop agility, body balance, evasive running techniques, and to practice shifting the football from one arm to the other.

Procedure: Same as (7) Shake-the-Tackler or Evasive Running Drill, only upright dummies are arranged in a circle twenty yards in diameter. The coach stands in the middle and specifies which technique is to be used.

Coaching Points: Same as for Drill 7. The players should not touch the dummies. A manager sets up the dummies if any are knocked over.

DRILL 8

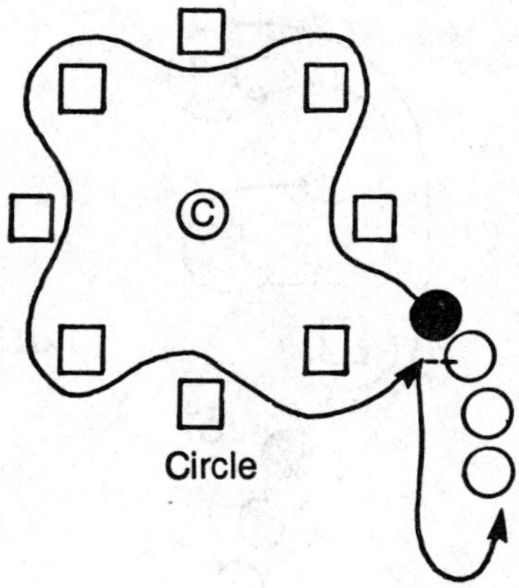

9. RUNNING–THE–SQUARE DRILL

Purpose: To develop agility and body balance, and to evade the tackler by using a shoulder drive or roll.

Procedure: Upright dummies are held at the corners of a ten-yard square. The first time through the ball carrier drives into the dummies alternating shoulders right, left, right, left, releasing outside and inside according to the shoulder that he uses to slam into the dummy. The second time through the ball carrier starts with the other shoulder. He should throw his weight forward, maintain a good base with his feet moving, protect the football with both arms upon contact, and keep his head up, eyes open, and drive through before breaking free releasing from the dummy.

Coaching Points: Stress hitting with the weight forward, keeping the feet chugging, protecting the football, and not fumbling.

DRILL 9

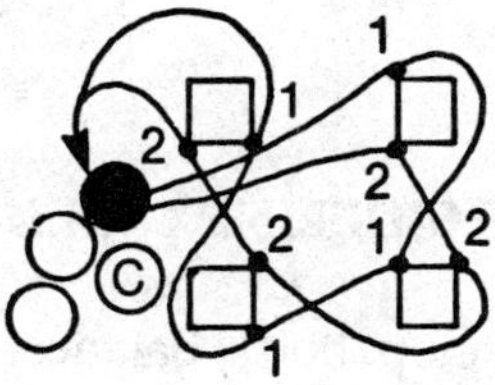

10. ZIG–ZAG RUNNING DRILL

Purpose: To develop agility and body balance, and to evade a tackler by employing a shoulder roll (and pivot) technique.

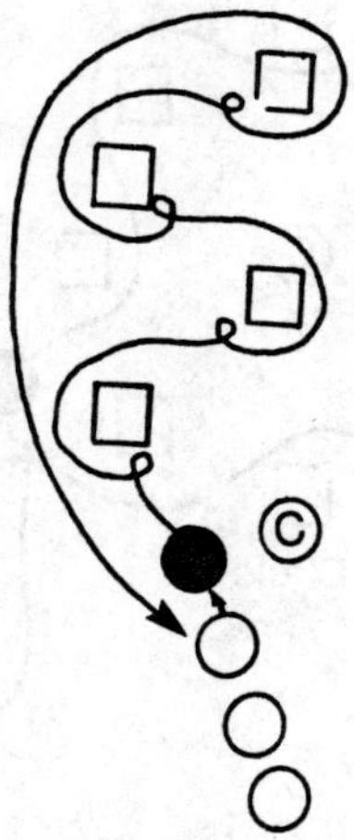

DRILL 10

Procedure: Same as (9) Running-the-Square Drill, only the upright dummies are held at staggered five-yard intervals in a zig-zag line. The ball carrier lowers his left shoulder and slams into the first dummy, sprints to the second dummy, and slams into it with his right shoulder, etc., alternating left and right shoulders until he gets to the end of the line. The second time through, he should shoulder roll and pivot, alternating shoulders. The ball carrier should throw his weight forward, meet maximum resistance from the bag holder, pivot quickly, maintain a low center of gravity, regain his balance quickly, and sprint downfield toward the next dummy.

Coaching Points: No effort should be made to shift the football from one arm to the other. Move the feet; do not hit and then stop moving the feet. In Drills 9 and 10 the ball carrier also should practice folding both of his arms over the football in order to protect it, slamming into the upright dummy simulating breaking a tackle, and charging forward to the next dummy.

11. BALL CARRIER'S SIDELINE DRILL

Purpose: To develop body balance, and to evade tacklers with a shoulder roll.

Procedure: Players (defenders) with upright dummies or air bags are stationed three yards apart and three yards from the sideline. They slam the dummies or air bags into the ball carrier, attempting to knock him out-of-bounds, while he employs a series of shoulder rolls as he moves forward

DRILL 11

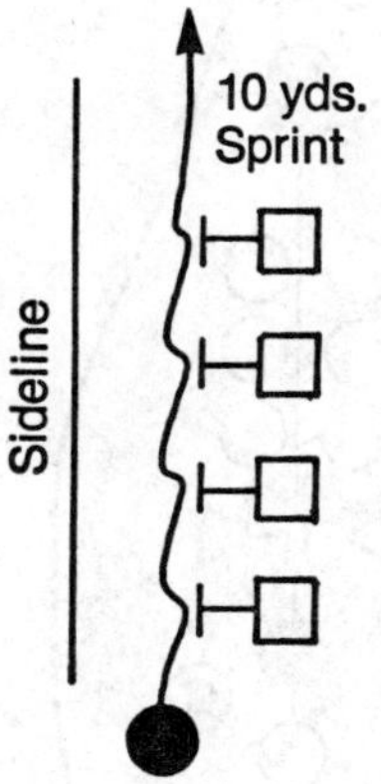

upfield. After getting by the last defender, the ball carrier sprints an additional ten yards.

Coaching Points: Stress hitting with the weight forward, keeping the feet moving, protecting the football, not fumbling, and continuing to fight toward the inside in order to remain in-bounds. If the ball carrier's foot touches the sideline, he is out-of-bounds. Run the drill in both directions so that the ball carrier can practice the technique using both his left and right shoulder as he counters resistance to advance the football, yet remain in-bounds.

12. GAUNTLET DRILL

Purpose: To develop protecting the football, body balance, and fighting through arm tacklers.

Procedure: Ball carriers line up ready to run through the gauntlet, with defenders in separate lines facing each other 1½ yards apart. At the head of the column are two defenders with air bags who slam the ball carrier, slowing him down, as he starts through the gauntlet of defenders. The other defenders attempt to pull out the football, or push or pull the ball carrier's arm holding the football as he fights pressure moving forward. A coach or manager stands at the far end of the line and indicates in which direction the ball carrier should break as the ball carrier approaches their position.

Coaching Points: Stress protecting the football. Control the drill and the flow of ball carriers. The defenders in the line should push or pull the ball carrier's arm or elbow, *not* punch the ball carrier. If offensive backs are

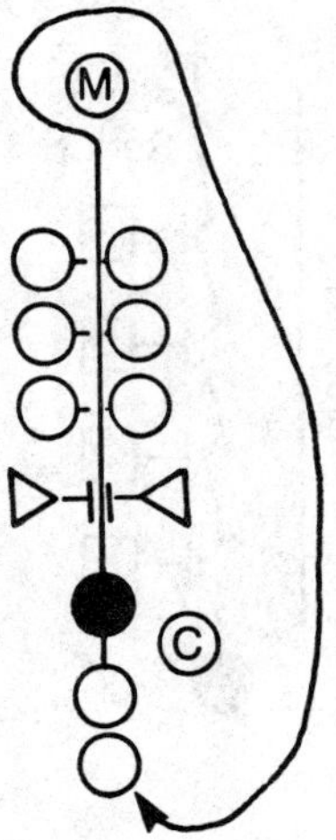

DRILL 12

utilized as defenders, rotate the personnel so they, too, can practice as ball carriers.

13. CIRCLE GAUNTLET DRILL

Purpose: To teach protecting the football, body balance, and fighting through tacklers.

Procedure: The ball carrier is in the middle of a circle of defenders, similar to (14) Bull-in-the-Ring, Chapter 11. Allow approximately 1½ yards between the players in the rim of the circle, who will grab the ball carrier's arm or the football or will close the gap and shoulder butt the ball carrier, but will *not* tackle him. The hub man tries to escape from the middle of the circle without fumbling the football, as he bounces back and forth from one side to the other if he meets strong resistance.

Coaching Points: Stress protecting the football. Same as Drill 12. Use a whistle to control the drill. Replace the ball carrier after not more than five attempts to penetrate the perimeter.

14. OBSTACLE COURSE DRILLS

Purpose: To develop agility and body balance, and to evade a tackler.

Procedure: The center, quarterback, and offensive backs run the dive play. a) The ball carrier must receive the hand-off and immediately leap

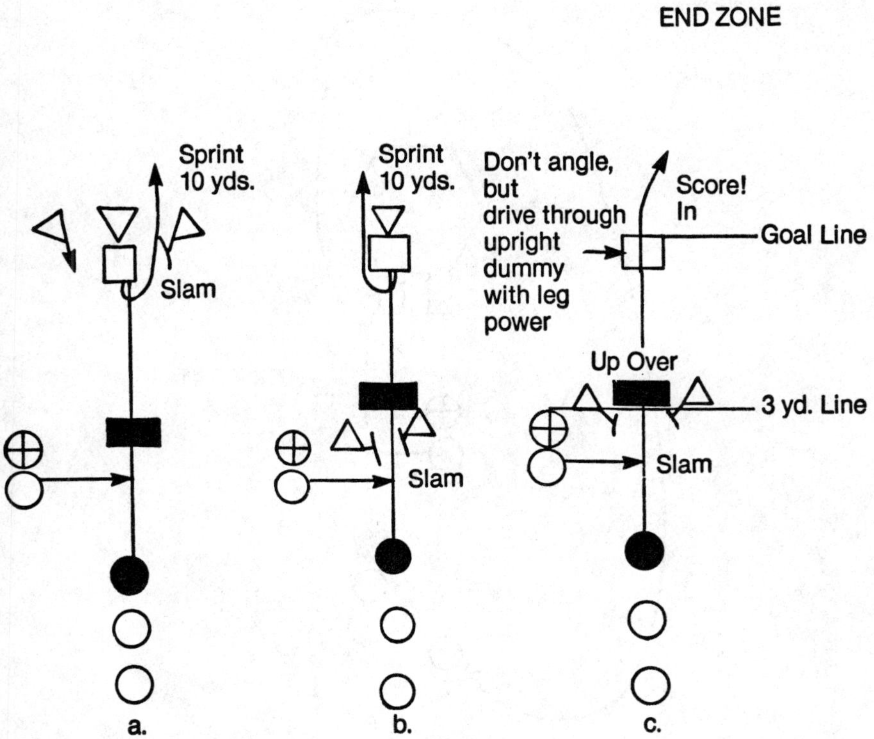

DRILL 14

over a horizontal dummy, then use an evasive tactic to get by a player holding an upright dummy, and be slammed by a player holding an air bag as soon as he breaks by the upright dummy. No effort should be made to shift the football from one arm to the other near the line of scrimmage. b) Reverse the procedure and slam the ball carrier with air bags as soon as he receives the hand-off. Then the ball carrier must jump over a horizontal dummy. In each case the ball carrier sprints ten yards at full speed after clearing the last obstacle. c) Move the football to the three-yard line, and score!

Coaching Points: Stress hitting with the weight forward, head up, eyes open, keep the feet chugging, both arms around the football protecting it, and not fumbling. The quarterback's responsibility is to get the football to the ball carrier, and it is the latter's responsibility to form a pocket properly for the reception of the football. In c) the ball carrier fights through resistance over, up, and in for the score. Run the dive plays right and left. (See (24) Up, Over, and In or TD Drill.)

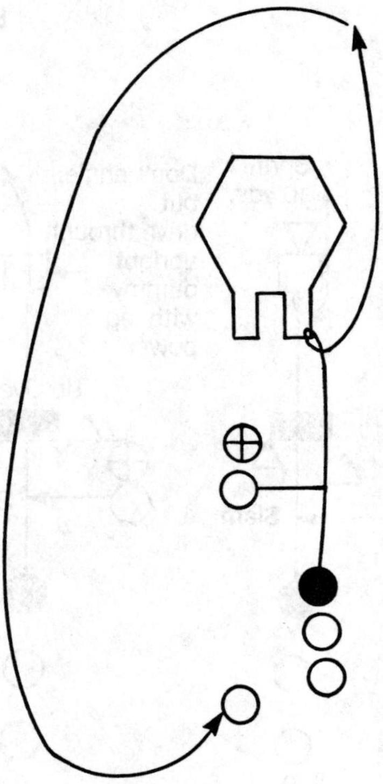

DRILL 15

15. TWO–MAN SLED SHOULDER DRIVE AND PIVOT DRILL

Purpose: To develop agility and body balance, and to evade a tackler with a shoulder drive and pivot technique.

Procedure: Same as (14) Obstacle Course Drills, only a two-man sled arm (pad) is positioned directly in front of the offensive back who is going to receive the hand-off. The quarterback gets the football to the back, who looks straight ahead at the arm (pad) in front of him. Upon receiving the football, the ball carrier drives into the pad on the sled (head on the outside), executes a shoulder roll and pivots away from the T or cross-bar on the two-man sled. After receiving the hand-off, the ball carrier should drive into the right pad with his left shoulder, and into the left pad with his right shoulder, pivot, and spin-out to simulate evading a tackler.

Coaching Points: The drill gives the backs poise and confidence, and teaches them not to look for the football. Stress hitting with the weight forward, head up, eyes open, keeping both feet chugging, both arms around the football and not fumbling. Do not run a deep arc course bowing away from the line of scrimmage when spinning-out; execute a tight pivot and turn upfield quickly. Always hit with the inside shoulder and the head outside of the pad. The center and quarterback must adjust right and left laterally for the ball carriers to align properly opposite the arm (pad) on the sled prior to receiving the hand-off. Permit the sled to run free so that on impact by the ball carrier the sled will "give" to a limited extent.

16. ONE–ON–ONE CHALLENGE DRILL (OFFENSIVELY)

Purpose: To teach the ball carrier to receive the hand-off, break-off of his offensive lineman's one-on-one block, and to evade the tackler.

Purpose: Same as (23) One-On-One Challenge Drill, Chapter 6, only the emphasis here is on teaching-coaching *offensive* backfield fundamentals and techniques, especially breaking-off of the offensive lineman's one-on-one block, and evading the tackler. The offensive center, quarterback, ball carrier and a lineman face the defensive lineman "live." Use the offensive starting count, and a whistle.

Coaching Points: Since this drill may be used either offensively or defensively, here stress *offensive* fundamentals. The ball carrier should follow his blocker's helmet, and break to the side the blocker places his head. Teach the ball carrier not to look at the quarterback or the football when receiving the hand-off, but to watch his blocker.

DRILL 16

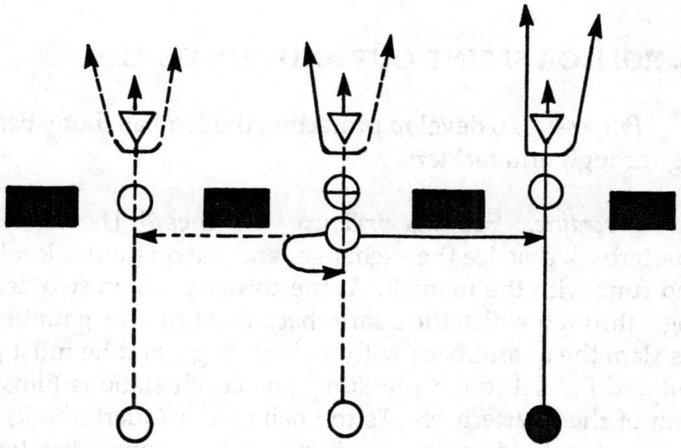

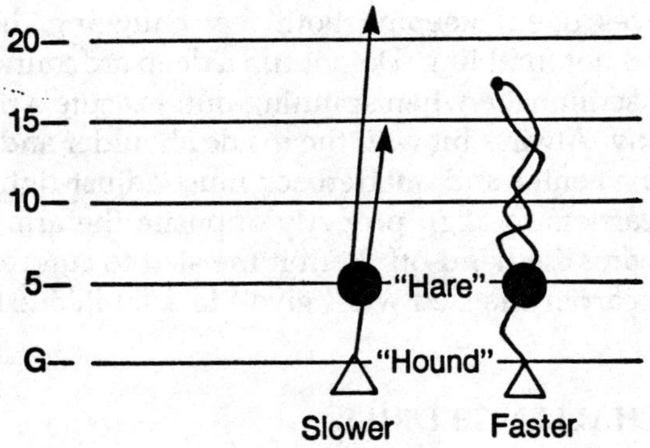

DRILL 17

17. HARE-AND-HOUND DRILL

Purpose: To develop open-field running techniques when being pursued by an opponent from behind.

Procedure: Pair off players with the "hare" on the five-yard line, and the "hound" behind him on the goal line. The tackler attempts to tag the ball carrier, overtaking him as quickly as possible. Both men start running at the same time on the coach's command. If the "hare" is slower than the "hound," he should weave and break sharply, forcing the tackler to break stride and change direction, in an attempt to keep from being overtaken and caught.

Coaching Points: Stress changing direction, especially for a slower "hare." This drill is a good conditioner, competitive, and is fun!

18. ROLL OR SPRINT-OUT AND RUN DRILL

Purpose: To develop protecting the football, body balance, and fighting through arm tacklers.

Procedure: Set this drill up "on lines." The offensive center and quarterback practice the exchange, and the quarterback rolls or sprints out and runs with the football. At the corner position two defenders hold air bags, through which the quarterback must run the gauntlet. The bag holders slam the quarterback with their air bags, and he must protect the football and fight through pressure. The coach stations himself opposite the path of the quarterback. As the ball carrier (quarterback) comes between the two bag holders, the coach indicates in which direction he is to run.

DRILL 18

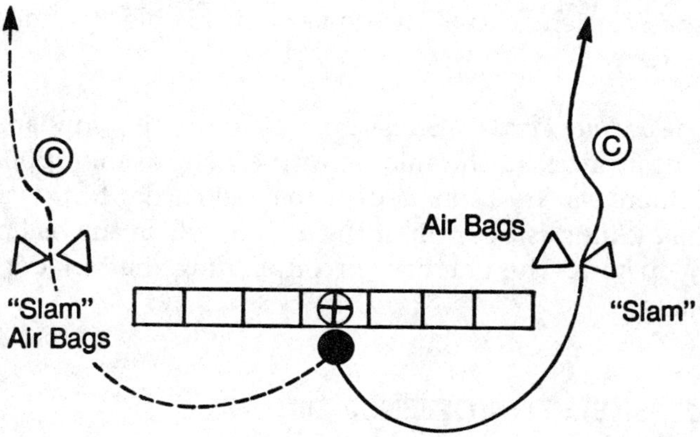

Coaching Points: Stress cutting sharply, putting the ball away, and running with power when going into the gauntlet. Caution the defenders *not* to be overly aggressive in their physical contact versus the quarterback, so as to minimize injury. Note: if you prefer *not* to have your quarterbacks physically challenge defenders by running with the football, teach them how to slide to the ground safely to protect themselves from injury from tacklers.

19. FOLLOW YOUR BLOCKER DRILL

Purpose: To teach the ball carrier to follow his blocker and to evade tacklers in the defensive secondary.

Procedure: The defensive secondary sets up so there are three tacklers versus one offensive blocker and the ball carrier. The blocker crosses the line of scrimmage leading the ball carrier who is three yards behind him. The blocker attempts to eliminate the first defender as he closes on

DRILL 19

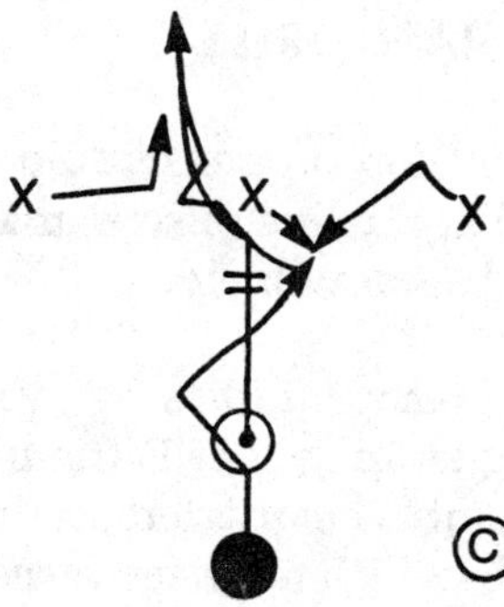

the ball carrier, who in turn breaks off his blocker and tries to evade the defenders.

Coaching Points: Stress open-field running fundamentals. Move from one hash mark to the middle of the field to the opposite hash mark so defenders can try to maneuver the ball carrier to the sideline if possible. If the tackling is poor, limit the area in which the ball carrier and blocker may operate. The emphasis is on eluding the tacklers, however, not on tackling.

20–21. SKELETON OFFENSE DRILLS

20. Ball Handling Drill

21. Skeleton Versus Live Perimeter or Outside (Offensive) Drill

Purpose: To teach play assignments, execution, timing and ball handling, and (21) to simulate game conditions in polishing the outside running attack.

Procedure: (20) The offensive center and complete backfield run through offensive plays, working on timing, execution, play assignments, ball handling, etc. (21) Offensive ends are added versus a live perimeter. The offensive team huddles and then executes its outside running plays and action passes.

Coaching Points: Use the offensive starting count and a whistle. The defense should react to keys. (See Chapter 6, (28) Offensive Inside Drill and (29) Offensive Half-Line Drill, for additional skeleton versus live defender drills with a similar purpose.) Use flash cards if working against your opposition's alignment tendencies.

22. FOLLOW-THE-BALL DRILL

Purpose: To develop proper huddle discipline and technique, alignment on the football at the line of scrimmage, team take-off, and a second effort following the ball downfield.

Procedure: The team huddles five yards from the seven-man blocking sled where the quarterback calls the pitchback (speed) sweep right or left and the snap-count. The quarterback breaks the huddle, and the team aligns on the football, which has been placed two feet from the middle arm

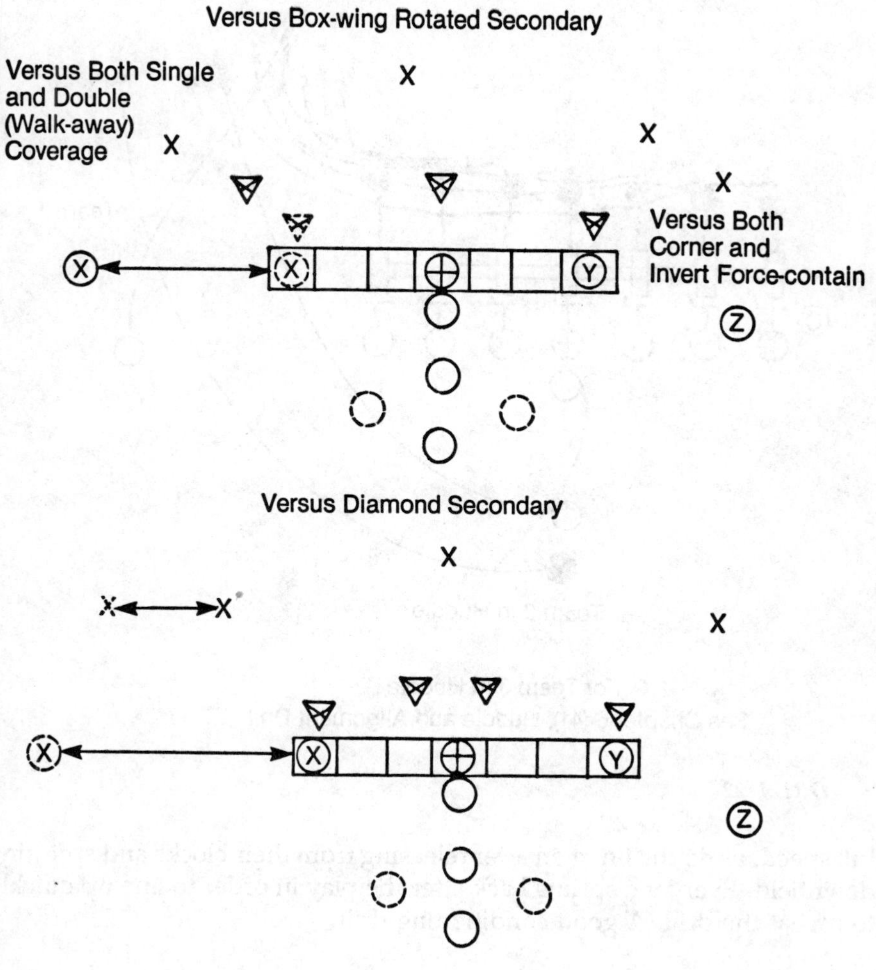

DRILL 21

(pad) on the seven-man sled. The quarterback calls the snap-count, and the team takes off together, with the line driving into the sled and the offensive backs running the sweep play. On the coach's command, all of the linemen release from their sled blocks and follow the football downfield approximately thirty yards. The entire team then runs back to the huddle. In the meantime team No. 2 has repeated the same procedure, and team No. 3 is huddling ready to follow team No. 2.

Coaching Points: Stress the proper huddle procedure and technique of breaking the huddle and lining up on the football. The line explodes together and the team takes off as a single unit. The backs run the sweep

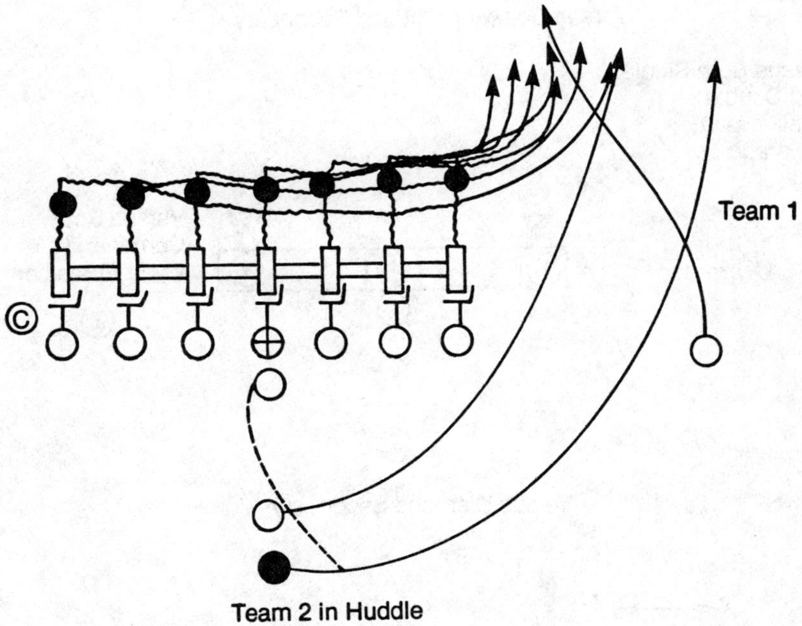

For Team 3 in Huddle,
See Chapter 6 (41), Huddle and Alignment Drill.

DRILL 22

full speed, as do the linemen after releasing from their blocks and sprinting downfield. Everyone sprints back after the play in order to line up quickly to repeat the drill. A good conditioning drill.

23. TEN (TWENTY OR THIRTY) YARDS–AND–IN DRILL

Purpose: To develop proper huddle discipline and technique, alignment on the ball, team take-off, and second effort following the football over the goal line.

Procedure: Same as for (22) Follow-the-Ball Drill, only a blocking sled is not used. After breaking the huddle, the offensive linemen align on the football on the 10- (20- or 30-) yard line, and run the play called in the huddle into the end zone, circle, and sprint back to form the huddle again. When the No. 1 unit is on the line running their play, No. 2 team is in the huddle in the middle of the field, and the No. 3 unit is on the opposite hash mark getting ready to huddle.

Coaching Points: Same as Drill 22. This drill is better to use than running laps or wind sprints. Specify the number of times your team will run the drill. Stress sprinting over the goal line, and hustling back to the huddle. (See Chapter 6, (41) Huddle and Alignment Drill.)

24. UP, OVER, AND IN, OR TD DRILL (See p. 182)

Purpose: To develop the ball carrier's ability to go up, over and in for the score.

Procedure: The box or "pit" is filled with sawdust, enclosed by sandbags, and has a depth of approximately thirty inches, fifteen feet wide and twenty feet long (inside dimensions). Alternating from each end of the pit, a quarterback gives a hand-off to the lead player in his column. The ball carrier simulates going in for the score over the offensive and defensive linemen by diving up, over and into the sawdust. He immediately rolls to the outside, and goes to the end of the opposite column of ball carriers. In the meantime, the other quarterback executes the hand-off to a ball carrier coming from the opposite end of the pit into the sawdust.

Coaching Points: If the fullback is taking the hand-off and coming over the middle, work left and right. By having the ball carriers roll to the outside and then go to the end of the opposite column of players, it is not necessary to move the center-quarterback combinations from one side to the other, although this could be done, too. Air bags may be placed on top of the sandbags, or upright dummies in front of the sandbags, in order to build up the front height of the pit, if one wishes to do this. (Cover the pit with a tarpaulin in order to keep the sawdust when not in use.)

25. RUNNING BACK (TAILBACK) BAG DRILL

Purpose: To develop the ball carrier's ability to meet resistance and break tackles, to evade tacklers, to develop and maintain body balance, to protect the football, and to gain extra yardage.

Procedure: Set up "on lines" to get proper and correct spacing, depth and perspective of defenders at the corner who are holding upright dummies approximately 1½ yards apart. The center and quarterback and running back or tailback practice either a hand-off or a pitch back exchange. As the ball carrier turns upfield running between the upright dummies, he is "shocked" by the bag holders. As the ball carrier squares up running directly toward a manager three yards beyond (either with or without a bag), he breaks opposite the direction indicated by the manager. Defenders

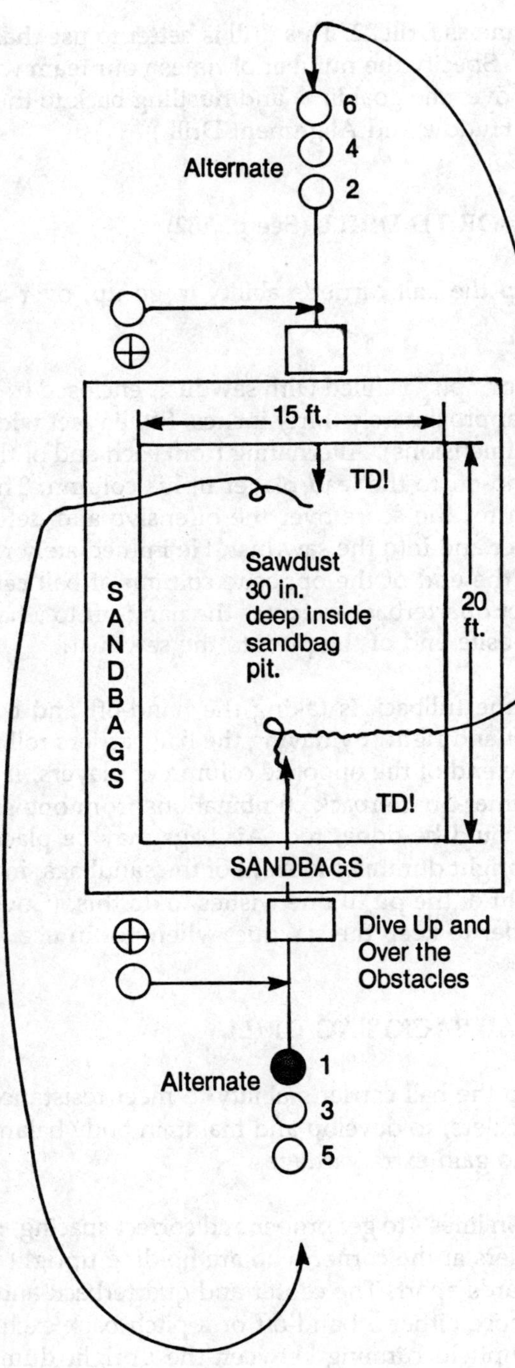
6
4
Alternate
2
15 ft.
TD!
Sawdust
30 in.
deep inside
sandbag
pit.
SANDBAGS
20
ft.
TD!
SANDBAGS
Dive Up and
Over the
Obstacles
1
Alternate
3
5

DRILL 24

DRILL 25

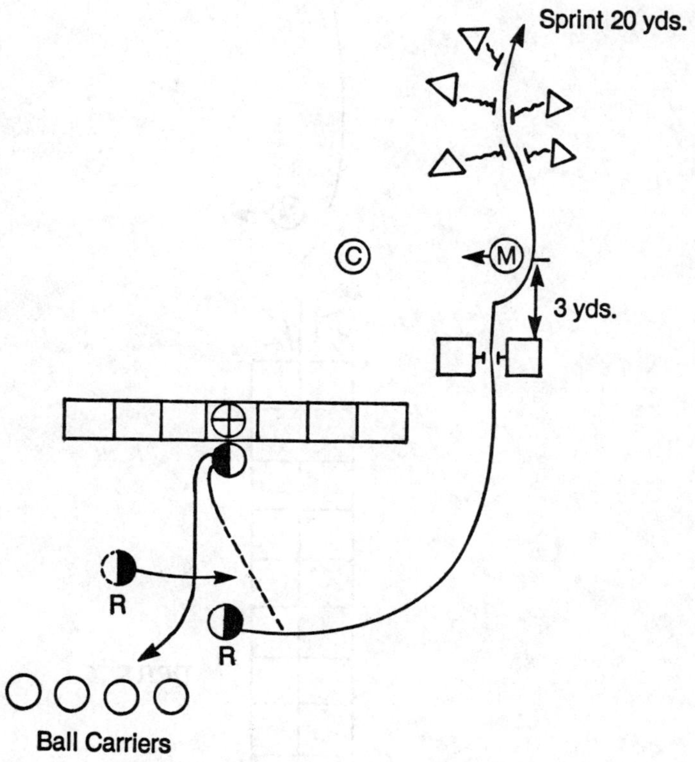

are spaced downfield with air bags or fight bags, and they push or shove the ball carrier, or throw the bags at him if he is too far away, while he must run and fight through this resistance. If the ball carrier does not shorten his stride, take choppy steps, and widen his base, he will either get knocked down or trip and fall down. After clearing the last obstacle, the ball carrier must sprint for an additional twenty yards toward his goal line before returning to the column of ball carriers.

Coaching Points: Stress "kicking through" the bags, maintaining body balance, and gaining extra yardage. After practicing the drill to the right side, move the bag holders and defenders to the left side so the drill is practiced both right and left.

26. RUNNING ROPES AND HAND–OFF DRILL

(See Chapter 5, Drill 35, for rope maze dimensions.)

Purpose: To practice receiving the hand-off from the quarterback, and to develop body balance, coordination and agility.

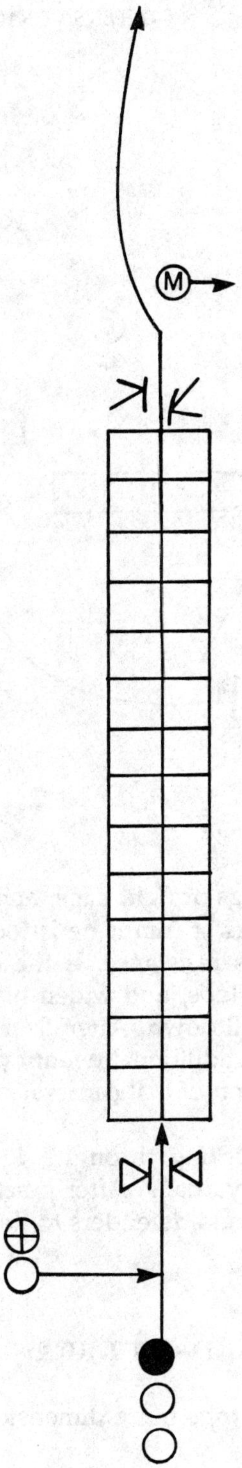

DRILL 26

Procedure: The quarterback makes the hand-off exchange to the ball carrier, who steps in every square on the first cycle of the drill, and then crosses over in every other square on the next cycle. The third cycle through the ball carrier hits every other square at full speed. (See Chapter 5, (33) Single Stepping Rope Drills.) Defenders with air bags may stand to the sides at the near end of the ropes to try to create a fumble on the hand-off exchange, and at the far end to offer resistance as the ball carrier comes out of the rope maze. They should not be added, however, until the ball carriers have gained confidence in running through the ropes after receiving several "hand-offs" successfully.

Coaching Points: Same as (12) Gauntlet Drill and (14) Obstacle Course Drill. The value of the drill is the teaching and practicing of a fundamental, along with developing and drilling for reaction and agility (Chapter 5).

27. OFFENSIVE SCRIMMAGE DRILLS

The following drills all involve offensive backs, but will not be repeated since they are explained in detail as follows:

See Chapter 6, (28) Inside Offensive Drill; (29) Half-Line Drill.

See Chapter 14, (12) Scoring Zone Offense Drill; (13) Danger Zone Offense Drill; (14) Touchdown Sequence or Clutch Offense Drill; (15) Stop (Kill)-the-Clock Drill; (16) Delay Offense Offense or Run-out-the-Clock Drill; (17) Racehorse or Go-Go-Go Offense Drill; (18) Giving-Up-a-Safety Drill.

PART IV

Drills for Teaching-Coaching Defensive Fundamentals and Techniques

10

Defensive Line Drills

Defense plays a greater role in present-day football than it ever has previously. Adverse weather and other physical conditions can seriously affect a team's offense, yet have practically no effect on a well-coached defense. Also, it takes longer and more practice time to install and coordinate all of the ingredients of a smooth-functioning, effective, synergetic offense, than it does to get a team ready defensively. A strong defense not only demoralizes the opposition by its unyielding tactics, but it also gives a tremendous lift to its own offense by securing the football in favorable positions on the field. It is not unusual in present-day football that a team's offensive attack is ineffective on long sustained drives, but the team still wins because of the points put on the scoreboard by the defense, and/or because the defense secures good field position and the offensive team starts within the four-down zone and must drive only a relatively short distance to score. Also, it is not unusual that a team will find it easier to stop the opposition than to score itself.

The objectives of defensive play are three-fold: to prevent the opposition from scoring the *easy* touchdown via a long pass completion or a long run; to obtain possession of the football; and to score. Defensive play is *reaction* football since the defenders must *react after* the ball has been snapped. The failure or a breakdown by the offensive team, specifically at the critical point of attack, usually means the offensive team suffers a loss of yardage, loss of the down, and perhaps loss of the football. The failure of a single defender to *react* properly, especially at the point where the offense is attacking, usually results in a long run or a long pass that scores or leads directly to a score. This pertinent fact cannot be minimized or overlooked, and it must be stressed frequently, if the objectives of winning defensive football are to be realized. Consequently, the following general principles, with their numerous ramifications, must be taught, practiced, and reiterated frequently, usually via practice drills: positive defensive morale must be built constantly; the correct angles of pursuit are imperative; gang tackling is essential for sound defensive play; and pass defense must receive adequate practice consideration.

Many experienced coaches, particularly at the collegiate level, consider pass defense to be the most important phase of defensive football. It is not only difficult to teach-coach, but it requires considerable time, practice, and patience to master individual and team techniques of coordinated play. Pass defense consists of four important phases: rushing the passer aggressively; delaying eligible receivers at or near the line of scrimmage; secondary pass coverage; and the intercepting or the breaking up of the pass, or tackling the receiver who makes the reception. Present-day football rules, particularly at the collegiate and professional levels, prohibit or restrict a number of pass rush and delaying receiver tactics and techniques that were permitted and taught several years ago. As a result, effectively teaching-coaching-learning the permitted tactics and techniques of pass coverage and intercepting or breaking up the pass are more important for successful defensive play today than at any time in the history of the game of football. Drills for teaching-coaching these and other techniques and fundamentals of defensive play are included in this chapter, and in the three chapters that follow. Specific defensive "systems" are beyond the scope of this book on drills.

In addition to the drills in Chapter 5, which may be used to teach and develop agility and reaction, the following drills are designed for teaching-coaching and developing defensive line fundamentals and techniques, as well as for creating game-like situations.

1–4. ONE–VERSUS–ONE DRILLS (PROGRESSIVE)

1. Stance and Alignment Drill

Purpose: To teach the defender to line up properly, taking the correct lateral and vertical alignment in a good defensive football stance.

Procedure: Players pair off one-versus-one. The defender assumes the proper stance the coach has indicated. The coach checks the alignment of the defender in relation to the offensive blocker: head-up or nose-on-nose; nose-to-ear, shoe-to-crotch or shoe-to-shoe; off-setting both to the outside and inside, depending on the individual player's defensive position and responsibilities.

Coaching Points: Stress the correct alignment and then the proper stance, indicating whether the defender's inside or outside foot should split the crotch of the blocker, or be inside, even with, or outside of the blocker's inside or outside foot. Stress the importance of a correct lateral and vertical alignment, depending upon the deployment of the defensive personnel, offensive splits and the tactical situation.

2. Block Protection Drills

Purpose: To teach and develop the defender's charge and block protection.

Procedure: The defender lines up in a proper stance after the coach has indicated the defensive alignment, charge, and type of block protection to be employed. No starting count is employed. The defender must react to the first movement of the blocker. After delivering his blow and destroying the block, the defensive lineman must be in a good football position ready to react to the coach's hand signal.

Coaching Points: The drill is controlled. The emphasis is to teach the defender to move on movement (the reason for not employing a starting count), to deliver properly a hand shiver or a forearm lift, and to maintain a good football position ready to react, i.e., control the blocker, locate the football, pursue and tackle.

3. Forearm or Shoulder Lift Drill

Purpose: To teach and develop using the forearm lift as block protection.

Procedure: The offensive player is on one (right) knee, back erect, head turned to the left, with the point of the chin on the (left) shoulder, right side of the body exposed. The coach stands behind the offensive player, facing the defender. The coach makes a quick hand movement indicating the snap of the football and the defender uncoils, coordinating his (right) foot and flipper, delivering a legal blow to the exposed shoulder of the blocker, attempting to bowl over the offensive lineman.

Coaching Points: Hand dummies or air bags may be held by the blocker, and the defender may boom these. Stress when the forearm or shoulder lift is employed to bring the feet under the body, maintain body balance, and react to the situation. Practice both left and right forearm lifts, coordinating the proper foot with each.

4. Reaction Drill

Purpose: To teach and develop the defensive principles of moving on movement (or on the snap of the football), delivering a blow, controlling the blocker, locating the football, pursuing and tackling the ball carrier.

Procedure: The coach stands behind the defender facing the blocker and the ball carrier (manager). The latter two are flashed the starting count, the type of block, and the direction the ball carrier will run. The defender is given his alignment, and the down and distance. On the coach's starting count, the blocker attempts to physically defeat the defender and vice versa. The defender must execute his defensive fundamentals properly, pursue and tag the manager, or tackle the ball carrier if the drill is live.

Coaching Points: Stress the correct alignment and stance initially. Stress disposing of the blocker quickly, and *not* wrestling with him. Stress the execution of the proper defensive fundamentals and techniques.

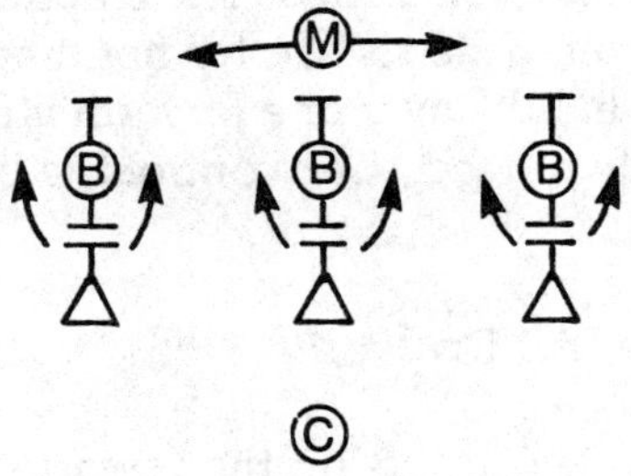

DRILL 4

5–7. TWO–MAN SLED DRILLS

5. Forearm Lift and Reaction Drill

6. Hand or Forearm Shiver and Reaction Drill

Purpose: To teach and develop block protection by using (5) the forearm lift and (6) the hand shiver, and reacting to the football.

Procedure: The defender lines up in a defensive stance opposite (5) the arm or pad or (6) the T-bar of the sled. The coach stands on the sled and shakes it quickly, simulating the snap of the football. The defender executes (5) a forearm lift or (6) a hand shiver, comes on body balance, and then reacts to the hand signal of the coach indicating left, right or pass rush.

Coaching Points: For the hand shiver, stress that the defensive linemen lock their elbows and wrists and follow through with short choppy steps until the direction of pursuit is indicated. The heels of the hands are driven forward and upward (under the blocker's shoulder pads in an effort to straighten him up in order to neutralize his charge). The defensive lineman should bring his back foot up first. If the forearm lift or boom is utilized, coordinate the forearm-shoulder-foot, then come to balance quickly, watching the coach for direction of pursuit.

7. Hit and Reaction Drill

Purpose: To develop the defensive fundamentals and techniques of the forearm lift, spin-out, ward-off, rushing the passer and making the tackle.

Procedure: Same as (5) Forearm Lift and Reaction Drill, only after throwing the flipper, the defender spins out, regains his balance, slams the nearest upright blocker with a coordinated inside forearm lift, and then slams the second blocker with a coordinated outside forearm lift, rushes the passer or tackles an upright dummy behind the sled, before returning to the end of the opposite line.

Coaching Points: Stress a coordinated foot-shoulder ward-off. Stress a good stance initially, and quick reactions. To develop punch from the buttocks, see Chapter 6, Two-Man Sled Drills 3 to 7.

DRILL 7

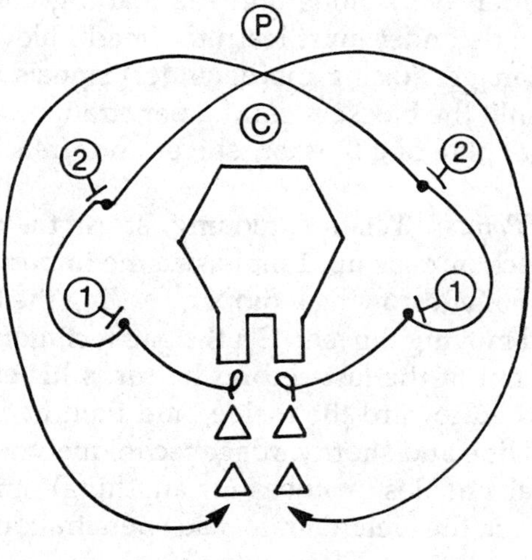

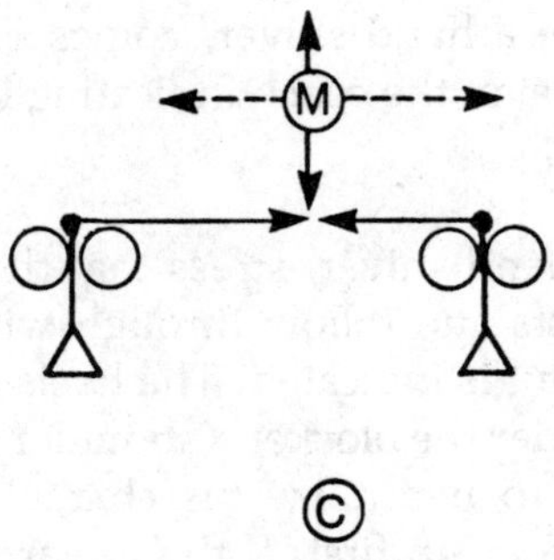

DRILL 8

8. EXPLOSION OR ONE-VERSUS-TWO DRILLS (PROGRESSIVE)

Purpose: To teach delivering an explosive blow, the gap charge, arm-leg sychronization; also, to read the block, to fight the pressure, and to react properly when a single defender versus two offensive blockers.

Procedure: For delivering an explosive blow two offensive linemen line up with their inside knee on the ground or on hands and knees, shoulder-to-shoulder, with the defender in the gap opposite them. The manager is behind the offensive blockers in the gap facing the defensive player, who will then explode into the target with his shoulder on the manager's hand signal. As contact is made, the defender then whips his tail down, with his legs extended straight, as the blow is completed. After getting the feeling of "popping" or exploding, without first raising up or drawing back, the defender repeats the drill, then brings his feet up under him, moving them quickly and rapidly, and holding in a position ready to react to the offensive linemen's block and the ball carrier's (manager's) movement. The coach is behind the defender facing the blockers and indicates by hand signals their offensive actions and the starting count. Then the drill is "live," and the defender must learn to "read" blockers and react to their blocks. The manager (facing the defender) signals whether the defender should try to split the blockers getting penetration, use a goal line or short yardage charge, play one blocker, shiver and "reach," etc.

Coaching Points: When exploding, stress the first move is forward; do not draw back or raise up. Emphasize the importance of a good stance, extending the body, throwing a flipper, reading the block, reacting, speed, quickness, and moving the feet. On the gap technique, the defender drives hard and low but at the last second he turns his shoulders and body so his belly is turned toward the inside, and then he scrambles through the gap. On a goal line and short yardage technique, the defender aims lower, penetrates, grabs ankles or knees (or anything), and fights upward. Occasionally permit the defender to fake penetration, and/or go over the blockers, if he has the ability to do so. Also loop, slant or veer into one blocker (simulated coordinated defense), then react accordingly to blockers. Also see (35) Gap Charge-Bag Drill to develop gap charge technique.

9. AROUND–THE–CIRCLE HITTING DRILL

Purpose: To develop arm-leg synchronization from a semi-upright position in delivering a blow in warding-off a blocker, and destroying the block; also, to give the defender a feeling of "hitting."

Procedure: Blockers line up in a semi-upright stance in a circle facing clockwise. The defender is *inside* of the circle in a semi-upright stance, working counter-clockwise. He synchronizes throwing the flipper with the proper (right) foot forward as he meets limited resistance, pushes off, sprints to the next blocker and repeats the procedure around the circle. After each defender has his turn, the drill is repeated with the defender going around the *outside* of the circle using the opposite (left) flipper and foot forward.

Coaching Points: Stress speed and quickness, and the proper arm-leg synchronization. A follow-up to Drills 8, 9, 10, and 14, Chapter 11.

DRILL 9

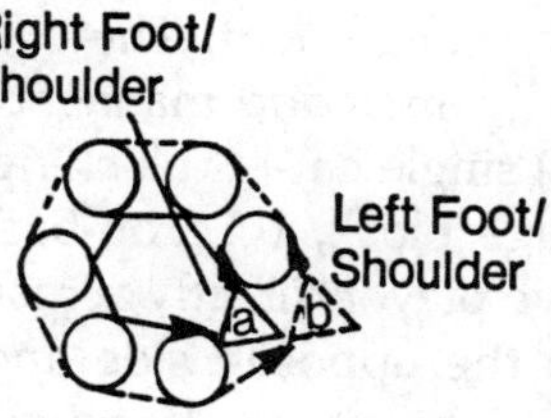

10. ONE–VERSUS–THREE DRILLS (PROGRESSIVE)

Purpose: To teach and develop reaction to the movements of the three offensive linemen in the interior defensive lineman's area, such as he will face under game condition.

Procedure: Similar to the interior offensive line drills (three-on-one) in Chapter 6, only here the emphasis is on developing defensive fundamentals and techniques for the interior linemen, especially for the middle guard and tackles in an odd defensive alignment or linemen over guards

Reading the Triangle/Blocking Scheme

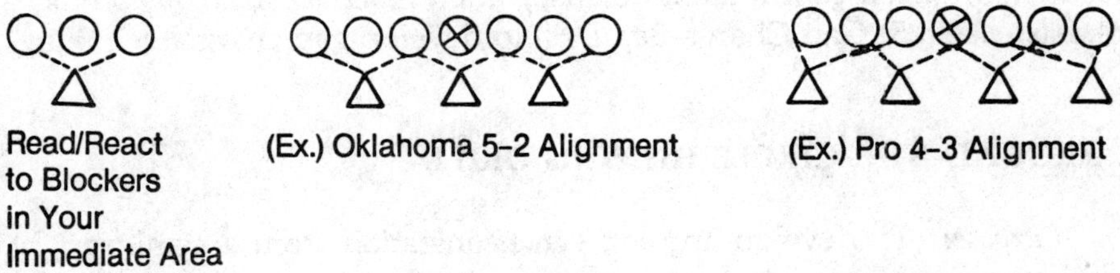

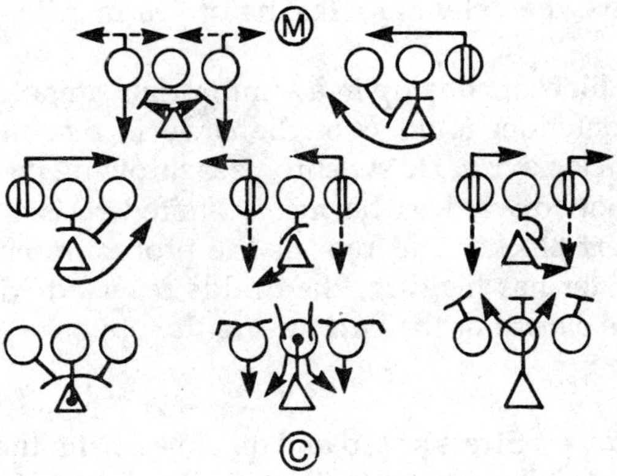

DRILL 10

and tackles in an even alignment. The coach starts behind the defender, facing the offensive linemen and manager (ball carrier), and indicates the starting count and a) single cut-off block right or left, b) double-team block right or left, c) wedge block, d) drop-back pass block, and e) influence block by the offensive player directly across from the defender, simulating the trap block from the opposite side and/or f) the reverse shoulder or straight shoulder block by either offensive lineman to the right and left of the defender. The ball carrier takes the path indicated by the coach so the defender can locate the football, pursue and tackle (tag), after having moved on movement and protected his territory first.

Coaching Points: Stress the proper defensive fundamentals and techniques. The coach may give the down and distance situation to make the drill more meaningful. Add a fourth blocker as a trapper.

11. DEFENSIVE REACTION MACHINE DRILLS

Purpose: To develop reaction to the movement of three simulated offensive linemen in the defender's area.

Procedure: Similar to (10) One-Versus-Three Drills, only by moving the helmet, which is mounted on a metal handle on the defensive reaction machine, the coach can simulate a straight ahead block, pulling or blocking to the right or left, a double-team block, or pass protection. When the mounted football helmet is slid laterally along the horizontal bar, a spring mechanism releases the wing pad on that particular side which pops forward at the defender.

Coaching Points: Stress the proper defensive fundamentals and techniques, keying on the (offensive) helmet. The machine may be used for practicing block protection drills, including forearm lift and hand shiver and reaction, such as in Drills 5 and 6 on the two-man sled. Also the machine may be used for the Linebacker's Key Drill, and for drilling the defensive end, simulating releasing from the wingback's block. In (11) Defensive Reaction Machine Drill and others, a ball carrier may be stationed behind the coach, and will run in the designated direction so the defender must pursue and tackle (tag) him after reacting to the movement of the pad(s), which has been triggered by the helmet mechanism. The value of using this and other similar equipment lies in the elimination of injury to personnel, while still practicing and perfecting the correct techniques under simulated game conditions.

12. TWO–VERSUS–THREE DRILLS (PROGRESSIVE)

Purpose: To develop reaction to the movements of the three offensive linemen in the two defenders' areas, such as they will face under game conditions.

Procedure: Similar to the offensive drills (three-on-two) in Chapter 6, only here the emphasis is on developing defensive fundamentals and techniques for the interior linemen, especially for the defenders playing opposite the offensive guards and tacklers in an even defensive alignment. The coach stands behind the defenders, facing the offensive linemen, and indicates the starting count, type of blocks that should be executed and the direction of the ball carrier (manager).

Coaching Points: Stress the proper defensive fundamentals and techniques. The down and distance situation may be given to make the drill more meaningful, as defenders covering the offensive guards seldom play head-up in every situation when employing an even defensive alignment. Then defenders may off-set to either crack (shoulder or gap), as they would do in a game situation depending on down and distance, and the offensive tendencies of the opposition.

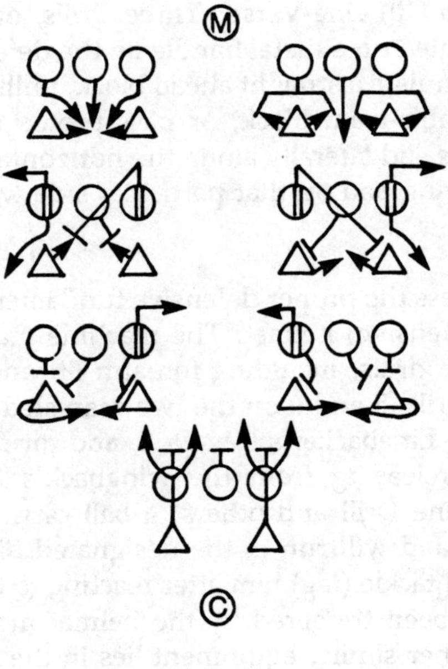

DRILL 12

13–15. DEFENSIVE LINE DRILLS (PROGRESSIVE)

13. Three-Versus-Five Drills

14. Five-Versus-Seven Drills (Odd Alignment)

15. Six-Versus-Seven Drills (Even Alignment)

Purpose: To teach and develop reaction to the movement of offensive linemen, such as defensive linemen will face under game conditions.

Procedure: Similar to the offensive line drills (five-on-three) in Chapter 6, only here the emphasis is on developing defensive fundamentals and techniques for the interior linemen from tackle to tackle, plus the linebackers in (15) Six-Versus-Seven Drills. In Drill 13 the offensive ends are not used, but are added for Drills 14 and 15. The coach uses the same procedure as explained in Drills 10 and 12.

Coaching Points: Stress the proper defensive fundamentals and techniques. In (13) the primary purpose of the drill is the reaction to the trap, and it should be run more frequently than the other situations. In (14) the defensive linemen react from an odd alignment, and in (15) from an even alignment versus the various offensive plays, similar to those illustrated in Drills 10, 12, and 13.

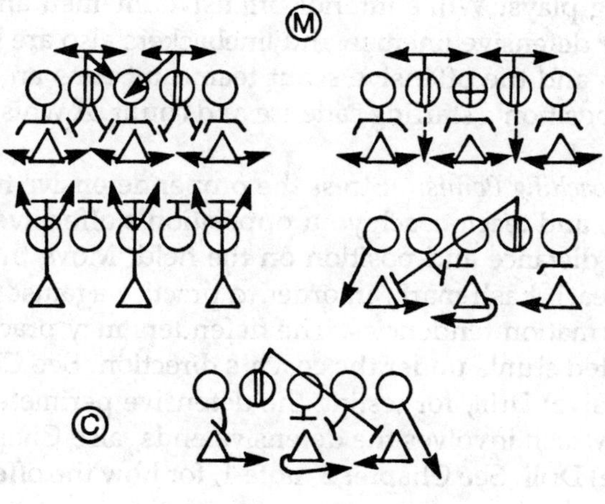

DRILL 13

16. INSIDE (DEFENSIVE) DRILL

Purpose: To recognize and defend against the opposition's inside running attack, and to test your defensive strategy and tactics.

Procedure: Similar to (28) Inside (Offensive) Drill, Chapter 6, only the emphasis here is on teaching-coaching the defensive fundamentals and techniques in order to recognize and stop the opposition's favorite inside

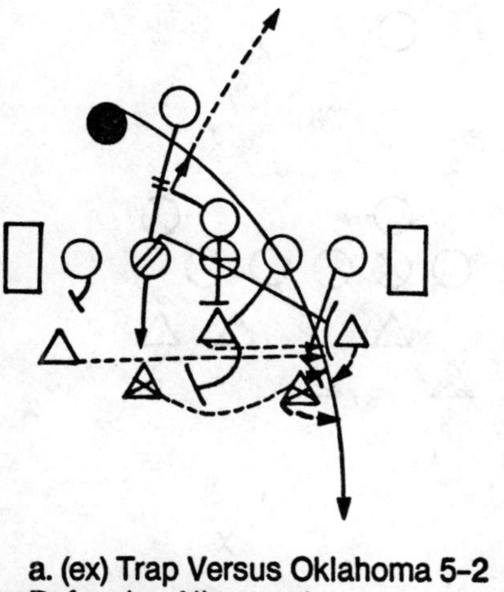

a. (ex) Trap Versus Oklahoma 5–2 Defensive Alignment

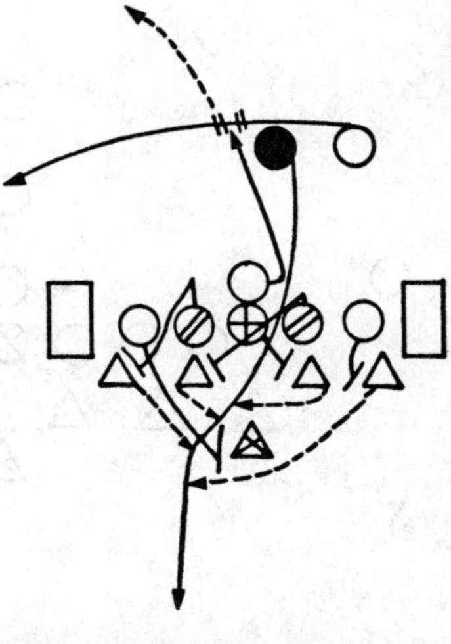

b. (ex) Quick (FB) Trap Versus Pro 4–3 Defensive Alignment

DRILL 16

running plays. While interior offensive linemen and backs are huddling, interior defensive linemen and linebackers also are huddling. The defense sets up and the offensive scout team unit runs an inside play live, using the opposition's starting cadence and count. A whistle terminates the drill.

Coaching Points: Stress the proper defensive fundamentals and techniques, and teach-coach your opposition's offensive tendencies, including down, distance and position on the field. Move the ball from the middle out to each hash mark, in order to practice against your opposition's field and formation tendencies. The defenders may practice individual and coordinated stunts under the coach's direction. See Chapter 12, (31) Outside (Defensive) Drill, for testing the defensive perimeter versus a skeleton offense, which involves the defensive ends; also Chapter 9 (21) Outside (Offensive) Drill. See Chapter 2, note 1, for how the offensive team may utilize flash cards.

17. DEFENSIVE HALF–LINE DRILL

Purpose: To recognize and defend against the opposition's favorite running and pass plays, and to test your defensive strategy and tactics.

Procedure: Similar to (29) Offensive Half-Line Drill, Chapter 6, in that half of the offensive and defensive lines are used, only the emphasis here is on perfecting defensive fundamentals and techniques and recognizing the opposition's favorite plays. One unit works right, while the other unit

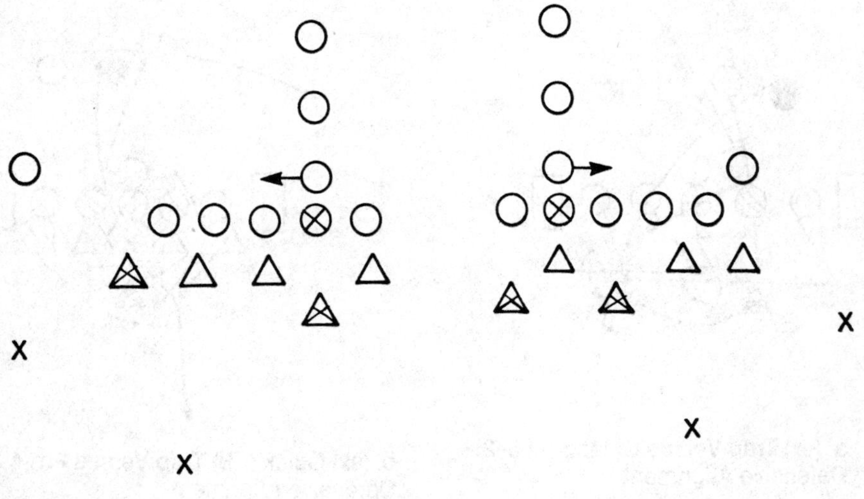

DRILL 17

works left. The No. 1 and No. 2 defensive units are divided up to work half-line at a time. The offensive scout team is limited to the opposition's favorite plays to each side (right or left), and counters and reverses are not run unless they hit inside of the off-side guard on the back-side of the play. Use the opposition's starting cadence and snap-count.

Coaching Points: Stress good execution by the offense in order to aid recognition and to get good reaction by the defensive units. Change defensive alignments. Rotate the off-side guard, the middle guard and the linebackers so they can practice working both right and left. The drill is live. Use a whistle to terminate the play. Give the opposition's offensive tendencies, including down, distance and position on the field. Move the ball from the middle of the field to each hash mark. Same as Drill 16. Offensive team utilizes flash cards.

18–19 DEFENSIVE LINE DRILLS

18. Seven-Versus-Seven Drill

19. Seven-Versus-Eight Drill

Purpose: To drill the forcing unit from even and odd alignment to get off on the snap of the football or to move on offensive movement, to coordinate individual and team stunts, and to test your defensive strategy and tactics.

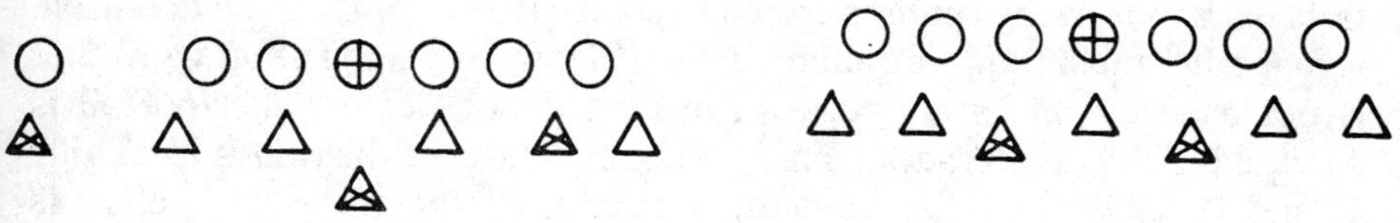

DRILL 18

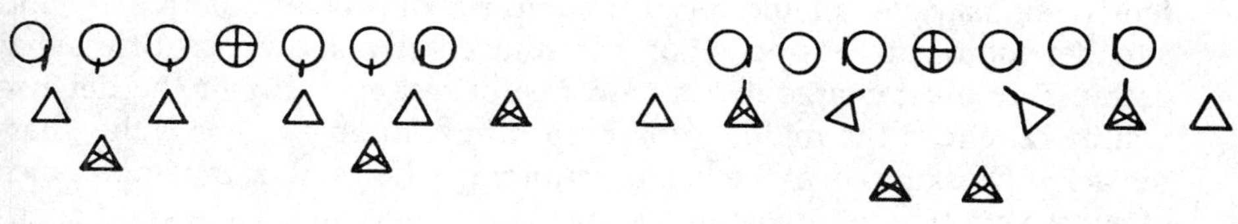

DRILL 19

Procedure: Similar to (30) Offensive Line Blocking Drill, Chapter 6, only here the emphasis is on developing defensive fundamentals and techniques, including coordinated individual and team stunts. Air bags are not used in this drill. The coach calls out the defensive alignment and/or stunts. He also calls the opposition's cadence and starting count, and the center simulates snapping the ball. The blockers merely raise their down hand from the ground, simulating offensive movement. The defenders must react quickly, each charging quickly to his point of responsibility.

Coaching Points: The drill is live for the defenders, but not for the blockers. Stress quickness, moving on movement or on the snap of the football, depending upon the opposition's starting cadence and count. The blockers should raise their hands from the ground quickly. Offensive backs are not used, and no effort is made to run the opposition's plays or to block defenders, as in (17) Defensive Half-Line Drill.

20. JUMPING DEFENSIVE ALIGNMENTS DRILL

Purpose: To practice showing one defensive alignment, and then jumping to another alignment before the offensive center snaps the football.

Procedure: The coach tells the defensive signal caller the defensive alignment and the new one to which he wants the defense to jump. The signal caller steps into the defensive huddle and might say, for example, "Jump 43 to 52 on 'Now,' " and the team breaks the huddle on his command. At the same time the coach gives the offensive linemen the starting count and cadence as they remain at the line of scrimmage. As the coach puts his hands in the center's crotch to accept the snap-back, the defensive signal caller must jump the alignment on "Now" (or some other word that is not used by the offensive team in its cadence), before the football is snapped to the quarterback (coach). The remainder of the drill is like Drills 18 and 19, as it is live for the defense but not for the offense. No effort is made to run the opposition's favorite plays. (See Drills 18–19 for diagrams.)

Coaching Points: Stress quickness. Vary the starting count. The defensive signal caller should give the jump signal ("Now") both early and late, depending on the opposition's starting count and cadence. Stress that each player must charge to his new area of responsibility or the defense will be caught in the middle of a jump. Stress double jumps if the quarterback is checking off at the line of scrimmage. Emphasize the importance of always starting with a good alignment, and ending up in a good alignment. Drills 18–20 precede defensive scrimmage. It is not necessary to use defensive backs in any of these drills, unless they are involved in defensive stunts, as when inside and corner blitzes are called.

21. PURSUIT DRILL

Purpose: To teach and develop the proper angles of pursuit against running plays.

Procedure: Proper pursuit is also taught in (16) Inside Defensive Drill, (31) Outside Defensive Drill (Chapter 12), and in (17) Defensive Half-Line Drill where a ball carrier or offensive backs are used. The defensive linemen and linebackers take their proper stance, position, alignment, and keys, and adhere to the defensive principles of move on movement, etc. (See *Coaching Points* Drill 2.) The quarterback (or manager) takes the snap from center and either rolls out right or left, attempts to run up the middle, or drops straight back to pass. He continues to run until every lineman has tagged him or the coach blows the whistle to stop pursuit. The drill is live for the defense, except for tackling.

Coaching Points: Stress the importance of the proper angles of pursuit and sprinting to tag the ball carrier. Change to different defensive alignments.

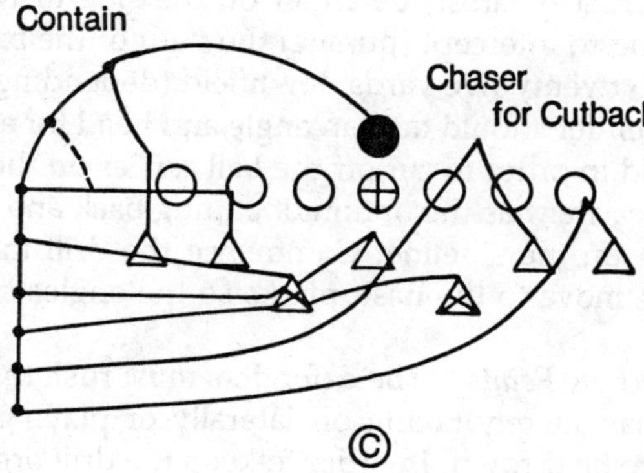

DRILL 21

22. SIDELINE PURSUIT DRILL

Purpose: To teach defenders to pursue the ball carrier at the proper angles keeping the same relative distance with each other.

Procedure: Similar to (21) Pursuit Drill, only a passer (coach) receives the snap-back from the center and either throws a quick pass or drops back

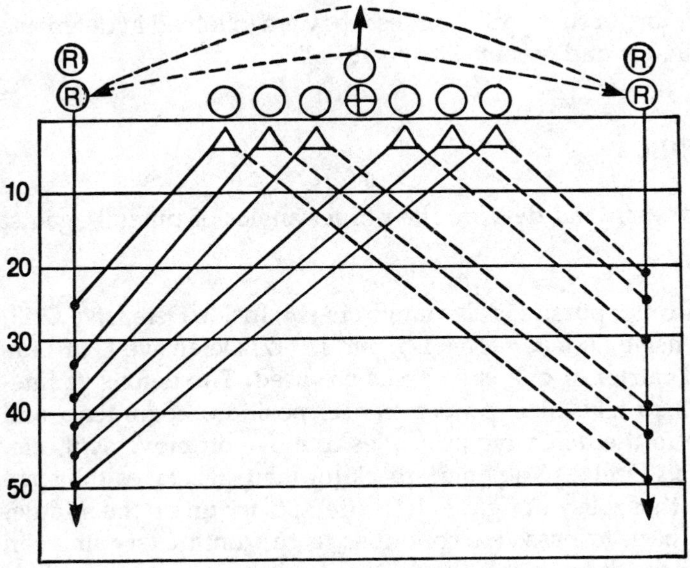

DRILL 22

and throws to a stationary receiver on the left or right sideline. The defenders must execute their proper defensive fundamentals and techniques with the first (nearest) defender on the side to which the ball is thrown attempting to intercept (pursue) the path of the ball carrier approximately twenty to twenty-five yards downfield (depending on his speed). The furthest defender should take an angle and head for approximately fifty yards downfield in order to cut off the ball carrier on the opposite (far) sideline. The ball carrier has the option of cutting back and changing direction if he is cut off on the sideline. Commence the drill in the middle of the field and then move to the hash marks so the angles of pursuit will change.

Coaching Points: The defenders must rush the passer if he fades back, rather than merely taking off laterally or playing "soft" waiting for the football to be thrown. In order to keep the drill organized and moving, the receiver must run downfield regardless of whether or not he catches the football, and the defenders must pursue until they tag him.

23. PASS RUSH–AND–PEEL DRILL

Purpose: To teach and develop rushing the passer, and then peeling back in the event of an interception or pass completion.

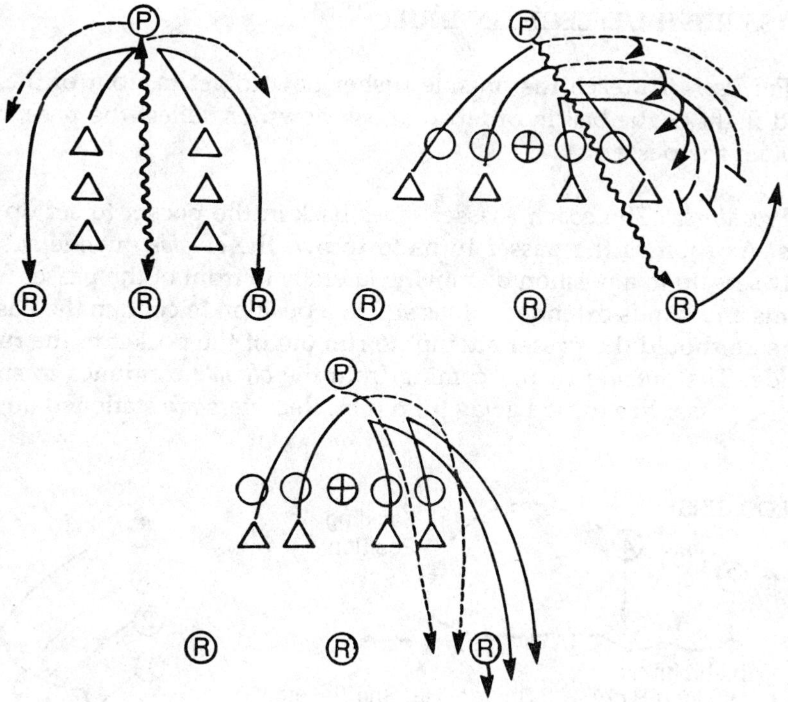

DRILL 23

Procedure: Similar to (21) Pursuit Drill, which may be used as a pass rush-and-peel drill, in that the defenders must immediately rush the passer (coach) when he raises the football signalling, ''Pass.'' The rushers extend their arms upward as they near the passer, attempting to deflect the ball or block the pass if possible. (See *Procedure,* (24) Pass Rush Deflection Drill.) The passer throws the football to one of the three stationary receivers downfield. If the receiver sounds off with the interception signal, ''Block!'' (or ''Bingo!''), the rushers peel back for the return. If he does not sound off after catching the ball, it means the pass has been completed (or is incomplete) and the rushers must sprint to tag the receiver as he jogs toward the goal line.

Coaching Points: Stress peeling back to the same side. If the football is thrown to the side opposite from where a defender rushes, he should continue through his course of peeling back. If the football is thrown down the middle, indicate whether the rusher should turn and peel (as illustrated), or continue on through to the opposite side and then peel. (See (24) Pass Rush Deflection Drill.)

24. PASS RUSH DEFLECTION DRILL

Purpose: To teach the on-side rusher how to get in front of the intended flight of the ball in order to knock down or deflect the pass, and to contain the passer.

Procedure: The coach (passer) goes back in the pocket to set up for a pass. As soon as the passer turns to throw, the *on-side* outside rusher quickly sets up in a position by moving laterally in front of the passer with his arms and hands extended. He is still in a position to contain the passer to his side should the passer attempt to run out of the pocket to the rusher's side. The outside rusher coming from the *off-side* continues to rush, since the passer has turned away from him. Receivers are stationed down-

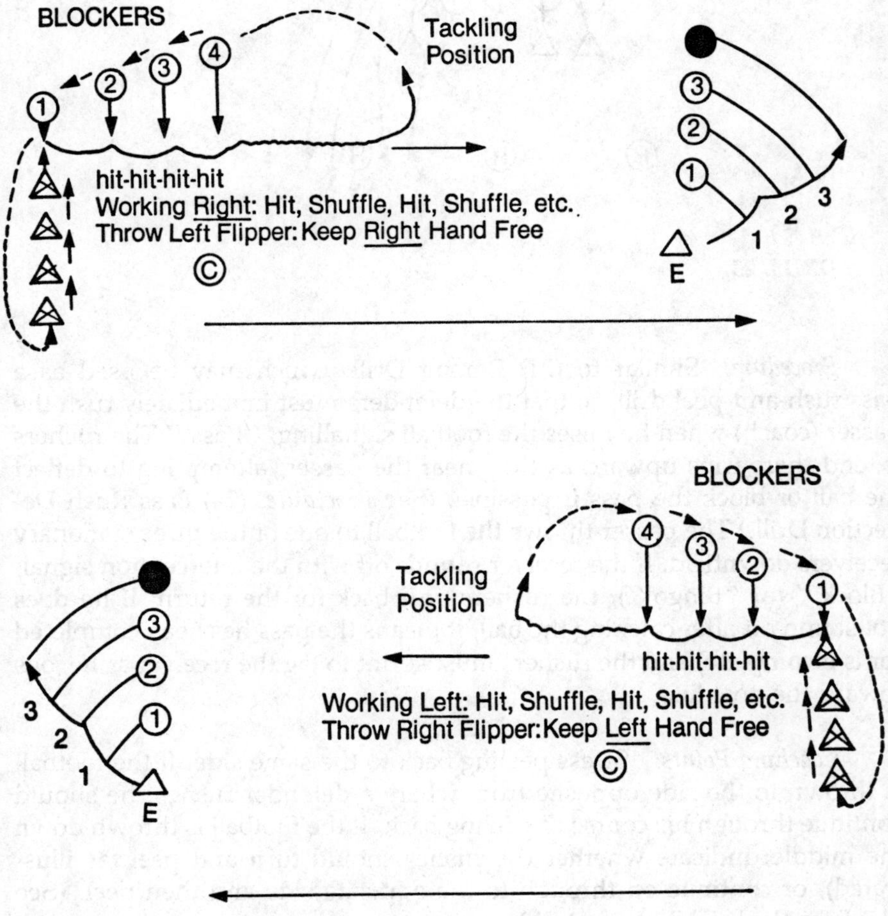

DRILL 25

field approximately ten yards. If the passer attempts to throw to the receiver on the side to which he has turned, the defender is in front of him with his hands and arms extended. The off-side rusher continues to come hard, tagging the passer before he releases the football.

Coaching Points: Stress the on-side rusher moving laterally in front of the passer when he turns and sets up to pass. The defenders still peel back if the ball is thrown and the pass is completed or intercepted.

25. LEVERAGE DRILL

Purpose: To develop warding-off and shedding blockers, maintaining leverage, pursuing and tackling the ball carrier.

Procedure: The diagrams illustrate linebackers or ends, but any interior defender may be used in the drill by using a hand shiver (or forearm block by the end) to ward-off the first blocker, moving laterally to ward-off the second until he tackles or tags the ball carrier. The drill may be half or full speed, with the blockers or coach controlling the flow. As soon as the first blocker charges, the second leaves, then the third. The defender must hit, shuffle, hit, shuffle, hit. He must maintain leverage on the ball carrier throughout the drill, not losing his contain position.

Coaching Points: The drill may be set up with the blockers in a vertical, diagonal and/or a horizontal line, depending upon the situation the defenders will face in a game. Stress hitting and shuffling, not wrestling with the blockers, and always maintaining leverage on the ball carrier.

26. THREE–ON–THREE (ONE–ON–ONE) CHALLENGE DRILL (DEFENSIVELY)

Purpose: To teach a defensive lineman to defeat a one-on-one block by charging, controlling the blocker, locating the football, pursuing and tackling the ball carrier.

DRILL 26

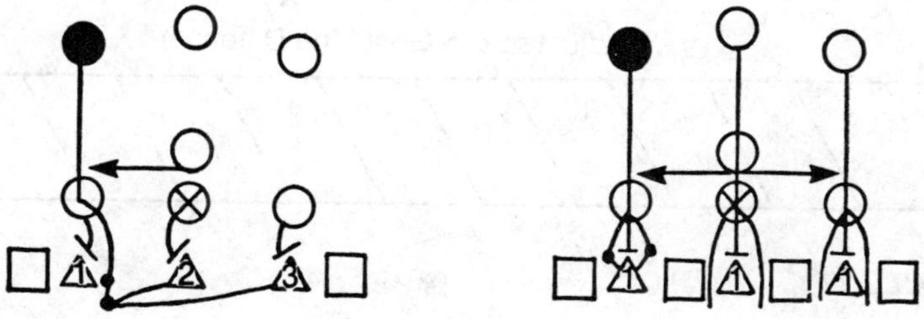

Procedure: Same as Chapter 6, (23) One-On-One Challenge or All-Purpose Drill, only the emphasis here is on defensive fundamentals and techniques. The ball carrier may try to break off of his offensive lineman's block and evade one (right illustration) or three tackles (left illustration). If three blockers and defenders are used, the inside upright dummies are removed.

Coaching Points: Stress defensive fundamentals and techniques. Use an offensive starting cadence and count, and a whistle. The drill may be used offensively for linemen and backs, or defensively. However, coach-teach (drill) only one phase at a time (here defensive line).

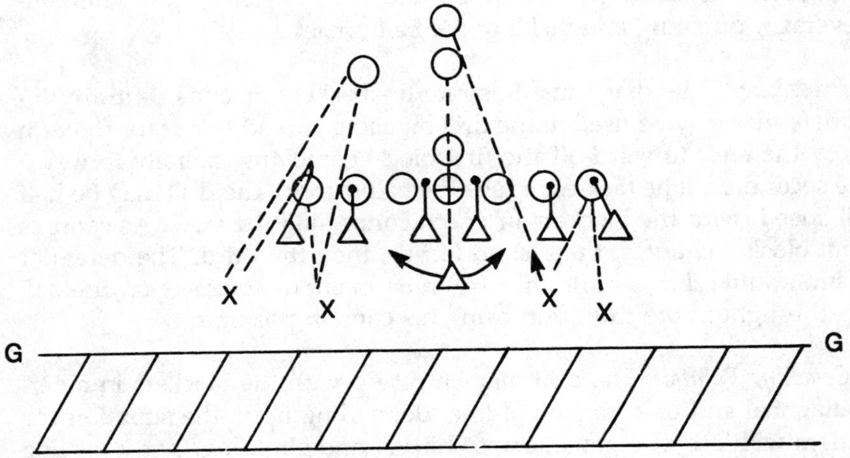

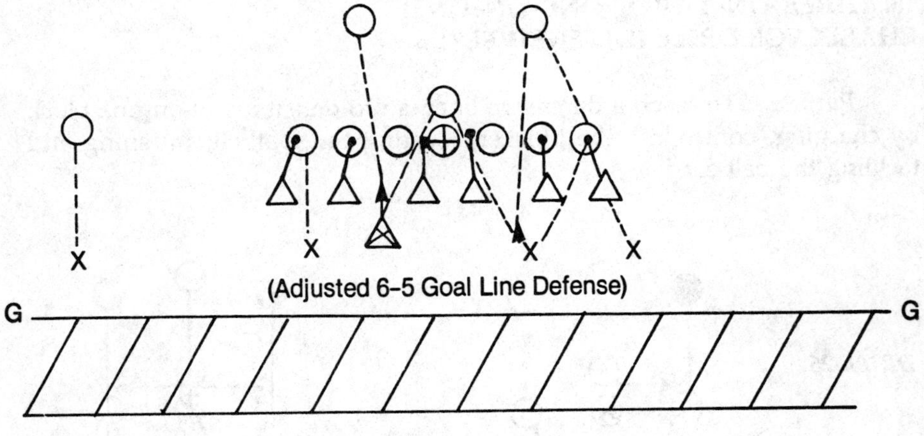

(Adjusted 6–5 Goal Line Defense)

DRILL 27

27–29. DEFENSIVE SCRIMMAGE DRILLS

27. Goal Line (Six–Five) Defense Drill

28. Slow Whistle Drill

Purpose: To test and practice goal line defense versus the opposition's favorite Scoring Zone plays and passes, (28) including pursuit and gang tackling.

Procedure: The football is moved from the middle of the field to each hash mark versus opposition's offensive tendencies. Simulate game conditions, including penalties against the defensive team. When the ball is placed in the Scoring Zone to drill against stopping the opposition's favorite scoring plays, use a slow whistle in order to check second reaction, pursuit and gang tackling (28).

Coaching Points: Stress perfection of coordinated goal line defenses, stopping the opposition and getting the football. *Call out the tactical situation on every play and stress recognition of your opposition's favorite running and pass plays.* Do not permit piling on after the whistle stops the play. (If a coach permits the use of a fast whistle all of the time, the players will become accustomed to it and will not hustle to assist with the tackle. In a game this will permit opposing backs to drive for extra yardage or even break loose for extra yardage and touchdowns.) Your opposition's Scoring Zone plays should be run off of flash cards by the demonstration team (see Chapter 2, note 1).

29. Special or Critical Situation and "Fringe" Drills

Purpose: To recognize and adjust quickly in order to defend correctly against unusual offensive sets and special or critical situations, sometimes referred to as defensing the "fringes."

Procedure: Scouting and knowledge of the opposing coach's offensive strategy, along with the tactical situation, will determine defensive alignments and most adjustments, especially after analyzing the opposition's offensive tendencies. In addition to an automatic spread, prevent and/or victory defense must be prepared and practiced under simulated game conditions, as well as defensing the field goal lineup, and the fourth down play in a short yardage situation, especially near the 50-yard line, or when the opposition must retain possession of the football in order to win the game. In order to remove the element of surprise and to adjust quickly to the situation, the defensive team should have some practice versus the situations described in Chapter 14, (14) Touchdown Sequence or Clutch Offense Drill; (15) Stop (Kill)-the-Clock Drill; (16) Delay Offense or Run-Out-the-Clock Drill; (17) Racehorse or Go-Go-Go Offense Drill. Unusual offensive sets, such as the 5-1, "swinging gate," spreads, and the "special situation" offense mentioned above are successful as the result of confusion, surprise and the failure to recognize, adjust and defend against them properly. Set up "specials" and "fringes" on flash cards so the demonstration team can run them quickly (see note 1, Chapter 2). The drills may be live or dummy.

Coaching Points: Review and practice situations, including calling out the defensive alignments and adjustments at the line of scrimmage instead of huddling versus (14) Clutch Offense and (17) Racehorse Offense, since the offensive team is calling the play at the line without benefit of a huddle first. Versus (15) Kill-the-Clock, defenders should try to force the opposition to waste a down or call a time-out and not permit the ball carrier to run out of bounds in order to stop the clock. Defenders should unpile slowly in order to consume time. Versus (16) Delay Offense, the defensive team may have to sustain a penalty in order to stop the clock. (Handling the blocked and partially blocked punt and the on-side or short kick on the kick-off are also on the "critical situations" checklist, but will not be treated separately here.)

30–33. SEVEN–MAN SLED DRILLS (PROGRESSIVE)

30. Forearm or Hand Shiver Drill

31. Forearm Lift or Flipper Drill

32. Roll-Out or Spin-Out Drill

Purpose: To develop the major defensive techniques of the hand shiver, flipper, spin-out, and lateral movement, balance and reaction.

Procedure: From a good defensive football position in a semi-upright stance, start chugging the feet and move into the first pad on the seven-man sled using (30) the hand shiver. The tail should be down, the head up, elbows and wrists locked, hit on the rise, then shuffle laterally down the line shivering every pad. Repeat coming back from the opposite direction. The flipper (31) is employed next moving to the right; then repeat coming back to the left. The roll-out or spin-out (32) is the third progression and the defender should hit, spin, recover, repeat on every other pad. Moving to the right, he hits the machine with his right shoulder, then

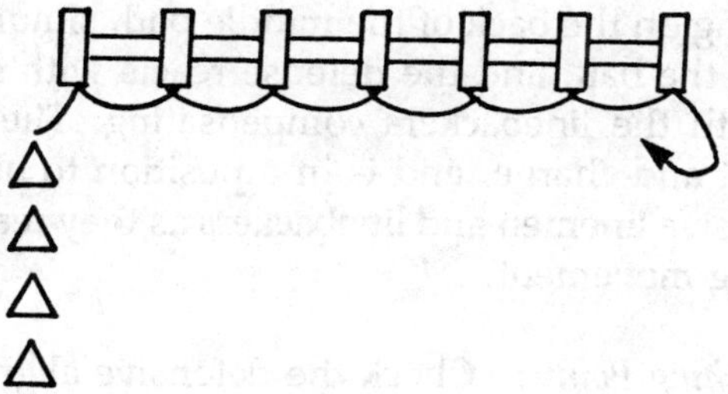

DRILL 30

spins to his right. Coming from the left side, he hits with his left shoulder, whirls to his left, and hits every other pad.

Coaching Points: Stress quickness, and the proper execution of the defensive techniques. On the spin-out techniques indicate whether he is to go to the ground when he arcs back on the quick spin, simulating being knocked down and getting up for a second effort, or whether he should collapse his near knee, drop step with his far foot, take a short arc, regain his balance, and hit every other pad.

33. Team Reaction Drill

Purpose: To drill the forcing unit from even and odd alignments to react to movement or the snap of the ball, and to coordinate individual and team stunts.

Procedure: Similar to (35) Team Starts or Take-Off Drill, Chapter 6, only here the emphasis is on the defensive team getting off with the ball or on offensive movement. The coach stands on the seven-man sled opposite the back of the middle pad facing the defensive players who have set up in an odd or even alignment facing the coach. The coach shakes the

DRILL 33

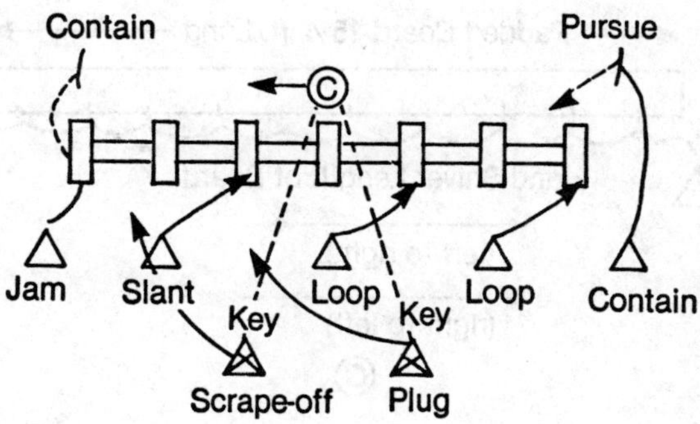

(ex) "52 Right" (Stunt)

steel spring on the back of the middle pad, simulating the offensive center snapping the ball, and the defense reacts with stunts, slants, loops, and veers, with the linebackers compensating. The coach first calls out the alignment and charge, and is in a position to observe the movements of the defensive linemen and linebackers as they react to his shaking the sled, simulating movement.

Coaching Points: Check the defensive alignments and stunts. Stress quickness, and getting off with the ball or on offensive movement.

34. DEFENSIVE BUCKER BOARD DRILL

Purpose: To develop the techniques of hand shivering, lateral movement, balance and reaction.

Procedure: Similar to (30) Forearm or Hand Shiver Drill on the seven-man sled, only this drill is performed on a large bucker (coil springs) with a padded 15½ foot board 10 inches wide about 30 inches off the ground. The linemen execute a hand shiver technique on the board from one end to the other (left to right), spin-off at the end and hit the ground with a seat roll as in Drill 32. They come up with a forearm lift or a flipper ward-off to the player in front facing them, and then turn to meet the player coming from behind. The lineman next moves to the end of the line to get ready to shiver going in the opposite direction (right to left).

Coaching Points: Stress quickness, including getting up quickly from the ground.

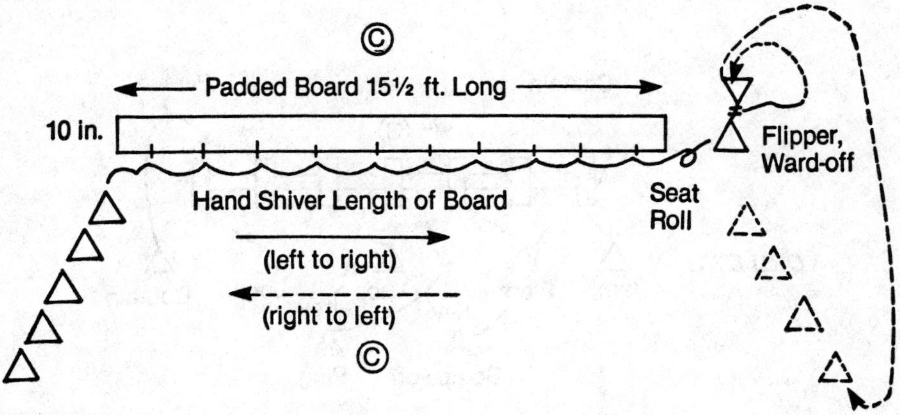

DRILL 34

35. GAP CHARGE–BAG DRILL

Purpose: To teach and develop the gap charge technique, getting penetration.

Procedure: Similar to (8) Explosion or One-Versus-Two Drills, only large dummies are held approximately two feet apart and the defender tries to penetrate the gap as the dummies are slammed together. The coach gets down on his knee behind the dummies facing the defensive player who is down in a 3–4 point stance facing the coach. The coach moves his hand or the football, simulating offensive players charging or the snap-back exchange. The defensive player uncoils, popping forward, turning his shoulders and body as he drives hard and low through the seam and scrambles through to get to the coach. The latter gives a hand signal for a second reaction, simulating the direction of pursuit.

Coaching Points: Stress quickness, exploding forward, and scrambling to get the feet up under the body. On a goal line and short yardage charge, the defender should angle slightly inward and aim for a spot one yard deep in the offensive backfield. As he makes penetration he should fight upward from his low penetrating position and charge.

36. DEFENSIVE LINE DRILLS (ADDITIONAL)

Additional drills for teaching-coaching defensive line kicking game fundamentals and techniques are included in Chapter 16. Additional tackling drills are in Chapter 13.

11

Linebacking Drills

The real heart of any defense is good linebacking. There never has been a strong defensive team with incapable linebackers. A team must have good linebacking in order to have a strong defense. A linebacker who is not sound fundamentally will make any kind of defensive line look weak, and outstanding linebacking can strengthen a mediocre line. In building a defensive unit, therefore, prime consideration must be given to the selection of good athletes for the linebacking positions. After that it becomes a matter of teaching-coaching.

The typical linebacker should be a combination of a defensive back and lineman, particularly in collegiate and professional football where the forward pass is prominent in the modern-day game. Since under normal conditions a linebacker is part of the forcing defense, he must be able to handle the running play to his area. If the play does not hit in his immediate area, then he must keep himself free and maintain proper leverage on the ball carrier.

A linebacker does not have to possess great speed, but he should have first-step quickness. Assuming he is keying and not gaming or stunting, he must react and move quickly after reading his key, without first false-stepping. When involved in defensive stunts, a linebacker must move and react quickly. On practically every offensive play someone will try to block the linebacker and he must be able to shed or ward-off blockers and react quickly to the football.

Pass defenders must be able to react quickly and have good mobility. With more emphasis on the passing game in present-day football, additional attention must be given to the linebacker's ability to defend against the forward pass. The linebacker is an integral part of pass defense whether dropping back to cover a zone or playing man-for-man coverage, "dogging" in rushing the passer, or holding up an intended receiver. Also, the linebacking corps must be good tacklers. Slow-footed linebackers will not only encounter difficulty versus your opposition's passing attack, but will have similar problems getting to the point-of-attack away from their defensive alignment to make the tackle versus your opposition's running game. It is imperative to select "good" athletes for your linebackers.

The drills explained below, in addition to those listed at the conclusion of this chapter that are discussed elsewhere, should prove more than adequate for training the linebacker in the individual skills and techniques his position demands.

1. LATERAL RUN BAG DRILL

Purpose: To teach and develop agility, body balance and foot quickness in stepping over and around simulated supine players in pursuing the football.

Procedure: Five or more blocking dummies are laid side by side on the ground one yard apart. Moving laterally left to right or vice versa, and then coming back in the opposite direction, with high knee action, each player shuffles laterally over the bags. Players should lead or set step all the way or cross step only with the off foot after lead stepping each time with the on-side foot, keeping the shoulders square with the line of scrimmage and the coach who is facing the players out in front of the bags. Each player's head should be up, his eyes focused on the coach, with his hands and arms extended forward in a ward-off position or to assist him in getting over the dummies (supine bodies).

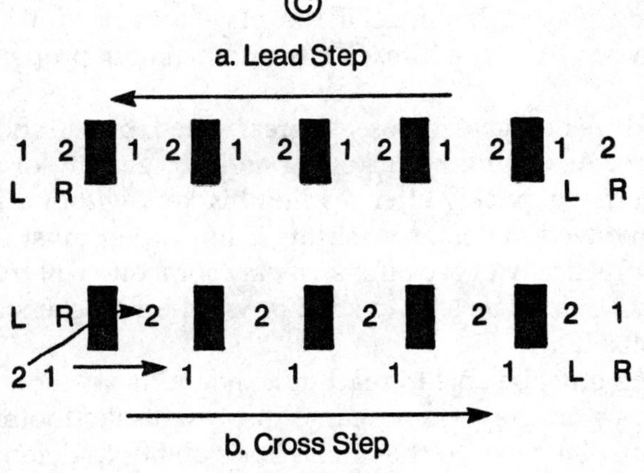

DRILL 1

Coaching Points: Commence the drill slowly permitting the players to watch their feet initially in order to emphasize the correct method of lead or set stepping all the way where the feet are *not* crossed, and then cross stepping where only the lead (back) foot goes into the hole and the off (opposite) foot crosses over all the way through. The latter method is quicker than lead stepping all the way, although a player may be more likely to trip over a supine body when cross stepping. The players should move rapidly one after another, and if a player trips and falls to the ground those following should *not* stop but should step around or over him and continue to pursue to the end of the line. The coach should indicate which method the players are to utilize, i.e., lead step all the way or lead-cross-over, and then speed up the drill encouraging the players to perform the drill correctly as rapidly as possible.

2. BACKWARD AND FORWARD ZIG-ZAG BAG DRILL

Purpose: To teach and develop agility, body balance and foot quickness in stepping around (instead of over) a simulated supine player.

Procedure: Same as (1) Lateral Run Bag Drill, only the line of players moves backward and forward in and out, around and between the dummies on the ground, not stepping over them laterally.

Coaching Points: The line of players should always be facing the coach as they move backward and forward around and between the dummies as quickly as possible.

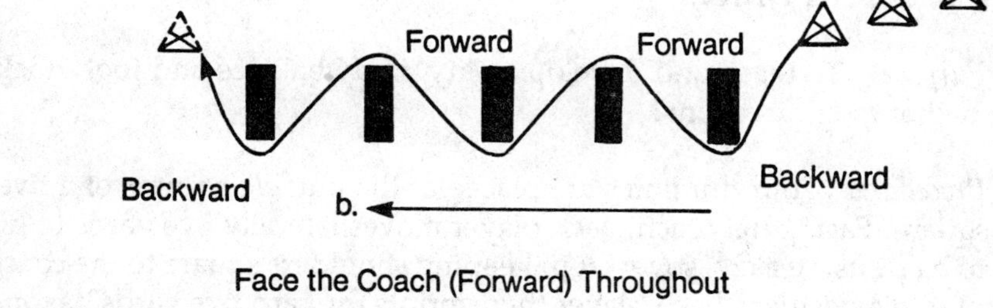

DRILL 2

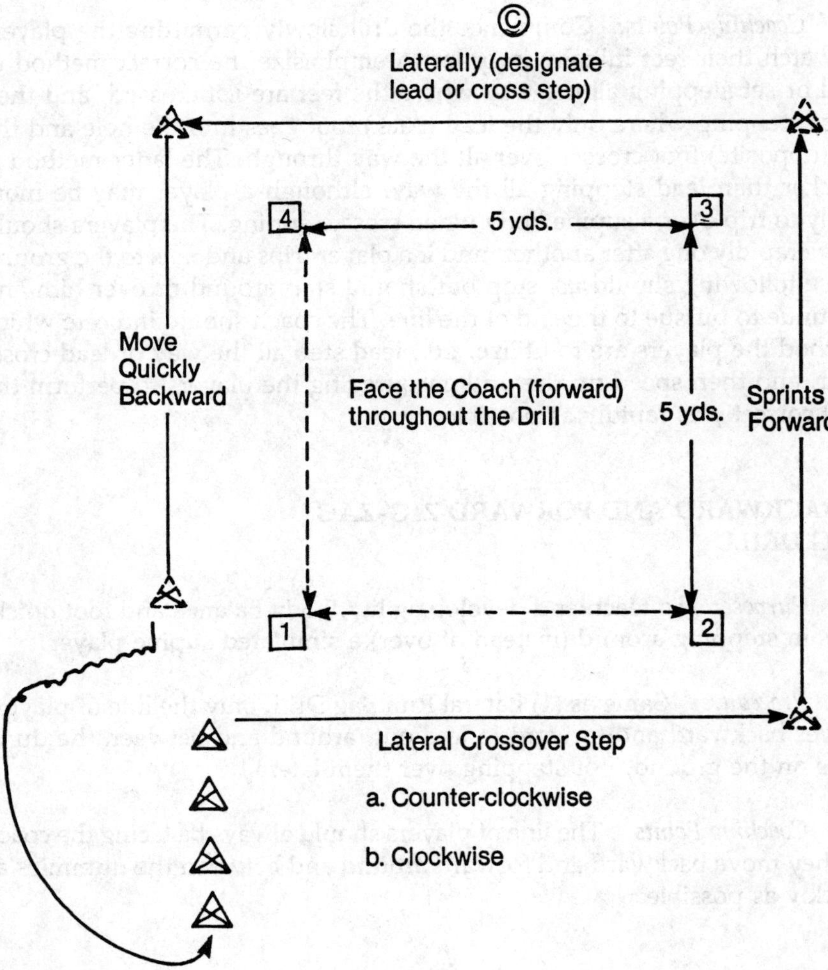

DRILL 3

3. SQUARE BAG DRILL

Purpose: To teach and develop agility, body balance and foot quickness in changing directions.

Procedure: Four dummies are placed at the outside corners of a five-yard square. Facing his coach, each player moves laterally five yards to his right to bag 2 using a crossover step, keeping shoulders square to the coach in front of his position. Each player then sprints forward five yards beyond bag 3, moves laterally to his left to beyond bag 4, and backs up as quickly as possible beyond bag 1. Reverse the procedure moving clockwise: from bag 1 each player sprints forward to 4, moves laterally to 3, backward to 2, and moves left laterally returning to his starting position at bag 1.

Coaching Points: Stress quickness, no false-stepping, breaking at right angles instead of arcing or bowing (same as (19) Lateral Wave Drill, Chapter 5).

4. COMBO ZIG–ZAG AND LATERAL RUN BAG DRILL

Purpose: A combination of Drills (1) and (2), for developing agility, body balance and foot quickness.

Procedure: Commence and finish the drill the same as (2) Backward and Forward Zig-Zag, with (1) Lateral Run positioned in between those dummies stationed to the outside.

Coaching Points: Same as those in (2) and (1) above. Conduct the drill both to the right and to the left.

DRILL 4

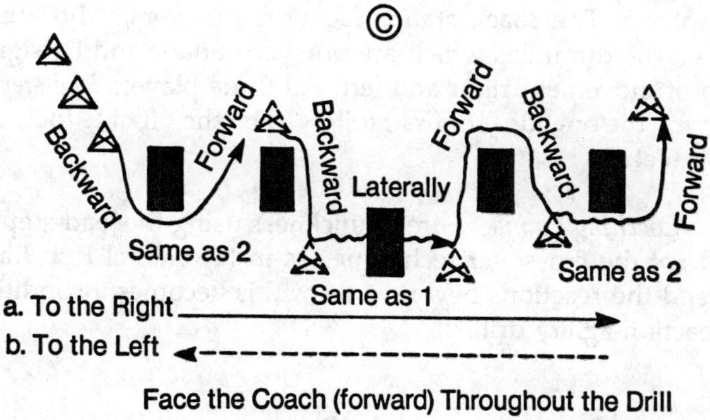

5. COMBO LATERAL OVER AND AROUND RUN BAG DRILL

Purpose: A combination of Drills (1) and the lateral movement in (3), for developing agility, body balance and foot quickness.

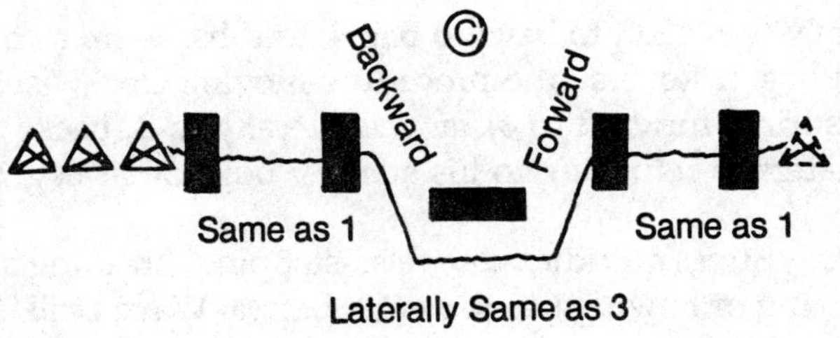

DRILL 5

Procedure: Commence and finish the drill the same as (1) Lateral Run Bag Drill, with (3) moving laterally around the bags in between those stationed in outside positions.

Coaching Points: Same as those in Drills 1 and 3 above.

6. BAG WAVE DRILL

Purpose: To teach and develop agility, body balance and foot quickness.

Procedure: Using six large dummies lying lengthwise on the ground with open one yard spaces to each side of the three players to minimize the danger of ankle and foot injuries from teammates stepping on each other's ankles and feet, this drill is conducted like (19) Lateral Wave Drill, Chapter 5. The coach stands facing the players, who are positioned between the dummies which are one yard apart, and he signals their direction of movement right and left. All three players *lead step* over the bags, moving the on-side foot first, followed by the off-side foot, and *not* crossing their feet.

Coaching Points: Stress quickness using the lead-stepover technique, and *not* the crossover technique, as in (1) Lateral Run Bag Drill. Do not extend the reactions beyond five or this becomes a conditioner instead of a reaction-agility drill.

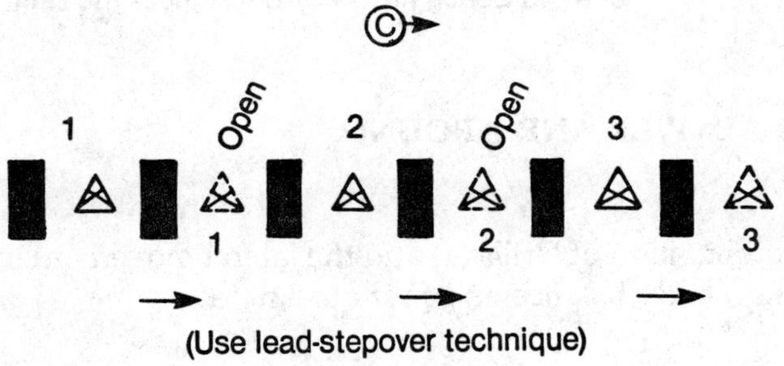

DRILL 6

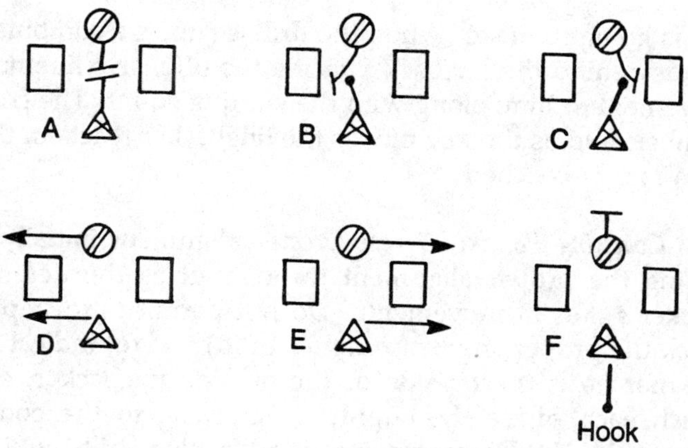

DRILL 7

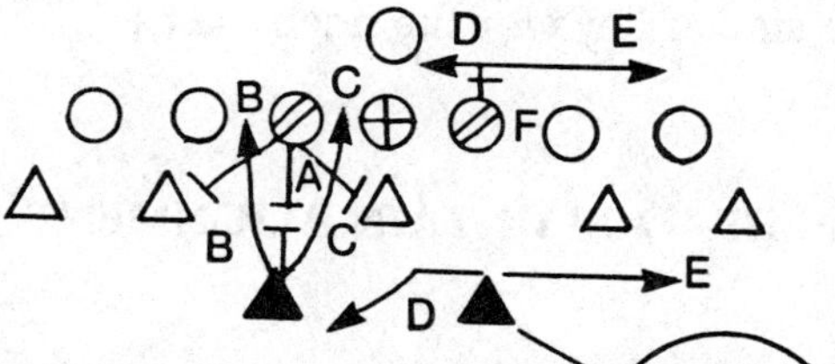

Linebacker Keys through Guard to Near Back

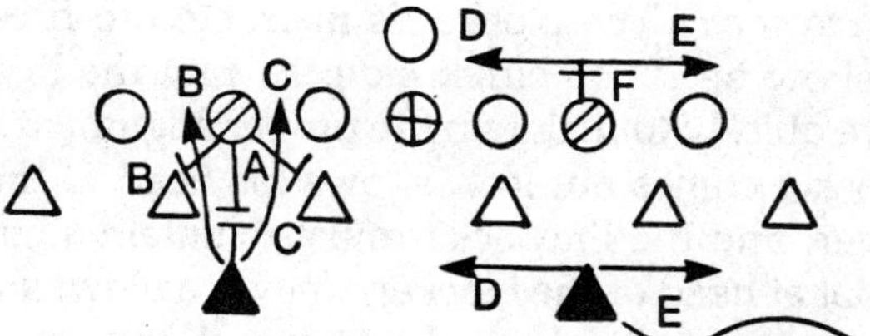

Linebacker Keys through Tackle to Near Back

7. KEY–REACTION DRILLS (SEPARATELY; THEN COMBINED, ONE DRILL)

Purpose: To teach the proper alignment, keys and reaction to (a) key firing-out straight; (b) key blocking to his right; (c) key blocking to his left; (d) key pulling to his right; (e) key pulling to his left; and (f) key setting up for drop-back pass blocking.

Procedure: Each segment of the drill is done separately and after the linebacker becomes proficient, then all of the reactions are combined into one drill so the linebacker does not know in advance the movement his key is going to make. When the drill is run as a combined drill, the coach stands behind the linebacker facing the offensive lineman and flashes his movement to him, along with the starting count. The coach calls the snap number, and as the key moves the linebacker reacts in the manner he has been taught-coached.

Coaching Points: Stress proper alignment initially, and then maintaining the proper alignment throughout as the defender reacts to the blocker's (key's) movements. Do not permit false-stepping, and always check the proper angle of pursuit. In (d) and (e) indicate to the linebacker whether he is the on-side or the off-side linebacker, and practice both. Coach each phase thoroughly progressing to the combined drill. (See Chapter 10, (11) Defensive Reaction Machine Drills, which may be used to simulate similar keys for the linebacker.)

8. SHOW HEAD–MAINTAIN ALIGNMENT DRILL

Purpose: To teach and develop maintaining proper alignment to (a) key firing-out straight with the blocker's head on either side, Drill 11.

Procedure: The blocker is instructed to fire-out (walk through first) and "show head" to either side. At first the linebacker is taught merely to move quickly to maintain the proper alignment. When the drill is "live," the blocker comes out low, shows his head to the right or left side of the defender, and the linebacker must maintain alignment, jab step with the near foot at head of the blocker, deliver a blow, shed the blocker, and fight pressure. Left and right linebackers each line up opposite a blocker, taking proper lateral and vertical alignment.

Coaching Points: A common error is for the linebacker to jab step forward when the blocker is stepping for position right or left on him. He must move the proper foot first to maintain alignment and leverage. The linebacker should not step back when the blocker fires-out or comes to the side of his position.

9–11. PROGRESSIVE HITTING DRILLS

9. Hit-Hit-Hit Drill

Purpose: To teach and develop delivering a blow (block protection) to destroy the offensive man's block.

DRILL 9

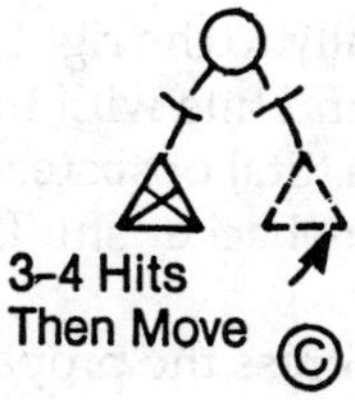

Procedure: Same as (7) Key-Reaction Drill, (a). The linebacker takes his proper alignment laterally, with both players in the "ready" position. The blocker steps toward the linebacker, who jab steps and throws a flipper and delivers a controlled forearm lift, simulating the aggressive technique in delivering a blow in order to nullify the block. The blocker steps back and comes forward again, and the linebacker recoils and uncoils for a total of three times. Both men sort of "bounce" up and back, with the linebacker practicing delivering a controlled blow to the chest of the blocker. The (left) linebacker moves to a position opposite the blocker's other shoulder and repeats the drill three times, simulating the block is coming from outside-in, whereas the initial block was from inside-out. He should not reverse the position of his feet if he is using a staggered stance, but he must deliver a blow (block protection) with the same shoulder and foot forward, especially when the blocker is coming from outside-in or blocking down on him.

Coaching Points: Stress the proper fundamentals and techniques of delivering a blow in order to destroy the offensive lineman's block. Control the drill so that the emphasis is on foot quickness and arm-leg synchronization.

10. Hit-Shuffle-Hit Drill

Purpose: To teach and develop delivering a blow in order to destroy (nullify) the offensive player's block.

Procedure: Same as (7) Key-Reaction Drill (a), and (9) Hit-Hit-Hit Drill. The linebacker is in "ready" position and he "hits" with his right

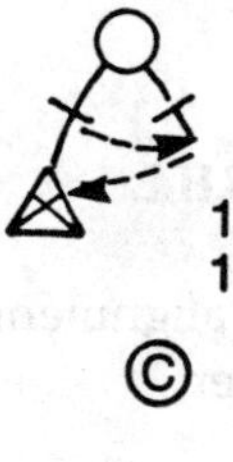

DRILL 10

shoulder, shuffles laterally to the right and hits with his left shoulder, shuffles laterally to the left and hits with his right shoulder. Repeat three times with each shoulder for a total of six reactions. The players sort of "bounce" up and back with the linebacker shuffling laterally back and forth quickly.

Coaching Points: Stress the proper fundamentals of delivering a blow, and the proper arm-leg synchronization. If false-stepping occurs, correct this error.

11. Ricochet and Triangle Drills

Purpose: To teach and develop delivering a blow, and arm-leg synchronization.

Procedure: The offensive men are in a semi-upright position twelve to eighteen inches apart and the linebacker is in a "ready" position about two feet from the blockers. The one blocker (right) steps toward the linebacker, who steps and delivers a blow to the blocker with the same shoulder and foot forward, and they step back; then the linebacker steps toward the left blocker with proper shoulder and foot forward, who has stepped forward, and they step back. The same procedure is repeated six times. Next the coach stands behind the linebacker and indicates which of the two offensive players is to stay forward to block the defender. The linebacker starts from a "ready" position, jab steps to meet the designated blocker with his proper shoulder and foot, and returns to his original position ready to meet *either* blocker again. Repeat this segment of the drill six times.

Coaching Points: Stress the proper arm-leg synchronization. The linebacker must recoil each time after delivering a blow. Follow up with (9) Around-the-Circle Hitting Drill, Chapter 10.

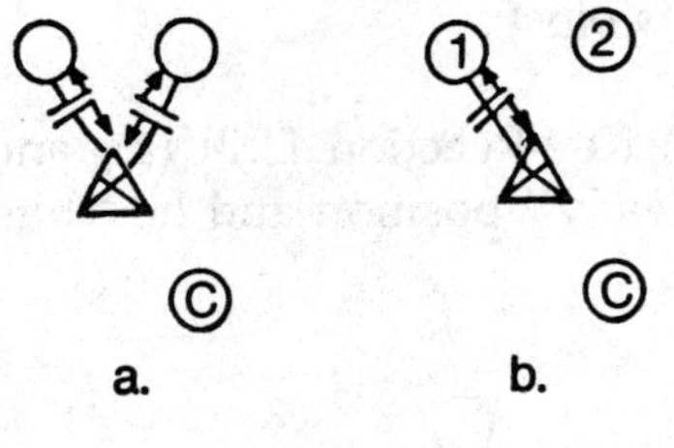

DRILL 11

12. KEY–REACT–TACKLE DRILL

Purpose: To teach proper alignment, keys, "reading" the football and reacting to it and the ball carrier.

DRILL 12

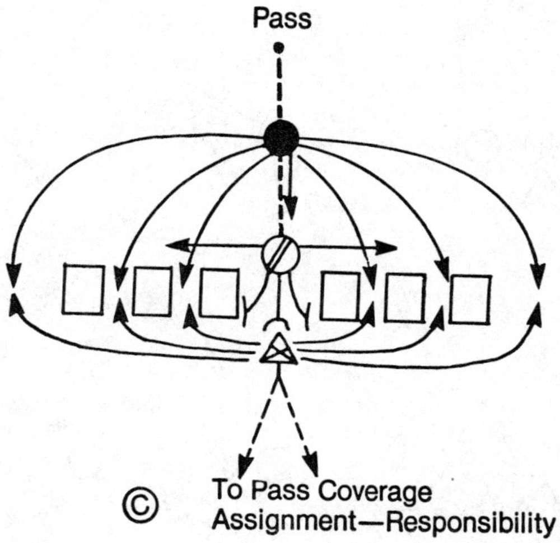

Procedure: Same as (7) Key-Reaction Drills (a–f), only a ball carrier is added so the linebacker can pursue and tackle him. The linebacker assumes a "ready" position in the proper alignment. The coach is facing the blocker and the ball carrier but is behind the linebacker. The coach indicates the starting count, the movement of the offensive blocker, and the hole where the ball carrier should hit. The linebacker must react as previously indicated in (7) Key-Reaction Drills.

Coaching Points: Stress the proper alignment, key-reaction, and the correct angle of pursuit and tackling.

13. WHAM OR DIVIDE DRILL

Purpose: To teach the proper alignment and reaction when the key blocks inward or false keys.

Procedure: Same as (7) Key-Reaction Drills (b and c) (left linebacker), only the center, the interior linemen and several offensive backs are added for this drill. Appropriate defensive interior linemen are added, too. The linebacker must jab step in the direction of his key, then bring up his back foot and the same forearm to protect himself from the outside-in block of the tackle (d), or the offensive back(s) (a and c); then he must bring up the inside foot and forearm to be ready for the trap (b) if the block does not come from the outside. The linebacker should quickly play (expect) the inside trap first, and then react quickly in order to protect himself from the outside-in block.

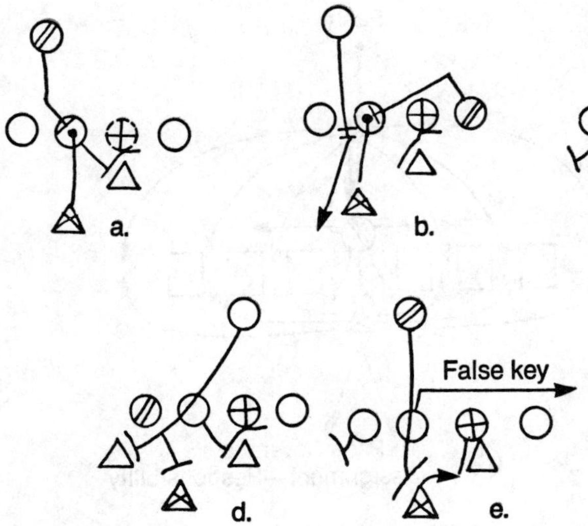

DRILL 13

Coaching Points: Add a quarterback and occasionally give the ball to the halfback on a straight dive play with the offensive blocker firing-out in a one-on-one situation, as in Drill (7), reaction (a). The linebacker must shed the blocker and make the tackle. Stress reaction to outside-in blocking in particular (d), and the correct method of playing the power or isolation block (c), Drill 13.

14. BULL–IN–THE–RING SHED DRILL

Purpose: To develop arm and leg coordination, rapid footwork, body balance, and to shed a blocker.

Procedure: The "bull" (linebacker) is in the center of the circle, pumping his arms and legs, and moving in a counter-clockwise direction slowly. The "bull" may point at the blocker whom he wants to attack him. The coach may indicate the blocker. Or the blocker may come from the rim on his own and try to drive the linebacker out of the circle with a running shoulder block. The defender meets the blockers, one at a time, synchronizing the proper arm-leg and delivering a blow to the blocker with force. He should shed the blocker, using the properly taught-coached techniques, and continue to turn to meet other blockers (one at a time). Four or five repetitions will be sufficient before replacing the linebacker in the middle.

Coaching Points: If either the "bull" or the coach indicates the blocker, the blocker to either side of the one indicated may charge in order

DRILL 14

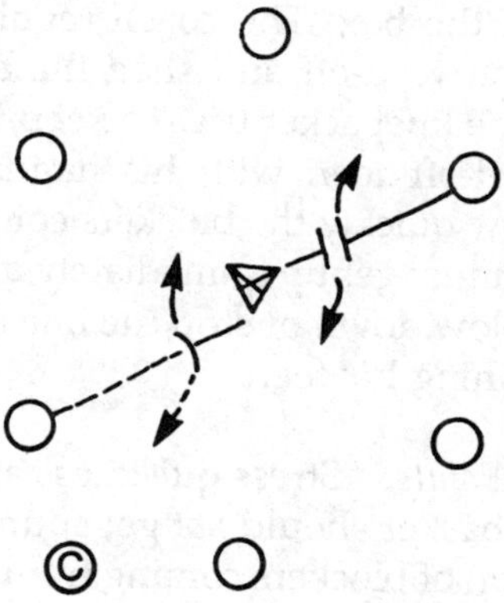

to get a better reaction. (Explain which method will be utilized before the drill commences.) If the blocker comes on his own, the player who is going to block should yell "Here!" before charging the "bull." Stress quickness, proper arm-leg action, and shedding the blocker immediately. Do not wrestle with the blocker. Alternate forearm-shoulder lifts so the linebacker cannot favor his strength and protect his weakness. *No clipping from behind.* Follow up with (9) Around-the-Circle Hitting Drill, Chapter 10.

15. KNIGHT–THE–LINEBACKER DRILL

Purpose: To develop arm and leg coordination, and to shed blockers.

Procedure: Upright dummies are set up outside of a three-yard square. The linebacker assumes a "ready" position a foot inside of the front line of his box. The blockers line up in a column a yard behind the

DRILL 15

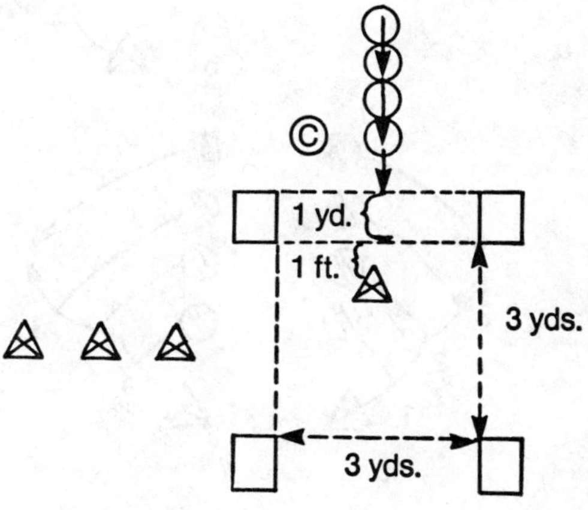

line outside of the box. The coach regulates the flow of blockers so the linebacker must ward-off and shed the blockers just as fast as the coach sends them. The linebacker tries to keep from being driven out of the box, and must ward-off men with his hands, knees, elbows, forearms, depending on how quickly the blockers come at him. If he is knocked down, the linebacker must get up immediately and keep fighting to shed on-coming blockers. Slow down or stop the line of blockers if the linebacker reacts slowly in regaining his feet.

Coaching Points: Stress quickness and meeting the blockers from the front. The linebacker should *not* get spun around and turn his back on the flow or direction of blockers coming from the front of the box. The blockers should *not* clip from behind if the linebacker gets turned around. When the blocker gets even or beyond the linebacker, he should continue on to the opposite side of the box. Do not permit piling on. Stop the flow of blockers if the linebacker is knocked off his feet. Caution the blockers *not* to block the defender if he is already down, i.e., *no* piling on.

16. WARD–OFF LEVERAGE OR OUTSIDE SHED DRILL

Purpose: To develop shedding blockers, pursuit and tackling.

Procedure: The drill is either one-half or full speed, with the blockers regulating their flow. As soon as No. 1 blocks, No. 2 leaves, then No. 3. The linebacker must deliver a blow, ward-off, shed and make the tackle.

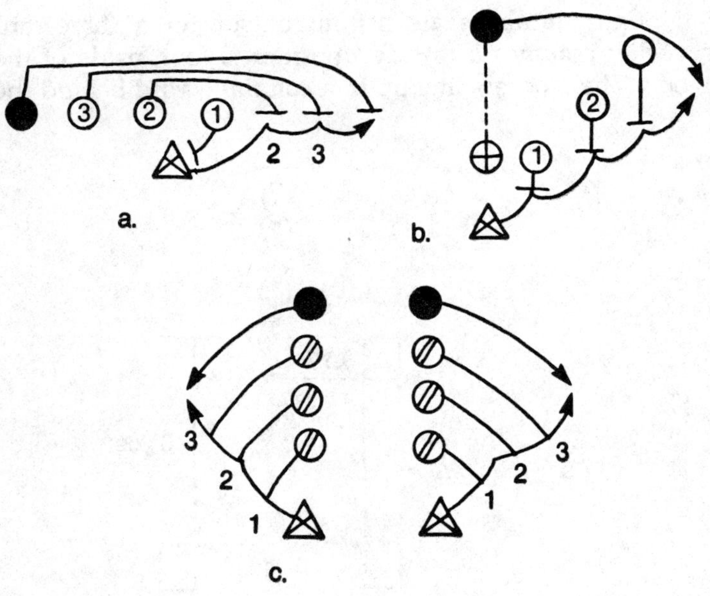

DRILL 16

Restrict the area in which the ball carrier can run laterally, favoring the linebacker. The latter has more opportunity to make the tackle than if blockers must pull and block because the ball carrier has further to run to evade him, and the drill is not as fast (a). If the ball carrier is lined up four yards opposite the linebacker, he can get outside quicker. The linebacker must react more quickly in (b) and (c) drills.

Coaching Points: Stess taking an inside-out pursuit angle, maintaining proper leverage throughout. Drill may be set up with blockers in a vertical, horizontal or diagonal line. (See Chapter 13, (18) Ward-Off Leverage Tackling Drills, and Chapter 10, (25) Leverage Drill.) Stress hit, shuffle, hit, shuffle, hit, shuffle, not wrestling with the blockers in pursuing and maintaining leverage on the ball carrier.

17. INSIDE SHED DRILL

Purpose: To develop reaction to a blocker firing-out straight one-on-one, delivering a blow, shedding the blocker, and tackling the ball carrier.

Procedure: Same as (7) Key-Reaction Drill (a), only a ball carrier is added. On the starting count the blocker attacks the linebacker blocking one-on-one. The ball carrier is at a depth of four yards, and approaches the rear of his blocker slowly, then breaks quickly. The linebacker must deliver a blow to the blocker nullifying his block, shed him, and make the tackle. A second linebacker may be added if the coach wishes to use this as a tackling drill, too. (Or this may be used as a tackling drill by positioning a defensive lineman nose-on the blocker on the line, with or without the linebacker stacked behind him.)

Coaching Points: If one-on-one, have the linebacker in his proper alignment (nose-on-ear) and not nose-on-nose (as illustrated). Stress the

DRILL 17

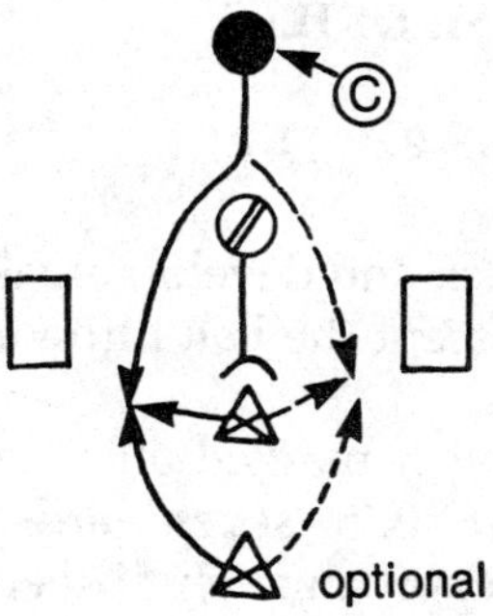

proper fundamentals of maintaining position, jab step and forearm lift, shedding, and tackling.

18. EYE–OPENER OR OUTSIDE SHED DRILL

Purpose: To teach maintaining proper leverage on the ball carrier and the football, shedding the blocker, and making the tackle.

Procedure: Upright dummies are placed on a straight line, allowing five feet between each dummy. The linebacker is in a "ready" position at one end of the dummies, across from a blocker and a ball carrier who is three yards behind his blocker. The blocker turns and informs the ball carrier which hole he is going to lead him through, and the ball carrier must go into the hole. The coach flips the football to the ball carrier, who follows his blocker into the designated hole. The linebacker meets the blocker in the hole, sheds him, and makes the tackle from an inside-out position.

Coaching Points: The blocker may run directly into the hole, or he may fake once and go through the next hole. Work left and right. Stress proper leverage, shedding the blocker, and tackling fundamentals. Chapter 13 (7) Lateral Fill Tackling Drill, without a blocker leading the ball carrier, should precede this particular drill so the teaching-coaching is progressive.

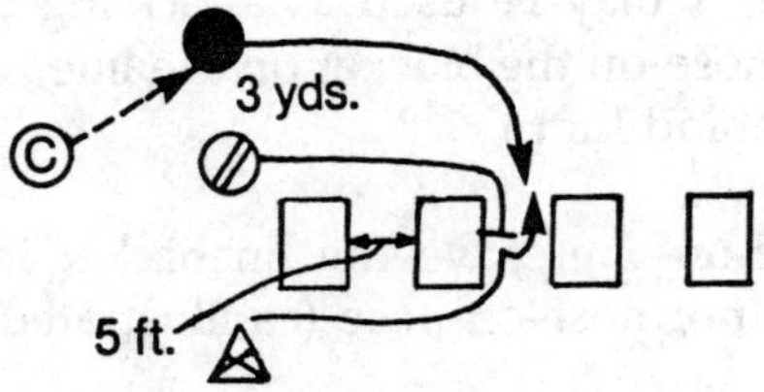

DRILL 18

19–28. PASS DEFENSE DRILLS

19. Going-for-the-Ball Drill

Purpose: To teach and develop breaking at the proper angle (90°) on a straight line to intercept the ball thrown to either side of the defender.

Procedure: Using a marked-off area the linebacker sets up at ten yards, and the passer six to seven yards, from the line of scrimmage so there is a distance of approximately sixteen yards between the two players.

DRILL 19

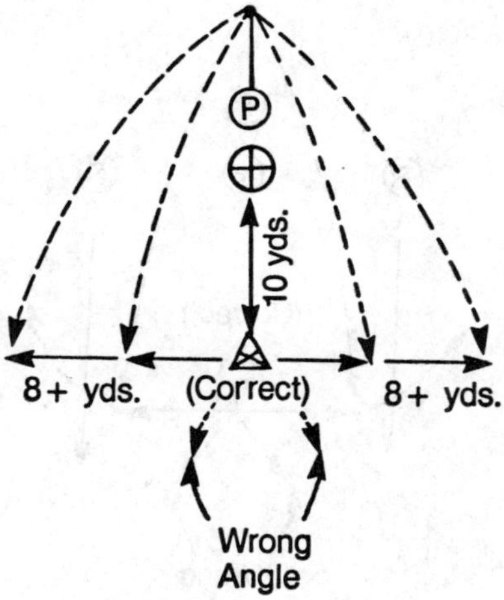

The passer raises the football, indicating pass, and the linebacker yells, "Pass!" The passer throws the ball to the right or left of the linebacker, who must break at a 90° angle for the football in order to reach the interception point. On catching the football, the linebacker sounds off with the interception signal, "Block!" "Bingo!" or some other designated word.

Coaching Points: In *all* drills the defender yells "Pass!" as soon as a pass is indicated, and the appropriate interception signal when he or a teammate catches the football. Build the confidence of the linebacker by first throwing the football directly to his right and left, and work outward until the linebacker can react quickly, going on a straight line, and intercepting the pass thrown approximately eight yards or more on either side of his initial position. Check his feet so he does not run in an arc for the interception. Emphasize catching the football at its height, not when it is descending, and catching with the fingertips.

20. Back-Up and Going-for-the-Ball Drill

Purpose: To teach and develop breaking at the proper angle on a straight line in order to intercept the football thrown to either side of the defender.

Procedure: Same set up as (19) Going-for-the-Ball Drill, only the passer and the linebacker are approximately ten yards apart, and two receivers are added, who are five yards apart (working outward until they are fifteen yards apart). The passer takes two short steps backward and raises the football. The linebacker drop-steps with his outside foot first, and then crosses over with his inside foot and squares off so he is facing the passer when the latter raises his arm to pass the football. From his

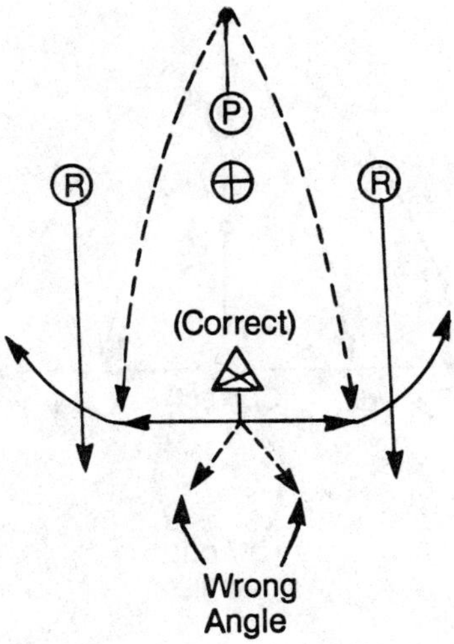

DRILL 20

"ready" position the linebacker breaks immediately to intercept the pass when it is thrown. The linebacker must yell "Pass" when the ball is raised in the air by the passer.

Coaching Points: Same as for Drill 19. The linebacker must stop and set up when the passer stops and raises the ball to pass. The passer *cannot* fake a pass, since the linebacker is playing his first passing motion. Check for false-stepping, and running incorrectly in an arc. Build the confidence of the linebackers by regulating the drill so they will succeed.

21. Going-to-the-Spot Drill

Purpose: To develop reaction to the key and the football, indicating a drop-back pass, as in (7) Key-Reaction Drills (f).

Procedure: The center, an offensive lineman, and the quarterback have the starting count. The linebacker's key indicates a drop-back pass. The linebacker sounds off, indicating "Pass," and immediately shifts his attention from the offensive lineman (key) to the quarterback and the football. The linebacker sets up at ten yards, or sooner if the passer stops and sets up before the linebacker gets back to a depth of ten yards. The passer attempts to throw to one of two stationary receivers, who are five yards apart (work outward until they are fifteen yards apart) at a depth of approximately eleven yards from the line of scrimmage. The linebacker should be in a good football ("ready") position, and break for the football on a straight line at a 90° angle to catch it at the interception point.

Coaching Points: Use a marked-off area to determine the correct depth for the linebacker (his heels should be on the line). Emphasize breaking in

DRILL 21

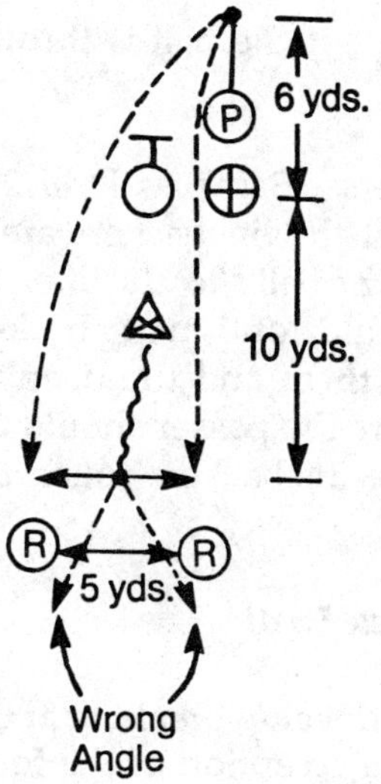

a straight line for the football, and do not permit the linebacker to run in an arc. The passer is *not* permitted to first fake a throw as the defender will play the passer's first passing motion.

22. Five Spots Drill

Purpose: To develop reaction to the quarterback and the football indicating a drop-back pass.

Procedure: The quarterback turns and sprints back, setting up for a drop-back pass. The linebackers drop off to cover their zones, as they sound off, "Pass." Five stationary receivers face the passer, and he tries to throw the ball to one of them. The receivers are eleven yards from the line of scrimmage, and ten yards apart between receivers. The linebackers must

DRILL 22

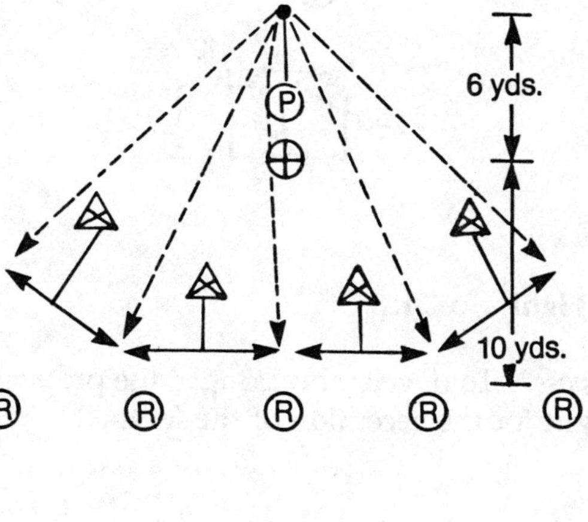

break at a 90° angle if the ball is thrown toward a receiver stationed between them.

Coaching Points: Same as Drill 21. Check the defenders' positions every time to see if the linebackers are getting the required depth. If the quarterback holds the ball *after* the linebackers have sprinted back ten yards, ordinarily they would continue to back-pedal and get additional depth, or the zone between them and the deep defenders would be extended and stretched. Therefore the passer should time-out his throw, passing as soon as the heels of the linebackers touch the line ten yards from the line of scrimmage.

23. Fight–Back Drill

Purpose: To develop breaking at the proper angle to intercept a pass, and to fight for the reception of the football.

Procedure: Same as (21) Going-to-the-Spot Drill, only the football is thrown between the two linebackers and they break at a 90° angle on a straight line to intercept the ball.

Coaching Points: Same as for Drill 21. Also use (4) Back-Up Interception Drill, Chapter 12. The objective of this drill, and (24) Fight-Up Drill is *not* for the linebackers to crash into each other but for one to snatch the ball from the other, simulating intercepting the pass from the intended receiver.

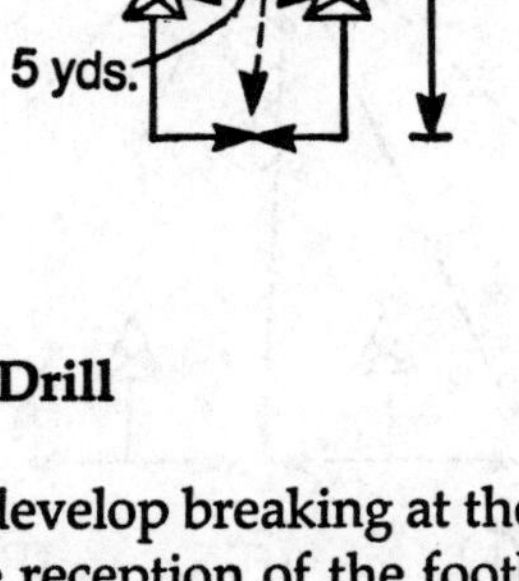

DRILL 23

24. Fight–Up Drill

Purpose: To develop breaking at the proper angle to intercept a pass, and to fight for the reception of the football.

DRILL 24

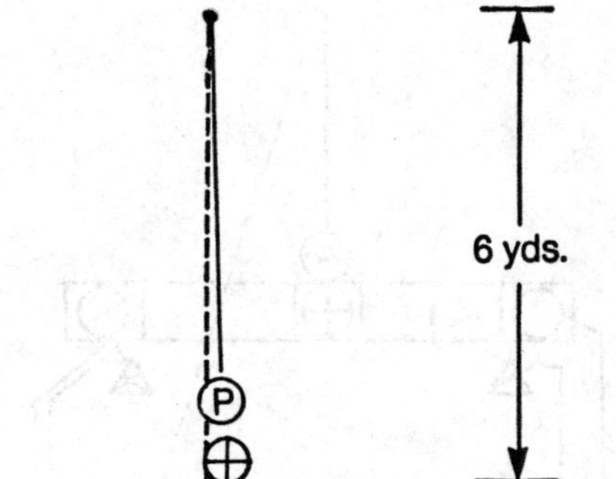

Procedure: Same as (19) Going-for-the-Ball Drill, only two linebackers are used and are stationed ten yards from the line when the drill starts. The ball is thrown high, low, hard or soft toward the two linebackers, who must change direction quickly to intercept the pass.

Coaching Points: Same as Drill 23. Also use (6) Straight-Ahead Interception Drill, Chapter 12.

25. Chugging Receivers Drill

Purpose: To "chug" receivers, temporarily deterring their quick release from the line of scrimmage and then cover one's zone area of responsibility on pass defense.

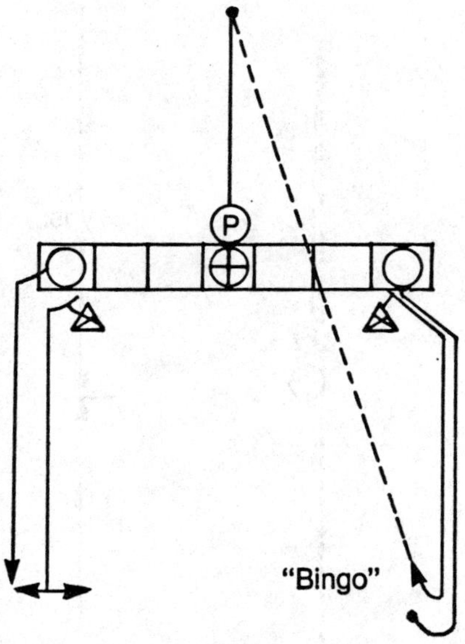

DRILL 25

Procedure: The linebackers take an alignment on the inside shoulder or head up over the ends, depending on the defensive alignment, such as Eagle, 4–3, 5–3. Do not permit the receivers to release inside, but attempt to jam them legally at the line of scrimmage. If offensive ends are forced to release outside, they should still run a hook at twelve yards. The linebackers must cover their hook zone responsibility, and the passer must throw the football before the intended receivers get a depth of fifteen yards.

Coaching Points: Defenders must use only legal tactics to chug and jam intended receivers. Force the ends outside, with the linebackers turning to the outside facing the receivers when going back to their hook zones. They should square off and slide laterally after getting to their hook zone area of responsibility. The passer cannot fake a pass, but must cock and throw the football.

26. Man–For–Man Coverage Drill

Purpose: To teach man-for-man pass coverage.

Procedure: The linebackers are assigned man-for-man coverage on the remaining backs. The passer sets up to pass. If their key (back) sets up to block, the linebacker covers in the hook zone on his side in order to help on underneath patterns since he is "free." If his key releases and goes out for a pass, or sets up and then releases, the linebacker covers the offensive back man-for-man. The passer should throw quickly and *not* try to beat

DRILL 26

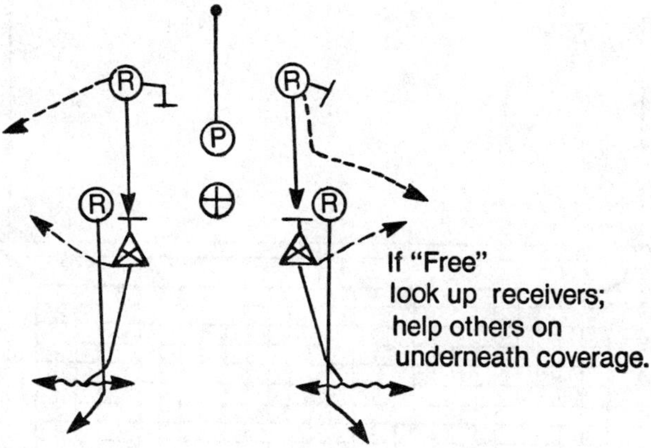

the linebacker deep by running an offensive back down the middle, although a linebacker must attempt to cover a receiver deep. If the key (back) comes to the inside through the line, the linebacker "chugs" him and stays with his potential receiver.

Coaching Points: Stress watching the key and taking off quickly to run with the back who releases. Throw delays, flares and swing passes to offensive backs coming out of the backfield; also teach-coach to correctly cover or check-off a key (back) in motion (depending on secondary alignment and pass coverages).

27. Defender's Quick Hands Drill

Purpose: To develop quickness in reacting to an oral command, and to intercept the pass.

Procedure: The linebacker (or any secondary pass defender) is stationed directly in front of and *facing* a net, which hangs down from the crossbar between the goal posts and serves as a backstop. The passer (coach) is fifteen yards away with the football cocked, ready to throw as soon as he shouts, "Now!" The linebacker whirls around when he hears the command, and immediately tries to intercept the pass coming toward him.

Coaching Points: As soon as the coach shouts, "Now!" he throws the football; he does *not* wait until the defender turns around. Stress the proper fundamentals of catching a football. After the linebacker (defender) becomes proficient, the passer will throw the football to any area under the crossbar between the posts.

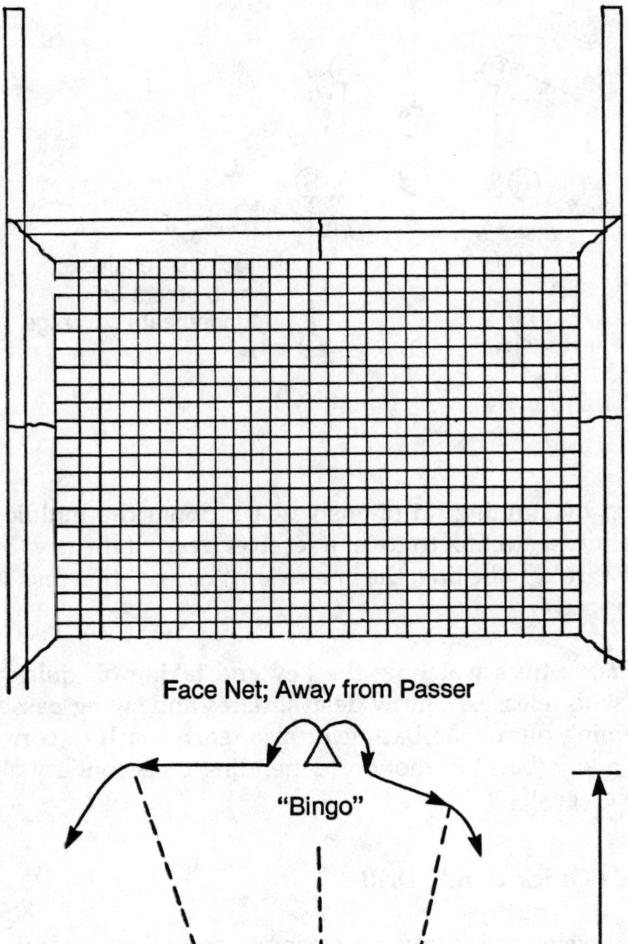
Face Net; Away from Passer
"Bingo"
Hard, High
Soft, Low
15 yds.
"Now!"
P (Coach)

DRILL 27

28. Defender's Net Drill

Purpose: To teach and develop breaking on a straight line to intercept the pass thrown to either side.

Procedure: Same as (27) in using a net covering the goal posts, only the linebacker is head-on the center, keying the quarterback, and the line of scrimmage is the five-yard line. The quarterback takes the snap-back from his center and goes to the pocket to set up for a drop-back pass. The linebacker uses a drop-step, cross-over sprint back technique to set up in a good defensive football position in the middle of the net approximately fifteen yards from the passer. The passer can throw the football to any area under the crossbar between the posts, and the linebacker must break at a 90° angle on a straight line to intercept the pass.

Coaching Points: The linebacker must stop and set up when the passer stops. Check for false-stepping, and running incorrectly in an arc. The passer cannot fake his pass as the linebacker is playing the passer's first throwing motion.

29. UP, OVER, BUT NOT IN OR NO TD DRILL

Purpose: To teach linebackers (and defensive backs) to meet and physically defeat the ball carrier trying to go up, over, and in for the score at the goal line.

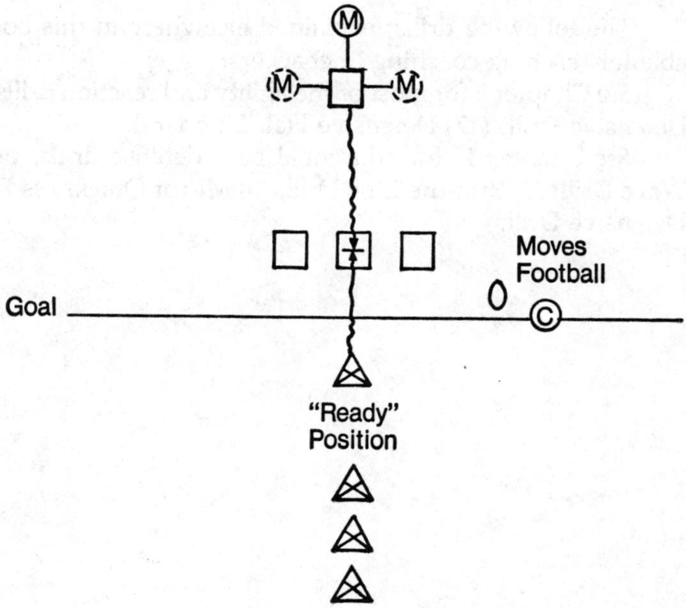

DRILL 29

Procedure: This is the counterpart of (24) Up, Over, and In or TD Drill, Chapter 9, but it is organized differently to minimize the possibility of injuring the ball carrier. Three upright dummies are positioned one yard from a line (simulated goal line), with a linebacker (or defensive back) one yard away from the dummies in a "ready" position. The coach is at the goal line on one knee with a football so he can move the ball indicating the offensive snap count, and can observe from his side view position the tackler meeting the (simulated) ball carrier at the line and indicate whether or not there is a score. Behind the middle upright dummy a manager holds a smaller dummy, and when the coach moves the football the manager runs forward and hurls the smaller dummy up and over the upright dummies. The linebacker should move forward, go up, drive the dummy back, and deny the "ball carrier" from scoring.

Coaching Points: Instruct the manager(s) to run forward and bring the smaller dummy up behind the upright dummies at an *upward* angle, simulating the ball carrier going up over his linemen. (An air shield is not suitable.) If a regular upright dummy is used, have managers carry it by the straps at the top, drag it low on the ground, and then as they bring it up and over release their hold of the straps so it is airborne when the linebacker meets the "ball carrier." The defender should be square when he hits, and he should meet the bag high so the (simulated) ball carrier does not lean forward and cross the plane of the goal line for a touchdown.

30. LINEBACKING DRILLS (ADDITIONAL)

The following drills, explained elsewhere in this book, are also suitable for teaching-coaching linebackers:

See Chapter 5 for most of the agility and reaction drills, plus (16) Inside Defensive Drill; (17) Defensive Half-Line Drill.

See Chapter 12 for additional pass defense drills, plus (1) Defensive Wave Drill; (2) Run-the-Line Drill; (3) Mirror Quickness Drill; (31) Outside Defensive Drill.

12

Defensive Secondary Drills

Secondary defenders must be able to move and react, fight a receiver for possession of the football, and make the tackle in open field. These skills are taught through repetitive drills. However, such drills are of little value if the defender lacks a burning desire to play pass defense and to excel in his secondary play. A good defensive back not only wants to intercept every pass that is thrown, but he wants to make the tackle as close as possible to the line of scrimmage on running plays. Therefore, he must know well the responsibilities of his position and react properly with quickness and speed, since a secondary defender's failure to react correctly may mean his teammates will be penalized six points. In no other phase of football is the penalty as severe as when the secondary defender fails to react as taught-coached, and through his faulty play the opposition scores an easy touchdown. Therefore, pass defense is undoubtedly the most important phase of defensive football. Tackling will be discussed in the chapter that follows, including tackling drills for teaching-coaching secondary defenders.

Only through drills can a team's pass defense be improved. Through drills the following basic fundamentals of pass defense can be taught:

- How to be in the proper position at all times.
- How to lengthen the interception distance in getting to the football.
- How to play the football in the air after it is thrown.

A football team, regardless of potential, will never become great defensively if it permits its opposition to make their "must" play on the key down. Frequently the key or "must" play is a pass on a third (or fourth) down situation, i.e., the team "must" make the necessary yardage. Defensing the key play properly means the opposition gives up possession of the football; failure to do so means the opposition retains possession. If a team cannot stop the "must" plays, generally the opposing team will win the game. Consequently, pass defense is the most important phase of defensive football.

Drills for teaching secondary pass defense fundamentals and techniques are as follows:

1. DEFENSIVE WAVE DRILL

Purpose: To improve the individual defender's fundamentals to be in the proper position at all times, to increase the interception distance, and to play the football after it is thrown; also to improve team pass defense.

Procedure: From a good defensive football position, the three defenders react to the arm motion of the coach, using a crossover step and moving at a diagonal angle backward. When the coach (passer) indicates a change of direction, the defender plants his away (far) foot, pushes off turning to the inside, and uses a crossover step going in the direction indicated. After four to five reactions, the ball is thrown and the defenders sprint to the interception point, with one man catching the ball and sounding off with the interception signal ("Bingo"), and the other two leading him back to the line of scrimmage.

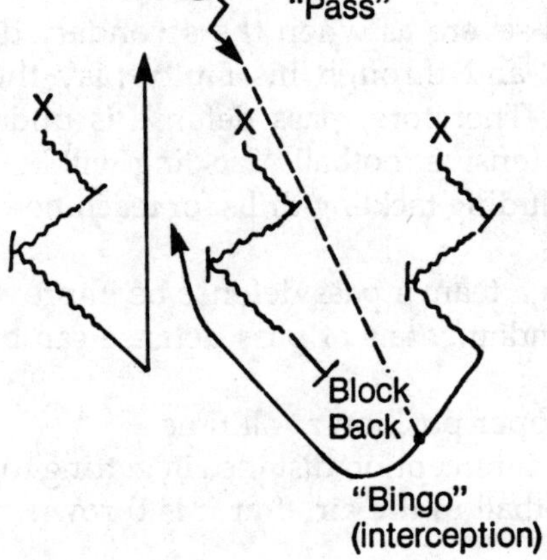

DRILL 1

Coaching Points (For All Pass Defense Drills): Recognize and identify, "Pass!"; sound off with the interception signal, "Block!" ("Bingo!"), and convey it to your teammates; sprint to the interception point; the defender nearest the interceptor peels-back and blocks the intended receiver or leads and blocks downfield. Stress the proper planting procedure; no false-stepping. Catch the football at its highest point with the arms, hands and fingers extended. Do not wait to catch the football on its downward path. Change quickly from defense to offense, and score!

2. RUN–THE–LINE DRILL

Purpose: To develop footwork, hip action, body balance and agility.

Procedure: The defender lines up in a position straddling a line, facing the coach, whom he will watch until the football is thrown or the coach signals the termination of the drill (forty yards downfield). Using a cross-over step, and reversing his feet as quickly as possible as he turns from side to side, the defender attempts to stay *on the line.* The objective is to run as fast, yet make as many turns from side to side as possible, while *watching the passer (coach) the entire time.* If a football is used, which is not necessary, the defender plants, sprints to the interception point, and returns the football to the coach (passer). If a ball is not used, the coach signals the end of the drill, and the defender turns around and starts back down the line coming toward the coach but facing in the opposite direction.

Coaching Points: The defender should *not* angle off the line as in (1) Defensive Wave Drill. Stress watching the coach (passer) or looking straight ahead, and *not* looking downward watching the feet. Work up to an all-out effort, *staying on the line,* turning from side to side as quickly and as many times as possible in the forty yard distance.

DRILL 2

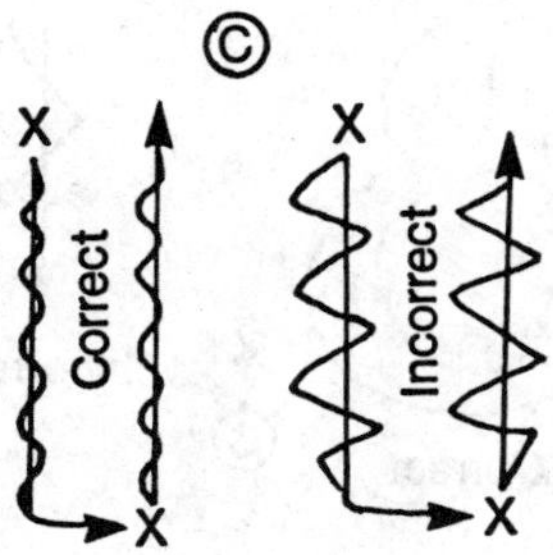

3. MIRROR QUICKNESS DRILL

Purpose: To develop footwork, agility and body balance, while reacting to the passer's (coach's/manager's) movements.

Procedure: The coach and a manager are forty yards apart, facing each other with footballs. When the offensive player (receiver) is coming toward the coach and the defender has his back to the coach, the coach controls the drill with his football by indicating the diagonal movements the offensive player should take. The manager (passer) "mirrors" the coach's movements with his football, and the defensive player reacts to these, similar to (1) Defensive Wave Drill. The procedure is reversed when the defender is facing the coach (passer) and the receiver is facing the manager, as the manager controls the drill with his football and the coach "mirrors" the movements for the defender with his football. Although the defender will watch the passer (coach or manager) and not the receiver, his movements should "mirror" the receiver's movements.

Coaching Points: Stress quickness, changing direction frequently, and positioning the receiver properly. The defender should not play the receiver too loosely or merely retreat straight back; he should react to the movements of the passer and the receiver. The defender's first step should be backward when the passer raises the football, and he should maintain a three-yard distance from the receiver throughout the forty yard distance.

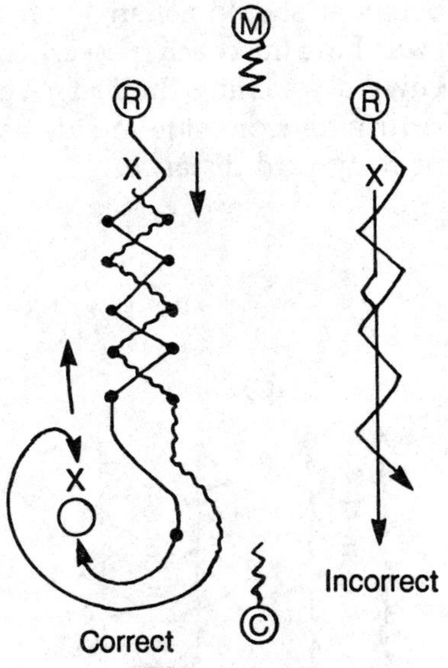

DRILL 3

4. SPRINT–BACK INTERCEPTION DRILL

Purpose: To develop reaction, footwork, agility in going backwards to catch the football.

Procedure: The coach raises the ball indicating "Pass." The defender sprints backward as fast as possible, turning his body outward and looking over his inside shoulder. The ball should be thrown high and hard so the defender must stretch to catch it, playing the ball at its highest point, yet maintaining his balance. The defender should not false-step. He should tuck the ball away securely and reverse his field immediately after catching the football. A stationary receiver (manager) may be placed behind the defender ten yards. The coach (passer) uses him as a target when throwing the ball high and hard. Occasionally, throw a soft pass so the defender must plant his far foot and come back immediately to catch the pass thrown in front of his position.

Coaching Points: Stress the proper fundamentals of catching the football, putting it away, and running hard after intercepting the ball. Follow-up with (23) Fight-Back Drill, Chapter 11, simulating the defender and receiver fighting for the football thrown between them while going away from the passer.

DRILL 4

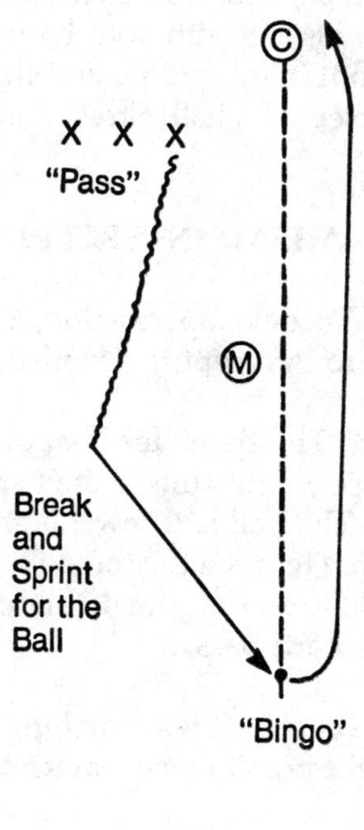

5. FORWARD–BACKWARD–DIAGONAL DRILL

Purpose: To develop reaction, footwork, agility in changing direction in order to catch the football.

Procedure: The defender faces the coach (passer) six to eight yards apart, with two upright dummies half-way between them two to three yards apart. On the coach's signal the defender comes forward between the dummies with body under control, plants his foot and moves laterally several steps, breaking at a 90° angle until the coach raises the football as if to pass. The defender yells "Pass!", plants his outside foot and sprints backward as fast as possible, yet watching the passer the entire time. The ball may be thrown at any time the defender starts backward, as the drill is then like (4) Sprint-Back Interception Drill. Or the coach may point left or right any time after the defender starts backward, and the player must break on a diagonal angle for the football which should be thrown immediately after pointing in the direction the defender should break. On intercepting the football, the defender sounds off.

Coaching Points: Stress breaking at sharp angles, and the proper planting procedure. The defender does not move a great distance, as the emphasis should be on changing direction forward, laterally, backward, diagonally. Conduct the drill as follows: the coach (passer) stands with his feet staggered and pulls the football to his stomach indicating the snap-back from his center; the defender comes forward between the dummies (three to four steps) and moves laterally several steps; the passer raises the football behind his ear with both hands on the football simulating a pass, removes his front hand, points and throws the football; and the defender sprints to intercept the ball. Stress catching the ball properly.

6. STRAIGHT–AHEAD INTERCEPTION DRILL

Purpose: To develop reaction, footwork and agility while running straight ahead to intercept the football.

Procedure: The defender is approximately twenty yards away from the coach (passer), and runs at half-speed directly at him, with his body under control. The ball is thrown high and hard directly at the defender, who must stretch to catch the football. Occasionally, throw a soft high pass or a low line drive so that the defender does not "hang back" in order to catch the high, hard pass.

Coaching Points: Stress catching the football with the fingers at the maximum height possible, not on its downward path. Follow-up with (24)

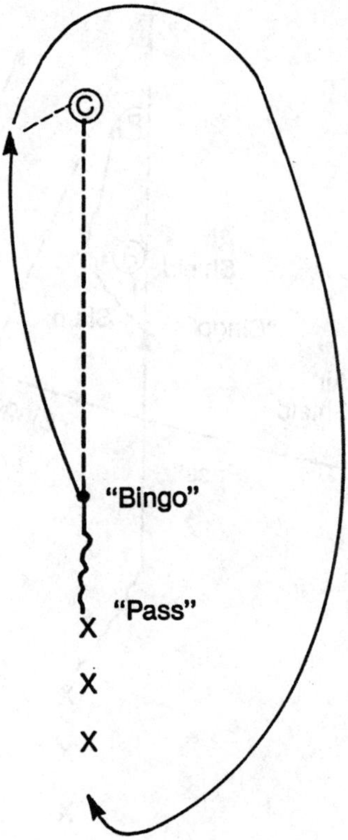

DRILL 6

Fight-Up Drill, Chapter 11, simulating a receiver and a defender fighting for possession of a football that is thrown between them when they are coming toward the passer.

7. AGGRESSIVE INTERCEPTION DRILL

Purpose: To teach the defender to concentrate on catching the ball, competing aggressively to intercept the football when it is in the air—"the ball is mine!"

Procedure: Three players with air shields are positioned as targets for the passer (coach). The player in the middle faces away from the coach; the other two players face each other at the wings. Only the middle defender will come straight forward, as in Drill 6. The other defenders, *one at a time,* will move laterally toward the opposite side to try to intercept a lead pass thrown by the coach. The coach signals which player is involved in the drill. As that secondary defender starts moving toward the player

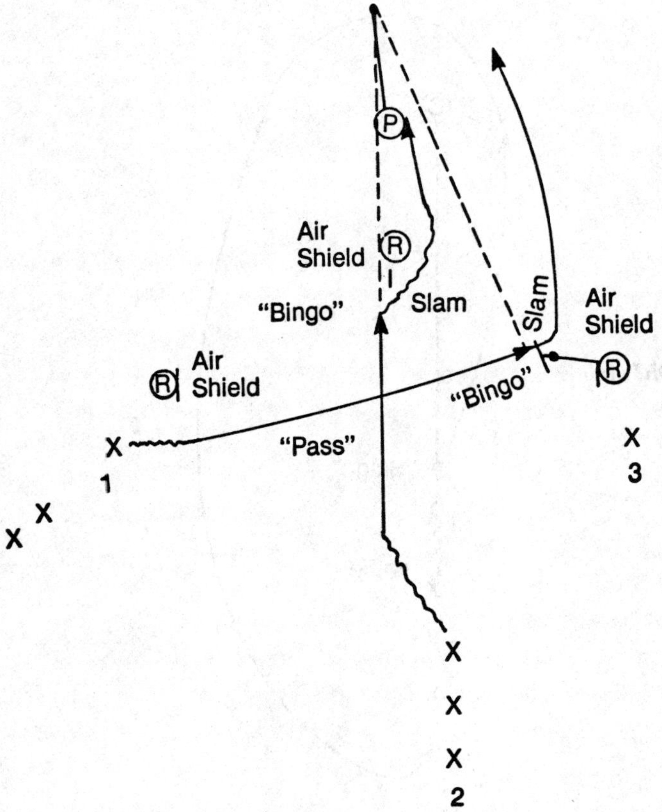

DRILL 7

holding the air bag, the coach (passer) tries to time his pass so that as the defender intercepts he will be slammed with the air bag trying to force a fumble. The interceptor should immediately tuck the ball away securely, lower his shoulder and use his body to ward-off being slammed by the player (the intended receiver) with the air bag.

Coaching Points: Stress intercepting the pass and safely tucking away the football. Stress playing the football, ignoring the opponent (the theoretical intended receiver) as the defender goes for the interception. Try to time throwing the football so the interception and shock with the air bag are almost simultaneous.

8. AGGRESSIVE LIVE INTERCEPTION DRILL

Purpose: To compete aggressively to intercept the football when it is in the air—"the ball is mine!"

Procedure: Using a marked-off area, a receiver is stationed fifteen yards away facing the coach (passer), either at a left or right oblique angle (for the defensive halfbacks) or straight ahead (for the safety man), with the defender five yards behind the receiver. The passer drills the football toward the intended receiver. The defender cannot break to attempt to intercept or deflect the pass until the football leaves the passer's hand. The defender should compete aggressively for the football, playing the football in the air, *not* playing the potential receiver.

Coaching Points: Probably the most difficult of all passes to intercept is the one that is rifled at the receiver; therefore, this is an excellent drill! The defender cannot "creep" up, and he cannot play the arm motion of the passer. Occasionally the passer should throw high or wide to determine if the defender is playing the receiver or the football. Occasionally the passer should fake pump, and the receiver should run and attempt to get behind the defender to determine if the defender is playing the receiver or the ball.

9. BREAK–OFF INTERCEPTION DRILL

Purpose: To develop reaction, footwork and agility while running straight ahead, then breaking to intercept the football.

DRILL 9

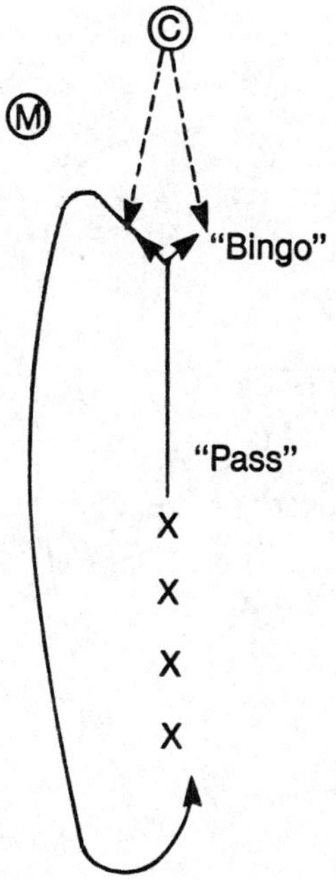

Procedure: Same as (6) Straight-Ahead Interception Drill, only the passer throws the ball to the left or right of the defender coming straight toward him, who must break-off at a sharp angle to intercept the pass.

Coaching Points: The defender should not guess. Occasionally throw the football straight ahead in order to determine if the defender is keeping his eyes on the football. Stress catching the ball away from the body; sprinting to the interception point.

10. ANGLE INTERCEPTION DRILL

Purpose: To develop reaction, footwork and agility while running at an angle to intercept a pass.

Procedure: Same as (9) Break-Off Interception Drill, only after moving forward for several yards the player then breaks right or left and runs at an oblique angle toward the line of scrimmage before the ball is thrown toward him.

Coaching Points: Stress catching the football properly. The defender comes forward about five yards, then breaks on an angle before the ball is thrown. Increase interception distance by leading the defender, forcing him to sprint to catch the football.

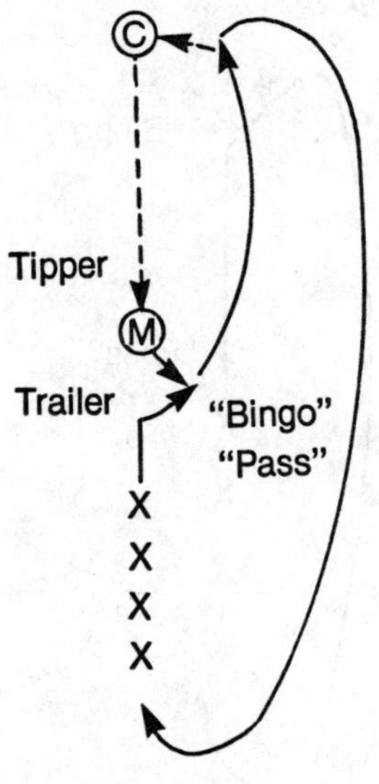

DRILL 12

11–14 TIP INTERCEPTION DRILLS

11. Straight-Ahead Tip Drill

12. Stationary (Manager) Tip Drill

13. Criss-Cross Tip Drill

14. Side Tip Drill

Purpose: To improve body control and reaction by getting the interceptor (trailer) to play the ball better by keeping his eyes on it.

Procedure: Same as (6) Straight-Ahead Interception Drill, only the second man trails five yards behind the tipper, who runs three-quarters speed toward the passer in (11) Straight-Ahead Tip Drill. A variation (12) is for the manager to be stationed seven yards in front of the coach (passer), facing him, with a football in his hands extended upward. The coach throws another football toward the one held by the manager, who deflects it backward into the air for the defender running toward him from

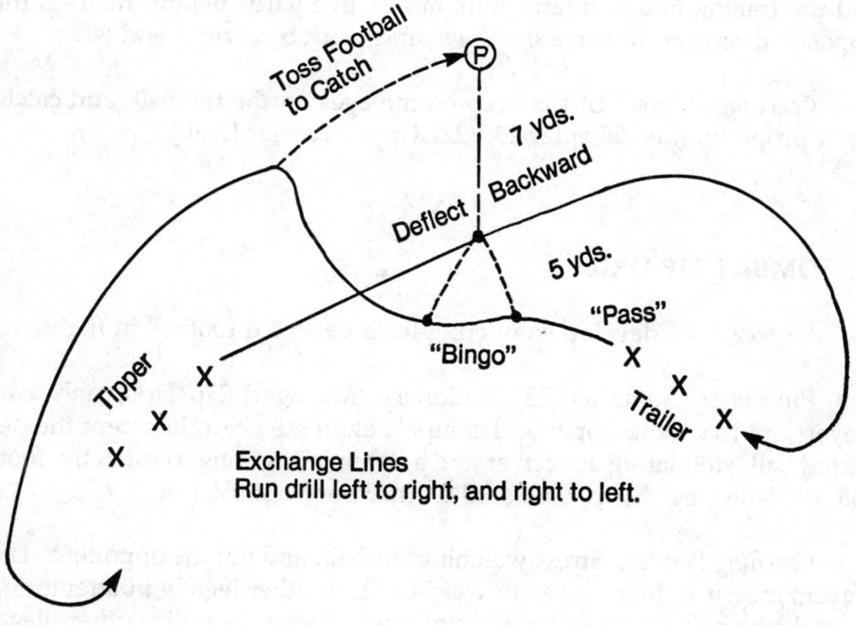

DRILL 13

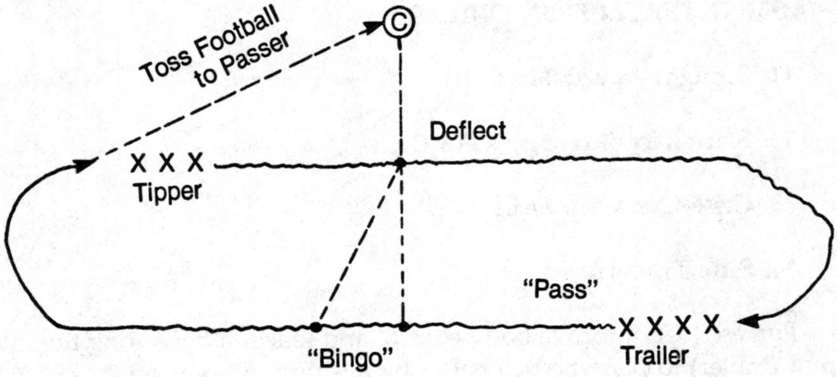

DRILL 14

behind to intercept. In (13) Criss-Cross Tip Drill, the tipper crosses at an angle seven yards in front of the coach (passer), and tips the ball backward to the trailer crossing at an angle five yards behind him. In (14) Side Tip Drill, the line of players tipping the football moves in a designated direction parallel to the line of scrimmage seven yards away from the coach, and the trailing line of interceptors moves five yards behind them in the opposite direction. Reverse the lines, and work both right and left.

Coaching Points: Stress keeping the eyes on the football, and catching it properly. (See Chapter 13, (22) Tipper-Tackler Drill.)

15. COMBAT TIP DRILL

Purpose: To develop competing for a deflected football in flight.

Procedure: Same as (12) Stationary (Manager) Tip Drill, only two players approach the tipper and compete aggressively to intercept the deflected ball, simulating a receiver and a defender fighting to catch the football, or deflecting the football so the other does not catch it.

Coaching Points: Stress watching the ball, and not the opponent. The players may use their bodies to ward-off each other legally in attempting to catch the ball, but they should not push, shove, or utilize other illegal means in competing for the ball.

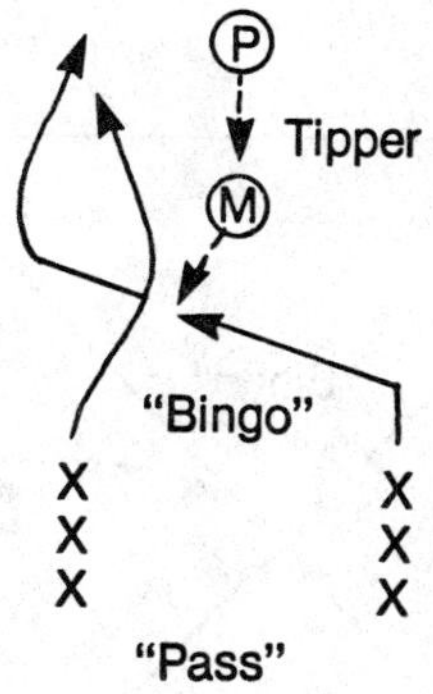

DRILL 15

16. DEFENDER'S (RECEIVER'S) CROSSBAR DRILL

Purpose: To develop leaping into the air to catch the football.

Procedure: A single column of defenders (receivers) start on the five-yard line and sprint toward the goal posts. On the first progression, the defender (receiver) tries to touch the crossbar (ten feet from the ground) with his right hand; the second cycle, his left hand; and the third time, with both hands, simulating leaping into the air to catch or defend against the high pass.

Coaching Points: Stress gathering and leaping into the air without stopping, timing the take-off and touching the crossbar. The defender (receiver) should not grab the bar and/or attempt to swing on it, which is a rule violation. Also have the players stand under the crossbar and attempt to jumb vertically from a stationary position and touch the crossbar. This is a good pre-practice drill as part of their warm-up after the players are loose.

17. DEFENDER'S (RECEIVER'S) SQUARE DRILL

Purpose: To develop defenders (receivers) in competing for the football when it is in the air, using their bodies to ward-off opponents.

Procedure: The drill is similar in principle to (16) Receiver's (Defender's) Three-Man Square Drill, Chapter 8, although twelve players are involved there, whereas only four players are used in this square drill. The defenders are stationed on the corners of a five-yard square, with the coach outside of the square area. The coach moves around the outside of the

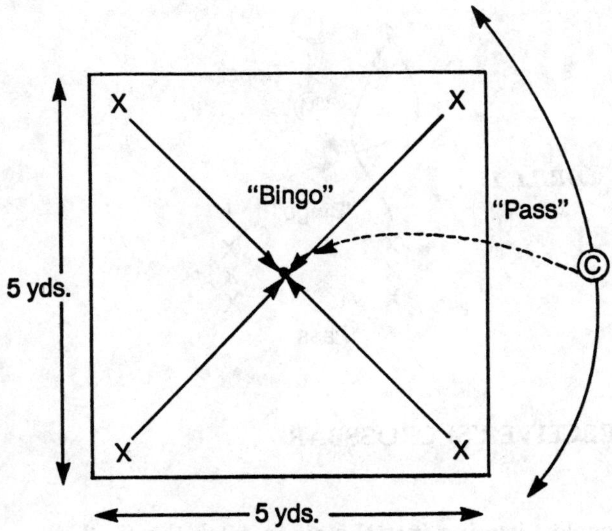

DRILL 17

square, throwing high passes into the middle of the square. All four players move from the corners to compete in catching the football, using their bodies to ward-off each other.

Coaching Points: Do not permit pass interference, such as holding and shoving but teach the defenders to use their bodies to ward-off each other without violation of the rules. The drill is aggressive, and players should be alert to catch the deflected ball. Stress jumping and playing the football at its height, and tucking the ball away securely after intercepting. Do not permit any player to "creep" toward the middle before the ball is released.

18. FIGURE 8 INTERCEPTION DRILL

Purpose: To develop catching the ball at various angles, and to give the interceptor maximum practice in catching the football in a short period of time.

Procedure: A defender lines up ten yards away from the passer (coach), who has a manager on either side of him. The defender jogs through a Figure 8 pattern going back and forth toward each sideline in an area approximately 10 × 10 yards, and crossing at a point ten yards in front of the coach each time. The passer throws the ball at any time and so the intercepter is taking the football over either shoulder, coming to or

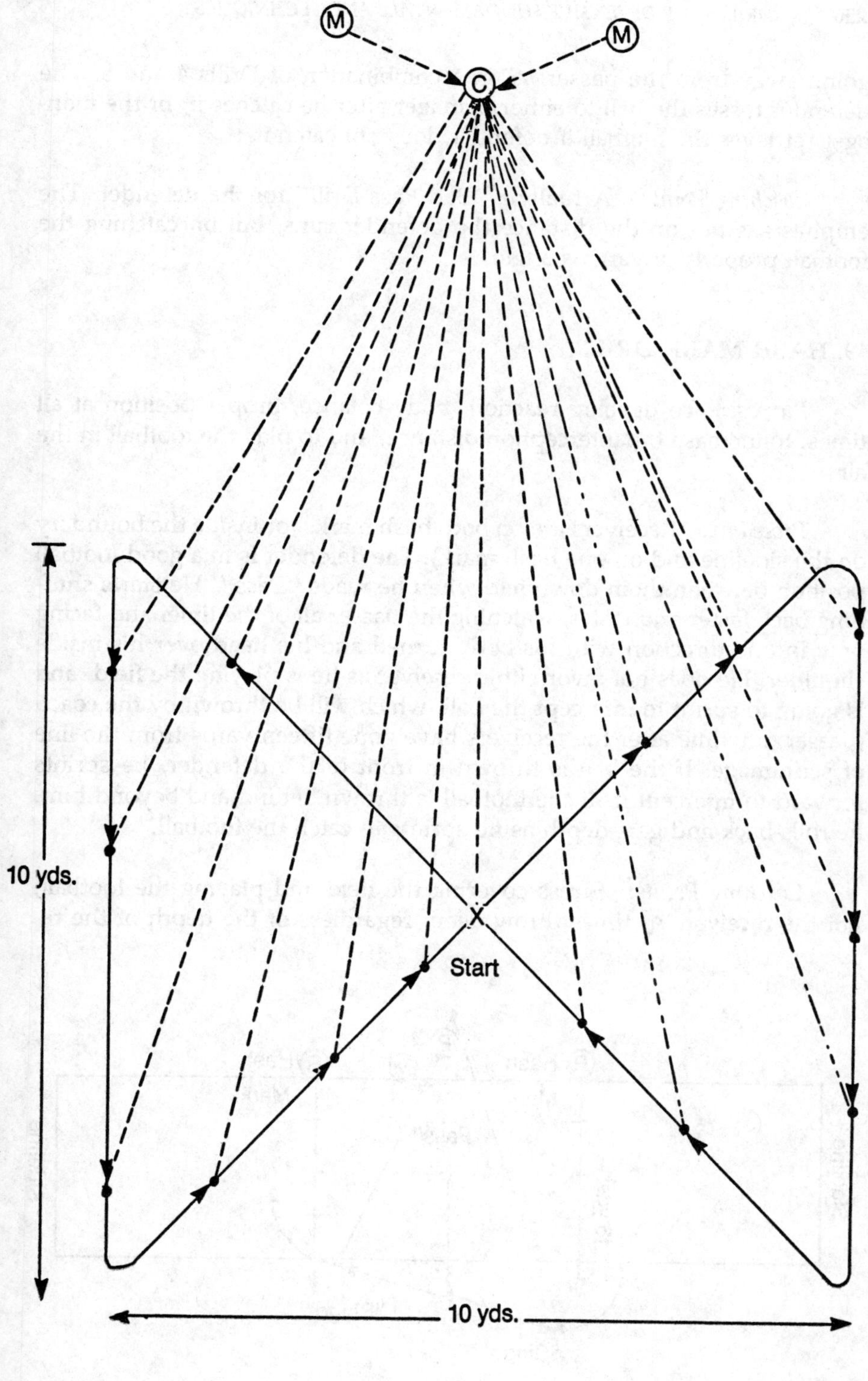

DRILL 18

going away from the passer, as in a combination of Drills 4 and 5. The defender tosses the ball to either manager after he catches it, or the manager retrieves the football if defender does not catch it.

Coaching Points: Actually a "Bad Pass Drill" for the defender. The emphasis is not on the distance the defender runs, but on catching the football properly at various angles.

19. HASH MARK DRILL

Purpose: To develop reaction, body balance, proper position at all times, to increase the interception distance, and to play the football in the air.

Procedure: Receivers are on both hash marks (or inside the boundary on the sideline and on one hash mark). The defender is in a good football position between them downfield when he reads "Pass." He starts shuffling back faster and faster, watching the passer all of the time, and facing only in one direction with his body turned and his head over his inside shoulder. He does not favor either receiver as he is playing the field, and is going to sprint to intercept the ball, which will be thrown by the coach (passer) anytime after the receivers have gone fifteen yards from the line of scrimmage. If the ball is thrown in front of the defender, he sprints forward to intercept it. If the football is thrown behind and beyond him, he rolls-back and gets depth as he sprints to catch the football.

Coaching Points: Stress covering the field and playing the football, not the receiver. At times throw deep, regardless of the depth of the re-

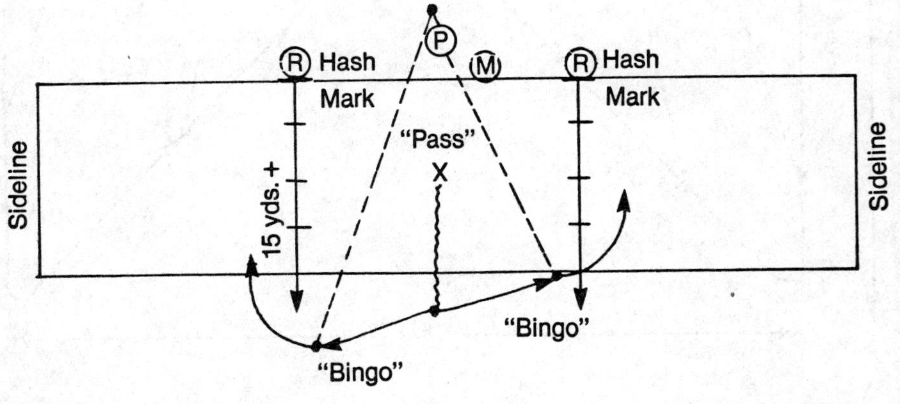

DRILL 19

ceivers, so the defender has to sprint hard to catch the football. Build confidence by "hanging" the ball in the air to show the defender how much distance he can cover while sprinting to the interception point.

20. ROLL–BACK DRILL

Purpose: To teach playing the football and intercepting the pass thrown beyond and behind the defender.

Procedure: The defenders set up in a three-deep or a semi-rotated, three-deep position from the box-wing secondary alignment. Start with the football in the middle of the field, and move out to the hash marks. The passer should look at one of the defenders and signal him to move deeper in his defensive area. The ball is thrown *behind and beyond* the defender or in front of him. If the former, the defender will roll-back toward the football as he drops his far shoulder and turns his head, gains depth and sprints to the interception point. If the ball is thrown in front of the defender, he must be taught-coached to change his direction immediately without false-stepping. He should use his arms to aid in reversing his direction and sprint to the interception point.

Coaching Points: Stress catching the football at the highest point possible, and not waiting to catch it on the downward descent. Check the defender's steps after the ball is thrown to determine how much ground is lost before he reacts forward toward the football thrown in front of his position.

DRILL 20

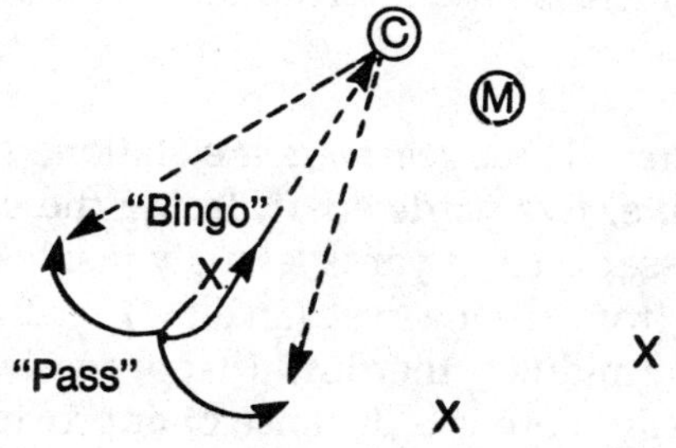

21. SECONDARY'S BACK–UP DRILL

Purpose: To develop reaction, body balance and proper position at all times, to increase the interception distance, and to play the football in the air.

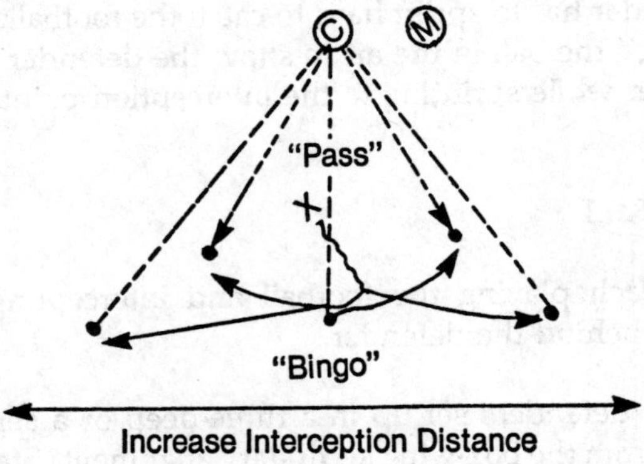

DRILL 21

Procedure: The defensive player sets up in a good football position and starts moving back as the coach raises the ball signalling pass. The coach throws the football directly toward the defender, high or low, or to either side of him. The defender must use the proper techniques in playing the football in the air as he sprints to the interception point.

Coaching Points: Stress breaking at the correct angle for the football, and not false-stepping. Build player confidence by gradually increasing the defender's interception distance.

22. DEEP–MIDDLE–SHALLOW DRILL

Purpose: To develop reaction, body balance and proper position at all times, to increase the interception distance, and to play the football in the air.

Procedure: Three receivers are stationed inside of the boundary line on the sideline, five yards apart, facing the coach (passer) at oblique angles. The passer is eight yards laterally inside of their positioning, and ten yards away from the nearest (shallow) receiver. A second receiver is at fifteen yards (middle); the third (deep) receiver is twenty yards from the passer. Initially there is a distance of approximately twenty-five yards between the passer and the defender. The drill may be used with the defender coming forward or going away from the passer. On the coach's command the defender starts forward at three-quarters speed, body under control. At any time the coach may yell, "Deep!" "Middle!" or "Shallow!" and pass immediately to that receiver. As a variation, the defender is started nearer the coach and goes away from the passer before the com-

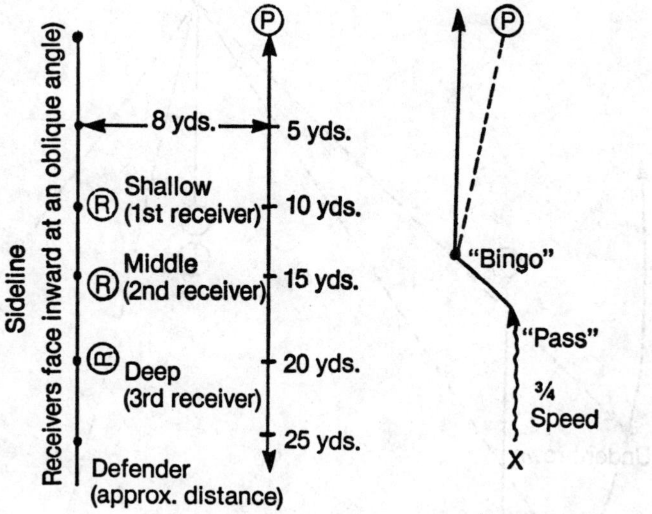

DRILL 22

a. Basic alignment

b. (ex.): "Middle"—
going forward

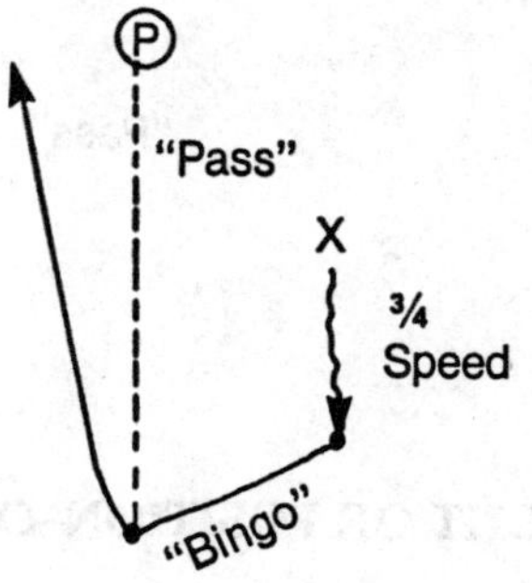

c. (ex.): "Middle"—
retreating backward

mand is given to the receiver to whom the ball will be thrown. In either case, the defender must take the correct angle to get to the interception point without first false-stepping.

Coaching Points: Stress the proper footwork and catching the ball properly. Vary the length of commands bringing the defender forward and then forcing him to cover deep, and vice versa. Run the drill both ways, (b) forward and (c) backward.

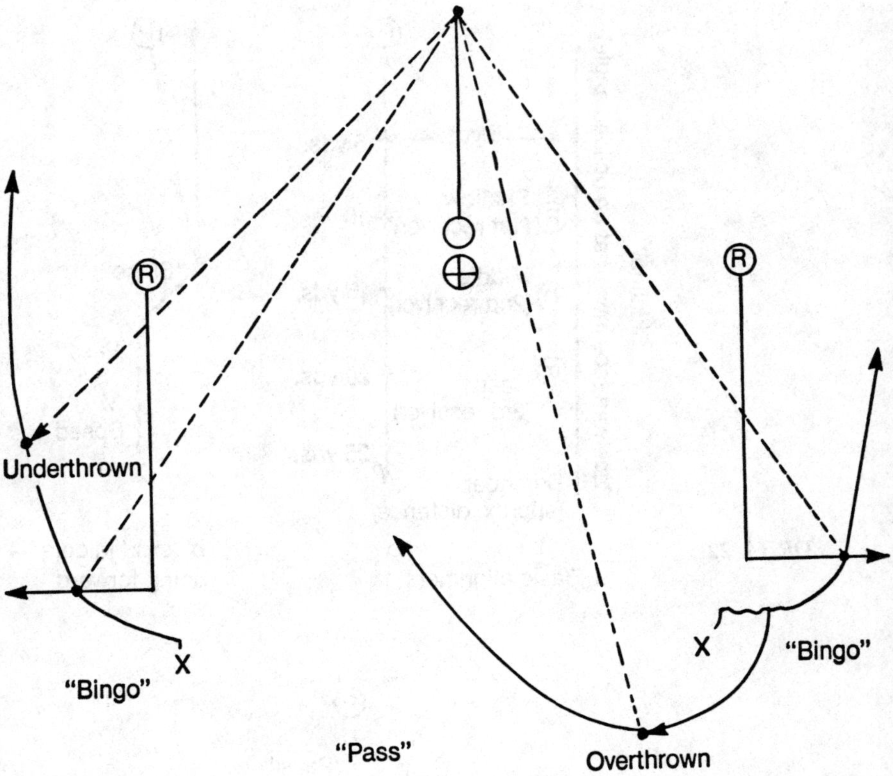

DRILL 23

23. DOG FIGHT OR POSITION–ON–RECEIVER DRILL

Purpose: To teach the defender always to have a proper position on the receiver.

Procedure: The defender sets up in a good defensive football position and reacts when the coach raises his arm indicating pass. The receiver runs a square-out pattern and the passer (coach) places the ball so the defender must play the ball in the air aggressively in order to intercept or break up the pass. At times the ball should be thrown so the defender can break past the receiver and intercept the pass, in order to build the defender's confidence.

Coaching Points: The defender should maintain an approximate cushion-position of three yards vertically and two yards laterally inside-out on the receiver, until the ball is released. Check for false-stepping, and running an arc when going to the football. At times underthrow and overthrow the receiver to determine if the defender is playing the passer and the ball, or merely covering the receiver.

24. OVERLAP DRILL

Purpose: To teach and develop overlapping the flight of the football on a pass.

Procedure: The coach (passer) raises the football indicating a pass, and the defenders start shuffling back to cover their zones. Two defenders should be able to overlap the ball when it is thrown in the middle to either halfback's position, and the halfback should be able to overlap the boundary when the ball is thrown outside of his position.

Coaching Points: Stress the proper angle and procedure in going to the interception point; also that overlapping defenders must communicate with each other.

DRILL 24

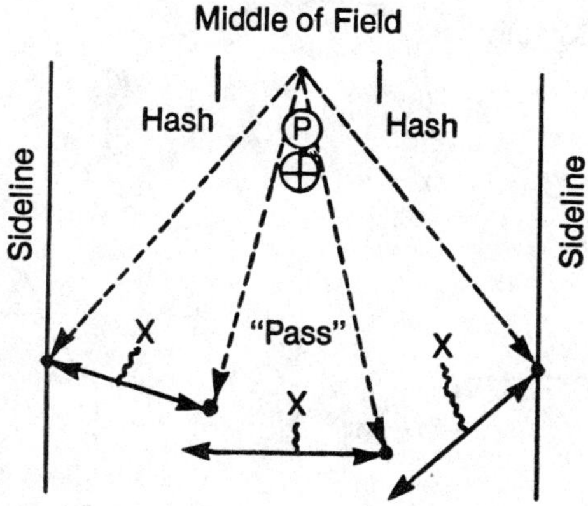

25. REACTION AND ROTATION DRILL

Purpose: To teach proper reaction and rotation on pass defense.

Procedure: The coach (passer) versus a skeleton defensive secondary. The ball is placed on a hash mark, in the middle of the field, and then on the opposite hash mark. The coach simulates receiving the snap-back from

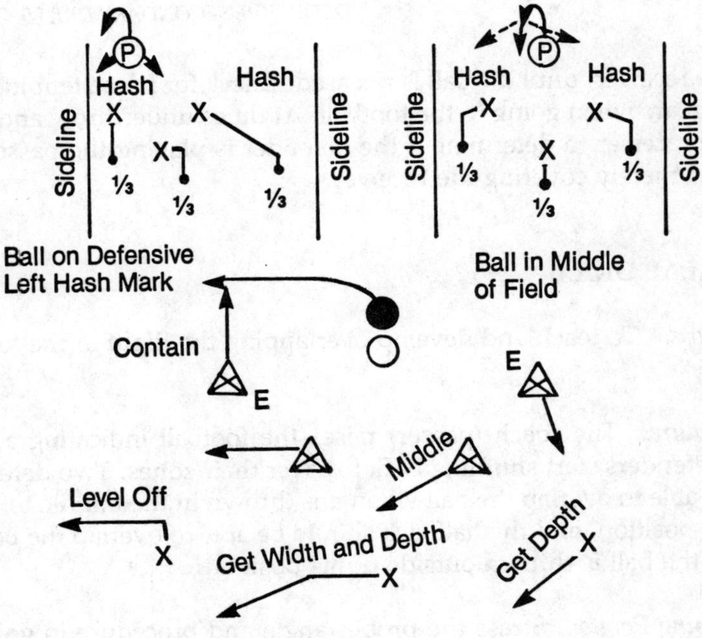

a. 3-deep zone.

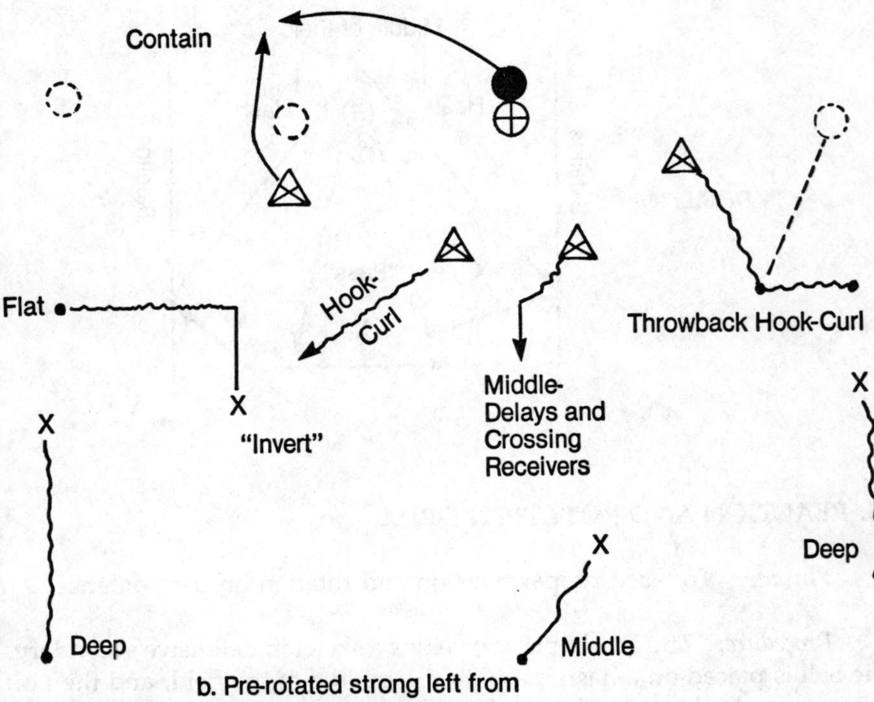

b. Pre-rotated strong left from 4-deep defensive secondary

DRILL 25

the center and goes to the pocket on a drop-back pass. The defensive secondary must react properly and cover their zones of responsibility. The drill is repeated with the quarterback (passer) rolling out simulating a flow pass. Defenders (ends and linebackers added) react and rotate properly. When the coach (passer) stops running, all secondary defenders should stop immediately so the coach can check their positions with each other and determine if they are getting width and depth and proper rotation. The emphasis is on maintaining proper field position in order to carry out the responsibilities of a coordinated pass defense.

Coaching Points: Individual responsibilities, fundamentals and techniques of stance, position, and alignment are taught during the Individual Period. They are then practiced during the Combination or Group Period, and scrimmaged during the Team Period. Stress a coordinated pass defense, proper positions initially, and correct angles in covering responsibilities (rotation). This drill precedes (30) Skeleton Pass Defense-Offense Drill, which is also a Combination or Group Period drill, where offensive ends and backs are added as receivers, and defenders must read and react to keys properly. Move the football laterally every time from the middle of the field to a hash mark.

26. BIG TIP DRILL

Purpose: To teach the defensive secondary to react to their pass defense responsibilities on the action of the passer, and to play for an interception of the deflected ball.

Procedure: Same as (25) Reaction and Rotation Drill, only the football is thrown directly toward one of the defenders who is rotating with the flow, or going to his zone versus drop-back passing. The defender purposely tips the ball in the air for a teammate to intercept. The interceptor sounds-off with the interception signal, and the other defenders lead the interference for the return.

Coaching Points: Stress a coordinated pass defense and the proper angles in getting to areas of responsibility while reacting to the quarterback (passer) key. Stress changing quickly from defense to offense, keeping one's eyes on the football, and playing for the deflection.

27. TEAM REACTION DRILL

Purpose: To teach and develop coordinated pass defense, and to change quickly from defense to offense on a pass interception.

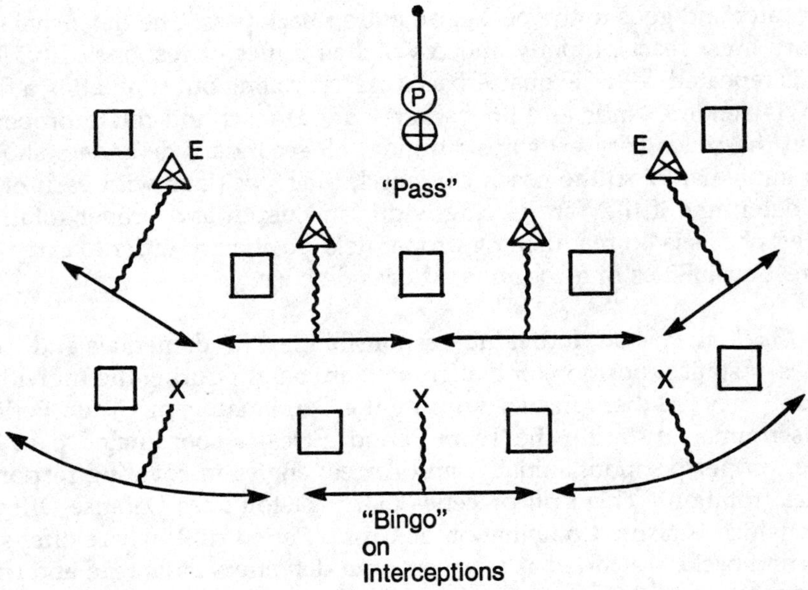

DRILL 27

Procedure: Same as (26) Big Tip Drill, only the ball is not deflected. When the interceptor sounds-off with the interception signal his teammates peel-back or block through the upright dummies stationed throughout the defensive secondary.

Coaching Points: Stress lining up quickly and accurately and taking the proper path to areas of responsibility. Stress scoring on the pass interception. Move from the middle out to hash marks, and change defensive alignments/coverages.

28. TWO–ON–ONE OR RELEASE DRILL

Purpose: To teach the defender to play his zone properly and the ball thrown in his zone.

Procedure: The defender is taught to play the deepest and widest receiver first, then the deepest; also to release from a deep receiver in his zone when the ball is thrown, and to come up to cover the short receiver, if necessary. In the latter situation, the defender releases from the deep receiver and either sprints to the interception point or "searches" the receiver, tackling him hard, and forcing a fumble if a receiver already has caught the ball and the defender cannot intercept or knock down the ball.

Also, the deep defender should be receiving underneath help from linebackers so that his assisting in short zones is secondary.

Coaching Points: Stress deep zone responsibility and not losing poise if passes are completed in front of the defender when he is covering deep. The passer should fake short and throw long to determine if the defender is playing the passer's arm motion instead of the flight of the ball, and if

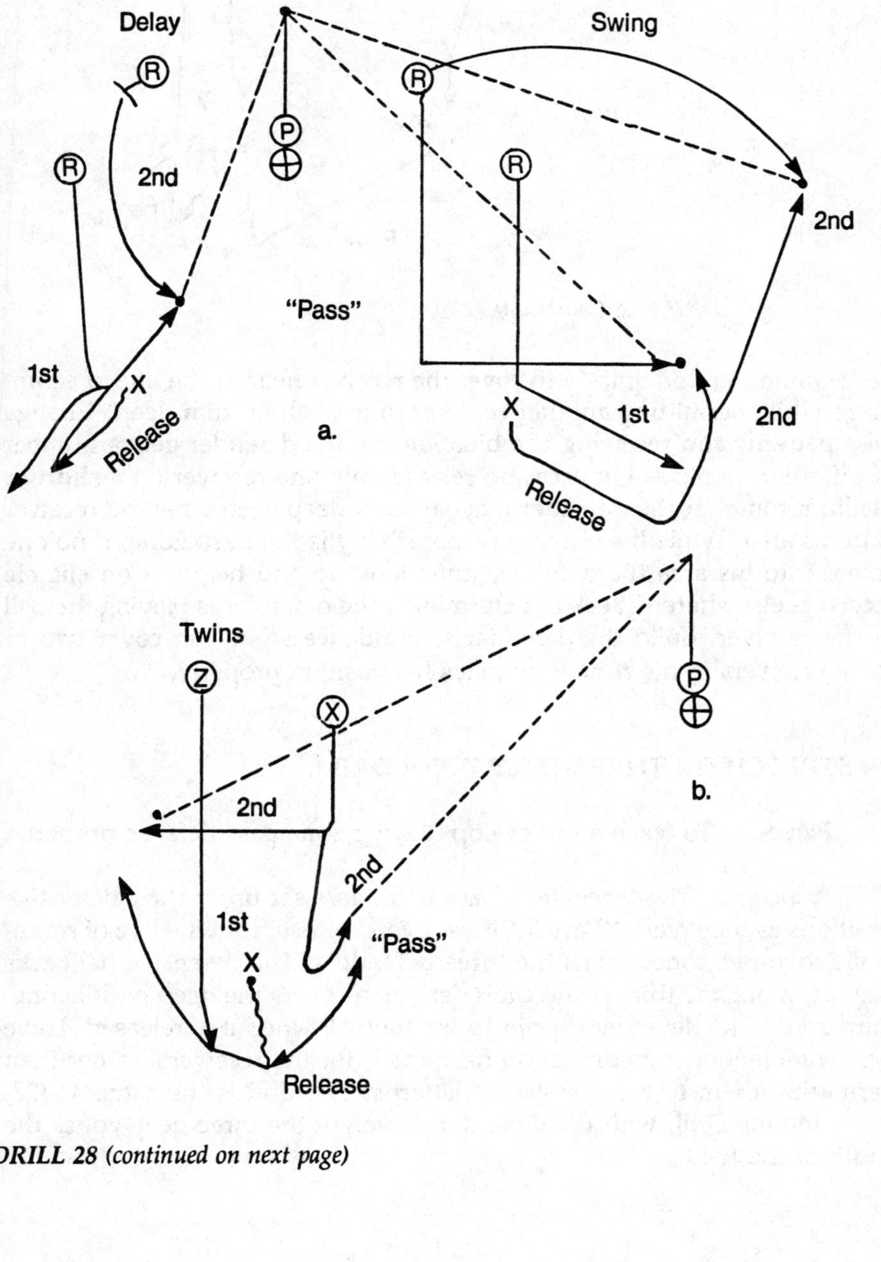

DRILL 28 (continued on next page)

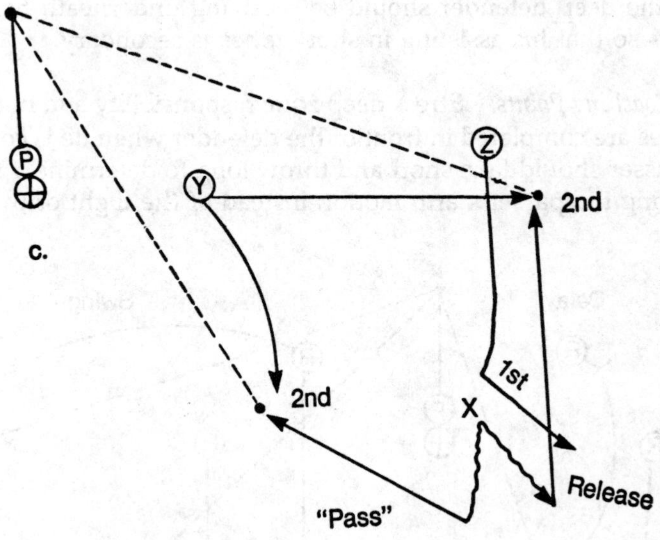

DRILL 28 (continued)

he is coming up too quickly to cover the receiver nearest the line of scrimmage while permitting another receiver to get behind him deep. Change pass patterns and receiving combinations so the defender gets a number of different "looks." On occasion release only one receiver on a short or medium route, or the defender may lay back deep even when no receiver is in his area. While his primary responsibility is the deep zone, if no one comes into his area the defender must look up and help out on eligible receivers elsewhere. Check to determine if the defender is playing the ball or the receiver. Build the defender's confidence so he can cover two or more receivers in his zone if he plays his position properly.

29. STRETCH OR THREE–DEEP ZONE DRILL

Purpose: To teach and develop playing zone pass defense properly.

Procedure: The three-deep pass defenders set up in their defensive positions as they read, "Pass." Six receivers release from the line of scrimmage, two per zone versus the three defenders. The defensive halfbacks play deep outside thirds, and the safety man covers the deep middle one-third zone. The defenders sprint to the football when it is released. Have pass combination cuts drawn on flash cards for the receivers, rather than permitting them to run free-lance patterns. The drill is the same as (28) Two-On-One Drill, with the defenders covering the three-deep zones the width of the field.

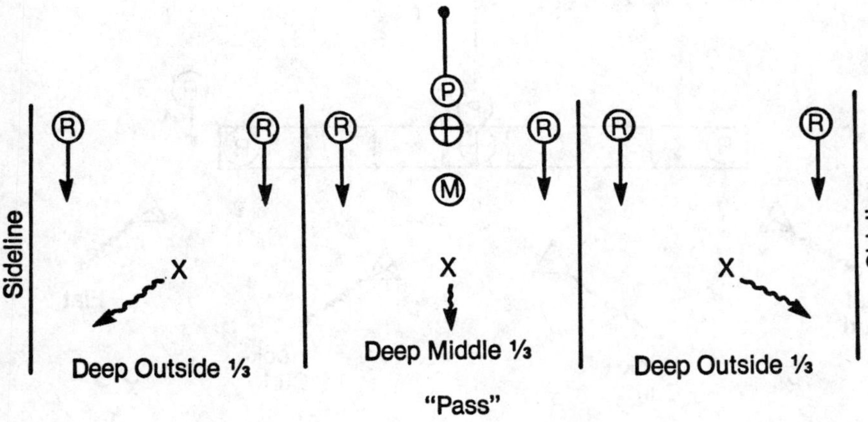

DRILL 29

Coaching Points: Same as (28) Two-On-One or Release Drill. Instruct the receivers to run deep patterns unless linebackers and/or defensive ends are used in the pass coverage underneath. Move the football from the middle out to the hash marks. The defenders should key the passer, taking the proper course to get to their areas of responsibility. Check that the defenders play the in zones and the ball properly, and pick up deep receivers. Build confidence that one defender can cover several men in his zone, and that three-deep defenders can cover the width of the field, as in (24) Overlap Drill.

30–31. DEFENSIVE PERIMETER VERSUS SKELETON OFFENSE DRILLS

30. Skeleton Pass Defense-Offense Drill

31. Outside (Defensive) Drill

Purpose: To check stance, position, keys, responsibilities, reaction, rotation, coverage, pursuit and tackling versus (30) opponent's pass offense, and (31) opponent's outside running offense.

Procedure: Same as Chapter 8, (22) (23) Skeleton Pass Offense-Defense Drills, and Chapter 9, (21) Skeleton Versus Live Perimeter or Outside (Offensive) Drill, only the emphasis is on the alignment and play of the defensive perimeter versus the opposition's favorite passes and outside running attack. If (31) a running play, the defenders should support in their proper pursuit; if (30) a pass, the defenders should play the ball ag-

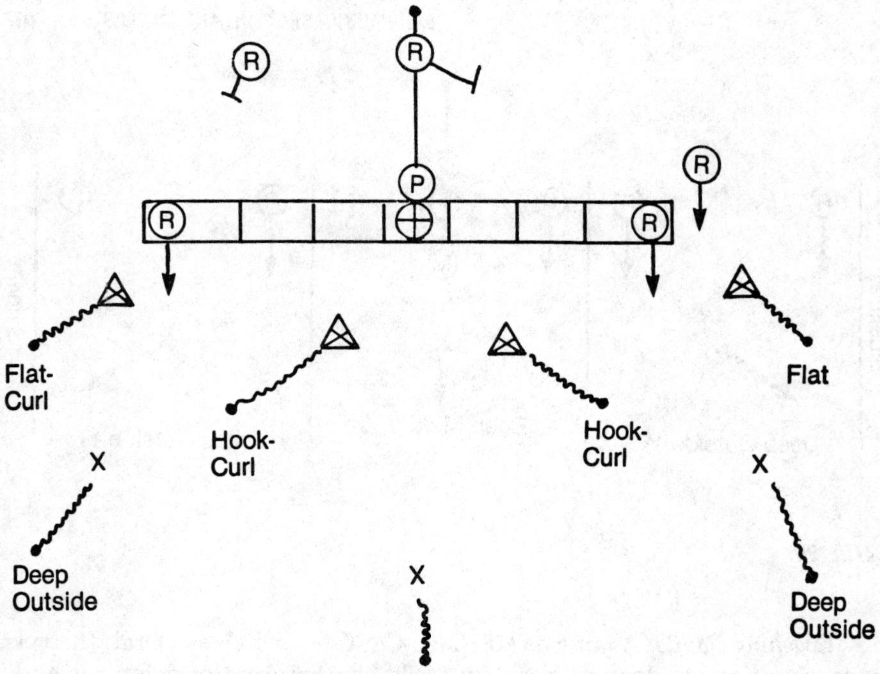

a. Deep Middle 3-deep zone

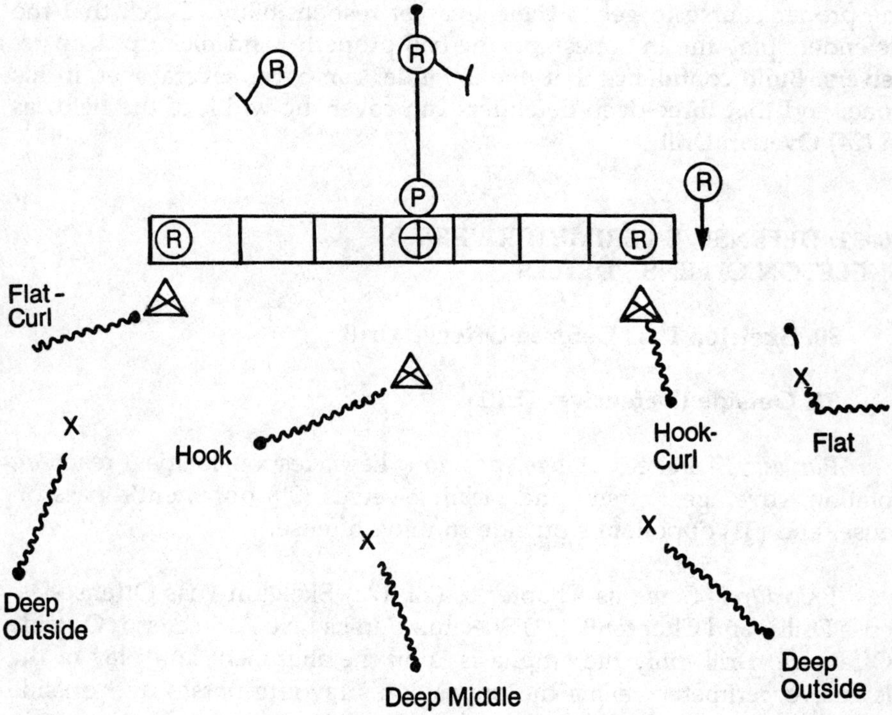

b. Pre-rotated strong right from 4-deep defensive secondary

gressively. If the drill is not live, use two skeleton offensive units so while one is running a play or pass, the other is huddling getting the next play. Use the opposition's cadence and starting count, and move the football from the middle to the right and left hash marks.

Coaching Points: Stress proper defensive play, including stance, alignment, and reacting to keys. Identify the opponent's field and formation tendencies to aid in play recognition for the defenders. Use a whistle to terminate the drill. See note 1, Chapter 2, on the use of flash cards when practicing against your opposition's tendencies.

32. DEFENSIVE SECONDARY DRILLS (ADDITIONAL)

The following drills all include defensive secondary fundamentals and techniques, but will not be repeated since they are explained in detail as follows:

See Chapter 8, (18) Outmaneuver-the-Defender Drill; (25) No. 1 Versus No. 2 Skeleton Pass Offense-Defense Drill.

See Chapter 10, (17) Defensive Half-Line Drill; (20) Jumping Defenses Drill; (27) Goal Line Defenses Drill; (28) Slow Whistle Drill; (29) Special Situations and "Fringe" Drills.

See Chapter 11, (23) Fight-Back Drill; (24) Fight-Up Drill; (26) Man-for-Man Coverage Drill; (27) Defender's Quick Hands Drill; (28) Defender's Net Drill.

See Chapter 13, (1) Straight-On Form Tackling Drill; (2) Sprint Tackling Drill; (13) Open-Field Tackling Drill No. 1; (14) Open-Field Tackling Drill No. 2; (15) Tackler Versus Ball Carrier Sideline Drill; (16) Tackler Versus Blocker and Ball Carrier Sideline Drill; (22) Tipper-Tackler Drill.

DRILL 30

13

Tackling Drills

Tackling is the ultimate of defensive football. A poor tackling team adversely affects the morale and reduces the effectiveness of its own offense by limiting its scoring opportunities when the defensive team fails to force the opposition to give up the football. On the other hand, an aggressively effective tackling football team usually is difficult to defeat, and limits the number of times its opposition has the football. Probably the best barometer of a team's morale is its tackling effectiveness. Defensively a football team is no better than its tackling, and probably the highest tribute that can be accorded is to identify it as an aggressively effective tackling team.

Coaches differ in their opinion of the best tackling techniques, although all agree that in most tactical situations the primary defensive objective is to down the ball carrier as quickly as possible and/or to prevent the offensive team from carrying out its specific objective. The offensive team's primary objective, depending on the tactical situation, is *not* always to score. On occasion the objective may be to make the first down. On other occasions the objective may be to "bleed" the clock or to stop it. From the defensive standpoint, however, in these and almost all other tactical situations, the immediate objective is to down the opposition's ball carrier as quickly as possible in order to gain possession of the football for its own offensive team.

To execute all of the defensive fundamentals correctly preparatory to the actual tackle, yet fail to make the tackle successfully and thus not stop the ball carrier from carrying out his team's objective, must be interpreted as failure. In reality it makes little difference how the defensive objective is accomplished. A tackle may consist of a defender hurling his body into the ball carrier, pushing an opponent into his own ball carrier, "riding" the ball carrier to the ground, or grabbing any part of the ball carrier's body or equipment (*excluding* his face mask). Although these methods or techniques of tackling generally are not taught, since they lack "form" and cannot be classified as "picture" or "master" tackles where the defensive player dominates, overwhelms and perhaps physically punishes the ball carrier, any legal means of downing the ball carrier is effective if the specific offensive objective is denied. Even unorthodox tackling methods and techniques can be improved if a player has the desire to learn and perfect his skill.

Tackling consists of two basic qualities, *desire* or effort and *form* or ability. Of the two attributes, *desire* is the more important requisite. The consensus is that desire is about three times as important as form. If a player has the "desire and fire," generally he has other qualities such as competitiveness and courage that are highly desirable for learning to tackle aggressively and effectively. If a football player lacks courage or "heart," no coach can give him this inherent quality.

Assuming a tackler is not "gun shy" and has "heart," tackling form or ability can be taught-coached so that an individual's tackling efficiency and effectiveness will improve to the extent of his physical limitations. There have been many changes in the game of football over the years. However, a team that displays desire, hustle and enthusiasm, and in which each defensive player works diligently to improve his quickness, speed and tackling skills to the limits of his ability, will produce a squad of players that will win more than its share of football games.

When drilling, a coach should strive to teach his players the proper form in tackling, without destroying their desire and determination. More than a dozen drills have been included already in other chapters with tackling as the ultimate skill or fundamental being taught-learned. While these will be referred to by number at the conclusion of this chapter, a description and explanation of them will not be repeated here. Additional drills for teaching-coaching tackling are as follows:

1. STRAIGHT–ON FORM TACKLING DRILL

Purpose: To teach and develop the fundamentals and techniques of tackling the ball carrier whose approach is head-on.

Procedure: The ball carrier lines up inside of a five-yard square approximately three yards from the front line. Opposite and facing him one yard away from the front line outside of the square is the tackler in a "ready" position, feet digging, eyes focused on the ball carrier's numeral.

DRILL 1

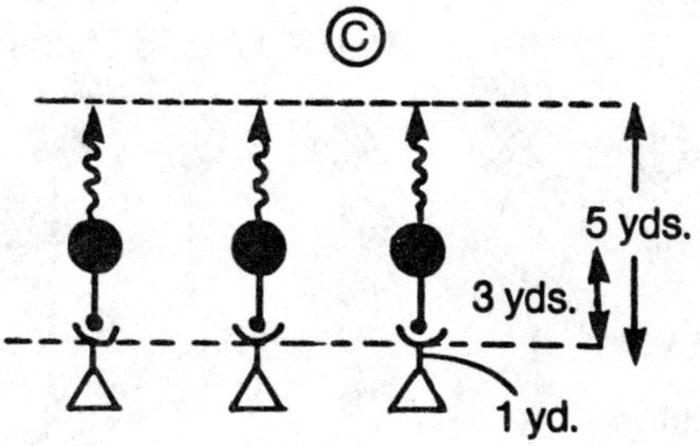

On the coach's command the ball carrier will move directly toward the tackler at about one-third speed. Prior to the initial contact between the ball carrier and tackler, the latter should take one step forward, flex at the knees and then make contact with the *front* of his shoulder pad on the ball carrier's upper torso at the numerals. The tackler's eyes should be open, his head up as he wraps his arms around the ball carrier's buttocks, picks him up, and carries him backward to the opposite side of the five-yard square. Each additional time the drill is repeated, the faster and tougher it becomes.

Coaching Points:[1] Stress the correct fundamentals of tackling. The tackler should *not* drop or turn his head as he shoulder tackles with the nape of his neck against the ball carrier's body. The helmet should *not* be used as the primary point of contact when tackling (and blocking). Stress accelerating the feet at contact (leg lift) to get maximum power. The ball carrier should not jump upward assisting the tackler. The tackler should *hit and lift,* sustaining his momentum forward, and *not* merely make contact with the ball carrier and then fail to move his feet.

2. SPRINT TACKLING DRILL (PROGRESSIVE)

Purpose: To teach and develop the fundamentals and techniques of tackling.

[1]"Face" tackling is no longer taught or advocated by the prudent coach, as it, along with "spearing" (and the various additional terms used to describe the use of the head in tackling and blocking, such as "face-to-the-numbers," "butt," "stick") have been legislated out of present-day football by scholastic and collegiate governing bodies. Face tackling is defined as "driving the face mask, frontal area, or top of the helmet directly into the runner." Spearing is "deliberately and maliciously driving the helmet into a player who is down or who is held so he is going down, or who is held so his forward progress is stopped, or who is obviously out of the play." "Spearing" is a disqualifying foul and brings automatic ejection from the game, plus a fifteen-yard penalty. "Face tackling" and "butt blocking" (Chapter 6) are personal fouls that carry a fifteen-yard penalty, too, but do not bring ejection for the errant player unless these tackling/blocking techniques are deemed flagrant violations.

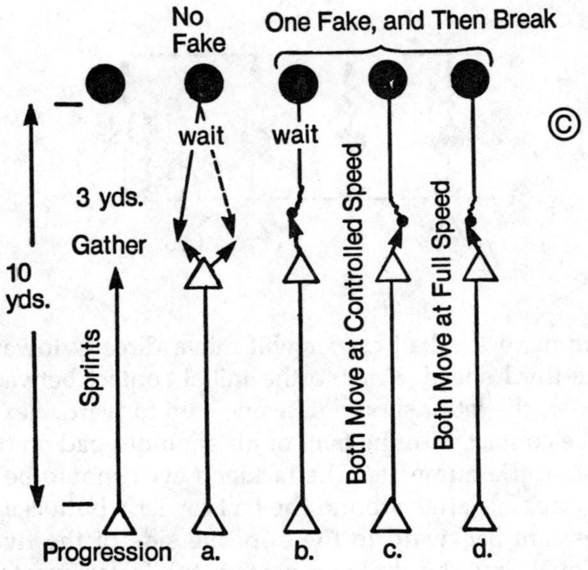

DRILL 2

Procedure: The ball carrier and tackler are ten yards apart facing each other. On the coach's command, the tackler sprints to within three yards of the ball carrier. The latter remains stationary until the tackler comes under control into a good defensive football position and "gathers" to tackle. The progression is as follows: a) the ball carrier breaks right or left immediately without any faking maneuvers; b) the ball carrier is permitted one fake, and then breaks; c) the tackler and ball carrier both move toward each other at controlled speed and the ball carrier is permitted to fake once, but then must break; and d) the tackler and ball carrier move at full speed, except the tackler comes under control and the ball carrier may fake once before attempting to break by the tackler. In all four progressions the defender *form shoulder tackles,* as explained in Drill 1, except he places the heels of his hands against the ball carrier's hips.

Coaching Points: As in Drill 1, stress getting into the proper position to tackle, including keeping the body under control, head up, eyes open, back straight, tail down, and "gathering."

3. ANGLE FORM TACKLING DRILL

Purpose: To develop the fundamentals and techniques of tackling a ball carrier from an oblique angle.

Procedure: The ball carrier runs back and forth laterally within a five-yard square, always remaining parallel to the front line. He switches the football to his off or far arm, i.e., to the side toward which he is moving laterally. From a position parallel to the ball carrier the tackler drives his shoulder into the ball carrier's body at the waist, keeping his eyes open and his head up. The tackler's head goes in front or "across the bow" toward the ball carrier's far arm. He "clubs" both arms, simulating all of the mechanics of a *shoulder* tackle, as he approaches the ball carrier at an oblique angle from the side. After several repetitions the coach can command the tackler to use the techniques and fundamentals of tackling mentioned in the previous drills.

Coaching Points: Stress quickness, movement, good football position and the correct fundamentals of tackling.

4. BACK–TO–BACK FORM TACKLING DRILL

Purpose: To teach and develop the fundamentals and techniques of tackling correctly.

Procedure: A ball carrier and a tackler line up back-to-back facing *away* from each other. On the coach's command both players walk slowly away from each other. On his second command, both whirl around and the ball carrier runs a pre-designated path at a right or left oblique angle, or approaches the tackler head-on. If at an angle, the mechanics of tackling are the same as in Drill 3; if head-on, the procedure and mechanics are the same as in Drill 1. After several simulated practice tackles, then speed up the drill and go "live."

Coaching Points: Stress the proper fundamentals and techniques of good tackling. When going "live," give the second command quickly so the players do *not* get too far apart before tackling. Conclude the drill "live" with the ball carrier being permitted to take any evasive course he wishes after the second command is given.

DRILL 4

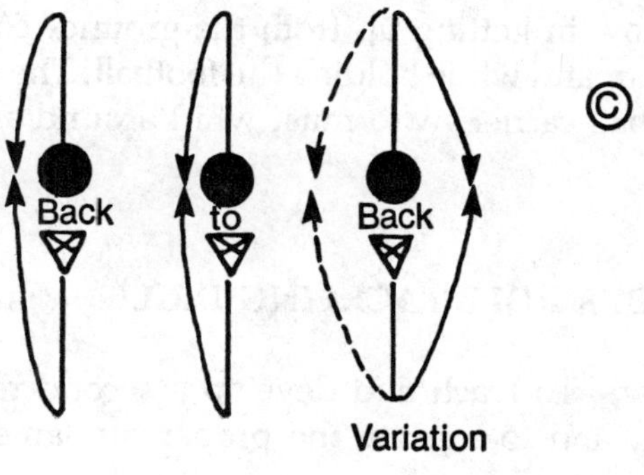

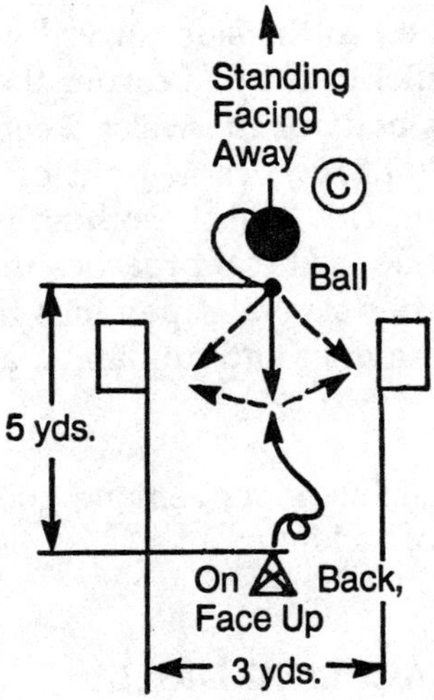

DRILL 5

5. SUPINE TACKLING DRILL

Purpose: To teach and develop a second reaction of getting up off the ground, and to execute the proper fundamentals and techniques of tackling.

Procedure: The tackler is in a supine position on his back with the top of his helmet touching the front line of a five-yard square. The football is placed five yards away on the back line of the square, at the heels of the ball carrier's feet, who is standing facing away from the tackler. On the coach's command the ball carrier must whirl around, pick up the football, attempt to evade the tackler, and try to get to the opposite side of the square. The tackler must roll over quickly on the same command, spring to his feet, get into a good hitting position and tackle the ball carrier. Upright dummies are stationed three yards apart so the ball carrier has a limited area in which to evade the tackler.

Coaching Points: Stress the proper fundamentals of tackling. If the tackler is slow in getting up from the ground, control the drill by giving him the command while holding the football. The coach then flips the football to the ball carrier, who must whirl around and attempt to evade the tackler.

6. SHOULDER ROLL TACKLING DRILL

Purpose: To teach and develop a second reaction of getting up off the ground, and to execute the proper fundamentals and techniques of tackling.

DRILL 6

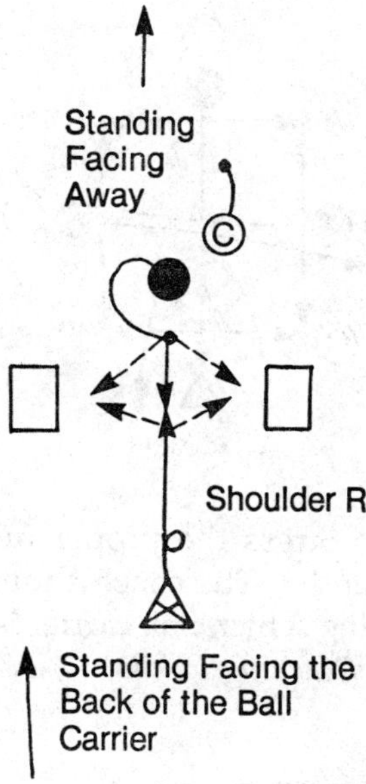

Procedure: Same as (5) Supine Tackling Drill, only the tackler is in an upright position *facing the back* of the ball carrier on the opposite side of the five-yard square, and is several yards away from the front line. On the coach's command, the ball carrier whirls around, picks up the football, and tries to evade the tackler while getting to the opposite side of the square. At the same time the tackler must execute a shoulder roll, come up into a hitting position, and tackle the ball carrier.

Coaching Points: Stress quickness, maintaining a low center of gravity, a proper shoulder roll, and the proper fundamentals of tackling. The coach can control the drill by favoring the tackler as in the previous drill, or by permitting the tackler to regain his feet before tossing the football to the ball carrier.

7. SOMERSAULT TACKLING DRILL

Purpose: To develop a second reaction, quickness and the proper fundamentals of tackling.

Procedure: The tackler is opposite a ball carrier in a five-yard square, two yards back from the front line. Also, to his left and right are ball carriers. On the coach's command, the tackler executes a somersault (forward roll or shoulder roll) and regains his feet, coming up into a good hitting position. The coach then calls the name of a ball carrier. The latter sprints to the opposite side of the square, or comes directly toward the tackler.

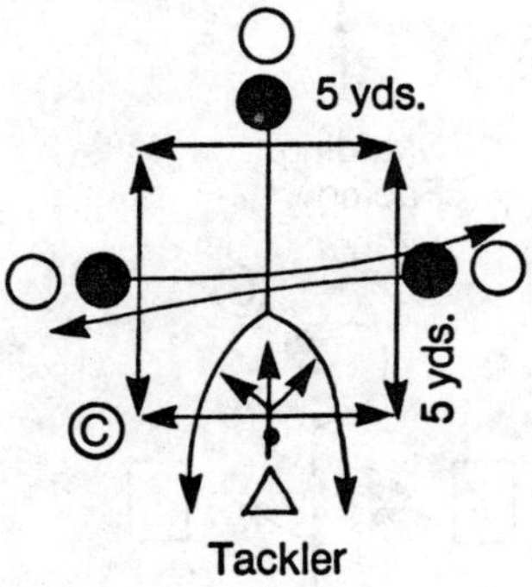

DRILL 7

Coaching Points: Stress the proper fundamentals of tackling as explained in Drills 1, 2 and 3. The coach should permit the tackler to regain his feet before indicating which ball carrier is to try and evade the tackling. See Drills 1, 2 and 3, *Coaching Points.*

8. WAVE–SHED–TACKLE DRILL

Purpose: To develop agility, reaction, and the proper fundamentals and techniques of tackling.

Procedure: The ball carrier and the tackler align ten yards apart, with a blocker five yards between them. The coach faces the blocker and the ball carrier standing behind the tackler. The blocker moves laterally side to side within his five-yard lateral boundaries, and the tackler must maintain a nose-on alignment with him. After several lateral movements, at the hand signal or command of the coach, the blocker attacks the tackler. The

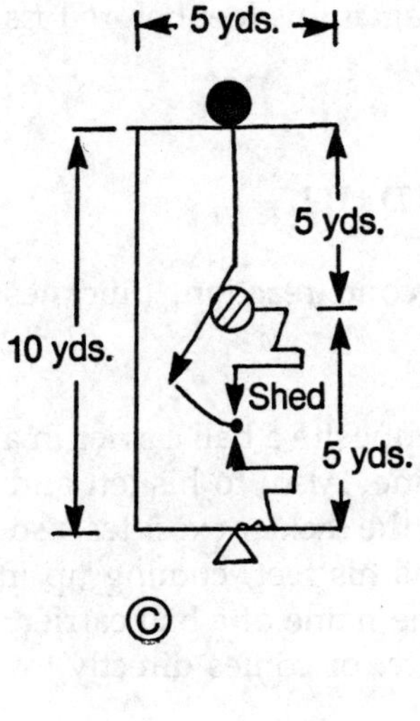

DRILL 8

ball carrier cannot move in an attempt to evade the tackler until the blocker gets to the tackler (and/or when signalled by the coach). The purpose of the drill is for the tackler to shed the blocker and make the tackle before the ball carrier crosses the boundary line nearest the defender's alignment.

Coaching Points: Stress quickness, body control, shedding the blocker, and the proper fundamentals and techniques of tackling. If a tackler is too slow to catch the ball carrier, control the drill by informing the ball carrier when to run, and limit his running lane to three yards in width.

9. LEADER WAVE–TACKLE DRILL

Purpose: To develop agility, reaction and the proper fundamentals of tackling.

Procedure: The ball carrier is ten yards away from a tackler, with another tackler three yards behind (if two tacklers are used in this drill). The ball carrier is the "leader" and the tackler(s) must "mirror" his movements laterally. On the coach's signal the leader does a somersault, comes up running, and attempts to get to the opposite side of the running lane, which is five yards wide and ten yards long. The tacklers must somersault when the ball carrier does, regain their feet, pursue and tackle. Once the ball carrier gets to the opposite side of the ten-yard zone, the defenders cannot tackle him.

Coaching Points: Stress quickness, direct angle movements, and good tackling. The "leader" should not extend his lateral wave movements beyond five, or the tackling is likely to be executed poorly. This is a defensive drill, not an offensive one; the purpose is to teach tackling fundamentals and not evasive running.

DRILL 9

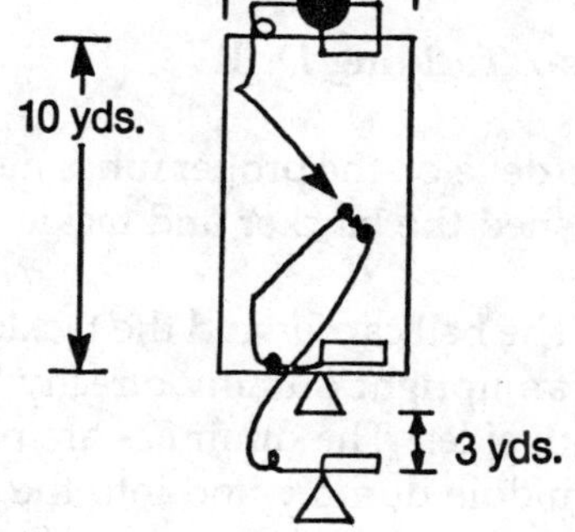

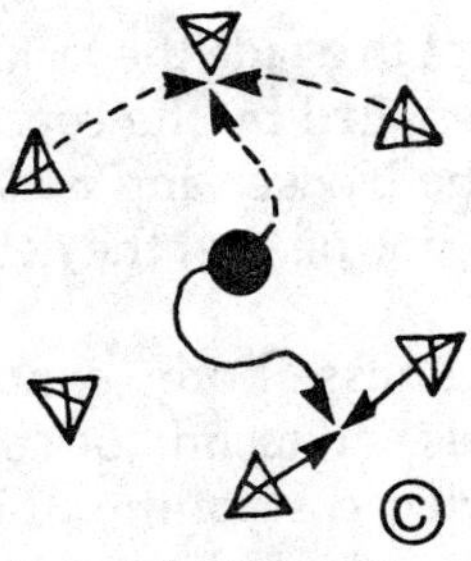

DRILL 10

10. CIRCLE–ESCAPE TACKLING DRILL

Purpose: To develop the proper fundamentals and techniques of tackling, including legalized gang or mass tackling.

Procedure: The ball carrier is in the middle of a twelve to fifteen-foot (diameter) circle. The rim men are tacklers, and they set up in a ready position, with their feet moving and their eyes on the target. The ball carrier either tries to run between two defenders, or runs directly at a defender, in order to "escape" from the circle. If he attempts to go between defenders, the men on each side of the gap must close it and both must tackle the ball carrier. If he runs directly at a tackler, the latter must meet him head-on, and the tacklers on each side should close to assist with the tackle. The player who lets a ball carrier "escape" replaces him in the middle of the circle.

Coaching Points: Since the drill is "rough" the ball carrier should not remain in the middle more than three times, if he does not "escape" sooner. Stress good tackling fundamentals and techniques.

11–12. IN–THE–HOLE TACKLING DRILLS

11. 1-Versus-1 Tackling Drill

12. 2-Versus-2 Tackling Drill

Purpose: To develop the proper fundamentals and techniques of tackling; also (12) to shed the blocker and tackle the ball carrier.

Procedure: The ball carrier and the tackler are five yards apart, facing each other, with an upright dummy directly between them and dummies three yards to both sides. The dummies are placed so the ball carrier must break off of the middle dummy and into the hole formed by it and either of the outside dummies. In (11) the coach flips the football to the ball car-

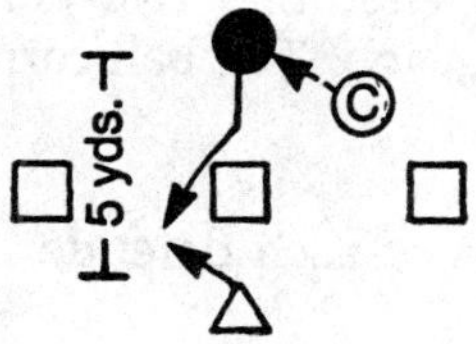

DRILL 11

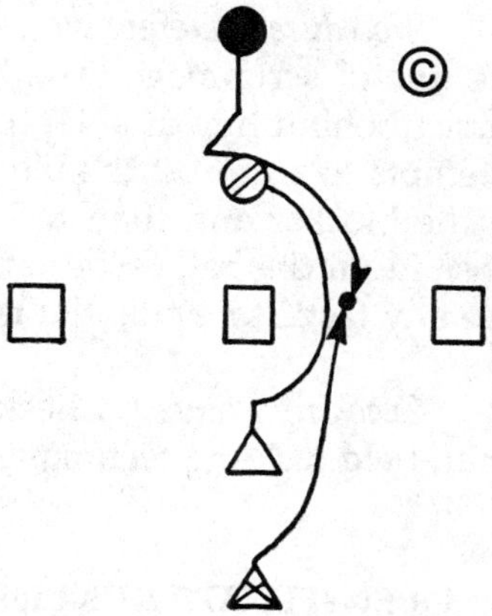

DRILL 12

rier. At the same time the tackler moves forward and sets up in a good football position, with his feet moving. He attempts to meet the ball carrier in the hole as the ball carrier veers left or right off of the middle dummy. In (12) the blocker tells the ball carrier which way to break, and he attempts to lead block for him through the hole. The tacklers may be in tandem or parallel with each other. The tacklers must shed the blocker and make the tackle in the hole.

Coaching Points: Stress the proper fundamentals and techniques of tackling. After flipping the ball to the ball carrier, attempt to watch the tackler's eyes. Getting into the proper position is the most important part of tackling, regardless of the player's size.

13. OPEN–FIELD TACKLING DRILL 1

Purpose: To teach defensive secondary men to ward-off or shed a blocker, control him, and then to make the tackle in open field.

DRILL 13

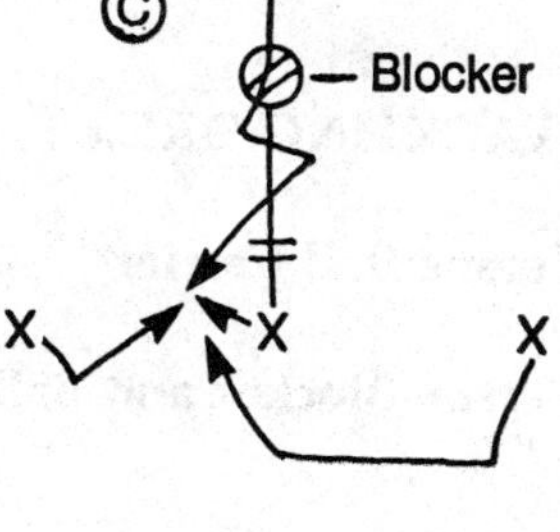

Procedure: Defensive secondary men set up in their positions from the line of scrimmage. The blocker goes for one defender, with the ball carrier behind him at a depth of approximately three yards. The defender attempts to ward-off the blocker, control him, keep his feet free, dispose of the blocker and then tackle the ball carrier. The other two defenders close in on the ball carrier and assist in tackling, too. The ball carrier can use any tactic to evade the tacklers.

Coaching Points: Check the pursuit angles of each defender. Stress open-field tackling techniques.

14. OPEN–FIELD TACKLING DRILL 2

Purpose: To develop reaction, pursuit and tackling in the open field.

Procedure: The defenders (linebackers or defensive secondary men) line up in a "ready" position on their fifteen-yard line, with the ball carrier slightly behind the twenty-yard line. The lateral distance may be increased until the defenders are attempting to protect the width of the field. The defenders move laterally with the ball carrier, but do not pursue him until he crosses the twenty-yard line and attempts to score. The defenders must take the proper pursuit angles.

Coaching Points: Stress proper pursuit and open-field tackling fundamentals and techniques.

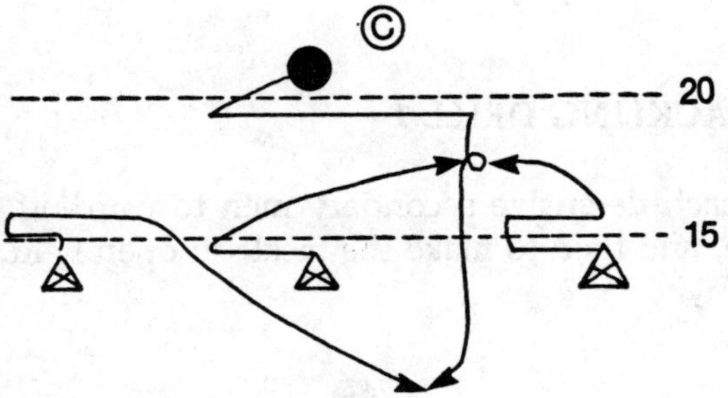

DRILL 14

15–16. SIDELINE TACKLING DRILLS

15. Tackler Versus Ball Carrier

16. Tackler Versus Blocker and Ball Carrier Drill

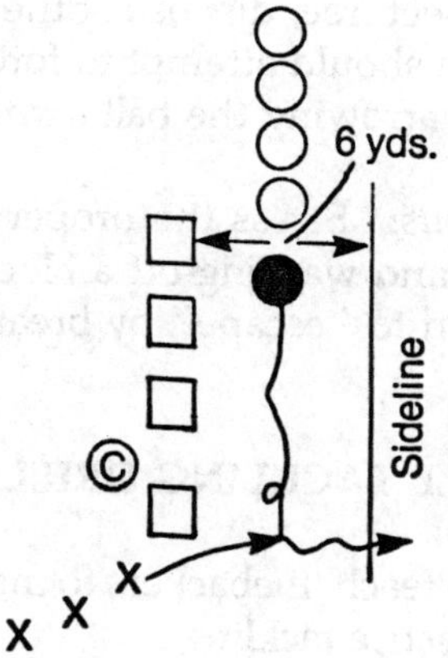

DRILL 15

Purpose: To teach defensive backs to employ the sideline as the "twelfth man" on their team, and to make the sideline tackle.

Procedure: The ball carrier has a six-yard running lane in which he may use any evasive tactic he wishes to get by the tackler (secondary defender). The tackler approaches the ball carrier from an inside-out position and either tackles him high or aggressively pushes him out-of-bounds. When a blocker is added, as in Drill 16, the defender must control the

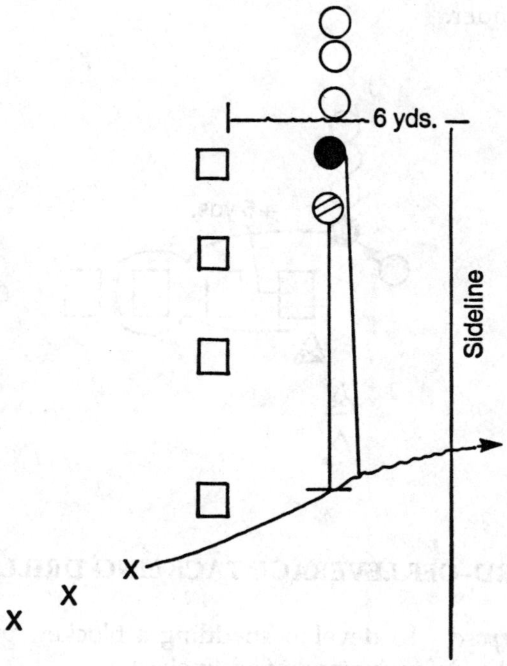

DRILL 16

blocker, keep his feet free, dispose of the blocker, and force the ball carrier out-of-bounds. He should attempt to force the blocker into the ball carrier from inside-out, narrowing the ball carrier's running lane.

Coaching Points: Stress the proper fundamentals and techniques of sideline tackling, and warding-off a blocker. Also, the ball carrier should never be permitted to "escape" by breaking back to the inside.

17. LATERAL FILL TACKLING DRILL

Purpose: To teach linebackers to maintain proper leverage on the ball carrier, and to practice tackling.

Procedure: Upright dummies are placed on a straight line, allowing five feet between each dummy. The linebacker is in a "ready" position at one end of the dummies, directly opposite the ball carrier. The coach flips or hands the football to the ball carrier. The ball carrier either runs directly between two dummies, or he fakes once and then must break into the next hole. The linebacker makes the tackle in the hole from an inside-out position, head across in front of the ball carrier, as in Drill 3.

Coaching Points: Stress maintaining proper leverage, and the proper fundamentals of tackling. Follow-up with (18) Eye Opener or Outside Shed Drill, Chapter 11, where a blocker leads the ball carrier into the hole versus the defender.

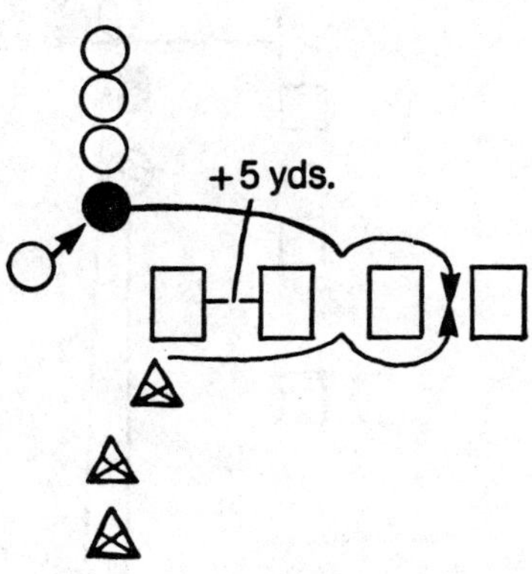

DRILL 17

18. WARD–OFF LEVERAGE TACKLING DRILLS

Purpose: To develop shedding a blocker, pursuit and tackling, especially by defensive ends and linebackers.

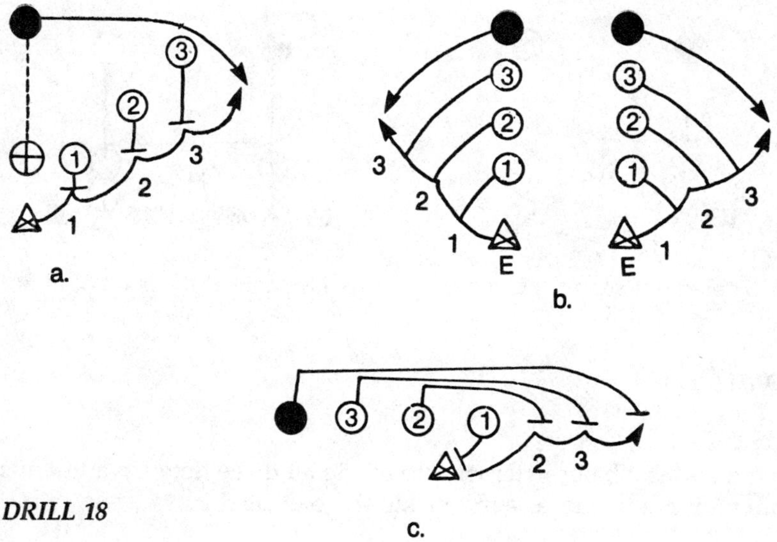

DRILL 18

Procedure: The drill is either half or full-speed, with the blockers or the coach regulating the flow of players moving toward the defender from diagonal, vertical and/or horizontal lines. As the first blocker makes contact, the second leaves, then the third, and finally the ball carrier. The defender hits, shuffles, hits, shuffles, hits and maintains leverage on the ball carrier as he moves to tackle him.

Coaching Points: Stress hitting, shedding blockers (*not* wrestling with the blockers), and moving from inside-out to maintain correct leverage on the ball carrier. Stress the fundamentals of proper pursuit, leverage and tackling.

19. THREE–ON–THREE (ONE–ON–ONE) CHALLENGE DRILL (DEFENSIVELY)

Purpose: To teach defensive fundamentals and techniques, including defeating the one-on-one block, controlling the blocker, locating the football, pursuing and tackling the ball carrier.

Procedure: Set up a full offensive backfield in a straight T-formation, plus an offensive center and two additional offensive linemen (tackles) versus three defensive linemen three-on-three (one-on-one) "live." The offensive back receiving the hand-off (counter, inside belly, drive, cross-buck) will be "live," and the other two backs will fake. All three offensive linemen execute one-on-one blocks, with the defensive linemen not at the point-of-attack pursuing and tagging the ball carrier. Inside dummies are

a. 3 defenders versus 3 blockers (all "live")

b. Live only at the point of attack (1-on-1)

DRILL 19

removed and the ball carrier tries to evade all three defensive linemen. All the linemen are trying to gang tackle the ball carrier.

Coaching Points: This is an "all purpose drill" which may be used either offensively or defensively; here it is used for teaching defensive line fundamentals and tackling. It is suggested that you *not* use your best running backs as ball carriers, since three defenders are likely to gang tackle him aggressively. Stress all of the proper defensive fundamentals and techniques.

20. ACROSS–THE–SQUARE TACKLING DRILL

Purpose: To teach the tackler to maintain proper leverage on the ball carrier, quickness, body control, and tackling from the side or at an angle.

Procedure: The ball carrier and the tackler line up directly opposite each other on two corners of the same side of a five-yard square. On the coach's command the ball carrier sprints diagonally across the square for the opposite corner. From his "ready" position, the tackler moves laterally, using the side tackling techniques discussed in Drill 3, and attempting to shoulder tackle the ball carrier before he gets to the opposite corner. The tackler is successful if he brings down his opponent inside the boundaries of the five-yard square directly to his right (or left). If the ball carrier gets to the opposite corner of the square, the tackler is unsuccessful. Occasionally instruct the ball carrier to break back to the inside instead of trying to run diagonally directly to the opposite corner. This will make certain the tacklers are maintaining inside-out leverage properly.

Coaching Points: Stress a good football position and the fundamentals and techniques of the tackle. Maintain proper leverage on the ball

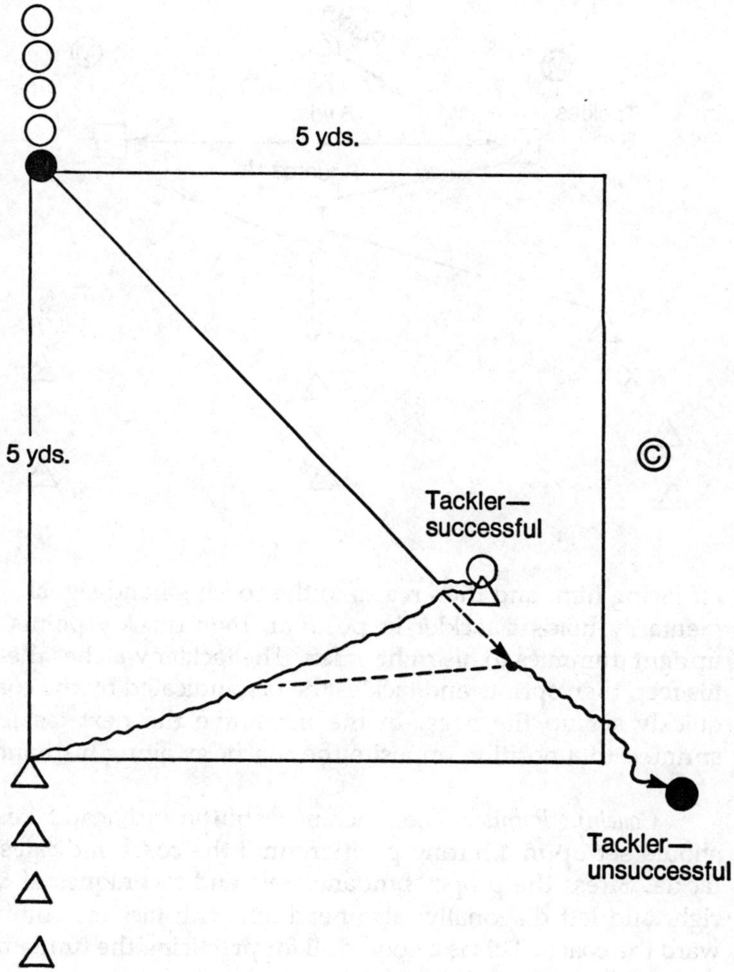

DRILL 20

carrier. Work the drill both left and right, so the defenders get practice tackling with both the left and right shoulder.

21. BAG TACKLING DRILL

Purpose: To teach pursuit, reaction and tackling, without going "live."

Procedure: Two upright dummies are five yards apart, with the coach in between but several yards beyond the dummies. In rapid succession one tackler after another sprints from the coach's left (or right), squares

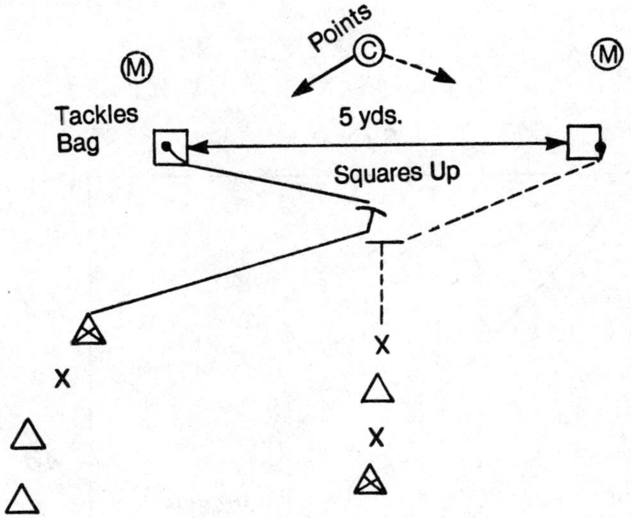

DRILL 21

off facing him, and then reacts to the coach's hand signal. The coach momentarily holds a tackler in position, then quickly points to one of the upright dummies to his right or left. The tackler watches the coach, pumps his feet, then sprints and tackles the bag indicated by the coach. Managers quickly set up the bags. In the meantime the next tackler has already sprinted to a position opposite the coach, awaiting his hand signal.

Coaching Points: The coach may shuffle and head fake. The defender should set up in a hitting position until the coach indicates which bag to tackle. Stress the proper fundamentals and techniques of tackling. Work right and left diagonally; also head-up, with tacklers coming directly toward the coach. This is a good drill for practicing the fundamentals of tackling, without the risk of sustaining injuries that may occur from always going "live."

22. TIPPER–TACKLER DRILL

Purpose: To react to the ball that is tipped, and to tackle the interceptor.

Procedure: The tipper (tackler) runs forward toward the passer (coach) and after tipping the football backward to the trailer, he turns and tackles him.

Coaching Points: Stress *either* tackling (this drill), or catching the deflected pass, as in (11) Tip Interception Drill, Chapter 12. In this (22) Tip-

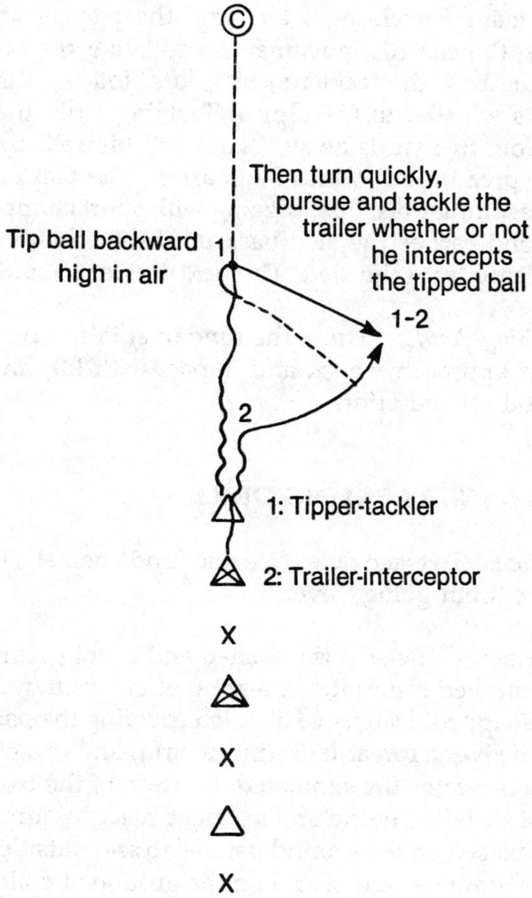

DRILL 22

per-Tackler Drill, the "tipper" turns and tackles the "trailer" regardless of whether or not he catches the deflected ball. The drill emphasis is on tackling.

23–24. TWO–MAN SLED TACKLING DRILLS

23. Close-Up Tackling Drill

24. Sprint Tackling Drill

Purpose: To teach and develop the fundamentals of tackling.

Procedure: The sled is allowed to run free and is not scotched or weighted for a single tackler. When working in pairs, the sled is weighted with one man. For close-up tackling, the players are in their defensive stance. On the coach's movement, simulating the offensive center snapping the football, the tackler(s) hits, lifts, follows through, and stops on the coach's whistle. In (24) Sprint Tackling Drill, the tackler approaches the sled from five yards away, "gathers" himself, comes to balance with feet well spread, and "clubs" his arms. The tackler's head is up, back straight, feet under his hips, digging with short choppy steps as he follows through, and carries the sled back until the coach's whistle indicates he should release from the sled. The next tackler should follow-up quickly.

Coaching Points: Stress the fundamentals of proper tackling, including proper approach, shock and impact with lift, and following through with a good second effort.

25. SLED–BAGS TACKLING DRILL

Purpose: To teach defensive line fundamentals, including pursuit and tackling, without going "live."

Procedure: The sled is scotched and is not permitted to run free. The coach on the sled rattles it, simulating offensive movement or that the ball has been snapped. Defensive linemen covering the pads (arms) on the two-man sled deliver a forearm lift (inside arm) and come to balance positions. The coach indicates the simulated direction of the ball carrier by hand signals, right or left. The defenders must react by jumping over horizontal dummies placed on the ground parallel to and outside the arms of the sled. Two other dummies are placed on the ground at oblique angles to the rear

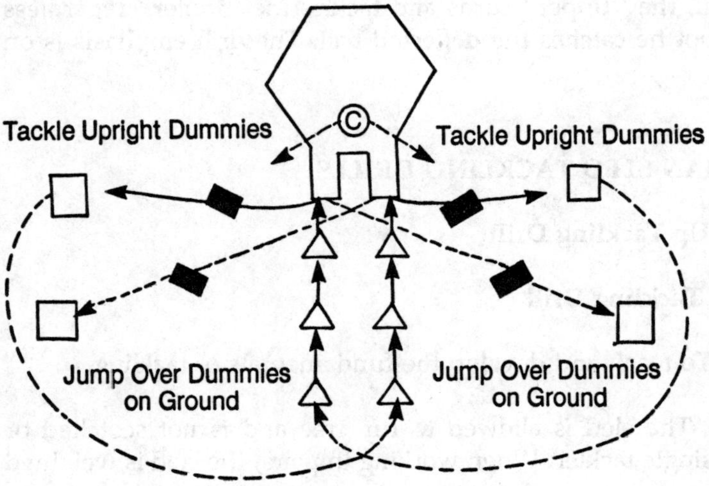

DRILL 25

of the defenders' initial positions. Each tackler, after jumping over a horizontal dummy, tackles an upright dummy.

Coaching Points: Same as (21) Bag Tackling Drill, in that the tacklers should each tackle a bag and roll it over. Stress the proper fundamentals of pursuit and tackling, after simulating neutralizing the offensive block and coming to balance. The drill should be done rapidly, but correctly. Managers should set up bags quickly in order to keep the drill moving rapidly. As in Drill 21, this drill permits "rough" work without going "live." Tacklers may each be signalled to pursue in the direction nearest their position, or to pursue on the same sides to tackle upright dummies. However, tacklers should *not* be signalled to cross, pursue and tackle the upright dummies *opposite* their initial alignments at the same time.

26. "BOUNCE" FORM TACKLING DRILL

Purpose: To teach and develop the fundamentals and techniques of tackling.

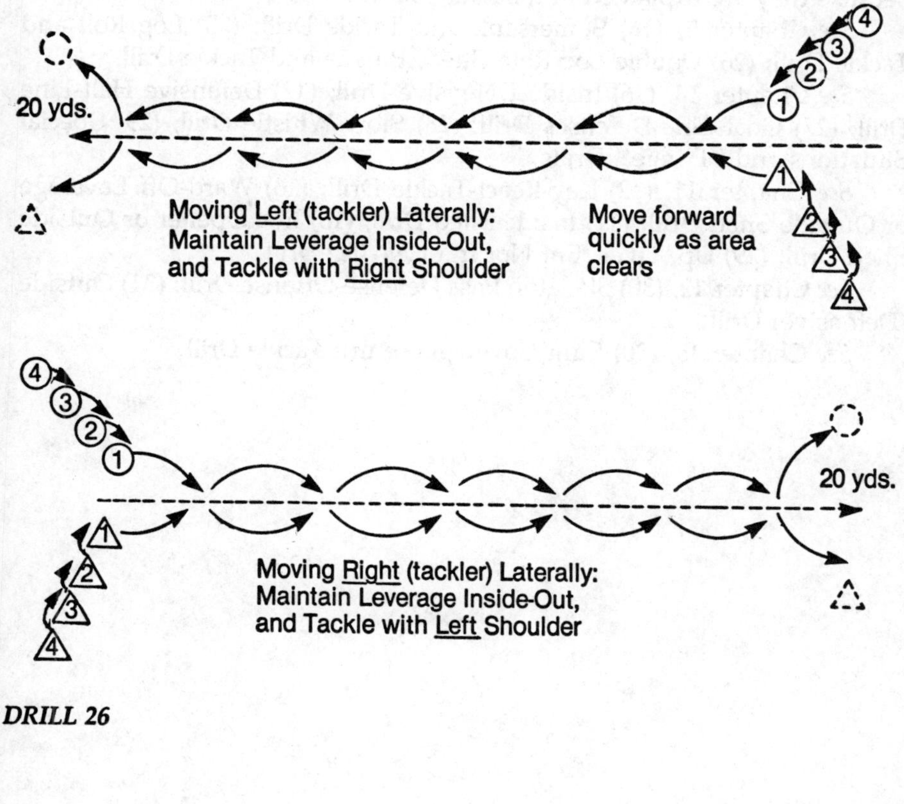

DRILL 26

Procedure: The ball carriers and tacklers are opposite and facing one another. If working left, on the coach's command the first ball carrier approaches a line approximately twenty yards in length at a slightly oblique angle. The first tackler also approaches from a slightly oblique angle, and simulates form tackling the ball carrier with his right shoulder, as in Drill 3. After clubbing the arms, both the ball carrier and the tackler bow ("bounce") back slightly from the line and then collide in controlled form tackling again and again for the entire twenty yards. Other ball carriers and tacklers follow as soon as the immediate area is cleared, so a number of tacklers are practicing form tackling at the same time, and each gets six or more opportunities to simulate shoulder-tackling to the far end of the line.

Coaching Points: Stress quickness, movement, good football position, and the proper fundamentals of shoulder tackling. Work on the line both left and right so the defenders can practice form tackling with both the right and left shoulder.

27. TACKLING DRILLS (ADDITIONAL)

The following drills all include tackling, but will not be discussed here because they are explained in detail as follows:

See Chapter 5, (16) Somersault and Tackle Drill; (25) Log Roll and Tackle Drill; (26) Double Log Roll, Shed, Pursue and Tackle Drill.

See Chapter 10, (16) Inside Defensive Drill; (17) Defensive Half-Line Drill; (27) Goal Line Defenses Drill; (28) Slow Whistle Drill; (29) Special Situations and "Fringe" Drills.

See Chapter 11, (12) Key-React-Tackle Drill; (16) Ward-Off Leverage or Outside Shed Drill; (17) Inside Shed Drill; (18) Eye Opener or Outside Shed Drill; (29) Up, Over, But Not In or No TD Drill.

See Chapter 12, (30) Skeleton Pass Defense-Offense Drill; (31) Outside (Defensive) Drill.

See Chapter 15, (20) Punt Coverage-Return-Tackle Drill.

PART V

Offensive and Defensive Drills for Teaching-Coaching the Signal Callers, and the Kicking Game

14

Drills for Teaching-Training Offensive and Defensive Signal Callers

Every head football coach must decide whether he, or a member of his staff, or the offensive and defensive quarterbacks, respectively, are going to call the plays and the defenses. A coach may prefer to use substitutes or to flash signals from the sideline to call all of the defensive alignments, stunts, and pass coverages, but train his offensive quarterbacks to make most all of the calls themselves. The coach may do the reverse, with all of the offensive calls being made for the quarterbacks, and the defensive quarterbacks being trained to make all of the defensive calls. Or the coach may make all offensive and defensive calls.

A problem usually arises if *both* the coach and the quarterbacks are calling the signals offensively and/or defensively. There are likely to be occasions when the signal callers expect or need help from the coach that is not forthcoming. Conversely, a coach may make a particular call when the signal caller would rather have made it himself. In the latter situation, if the call is the right one, the quarterback is apt to feel he could have done equally as well as the coach had he been permitted to try. If the call proves to be a poor one or wrong one, there may be the feeling among squad members that their signal caller would not have made the same mistake the coach made. While a coach always wants to build confidence and to provide opportunities for leadership, especially in his signal callers, he must exercise discretion when both he and his quarterbacks are making the offensive and/or defensive calls. It is very important for a head coach and his quarterbacks to understand that it is the coach's responsibility, right, and prerogative to call some, all, or none of the plays and defenses should he care to do so; also that second-guessing or criticizing coaching decisions by players is unacceptable. Most coaches feel strongly about this since it is the head coach who is ultimately responsible if the team does not win. Squad members don't always understand the pressures of coaching. However, if the issue is handled correctly and resolved tactfully ever before it arises in a game, it probably won't be a problem later on. To fail to resolve the issue in advance, however, is likely to create a number of problems, including poor team morale, especially if the team is not winning.

The frequency and extensiveness of off-the-field teaching via meetings and conferences, and on-the-field coaching-training of signal callers via practicing and drilling, depends on the method of signal calling utilized by the coach. If plays and defenses are sent in via substitutes or by flashing signals from the bench, then the signal caller merely repeats the call he receives or "reads" the signal and correlates it with his "ready" list of plays or defenses for that specific game. Some additional training-teaching is usually needed, however, to keep from running a poor offensive play or to get out of an improper alignment or pass coverage after a call has been sent in from the sideline. Typically the offensive signal caller is taught to automatic or check out of the bad or poorly selected play versus the overload defense, and to call a better play to take advantage of the defensive weakness away from the overload. Unless this is part of the quarterback's training, he is forced to run a poor play that has little or no chance of succeeding, and the offensive attack becomes ineffective, inconsistent, and inefficient.

With modern offensive attacks utilizing multiple formations, including the shifting of offensive backs and the tight end, and the use of motion, if defensive signal callers are not taught to check their team out of precalled alignments, stunts and/or coverages, the opposition will exploit the inherent weakness of defensive alignments and personnel via offensive overloading. While a poorly selected offensive play that should not be run against the strength of an overload defense may result in no gain, loss of yardage, or even loss of the football, catching a team in an improper defensive alignment, especially in a coverage that can be readily exploited, very likely will result in a long run or pass and/or a touchdown. Therefore, even if a coach utilizes substitutes or sideline signals to call plays and defenses, the offensive and defensive quarterbacks must be taught to check out of "bad" plays or incorrect alignments or coverages due to contingency variables. The other method is to train your quarterbacks to call all of the signals, and this takes time, practice, and patience. It cannot be accomplished in a week, or even in a season, depending on the extensiveness of the offense and/or defense. The training is progressive in nature, and can only be taught and learned through repetition and experience. The coach is confronted with finding suitable answers to the following questions:

- What should be taught?
- How much should I teach?
- Which are the most effective teaching methods?

TRAINING THE SIGNAL CALLERS

The *offensive* signal caller should be taught the following:

- A knowledge of defensive football, including the strengths and weaknesses of alignments, fronts, and coverages, as these affect directly his play selection.
- To know his offense thoroughly, including strengths and weaknesses and the capabilities of his teammates.
- To master certain principles relating to the selection of plays; to grasp the overall plan, concept, and philosophy of quarterbacking the offensive attack; and to learn the specific offensive game plan for the upcoming opponent.

The *defensive* signal caller should be taught the following:

- A knowledge of offensive football, including the strengths and limitations of the different offensive sets and systems of play, as these affect directly his selection of defensive alignments, stunts, and pass coverages.
- A thorough knowledge of the strengths and weaknesses of every alignment, stunt, and coverage utilized by the defensive team, plus the capabilities of his teammates.
- To master certain principles relating to defensive football; to grasp the overall plan, concept, and philosophy of quarterbacking the defensive attack; and to learn the specific defensive game plan for the upcoming opponent.
- To be always in the proper defense at the right time.

The Tactical Situation

It is imperative that both the offensive and defensive signal callers fully comprehend the complete tactical situation, as it has a direct bearing on the selection of all offensive plays and defenses. Such factors as the down, yardage necessary for the first down or touchdown, horizontal and vertical field position, time remaining to play, and the score must be considered as an entity, not as separate tactical factors, although some factors are more important than others in certain situations. Also, on occasion the wind, weather, and the condition of the playing field have a bearing on both offensive and defensive play, and these elements would have to be considered in signal calling. All of these factors are interrelated and have a direct bearing on each other. Considered separately they are of little value, since a football play is not an isolated entity. The tactical situation must always be taken into consideration.

Since the opposition is always just as vital a factor in the game as is your team, the offensive signal caller must consider such additional factors as the opposition's defensive strategy and tactics, including known and established tendencies, and the strengths and weaknesses of the defensive personnel. Also, he must know the capabilities of his team's offensive personnel. The defensive signal caller must consider the opposition's offensive strategy and tactics, including known and established tendencies, and the strengths and weaknesses of the offensive personnel. Also, he must know the capabilities of his team's defensive personnel.

Each should be taught how to automatic or check out of the bad offensive play and the improper defense, respectively. Probably the most important single factor for technically sound offensive and defensive football is for the signal callers to be cognizant of what their team or the opposition must accomplish in order to maintain possession of the football.

The proper training of the offensive and defensive signal callers, especially if the information is not sent in from the coach, requires teaching and testing, and constant review and reiteration until they can respond almost automatically to a given situation. Very few players think quickly and clearly in a stressful situation, especially when they encounter something of an unfamiliar nature and a decision must be made quickly. The signal caller's attitude toward his training and progress is very important. If he feels he is learning, and is becoming better each day, his interest and enthusiasm will not wane. His progress will be rapid, and he is likely to become a successful signal caller.

METHODS AND DRILLS FOR TRAINING THE SIGNAL CALLERS

There are a number of acceptable methods and drills that may be employed to train the signal callers, some better than others. No effort will be made to include all of the methods and drills, such as employing a tape recorder, metronome, etc. Much of the initial training and teaching must be done off-the-field at the blackboard, with lectures, notebook work, and film work. The latter is an especially effective teaching-training aid. Additional instructional aids may be used, several of which are listed. Much of the training-coaching will take place on the practice field.

The offensive signal caller's task is more difficult than his defensive counterpart. No coach can make any signal caller proficient and competent solely through chalk talks and lectures, or by sitting at their side telling them what to do in certain situations. While this method has merit initially while a coach is trying to teach his signal callers to "think like their coach" by imparting his philosophy and theory of offensive and defensive football, signal callers need to be tested on the field in practice and during actual game competition. You will not know whether you have a signal caller, especially a quarterback since his task and play are more varied, demanding and exacting, until he is tested under pressure. Only then will you get a true indication of his leadership qualities. Does he have the confidence and respect of his teammates? Does he have confidence in himself, and the spark, poise, and ability to lead the team? If he does, then additional experience is what counts. Initially there will be trial-and-error, including failure. As experience is acquired, trial-and-success is likely to follow if the signal caller maintains a positive attitude and continues to be enthusiastic about his training and progress.

The following are some methods and drills for training the offensive quarterbacks and/or defensive signal callers:

1. STARTING COUNT-HAND CLAP DRILL

Purpose: To teach recognition of and reaction to the offensive starting count and play, especially when employing automatics.

Procedure: The coach stands before the team and explains the method of changing the play at the line of scrimmage. Later the quarterback stands in the middle of a circle with his team around him. The coach (quarterback) starts through the offensive cadence, and may or may not change the offensive play and starting count called initially. The players stand with their hands apart ready to clap sharply when the coach (quarterback) says the correct starting count, indicating the team is getting off together with the count.

Coaching Points: Stand where you can observe all of the players and can determine which ones are slow in clapping their hands together, indicating they do not recognize and react instantly to the offensive starting count. Immediately ask a player the offensive play. He may recognize the starting count, even though it has been changed, but he may not realize the quarterback has changed the offensive play.

2. SLIDES OR TRANSPARENCIES DRILL

It is possible to devise slides to be used with a slide projector and/or transparencies to be used on an overhead projector that illustrate defensive alignments, stunts, and pass coverages, or offensive formations, plays and passes, or most anything else a coach wants to illustrate to teach his players. Much of this material has been commercially prepared and is available for purchase, although most coaches could prepare their own material. While preparing visual aids takes time initially, they can be used often and frequently without a coach being present if the teaching-coaching points are included on the transparencies-slides, too.

3. FILM-LOOPS DRILLS

Previous game film clips may be spliced together into separate reels or loops to be used to train your signal callers. For the best results, the segment of the game you want the signal callers to study and analyze should be carefully selected. The loop should not be too long or it will become cumbersome to handle. If a film is not edited, the signal callers will become interested in segments of the game you do not want them to spend time viewing. It is possible for the coach to record teaching-coaching points on an accompanying tape so players may view the film without a coach being present.

4. FLASH CARDS DRILL

Flash cards, 14 × 11 inches in size, may be devised for training the offensive and defensive signal callers. For the offensive signal caller, on the front of a single card draw a defense versus your basic offensive sets. Initially the purpose is to teach and test the quarterbacks in identifying the alignment, namely, odd, even, off-set, seven or eight man front, three or four deep secondary. On the back of the flash card have the same alignment as on the front of the card. In red ("Stop") mark the strength of the defense. In green ("Go") indicate the weakness of the defense. Use green squares to indicate where the quarterback should call running plays, and green ellipses where he should throw passes. At the bottom of the card you can indicate the specific plays in your offense the quarterback should call to attack the green-marked weak areas of the defense. Test the quarterback by going from the front to the back of the card, and then to the front again. Looking at the front of the card, he must fulfill the objectives stated previously.

The card(s) may be used similarly for defensive training, too, only the signal caller is taught and tested on identifying the offensive set, its strengths and limitations, and the best offensive plays or tactics for attacking the weaknesses of the defense(s). The same colors and symbols may be used on the back of the card to illustrate defensive strengths and weaknesses, and in which areas the opposition is likely to try to make yardage running and passing.

The flash cards are good teaching aids for the following reasons:

- The signal callers can use the cards for individual study and self-testing.
- The different color schemes and symbols facilitate learning.
- The signal callers have a starting point to begin learning, i.e., offensively where to commence attacking the alignment; defensively where the opposition is likely to direct its offensive attack, and which areas are more vulnerable than others. To attack intelligently offensively, the signal caller must learn the strengths and weakness of defensive systems of play; defensively, the signal caller must learn the theory and tactics of offensive systems.

5. DEFENSIVE AND OFFENSIVE TESTING DRILLS

Most coaches probably devise special sheets of common defensive alignments in order to teach recognition and play assignments or the application of blocking rules. (If a team were running the veer option, the numbering of the defensive players would be different and not correspond with those in the illustration. Therefore, the alignments would be the same, but the defenders would have to be renumbered.) This may be used as a worksheet, to test the quarterback by having him pencil in all of the assignments for a specific play. (It may also be used to test an offensive player

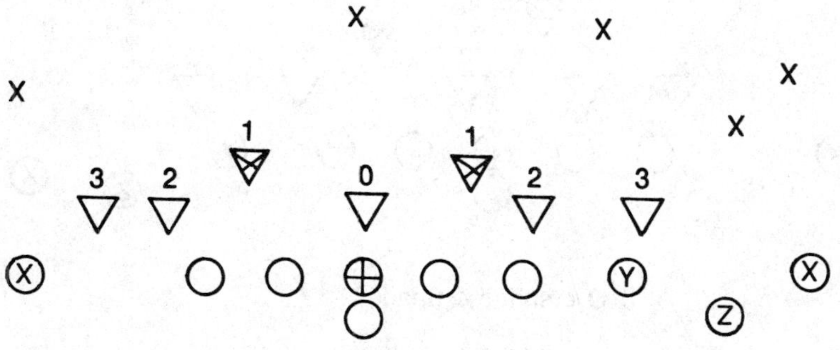

a. Oklahoma 5-2

DRILL 5

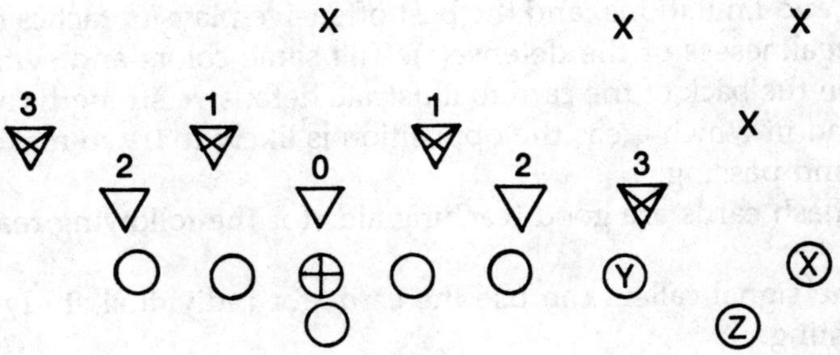

b. Pro 3–4

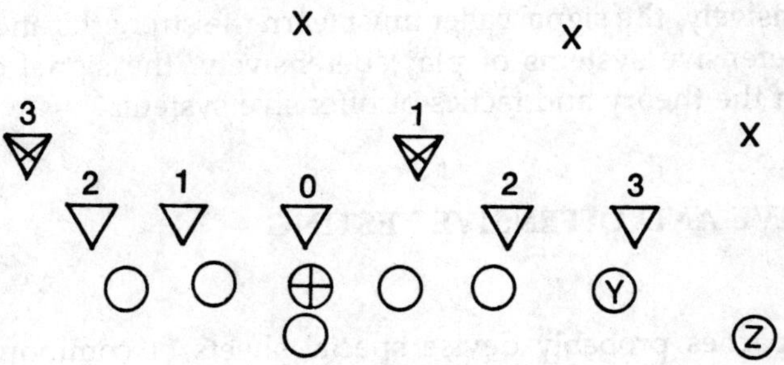

c. Oklahoma–Eagle (back-side)

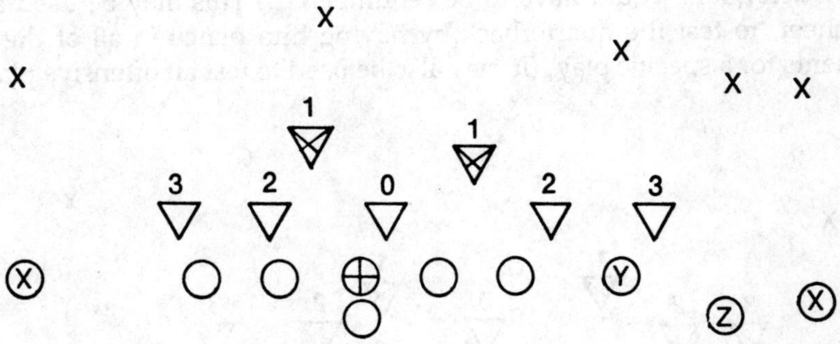

d. Overshift 5–2 Shade

DRILL 5 (continued)

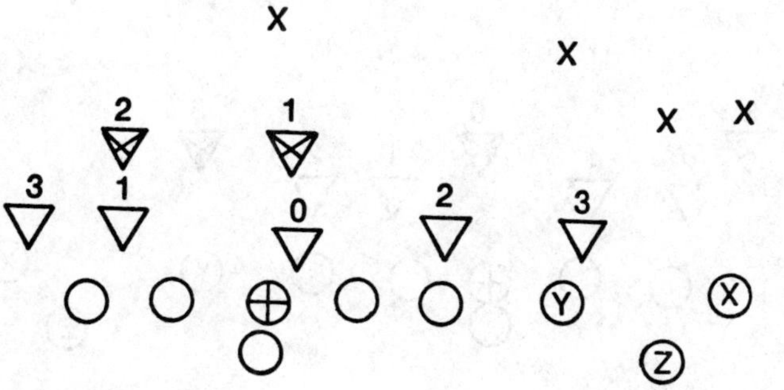

e. Oklahoma Stack (front-side)

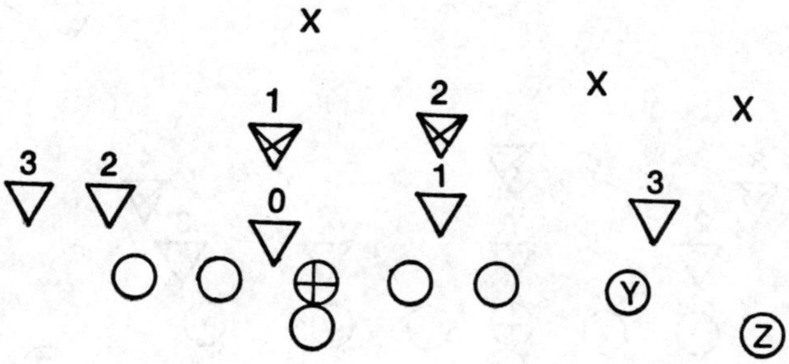

f. Oklahoma Stack (back-side)

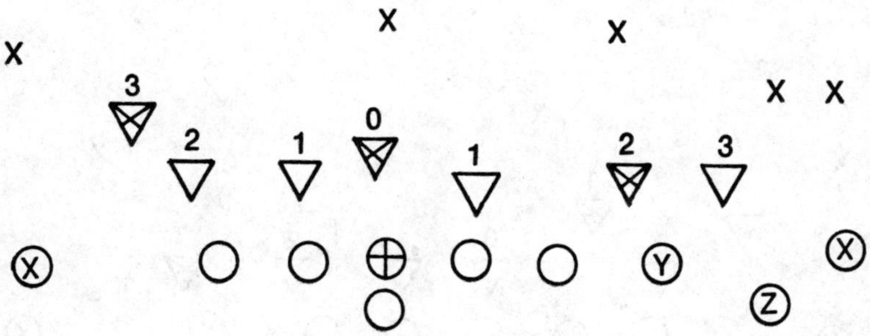

g. 4–3

DRILL 5 (continued)

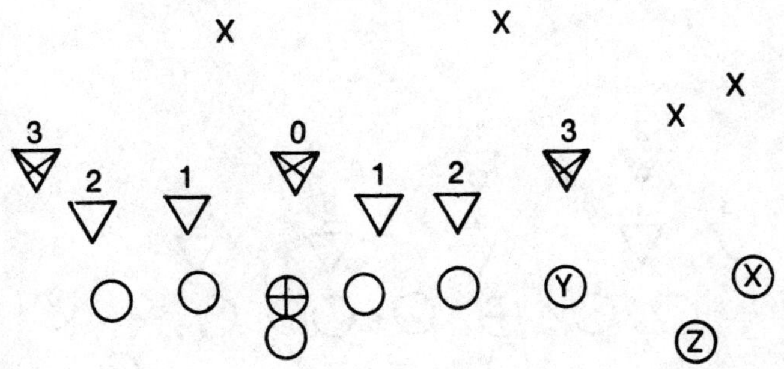

h. Pro 4–3 (standard)

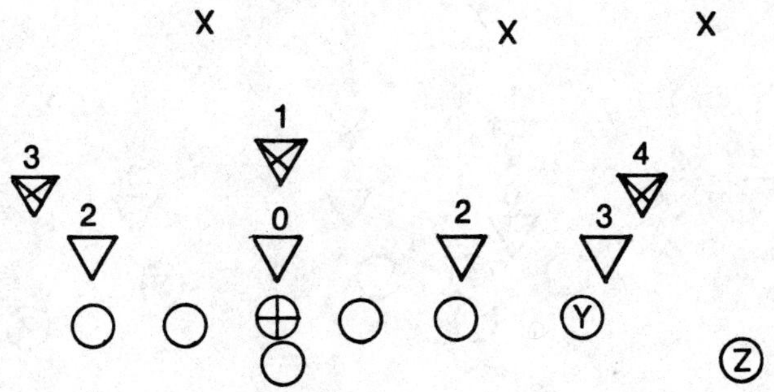

i. 4–3 Over (stack)

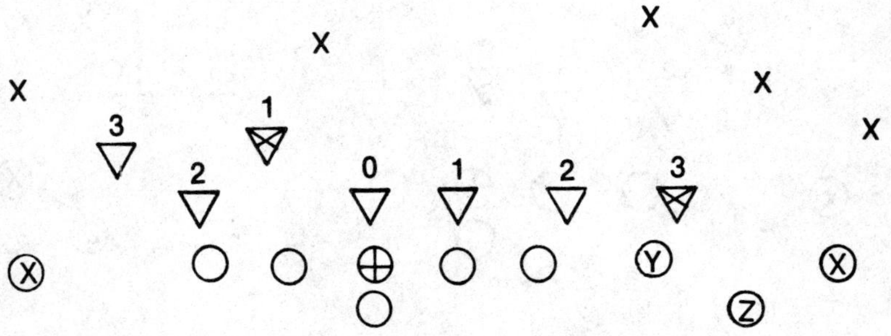

j. 4–3 Over (strong)

DRILL 5 (continued)

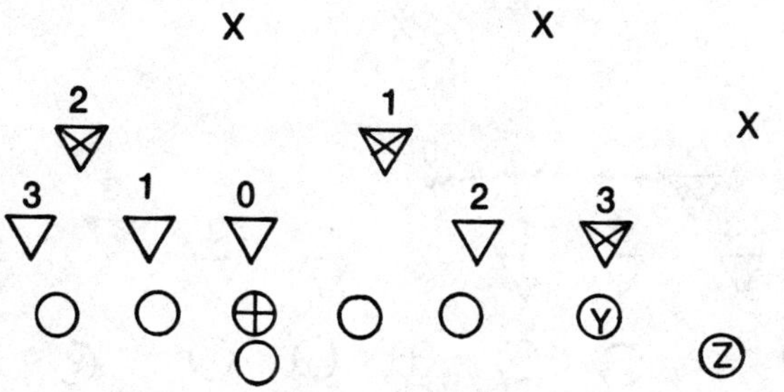

k. 4–3 Under (weak)

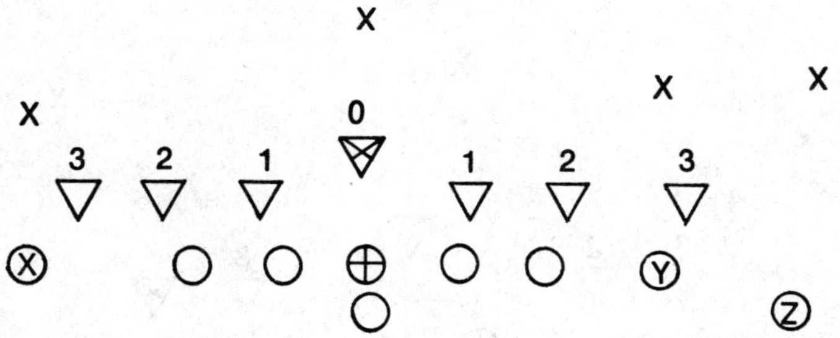

l. 6–1

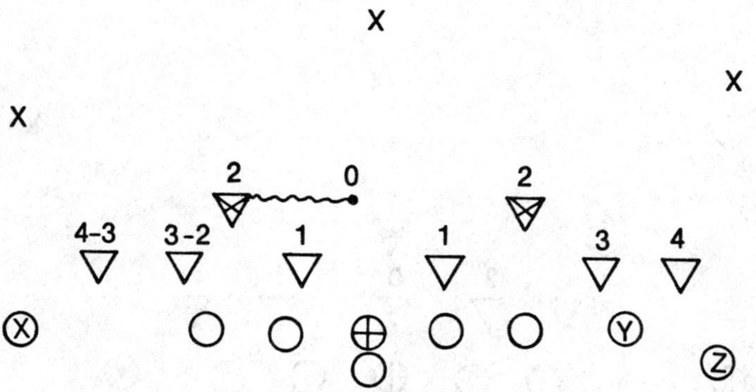

m. Wide Tackle 6–2

DRILL 5 (continued)

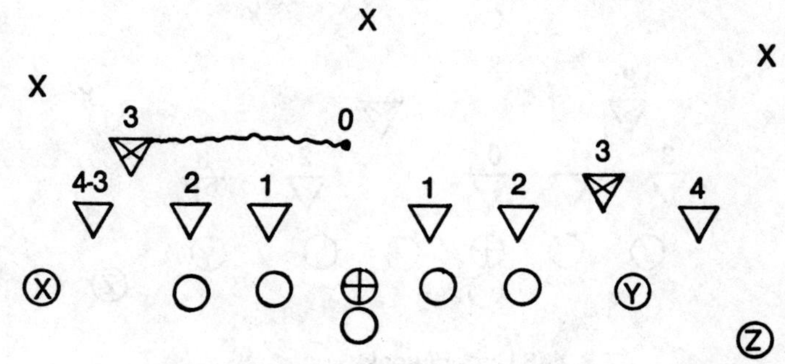

n. Tight Tackle 6–2

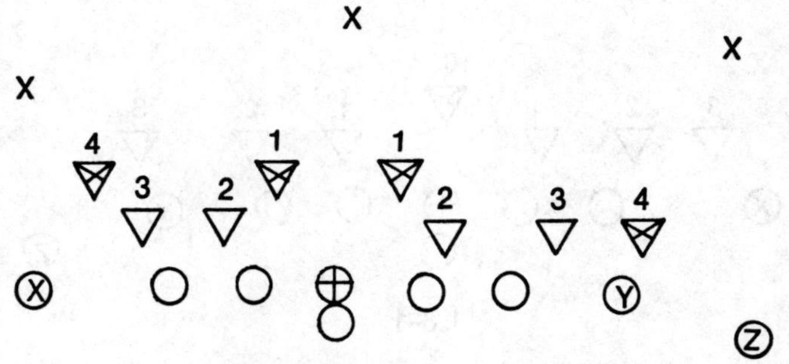

o. Split 6 or 4–4

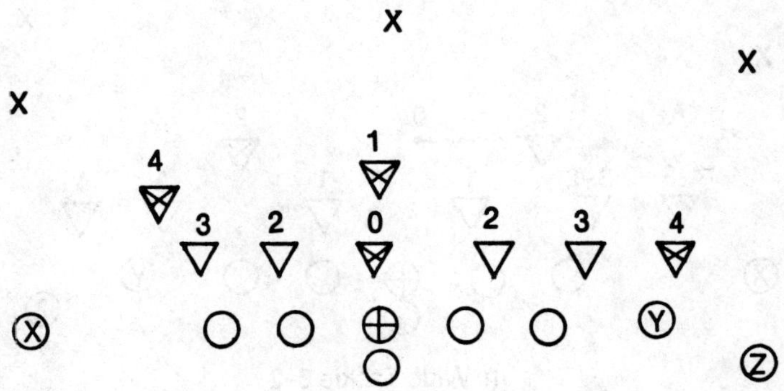

p. Split 6 odd (Gap 7–1)

DRILL 5 (continued)

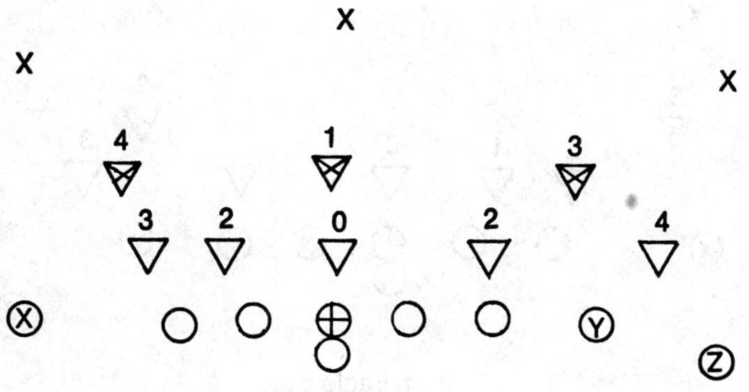

q. 5–3

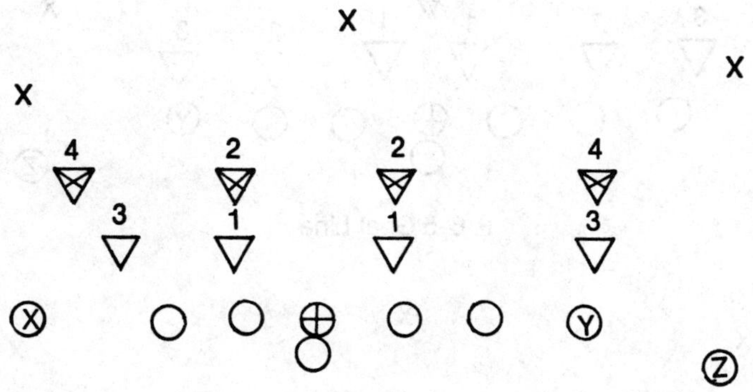

r. Stack 4–4

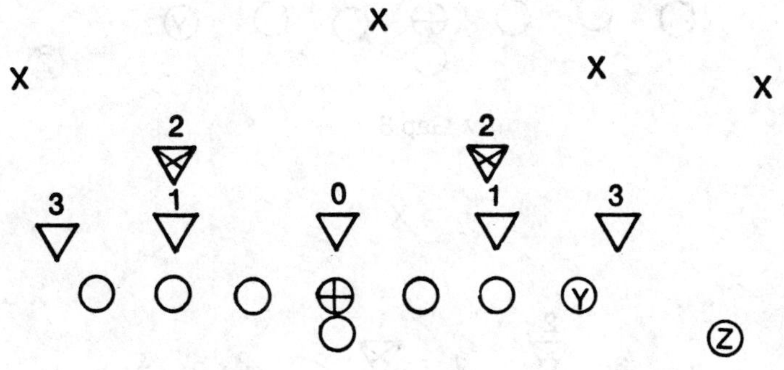

s. 5–2 Tandem

DRILL 5 (continued)

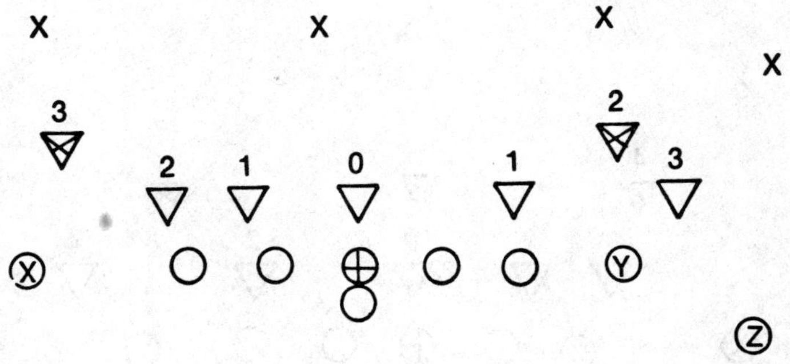

t. Eagle

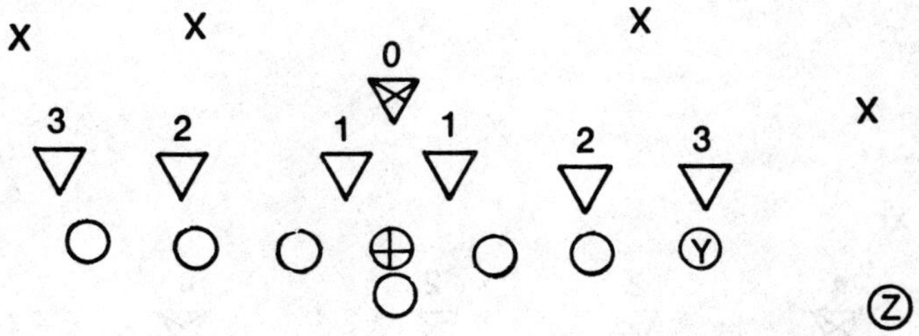

u. 6–5 Goal Line

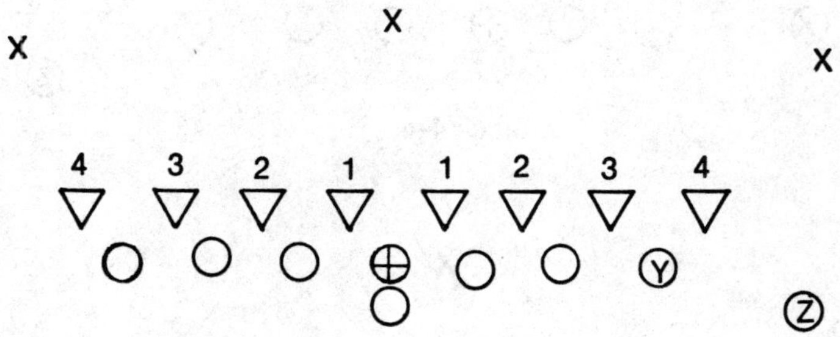

v. Gap 8

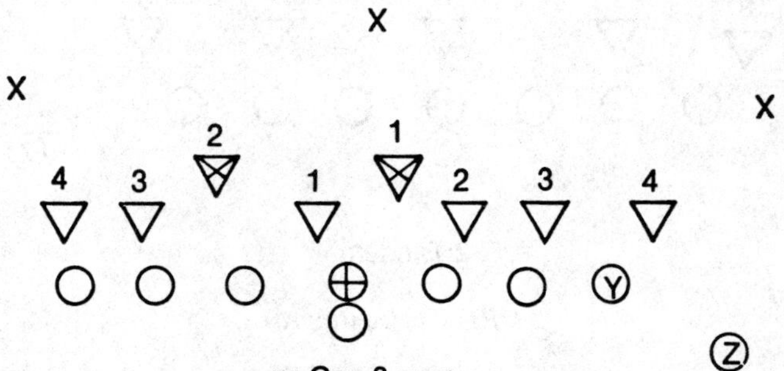

w. Gap 8 over

DRILL 5 (continued)

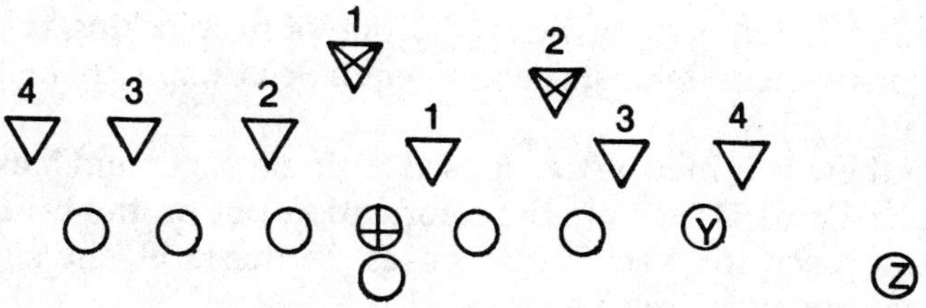

x. Gap 8 under

Versions of Alignments for Special Pass Coverages

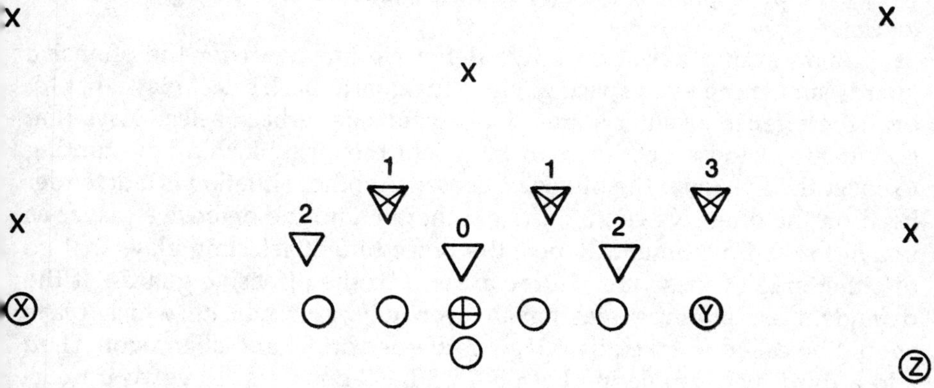

y. Nickel (5 under)

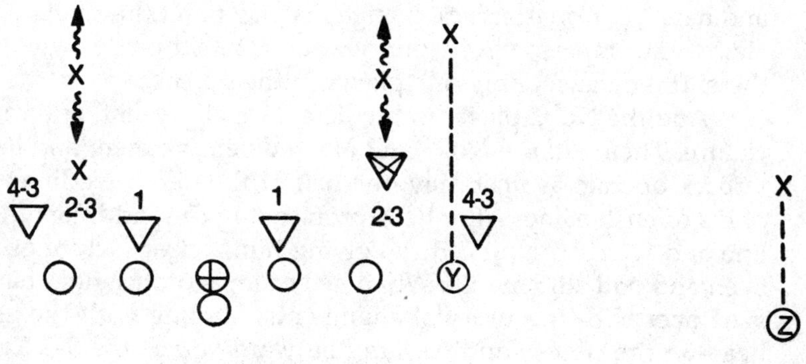

z. Dime (6 backs)

DRILL 5 (continued)

on his specific assignment or the application of his blocking rule on a specific play versus these defensive alignments. See Chapter 6, (30) Offensive Line Blocking Drill.)

Each of these sets may be transposed to single pages and handled much like (4) Flash Cards Drill, only the information put on the cards is placed there by the coach for teaching purposes. In this drill, the signal callers "take the examination" on paper.

6. SKELETON DRILLS

When teaching which offensive plays should be run versus the various defensive alignments, many coaches commence to train their quarterbacks by using only the interior linemen on defense. The drill generally progresses from off-the-field teaching to on-the-field coaching where actual players are substituted for the pencil and paper and the blackboard work. The principle is the same, and the sequence of teaching-coaching is logical.

As an example, put only two defensive linemen over the offensive guards simulating even spacing. Have the quarterback select plays that hit over the offensive center's area. Have your quarterback select plays that go outside of these defenders in the event they are pinching or stunting to cover the area over the offensive center. Another situation is a defender head-on the offensive center, and another behind the defensive player as in a 5–3 or 7–1 alignment. Repeat the procedure of selecting plays that go to either side of these men in the areas over the offensive guards. If the defenders are stunting making an even defense, indicate which plays should be called to take advantage of the personnel and alignment. Then add a third man simulating both 5–2 and 4–3 defenses. Have your quarterback select the proper plays if the defenders are playing straight and/or stunting. Then teach your quarterback how to change his play at the line of scrimmage, (11) Offensive Check Drill. After he has practiced the method and sequence, shift the three interior defensive players around and have your quarterback change his play to hit the weakness of the new alignment. Impress upon your quarterback that he does not have to whip the entire defense, only one player in the defense.

Add the No. 2 player in the defensive alignment, and repeat the procedure. Then add the No. 3 and No. 4 defensive men, and have the quarterback operate against only one-half of the defensive line with one-half of his offensive line. After he is proficient in this, add the other half of the line and repeat the procedure, giving him a clear picture of the standard even and odd alignments. When he becomes proficient in handling these, start over with the unusual alignments, starting with the zero defender head-on the center, and working outward versus the 5–2 Tandem, Eagle and other defensive alignments. (See Chapter 6, (24)–(27) Line Drills, (28)

Inside (Offensive) Drill, (29) Offensive Half-Line Drill, (30) Offensive Line Blocking Drill, (31) Offensive Scrimmage Drills; and Chapter 9, (21) Skeleton Versus Live Perimeter or Outside Offensive Drill.)

7. PAPER-AND-PENCIL AND BLACKBOARD DRILLS (See p. 312)

Much of what has been discussed already will be accomplished by special meetings, informal talks, blackboard and paper-and-pencil sessions with your signal callers. In addition, the coach can specify certain game and hypothetical situations and ask a quarterback to select the proper play. Or he can ask his defensive signal caller which alignment should be called. It is likely that the coach and signal callers will differ frequently in their opinions, particularly at the beginning of training. They should discuss the matter until both agree on the best play or the most logical defense for the given tactical factors. Such a method not only associates the correct play or defense with a specific situation, but also provides an excellent means of analyzing each play on the strengths and weaknesses of the defensive alignment. It also has merit because a coach can explain much of his philosophy in these sessions. However, it is not advisable to coach-teach offensive *and* defensive signal callers at the same time. Each group should be worked with separately for more effective teaching-coaching.

Some coaches give their offensive and defensive signal callers forms indicating specific zones of play. They ask them to write down the different plays or possible defenses for each zone, and then query the selections. In this manner the signal callers learn to associate certain plays and defensive alignments/coverages with certain spots on the field, and to identify the relationship of field position to possession by recognizing the three and four-down zones of play.

In order to give their signal callers better perspective on the horizontal and vertical zones of play, in addition to teaching, training and talking about hypothetical situations off the field, some coaches repeat the procedure on the game or practice fields with only the offensive or defensive quarterbacks and the coach walking from area to area. Although this is an informal exercise or drill, it is highly effective as a teaching-learning method for training the signal caller.

8. FILM STUDY AND ANALYSIS DRILL

Signal callers should study the play of their upcoming opponents by viewing game films, especially current films from a scouting exchange. For study and analysis it is best, but often impractical for many scholastic

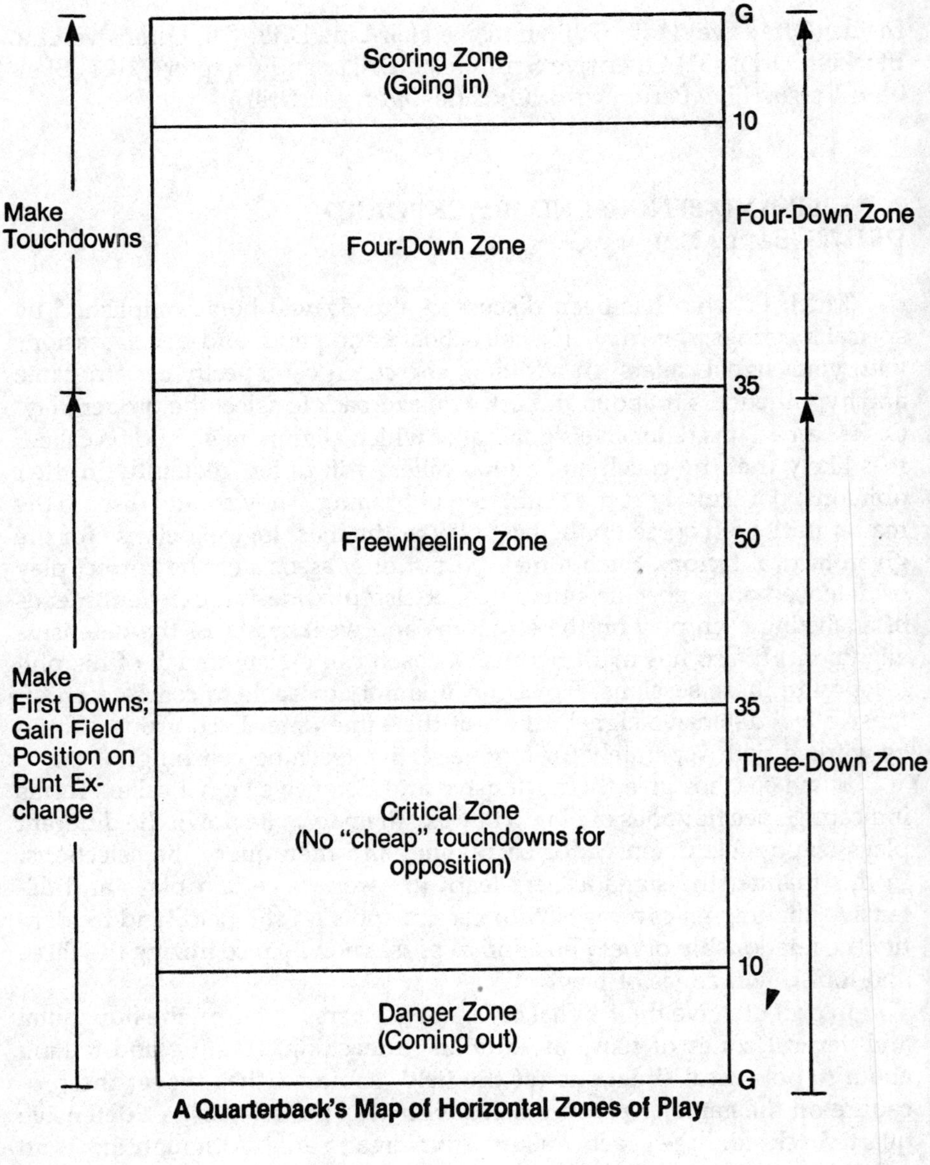

A Quarterback's Map of Horizontal Zones of Play

DRILL 7

coaches, if the films are broken down and spliced into offensive and defensive reels. When a coaching situation prevails where films are divided in this manner, your quarterbacks and offensive players need only view and study the opposition's defensive play, and your signal callers and players on the defensive unit need view and study only the opposition's offensive play.

Regardless of the coaching situation, however, coaches should provide a play-by-play and a complete statistical breakdown to their quarterbacks and defensive signal callers to facilitate teaching-learning while game films are being viewed. Quarterbacks need only be concerned with the opposition's defensive sets, coverages, stunts, tendencies and personnel. Defensive signal callers need only concentrate on studying and analyzing offensive formations, favorite running plays and passes, use of motion, tendencies and personnel. Signal callers typically do not have the time or the inclination to chart game films, so it should be done by the coaching staff for effective teaching-learning to occur. It must be acknowledged that due to multiple teaching-coaching responsibilities and other situational variables, the typical scholastic coaching staff often has difficulty time-wise compiling complete statistical information for film study and analysis. Still, in situations where play-by-play and other statistical information is provided by coaches to their signal callers, the quarterbacks can view the game films and verify the following:

- types of defensive fronts and coverages;
- types of defensive play, i.e., read and react and/or attack, penetrate, stunt, and in which situations they occur what percentage of the time;
- defensive adjustments versus offensive sets, and how motion is covered;
- the speed of the pass defenders, including linebackers, and overall team speed;
- defensive tendencies versus tactical factors;
- defensive personnel's strengths and weaknesses;
- tipoffs and "cheats";
- team strategy and tactics (game plan) versus your upcoming opponent.

This method can be a helpful aid to quarterbacks, particularly in their selection of third down plays where the choice made actually determines whether your team will maintain or give up possession of the football. (See (19) Third Down Calls Drill.)

Comparable statistical data also must be compiled by the defensive coaches pertaining to the opposition's offensive sets, plays, tendencies, strategy, tactics, and personnel. The defensive signal callers should have access to this data when they are studying and analyzing film in their preparation for making prudent defensive calls for an upcoming opponent. Remember, the defensive signal caller's primary objective is to be *always* in the proper defense at the right time.

9. GAME STUDY AND ANALYSIS DRILL

After a game careful study of the film will reveal much. Aside from the quarterbacks studying their play mechanics and techniques, coupled with a play-by-play statistical breakdown of the game, and an offensive drive chart, it is relatively easy to determine the answers to the following questions:

- How did our team gain possession of the football?
- Where did we gain possession, and what did we do offensively after we gained possession?
- How did we lose or surrender possession?
- Why did our offense bog down, and where?
- What stopped us?
- Why did I call such and such play in that particular situation?
- Did I (we) follow our game plan?
- If we deviated from our game plan, why?
- How did we win (or why did we lose)?

As the quarterback views the film, he can write down his observations, comments and answers using a "bingo" sheet so the answers can be quickly recorded, and the coach can evaluate and comment for teaching-learning purposes.

The statistics will also reveal to the coaching staff whether or not the team is getting the football its share of the time, the number/percentage of times the offensive team scored when they gained possession, the yards gained per play compared to the expected yardage of the play, each back's yardage gained, and other pertinent information such as any offensive tendencies of quarterbacking.

Similarly, comparable statistical data must be compiled by the defensive coaches of the opposition's running and passing offense versus team and individual performance. The defensive signal caller and each defensive team member must be graded from the film prior to viewing and analyzing his game performance. Was the team always in the correct defense and coverage versus the given specific tactical situation? If there was a "big play breakdown" was it because the defense was in the improper alignment? Was the alignment called incorrectly by the signal caller? Was it flashed from the sideline? Did the defensive signal caller fail to check to a correct alignment? Did the opposition crack the vulnerability of the alignment/coverage/personnel? Or did defenders commit individual errors and mistakes that caused the breakdown? Coupled with a play-by-play statistical breakdown of when your team was on defense, it is relatively easy (although time consuming) to determine the answers to these questions and to similar ones asked of the offensive coaches of your team's running and passing offense versus the opposition's defense. Despite the time involved in compiling this information, for effective coaching-learning to occur it must be done.

All of the above offensive and defensive information, after study and analysis, typically is used for teaching-coaching for the week's practice plans for your next upcoming opponent.

Defense Drive Sheet*

Date: 10–7 Game: Central Washington

Down	Distance	Yard Line	Defense Called	+/−	Comments
1	10	−30	44 BASE	0	Sam backer too close
2	10	−30	44 RUSH	+ 1	Exc. job
3	10	−31	41 STAR X	INTC	Exc. play—Bucky Hargrove
1	10	−29	50 SAM	+12	No contain by end
1	10	−41	51	+ 0	Good job—Mike
2	10	−41	44 BASE	+ 5	No reaction front
3	5	−46	44 FLEX STR.	INTC	Exc. rush and cover
1	10	+49	44 FLEX STR.	+ 2	Slow off ball
2	8	+47	44 BASE	+ 4	——
3	3	+43	44 BASE	+ 0	Exc.
4	3	+43	Punt Block	+35	Good rush

DRILL 9

*From Donald E. Fuoss and Rowland "Red" Smith, *Effective Football Coaching: Game Winning Techniques for Preventing Mistakes and Errors* (Boston: Allyn and Bacon, 1981), p. 117.

Illustration of an Offensive Game Plan

Game: State v. Tech
Note: Check and determine as quickly as possible:

1. What are their basic defensive fronts:
   V. RT/LT = ? V. Slot = ?
   V. RD/LD = ? V. Special = ?
2. When are they in *4–4 compared to 4–3?* Down distance or sets?
3. How and when are they in *man coverage?*
4. Who are the *inside LBers keying?*
5. Who are the *outside LBers keying?*
6. Are the *guards keying* guards or FBs' feet?
7. Are *LBers running through?* How and when?
8. Can we *screen?* When and how?
9. How about *squib pass?* (Pass from squib punt)
10. How about *end around?*
11. How about *fake FG screen?*

Running Game

V. 4–4: Run normal attack—favor short side option and 18–19 for outside game. No traps in middle if stacks on grds.

V. 4–3: Run powers and middle traps—favor short side. Also 30–31.

V. "Gap stacks": Traps away from—30–31 away from—pwrs towards.

V. 6–2: No 70 series—favor pwrs, middle traps, and 30–31.

V. 7–1: No 30–31. Otherwise normal attack. No middle traps if pure stack on center.

Passing Game

3 Deep Zone:
1. All hook
2. Option passes
3. Side line patterns

Pure Man Coverage:
1. FB counter passes
2. 52–53 pass "pick"
3. Cross patterns

Man with Two Free Safeties:
1. FB counter passes
2. 52–53 pass "pick"
3. Cross patterns

Man with One Free Safety:
1. FB counter passes
2. 52–53 pass "pick"
3. Cross patterns

Goal Line and Short Yards

RT/LT: 26–27, 56–57 Pr(Grd), 52–53, 52–53, Pwr

RD/LD: 58–59, 56–57 Pr(Grd) 52–53, 52–53Pr, 9, 52–53 opt., 52–53 pass "pick"

SLOT: Pwr RT or LT, Pitch to slot

Two-Point Plays

1. LO = 52 pass GL "pick"
2. Left Slot = Pitch right
3. Fake FG Screen

DRILL 10

Illustration of a Defense Game Plan

TEAM: Central Washington **DATE:** 10-14

GOAL	26 PWR – 26 PWR – 25 PWR – 25 PWR – 26 PWR – 25 PWR –		– 26 PWR – 40 TRAP	No gamble No blitz No big plays
−20	28 PITCH - 28 PITCH - 26 PWR	26 PASS 25 PASS	– 29 PITCH	Play conservative
−35	28 PITCH - 28 PASS 40 TRAP	41 TRAP		Attack some on first down
−50	28 PITCH	26 BLAST 28 PITCH	41 TRAP	Attack some on first blitz; some 3rd and long (poss. 2nd and long)
+35	48 PITCH 26 BLAST	41 TR 26 BLAST 56 PWR	56 PWR	
+20	26 PWR 25 PWR	20 BLAST 26 NEAR	20 BLAST 56 PWR	Attack in man coverage *Put out fire*
GOAL				

Tendencies *Downs*	
First	RUN 78% PASS 22%
Second	PASS 59% RUN 41%
Third	RUN 70% PASS 30%
Fourth	K.G. PUNT RUN 2 PUNT PASS 3

1. *Best Basic Defenses*:
   4 BASE
   4 FLEX STR
   4 TIGER

2. *Best Run Defenses*:
   44
   43 WIDE AND SHORT

3. *Best Short Yardage Defenses*:
   6 – 5 IN

4. *Goal Line Defenses*:
   6 – 5 NORMAL
   6 – 5 IN
   6 – 5 OUT
   6 – 5 PLUG

5. *Pressure Defenses (Pass Rush)*:
   44 – WHIP
   47 – THUNDER
   47 – LIGHTNING

6. *Maximum Coverage Defenses*:
   48 – 5 BKS
   49 – 6 BKS

7. *Play Action Situations*:
   ANY 2nd INSIDE
   −30 TO +30

8. *Screen and Draw Situations*:
   2 and LONG
   3 and LONG

9. *Automatic Defenses*:
   COVER 2 RED
   COVER 2 TRIPS

10. *Unusual Formations*:
    TRIPS R and L

11. *Formation–Set Tendencies*:
    60% PRO–RUN and PASS
    20% FLK ALL PASS
    10% RED and TRIPS ALL PASS

12. *Motion Adjustments*:

13. *Two-Point Play*:
    SPRINT PASS WK
    1 REC. SIDE

*Fuoss and Smith, *op. cit.*, pp. 106–107. (See "Game Preparation, Organization, and How to Avoid Mistakes, pp. 103–110.)

10. OFFENSIVE AND DEFENSIVE GAME PLAN DRILLS (See p. 316–317)

After offensive and defensive game plans are formulated, taught and practiced, the quarterbacks and defensive signal callers are given "ready" sheets outlining strategical plans and tactics to be employed against the opposition. The day preceding the game, the quarterbacks and defensive signal callers respond orally before the team at the squad meeting. Such a technique not only builds confidence and poise, since the quarterbacks and defensive signal callers must thoroughly familiarize themselves with the game plan information in order to respond correctly to the coach's questions, but it serves as a review for the squad members of their offensive and defensive objectives in the Scoring Zone, the Danger Zone, in short and long yardage situations, etc.

Many football games are won by well-planned, well-practiced reactions to tactical situations. Conversely, many games are lost as the result of poorly organized reactions to the same situations. The remainder of the drills in this chapter involve signal calling in a specific game situation. A former National Coach-of-the-Year said, "Go over with your football team the plays you are going to use. Walk or trot your men through what you want them to do on Saturday. Put them in a game situation on the field. The best way to teach the quarterback is to have a football team with him."

11. OFFENSIVE AND DEFENSIVE CHECK DRILLS[1]

Purpose: To teach the signal callers to change at the line of scrimmage the play or defense called in the huddle.

Procedure: Standing slightly behind his offensive center, simulating on offensive huddle, the quarterback either calls a specific play, or says, "At the line" or "Check with me." He then places his hands to receive the snap-back from his center, and the defensive signal caller jumps the defense to a different alignment. The quarterback either runs the specific play called, *if* it will still attack the new alignment effectively and accomplish the desired offensive objective, or else changes the play. His "at the line" or "check with me" instruction in the huddle means the offensive play will be selected and identified at the line of scrimmage after the signal caller checks out the defensive alignment. The defense is dummy but the offense runs the play or pass that has been called.

When the check drill is practiced defensively, the procedure is similar and the defense must adjust to multiple offensive sets, including shifting

[1]Donald E. Fuoss and Rowland P. Smith, *Effective Football Coaching: Game-Winning Techniques for Preventing Mistakes and Errors* (Boston: Allyn and Bacon, 1981), pp. 157–158; 183–188.

and/or motion. The stunt and coverage may be "on," or the signal caller may check the team out of the stunts and/or change the coverage. There is no blocking or tackling as the objective is to make certain the signal caller has his team in the proper defense and coverage.

Coaching Points: Always give down and distance. Do not try to combine the drills, i.e., teach and test offensively or defensively separately. Also, the same coaching points as in (1) Starting Count-Hand Clap Drill.

12. SCRIMMAGE-SCORING ZONE OFFENSE DRILL

Purpose: To polish and scrimmage a limited number of select offensive plays, including passes versus the opposition's goal line defenses, when the ball is in the Scoring Zone.

Procedure: The offensive team is given the football on the opposition's ten-yard line and has four plays in which to score versus your opponent's goal line defenses. Have the scout team run the opposition's defenses off of flash cards so they can easily follow the prepared script. (See note 1, Chapter 2.) The drill is live.

Coaching Points: Limit the offense to the game plan for a particular opponent. Give the quarterback the tactical situation for each series of plays, impressing on him that he must only average 2½ yards per play in order to score. Move the ball from the middle of the field to each hash mark after each series of plays, starting from the ten-yard line every time. The quarterback may or may not be permitted to use a field goal attempt, since the emphasis here is on polishing and scrimmaging the running and passing attack in the Scoring Zone.

13. SCRIMMAGE-DANGER ZONE OFFENSE DRILL

Purpose: To polish and scrimmage a limited number of select offensive plays, including punting, versus the opposition's defensive alignments and coverages, when trying to get the football out of the Danger Zone.

Procedure: The offensive team is given the football on its own one-foot line (two-yard line; five-yard line), and is given not more than three downs to make the necessary yardage (first down). Have the scout team run the opposition's alignments and coverages off of flash cards. (See note 1, Chapter 2.) The drill is live.

Coaching Points: Limit the offense to the game plan for a particular opponent. Give the quarterback the tactical situation for each series of plays, impressing on him that he must average so many yards per try (or punt on third or fourth down) in order to maintain possession of the football, depending upon the coach's kicking game philosophy. After each series of plays, move the football to a different field position inside of the ten-yard line near your own goal line. Stress the importance of a sound punting game; also stress in which situations the football will be punted on third down.

14. SCRIMMAGE-TOUCHDOWN SEQUENCE OR CLUTCH OFFENSE DRILL

Purpose: To polish and scrimmage a method of attempting to score in a critical situation in a limited period of time versus the opposition's defensing of your clutch offense.

Procedure: The football is placed anywhere on the field. The quarterback is given the tactical situation, including the fact his team must score (specify 3 or 6 points) to win the game, with only a limited amount of time (15 seconds, 30 seconds, 1 or 2 minutes) in which to do so. The quarterback is not permitted to call time-out (or is permitted only one time-out), and can stop the clock only by legally grounding the ball (Drill 15) or when the ball carrier gets out-of-bounds. Unless the clock is stopped, the quarterback yells, "Touchdown Sequence" or "Clutch Offense," and calls the plays aloud at the line of scrimmage without the benefit of a huddle first. (A two- or three-play sequence may be predetermined.) The drill is live.

Coaching Points: Stress poise, confidence, and the ability to make the critical play and score. Stress quickness in lining up after a play without huddling, the proper execution of the plays without busted assignments and/or penalties. Simulate game conditions, including penalties. Move the football to various spots on the field, changing the field position and other tactical factors after each series of plays. Also change the time remaining to play. If three points will tie or win, the quarterback must be drilled to set up the field goal, kill-the-clock, get the kicking tee from the bench, and permit his place kicker to be substituted if he is not already in the game. If not in the game, the place kicker must bring the kicking tee with him. Otherwise the quarterback must request the tee as it cannot be thrown on the field from the bench. The quarterback must be drilled to utilize every second of time after the official marks and signals the football is ready for play. Use a stopwatch.

15. SCRIMMAGE-STOP (KILL-THE-CLOCK) DRILL

Purpose: To teach the quarterback how to safely sacrifice a down and stop the clock in order to utilize the time remaining to play.

Procedure: The offensive team is given the football anywhere on the field, along with the tactical situation. *The time remaining to play is the most important tactical factor.* The quarterback wants to stop the clock, but has no time-outs remaining. He yells, "Clock Offense!" or "Red!" or some other word(s) to indicate his team will line up on the football without the benefit of a huddle in order to execute a predetermined play. To facilitate a quick offensive alignment, the team lines up automatically in a split right formation, with the exception of the wide flankers (X) and (Z), who both align *on the line of scrimmage* as soon as possible on the side of the field where they are at the conclusion of the previous play. (In few situations X and Z are on the same side of the field, and it makes little difference which side they line up on in this situation.) The football is snapped at the quarterback's command, and both wide flankers run sideline cut patterns. The quarterback drills the ball high and hard over the head of one of his flankers. It goes out-of-bounds, stopping the clock. The drill is live.

Coaching Points: Stress poise, confidence, and quickness in lining up and executing the offensive play correctly without sustaining a penalty. Use a stopwatch. Explain when it is necessary to stop-the-clock with this predetermined play. The quarterback should throw the ball high, so that it is impossible for a defender to intercept or deflect it, yet legally ground the ball (incomplete pass). Suggest yelling key word(s) other than "Stop-the-Clock" as the official might interpret this as requesting a time-out, and charge a time-out to the offensive team. The quarterback may not want a time-out charged against his team; only to kill-the-clock so he can punt with a strong wind before the end of a quarter, for example. Or a quarterback might be saving his team's last time-out for after he has run the next play, depending on the tactical situation. Stopping the clock may or may not be needed to run the Clutch Offense (14), i.e., it might not be feasible to waste a down.

16. SCRIMMAGE-DELAY OFFENSE OR RUN-OUT-THE-CLOCK DRILL

Purpose: To teach the quarterback how to slow down, "bleed," and control the game in the time remaining to play, including running-out-the-clock.

Procedure: The offensive team is given the football anywhere on the field, along with the tactical situation. *The time remaining to play is the most important tactical factor.* The quarterback wants to maintain possession of the football and consume as much of the playing time as possible without drawing a penalty. Depending upon the time remaining to play, it may not be necessary for the quarterback to make a first down to accomplish his objective. Then he should employ quarterback sneaks, merely falling to the ground with both arms wrapped around the football in order to protect it. He should arise very slowly consuming more time. On other occasions it will be necessary to make a first down to maintain possession of the football. The safest plays are sweeps, but the ball carrier should remain in-bounds so the clock will keep running. If he goes out-of-bounds he kills-the-clock. No attempt should be made to pass the football, as an incomplete pass will stop-the-clock. The drill is live.

Coaching Points: Stress poise and confidence. The quarterback has twenty-five seconds to huddle and put the ball in play after the official spots the ball and marks it ready for play. Practice stalling and consuming time when the football is marked ready for play. After your opponent has called time-out, time does not commence again until the football is snapped. In the first situation, a long huddle and extended cadence are of value, but in the latter this is of no important significance or value. Use a stopwatch. Limit the offense and specify which plays are to be used in which situation, and why.

17. SCRIMMAGE-RACEHORSE OR GO-GO-GO OFFENSE DRILL

Purpose: To teach the quarterback how to run several series of offensive plays rapidly without giving the opposition time to call their defensive signals and alignments properly.

Procedure: The offensive team is given the football anywhere on the field, along with the tactical situation. The quarterback tells his teammates in the huddle they are going to employ the rapid offense for several series of plays, assuming they are successful in moving the football. He gets his team in and out of the huddle quickly, attempting to speed up the tempo of the game and run their plays before the opposition can line up properly. The drill is live.

Coaching Points: Stress poise and confidence. The drill is not the same as (14) Touchdown Sequence or Clutch Offense Drill where plays are called at the line of scrimmage and the team must score in a relatively short period of time. Neither are plays called with the same urgency as in Drill 14.

The objective in the rapid offense is to "rattle" the opposition by running plays quickly before the defense can get set properly. The offense must move the football or force the opposition to call time-out to get organized, or the drill is not successful and has not accomplished its objective. Use a stopwatch. Stress quickness, and no busted assignments and/or penalties. A team must be in good physical condition and well disciplined to employ the racehorse offense successfully.

18. SCRIMMAGE-GIVING-UP-A-SAFETY DRILL

Purpose: To teach the quarterback how to give up a safety to the opposition, in order to put the ball safely in play with a free kick from the twenty-yard line.

Procedure: The offensive team is given the football in its Danger Zone (one-foot line, three-yard line, etc.), along with the tactical situation. The score and the time remaining to play are the critical tactical factors. The quarterback informs his teammates they will give up a safety, rather than attempt to kick the ball from the end zone or from deep in the Danger Zone. Everyone blocks for and protects the quarterback as he either takes the ball from the center or receives a direct pass, sprints back into his own end zone and downs the ball to the ground, protecting it with his body. If he wishes to consume more time, rather than downing the football immediately, the quarterback may move around in the end zone near the rear end zone line before stepping out of bounds as tacklers approach him. The drill is live.

Coaching Points: Stress poise and confidence. Explain when it is necessary to give up a safety, and how to line up to put the ball in play after a safety has been scored. Stress the importance of protecting the football, including not permitting the opposition to tackle the quarterback and possibly force a fumble. The quarterback must be disciplined to follow the procedure of either downing the ball or stepping out of the rear of the end zone. He must not give the opposition the opportunity to force a fumble and possibly score a touchdown on the recovery of the football.

19. THIRD-DOWN CALLS DRILL

Purpose: To teach the quarterback the importance of making the correct play call on the third down from various positions on the field.

Procedure: The drill is practiced both on and off the field. In the former, the coach and quarterbacks walk to various sections of the field and each time the coach gives the tactical situation, with third down being the determining tactical factor. From having studied the opposition's tendencies, the coach also indicates expected defensive alignments, stunts and coverages. The quarterback indicates an offensive play and why he has selected it. The coach evaluates and comments on the quarterback's play selection.

Coaching Points: Third down is considered the most important call in football, both offensively and defensively. The quarterback must understand thoroughly field position and zones of play. In the two-down zone he must average five yards per try or punt on third down. In the three-down zone he must average 3⅓ yards per try or punt (or go for very short yardage) on fourth down. In the four-down zone he need only average 2½ yards per carry. In the two-down zone, it is important for the quarterback to understand why he should punt on third down, if this is the coach's philosophy and theory of football. In the three-down and four-down zones, if the team does not make the prescribed yardage on the preceding downs, the quarterback's third-down call is very important since the success or failure of the play generally determines whether the team maintains or loses possession of the football.

20. WASTE DOWN DRILL

Purpose: To teach the quarterback how to recognize a "waste" down and to utilize it as part of his offensive strategy.

Procedure: Same as (19) Third-Down Calls Drill, with the determining factor being less than two yards to go for the first down and two downs remaining in order to get the necessary yardage. The coach may wish to consider second down and two yards to go in the four-down zone (with three downs to make the two yards) different from the "waste down strategy" below.

Coaching Points: Although the entire tactical situation must always be taken into consideration, *generally* on a waste down the quarterback tries to pass for the score. If the pass is incomplete and he wastes a down, he has another down to get the necessary two yards for a first down.

Although Drills 12 to 20 are presented for training the quarterback and the offensive team, for the most part similar drills set up for training the defensive signal caller and defensive team are equally as important and also should be practiced. They will not be duplicated here since Drills 12 to 20 need only be explained from the defensive viewpoint. The teaching-training would be for defensive objectives, and should be set up as defensive drills to counter and negate offensive strategy and tactics.

15

Offensive and Defensive Kicking Game Drills

The kicking game can be divided into the following parts: the punt, which includes the offensive phases of fundamentals, protection and coverage, and the defensive phases of fielding and returning the punt or blocking it; the quick kick, which is seldom used in present-day football and will not be discussed further, includes the fundamentals, protection and coverage, and defending against the quick kick; the place kick, which includes the fundamentals and protection of the point-after-touchdown placement, the field goal and its coverage, and defending it; and the kick-off, which is also a placement kick, including the lineup and coverage, and returning the kick-off. No effort will be made here to include the numerous details, techniques, and coaching points relevant to the entire kicking game. However, the individual and team kicking game drills that are included are considered some of the best ones available.

The majority of drills available on the kicking game involve the entire team working as a unit, either practicing returning the kick-off or punt, or protecting the kicker and covering the punt. Many coaches feel this method is the most desirable for several reasons. Offensive *and* defensive kicking game fundamentals are practiced at the same time in one drill. Secondly, only by working the team as a unit can timing and execution be perfected. However, since the incidence of knee injuries sustained by participants is significantly increased when working with full teams offensively and defensively, most coaches control the ''live'' kicking game drills closely. No effort will be made here to divide the kicking game drills into offensive and defensive phases, although only one phase at a time should be taught-coached. (See Chapter 2, Principles.)

DRILLS FOR THE PUNTER

A good kicker must have the patience to master the fundamentals of punting. The value of a punter is not in the distance he kicks the football, but in his dependability, consistency and accuracy. For the beginning punter in particular, punting should be taught step-by-step, and as simply as possible. Many kicking coaches suggest the beginning punter should be prohibited from kicking the football until he masters a series of pre-punting drills and mechanics. Drills for the punter are as follows:

1. PUNTER'S LOOSENING AND STRETCHING DRILL

Purpose: To warm up properly, stretching the necessary muscles prior to punting.

Procedure: The punter goes through a warm-up regimen on his own prior to punting: three-quarter knee bends, attempting to touch the palms of the hands to the ground without bending his knees, balancing on one leg and pulling the other knee and leg to his chest, and simulated kicking. He should also kneel on the ground with his toes extended and pointed to the rear, lean backward, and finally sit on his heels, stretching the muscles most important for kicking.

Coaching Points: Stress the importance and necessity of warming-up properly prior to punting. Only then is the punter ready to commence a series of quick drills, working with another kicker, his center, or by himself.

2. STANCE AND BALANCE DRILL

Purpose: To develop body balance and check the pre-kick position of the feet.

Procedure: After the punter takes his most comfortable pre-kick position, the coach or another player should merely push him gently from the side and front to test his balance. The punter should not brace himself flat-footed or exert pressure against the force of the push. He should maintain a good pre-kick position.

DRILL 2

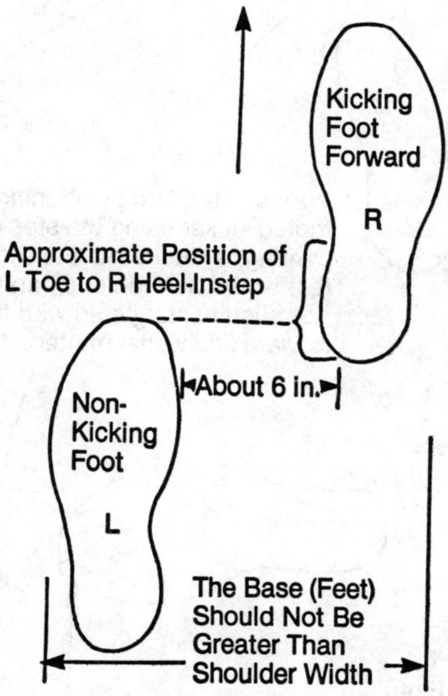

The Pre-Kick Standard Positioning of the Feet (Right-Footed Kicker) for Step-and-a-Half Method of Punting. The pre-kick position for the two-step punter is feet even and parallel [boxed], or with the non-kicking foot slightly in advance of the kicking foot [individual preference].

Coaching Points: Stress the pre-kick position and fundamentals, which include the positioning of the punter's feet, maintaining his balance, positioning the hands, and focusing his eyes on the football.

3. QUARTER-AND-HALF-TURN BALANCING DRILLS

Purpose: To develop body balance, and to maintain the pre-kick position.

Procedure: Same as for (2) Stance and Balance Drill, only on the coach's command the punter is to make a quick quarter-turn to his left or right. Repeat. The punter should land on balance and in a good pre-kick position. At first the punter is likely to be off-balance and his feet probably will not be parallel to each other. As he masters the drill, the punter should be able to make a series of one-half turns, facing in the opposite direction

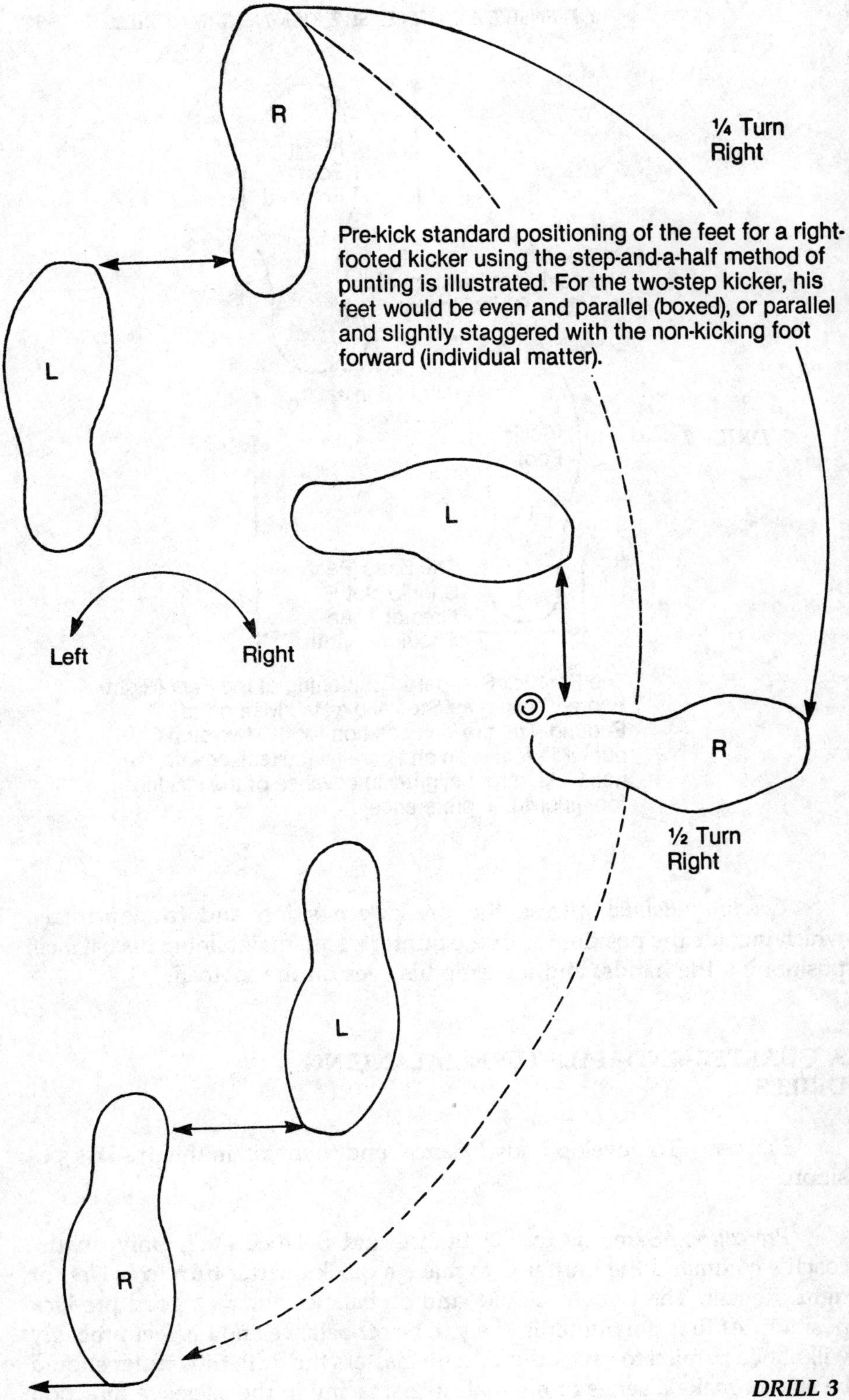
R
¼ Turn
Right
Pre-kick standard positioning of the feet for a right-footed kicker using the step-and-a-half method of punting is illustrated. For the two-step kicker, his feet would be even and parallel (boxed), or parallel and slightly staggered with the non-kicking foot forward (individual matter).
L
L
Left
Right
R
½ Turn
Right
L
R

DRILL 3

from his pre-kick direction and position, and still maintain his balance and the correct positioning of his feet.

Coaching Points: Stress the proper pre-kick position and fundamentals.

4. KICKING-BALANCING DRILL

Purpose: To teach balance and follow-through.

Procedure: Same as (2) Stance and Balance Drill, only a partner or the coach stands to the front and side of his kicking foot with hand extended, palm down and waist high as a target for the kicker. The punter attempts to swing his kicking leg and foot five times without stopping, attempting to touch the extended palm as the player or coach elevates it slightly each time. On the fifth kick, the punter should attempt to get the maximum follow-through. If the punter fails to maintain his balance, commence the drill again.

Coaching Points: A beginning punter will have difficulty maintaining his balance when he attempts to drive through with maximum effort, and

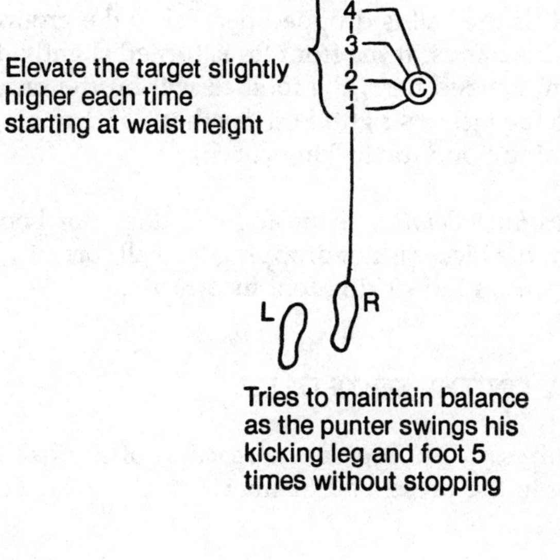

DRILL 4

even experienced punters fail to maintain their balance on some occasions. Stress that the punter must commence on balance if he expects to complete his kick on balance.

5. CATCH AND POSITION THE BALL DRILL

Purpose: To simulate catching all types of passes from the center, and to position the ball quickly prior to kicking it.

Procedure: The kickers work in pairs (or with a manager, center, coach) five to seven yards apart, facing each other. The football is flipped underhand to the kicker—high, low, short, soft, hard—simulating the types of pass the kicker is likely to receive from his center. The kicker must retrieve the football and position it quickly. If the errant pass is to his side, he must move laterally with a quick step or hop, keeping his feet in the same relative position as in his pre-kick stance. His objective is to keep his body in front of the flight of the football on the snap from his offensive center.

Coaching Points: Stress pre-kick position, catching the football and positioning it quickly.

6. HOLD AND DROP THE BALL DRILL

Purpose: To teach the correct position of holding the football and dropping (placing) it on the kicking foot.

Procedure: The punter merely positions the football in his hands and drops it. If the ball is dropped parallel to the ground, it will bounce back toward his hands. If the front tip is turned slightly downward and inward as recommended here, the football will hit the ground and bounce backward to the kicker's right. Both methods of dropping the football are used (depending upon the kicking coach).

Coaching Points: If the football does not bounce in the prescribed manner, the kicker is not dropping the ball correctly. This means it is being positioned on the kicking foot incorrectly.

7. BALL ON THE FOOT DRILL

Purpose: To observe the reaction of the ball after positioning it on the foot in the prescribed manner.

DRILL 7

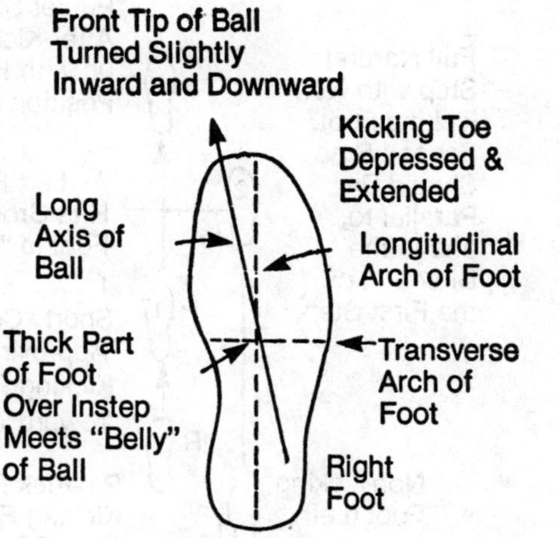

The Approximate Position of the Football on the Kicking Foot (right-footed punter)

Procedure: Punters stand in pre-kick position five yards apart facing each other. One kicker bends over and places the ball on his kicking foot in the manner he wishes foot contact to be made. He removes his hands as he raises his kicking foot and flips the ball to his partner. The two kickers continue to move away from each other 10, 15, 20 yards until they are getting the football to each other on a bounce.

Coaching Points: Stress positioning the ball on the foot properly. The punter should not "sling" the ball from his kicking foot. Note: When time is of the essence, select another drill since this one is of limited value. However, see that the position of the football on the kicking foot is correct regardless of the drill that is utilized.

8. WALK-THROUGH DRILL

Purpose: To practice the step-and-a-half method of punting without kicking the football. (See diagram notation for the two-step punter.)

Procedure: The punter works by himself, going through his steps and dropping the ball. Instead of making foot contact, the ball is dropped outside of the kicking foot, permitting the ball to fall to the ground. The cleat marks are checked to determine the length of the steps and to see if the steps are parallel to each other.

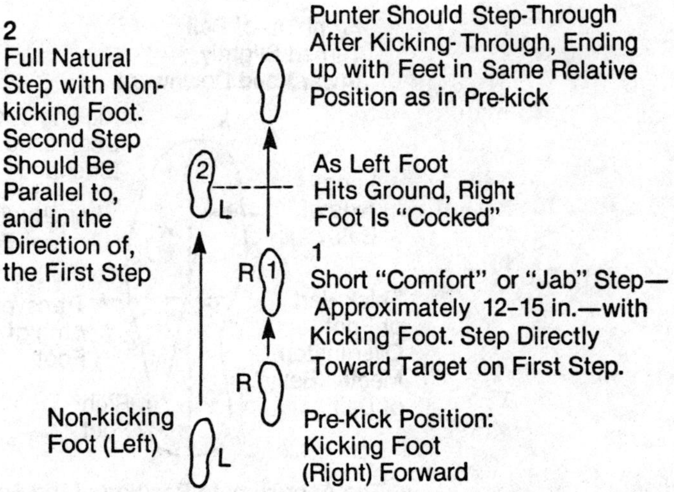

Normal Steps for a Right-Footed Punter Using Step-and-a-Half Method. The two-step punter usually takes a pre-kick position with his feet even and parallel (boxed), or parallel and slightly staggered with the non-kicking foot forward (individual matter).

DRILL 8

Coaching Points: Stress all of the fundamentals of punting. The drill is good for warming up to stretch the muscles, and to work on the follow-through.

9. CONTROL DRILL

Purpose: To observe how the football reacts to the impetus the kicker gives it as he learns to control his punts.

Procedure: A punter faces his partner ten yards away, and tries to kick the ball directly to his hands. After four or five times the partners move apart 15, 20, 30 yards. The difficulty of controlling the ball increases as the partners move farther apart.

Coaching Points: This drill involves most of the fundamentals of punting, only the punter does not exert a great deal of force in his leg swing and leg-snap.

10. SELF-RETRIEVING PUNTING DRILL

Purpose: To practice the fundamentals of punting.

Procedure: Working by himself the punter lines up approximately three to four yards from a portable kicking net or from a canvas or net hanging from the crossbar on the goal post (also used for centering, Chapter 7; passing-receiving, Chapter 8; pass defending, Chapters 11–12), and he practices the fundamentals of punting. The ball hits the net or canvas, drops, and does not ricochet into the kicker. The kicker is able to check his fundamentals, condition his leg, practice quickly, etc., without consuming much time retrieving the football. (Inside the gymnasium, especially during the off-season, the punter can practice kicking the football into the wall mats.)

Coaching Points: An excellent drill when a punter may be forced to practice by himself, such as during the summer months. It is good for maintaining condition of the kicking leg.

11. TOWEL OR FLAG DRILL (See p. 334)

Purpose: To develop kicking accuracy, if out-of-bounds punting is utilized to any extent.

Procedure: Towels, rubber cones, or flags are spotted at various places inside the twenty-yard line on the sidelines. With several retrievers to return the footballs, and a manager to make them available to the punter, they move to various spots on the field so the punter is kicking with and against the wind, from the middle of the field and from the hash marks. The kicker is also varying the distance of his kicks. A center may be used in the drill so the punter is employing all of the punting fundamentals, and the center is practicing the deep pass.

Coaching Points: The punter must step directly toward the target with his first step. His second step should be parallel to and in the direction of his first step. Emphasize that the punter must always kick over the core of his protection or his punt is likely to be blocked. This is especially true when angling the punt.

12. PRESSURE DRILLS

Purpose: To teach the punter to kick under pressure and to build confidence in his ability to do so.

Procedure: When practicing punting, your punters must learn that only the whistle stops play. Therefore, regardless of what happens, the punter must kick the football unless he hears the whistle. Put pressure on the punters in various ways, when they are least expecting it. The punter

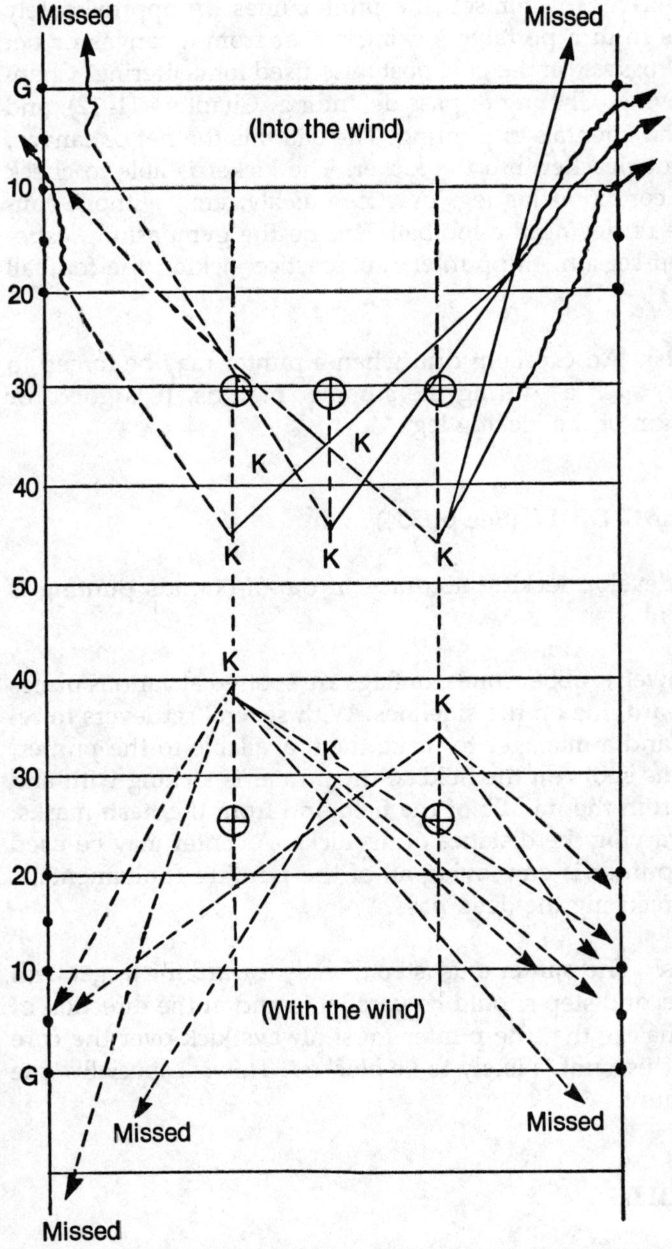

DRILL 11

• Denotes towel, rubber cone, or flag on the sideline (later punter should focus on sideline markers for his target).

DRILL 12

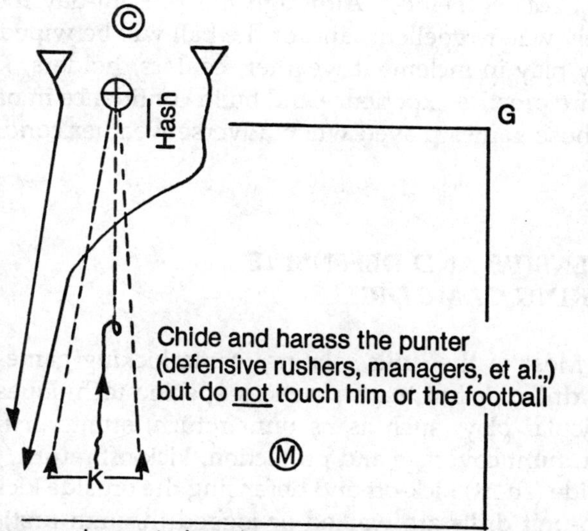

Most pressure is exerted on the punter when he must kick from deep in his own end zone, standing near the backline, especially if he cannot get the required depth of 13 yds. (tight punt formation must be utilized), and he receives an off-target pass from his center. Center-purposely on occasions, snap a one-bounce pass, and low, high, wide, and/or floater passes.)

should continue with his kicking despite shouting and veering linemen; despite the coach throwing his cap in front of the kicker just as he is ready to punt the football; despite receiving a high, low, wide, or bouncing pass from the center, etc. No one should push or touch the kicker, knock the football out of his hands or actually attempt to block the punt when they are applying "pressure."

Coaching Points: Stand in front of the punter by the center and check to see if his eyes are "skipping" after he receives the snap. Use a stopwatch to time the kick: the snap from center, seven-tenths of a second; kicker, one-and-three-tenths seconds, with punter standing at a depth of thirteen yards; overall time, two seconds. The drills are of little value if the kicker violates the principles and fundamentals of good punting.

13. WET FOOTBALL DRILL

Purpose: To teach the center and punter both to handle a wet football.

Procedure: Immerse a football in a bucket of water every so often and practice centering and punting a wet football.

Coaching Points: Although the present-day football is almost completely water repellent, and/or the ball will be wiped off or exchanged on every play in inclement weather, centers, holders, kickers, et al., should acquire practice experience and build confidence in handling a wet football for those games played when adverse weather conditions prevail.

OFFENSIVE AND DEFENSIVE KICKING GAME DRILLS

Most of the drills relating to the kicking game are situational team-unit drills. A full team practices specific techniques, just as if it were a particular play, such as its punt return, stunts or frame-up to block the punt, punt coverage and protection, kick-off return, kick-off coverage, the on-side (short) kick-off and defensing the on-side kick. Typically, complete team-unit drills are walked or jogged through first; then there may be a controlled "live" scrimmage under game-simulated conditions in order to get proper timimg and quasi-execution, while minimizing the possibility of sustaining unnecessary injuries. Kicking game drills that involve the entire team follow.

14–15. PROPER PUNT ALIGNMENT AND PROTECTION (BLOCKING RULES) DRILLS

14. Tight Punt Alignment and Protection Drills

15. Spread Punt Alignment and Protection Drills

Purpose: To teach offensive players to line up properly in (14) tight punt formation and (15) spread punt formation, getting their proper line splits, and applying their blocking rules correctly.

Procedure: This is a "show and tell" drill in that the offensive team lines up in (14) tight punt formation or (15) spread punt formation (the one indicated by the coach, i.e., inside its own three-yard line a team usually goes into a tight punt formation). From a semi-upright position every offensive player points out whom he is going to block. The defenders should move around and gang up in an attempt to confuse the offensive blockers in the application of their blocking rules. The drill is dummy initially, and if a rusher is not blocked he yells "Here," so the blocking rules can be checked and the coach can determine who failed to apply his blocking rule properly and how the rusher was able to break through freely.

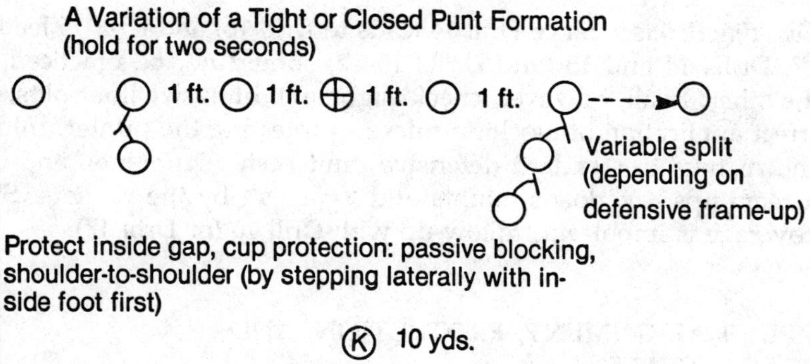

DRILL 14

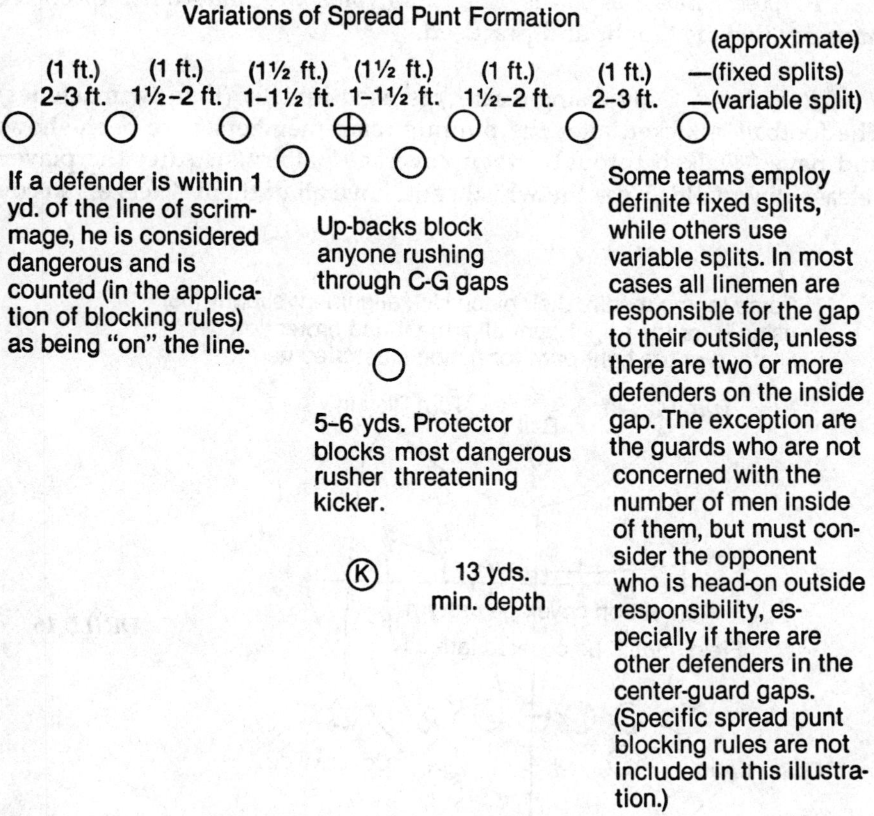

DRILL 15

Coaching Points: Since Drill 14 leads to Drill 16, and Drill 15 leads to Drill 17, Drills 14 and 15 (and Drills 16–17) should not be practiced one after the other. In all, however, check alignment, offensive line splits, and the correct application of blocking rules in protecting the punter. Initially limit the rushers to standard defensive punt rush alignments, and then permit team-ups, overloads, stunts and "games" by the rushers. Since punt coverage is important, follow-up with Drill 16 (or Drill 17).

16–17. PUNT ALIGNMENT, PROTECTION, AND COVERAGE DRILLS

16. Tight Punt Coverage Drill

17. Spread Punt Coverage Drill

Purpose: Same as Drills 14 and 15, plus the importance of correct punt coverage is taught and practiced.

Procedure: Only a single safety is used initially (then twin safeties). The football is kicked after the punting team members have been shown and have "walked through" their coverage pattern(s). After the players release downfield, blow the whistle and have all of them "freeze" so cov-

Some teams modify their place kick alignment slightly (36) using it for their tight punt alignment and protection (instead of the tight punt formation illustrated here).

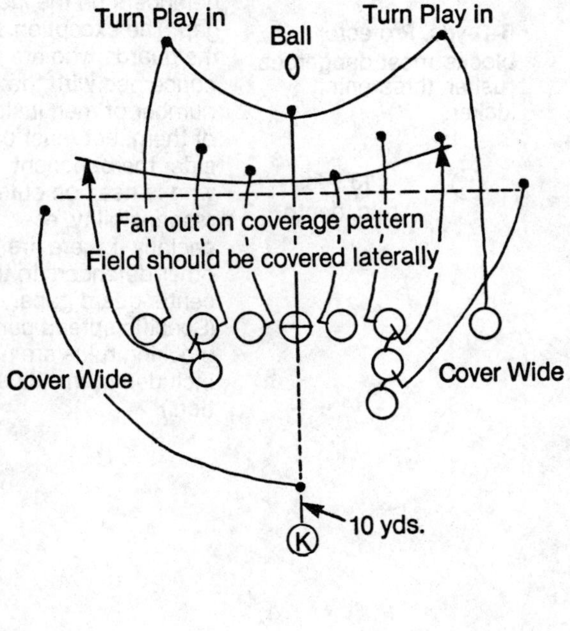

DRILL 16

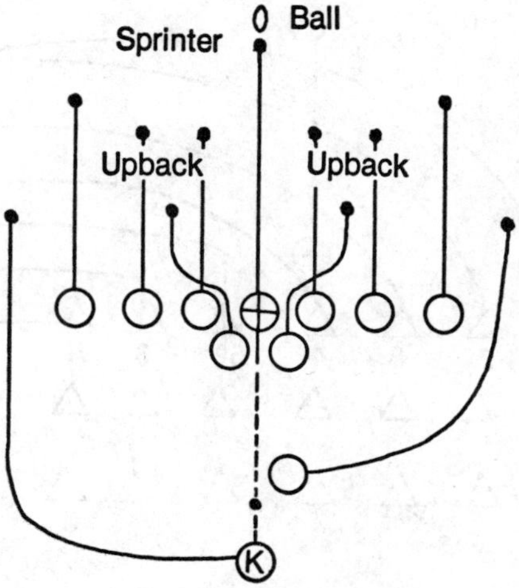

DRILL 17

erage patterns can be checked. Add defensive linemen, same as in Drills 14–15, so the blockers must apply their protection rules and then cover the punts. Finally practice Drill 16 (or 17) "live," with additional practice time being devoted to the spread punt rather than to the tight punt since it will be used more often in a game.

Coaching Points: Stress the importance of punt defense, i.e., not permitting a punt to be blocked, yet limiting the runback of the punt by not leaving a void in the coverage pattern for the ball carrier to pop through returning the punt.

18. DOWN 10-AND-IN PUNT COVERAGE DRILL

Purpose: To discipline players to cover and down punts before the football goes into the end zone, and to use as a conditioner.

Procedure: Depending on the ability of your punter, the football is placed on the 30- (35, 40) yard line, with the punter at his regular position thirteen yards deep in spread punt formation. When the center passes the ball to the punter, the line releases with the ultimate objective of downing the football in the field of play *before* it goes into the end zone for an automatic touchback. The punter attempts to kick the ball close to the goal line. However, he cannot stall in his punting, and he must punt the football within two seconds duration (overall). A manager (coach) stands near the goal line and will whistle the football dead if it goes over the goal line into the end zone before it has been touched. The players then fan to the sidelines and jog back as another group is ready to go. The squad must

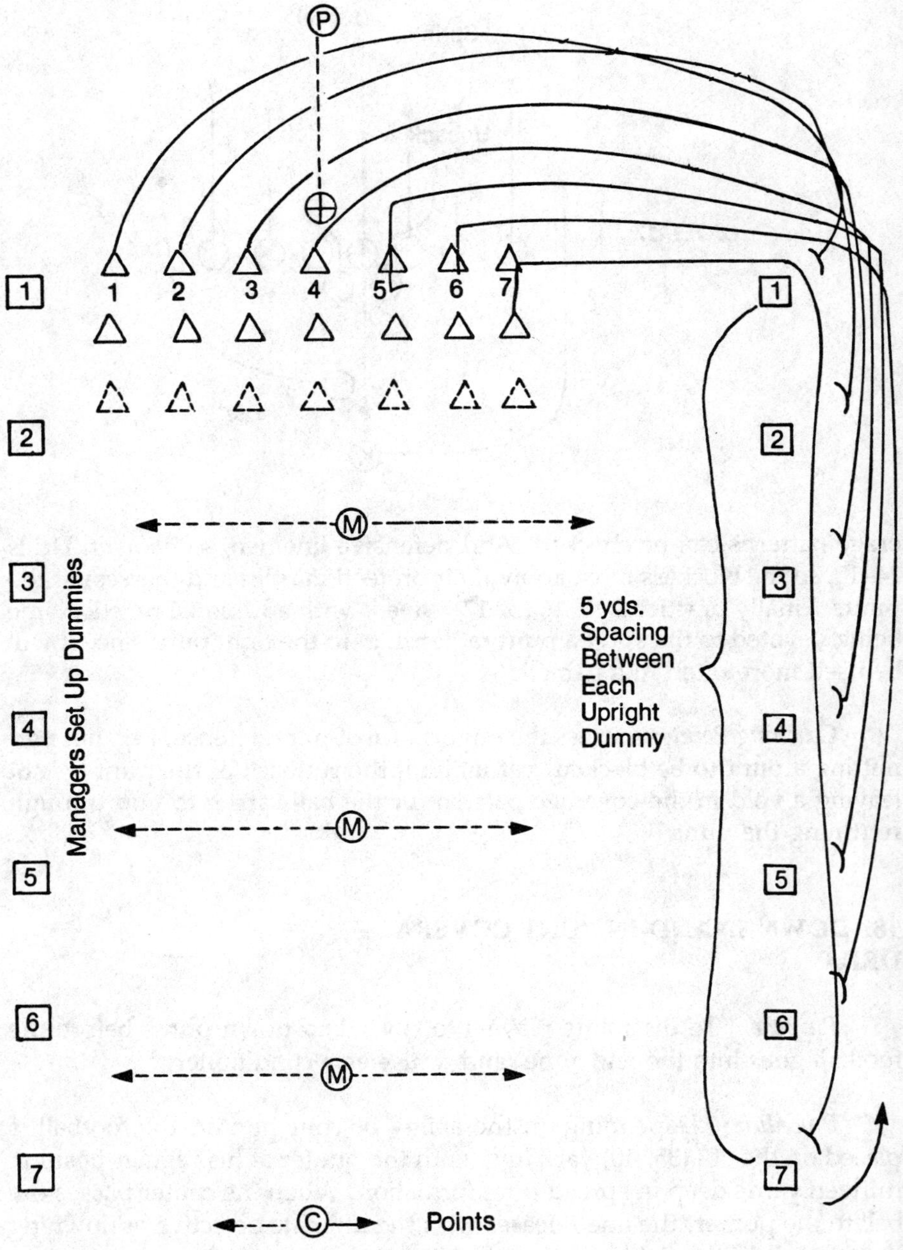
P
1
2
3
4
5
6
7
1
2
3
4
5
6
7
Managers Set Up Dummies
M
M
M
5 yds.
Spacing
Between
Each
Upright
Dummy
1
2
3
4
5
6
7
C
Points

DRILL 19

keep going until a total of ten punts have been downed in the field of play near the goal line.

Coaching Points: Use a stopwatch. The punter must get his punt off within two seconds or it does not count. The whistle signals the next group is ready to go. Stress hustle and hard running to cover the punts. (This is a good drill to finish practice with as players must down ten punts before the squad can leave the practice field.)

19. PUNT RETURN-UPRIGHT DUMMIES DRILL

Purpose: To teach and practice punt return techniques and responsibilities for the defenders at the line of scrimmage.

Procedure: Seven upright dummies are placed five yards apart on the hash marks at both sides of the field. Seven rushers line up in their positions opposite the punter (passer) on the defensive side of the line of scrimmage. On the snap of the football all seven cross the line of scrimmage and as soon as the football is passed (the drill is better controlled when the football is not punted), the defenders break laterally for the nearest upright dummy on the hash mark on the side indicated by the coach ("Right," "Left") and peel-off setting up their blocking wall. The lead blocker (the one nearest the side of the return) will block the furthest upright dummy downfield, and the rusher furthest away from the side of the return will take the dummy nearest the line of scrimmage (the last one in the chain). Each should block a designated dummy, coming back *toward* the line of scrimmage.

Coaching Points: Check to make certain each man blocks his designated upright dummy, driving his head in front as he comes back *toward* the line of scrimmage, otherwise he will clip illegally. No dummies should remain upright, and after a blocker throws and rolls, he should get up and lead. The second line moves up and is ready to simulate the return to the opposite side, while the first line of rushers return to await their turn again, and managers set up the dummies. Alternate sides, left and right.

20. PUNT RETURN DRILLS

Purpose: To practice specific punt return patterns as an entire unit.

Procedure: Indicate punt return alignment(s) and walk the team through the specific return(s). Initially offensive players should not release

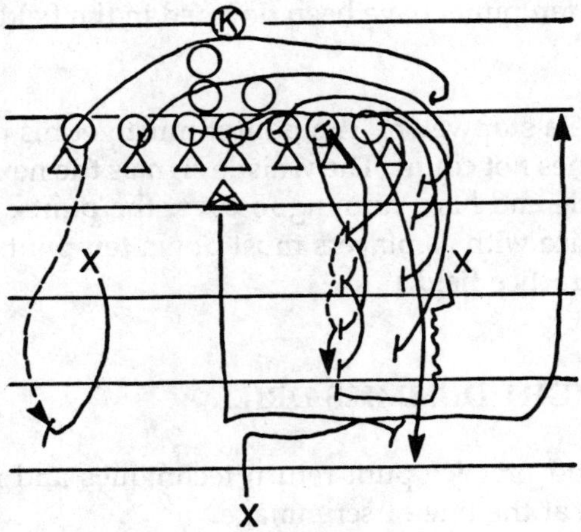

a. Return Right

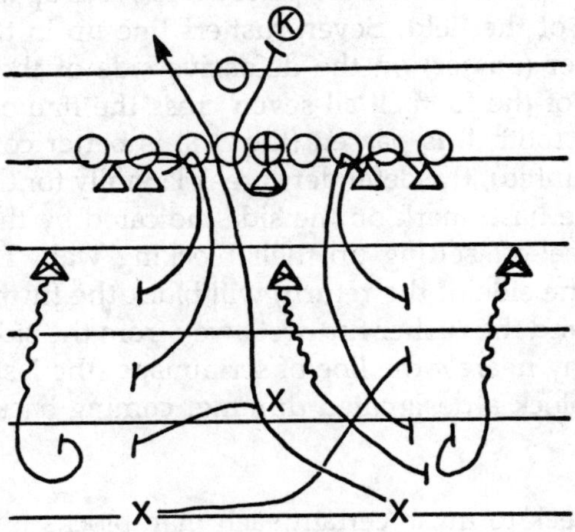

b. Middle Return

from the line of scrimmage, although the defensive players should sprint full speed, simulating there is punt coverage as they peel, set up the wall, exchange (or fake exchange) the football, etc. Use discretion if the drills are live, although they should be controlled because of the reasons mentioned previously. (Some coaches never practice live punt returns, but their teams still do well in games.)

Coaching Points: Stress not being offside, not clipping illegally, not roughing the kicker, and not permitting the football to strike the ground. Also stress setting up the wall, and having the ball carrier bring the pursuers to the wall in setting up their blocks. The blocker's head should go in front of the pursuer, so not to clip him.

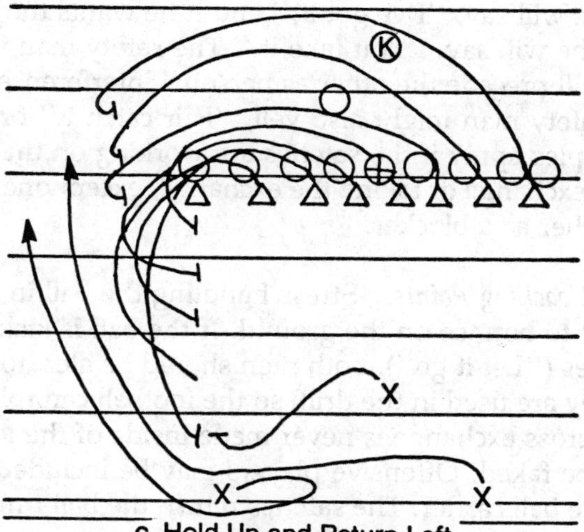

DRILL 20

c. Hold Up and Return Left

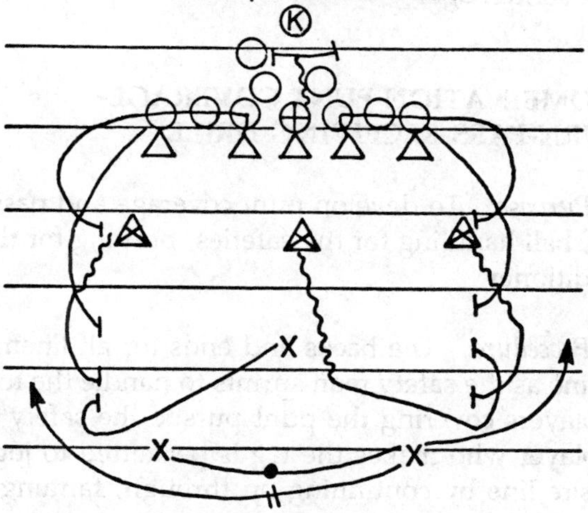

(Man with football goes in front and either fakes or gives hand-back exchange.)

d. Return Is Set Up to Both Sides

21. TWIN SAFETIES PUNT RETURN DRILL

Purpose: To develop handling the ball on a punt return, and to practice the techniques of the criss-cross exchange or faking the exchange.

Procedure: Two safety men are positioned twelve to fifteen yards apart at the ten-yard line, with the other safeties standing in the end zone ready to take their turn. The football is punted and the player at left safety *always* indicates who is to handle the football. If he is going to handle the ball he will say, "I've got it," and if he wants the right safety to catch the punt he will say, "You take it." The safety man who is not handling the ball will precede the other as personal interference and block for him. The left safety man might also yell, "Fair catch it" or "Let it go." The same principles apply if the safeties are working on the techniques of the criss-cross exchange or faking the exchange, except one safety does not precede the other as a blocker.

Coaching Points: Stress handling the ball in the air, and not permitting it to bounce on the ground. If the ball is kicked over the head of the safeties ("Let it go"), both men should be alert to block covering linemen (if they are used in the drill) so the football can roll into the end zone. The criss-cross exchange is never made inside of the ten-yard line, although it may be faked. Offensive players may be included in the drill to tackle or tag the ball carrier. The safeties return the ball running at full speed to the line of scrimmage.

22. COMBINATION PUNT COVERAGE-RETURN-PASS RECEIVING DRILL

Purpose: To develop punt coverage and pass receiving for ends and backs, ball handling for the safeties, punting for the kickers, and to use as a conditioner.

Procedure: The backs and ends (or all linemen) cover the punt two at a time as the safety man sprints to handle the football and return it. The two players covering the punt pursue the safety man until he is tagged. The player who makes the tag is permitted to jog back to the end of the opposite line by continuing on through, fanning wide to clear the area.

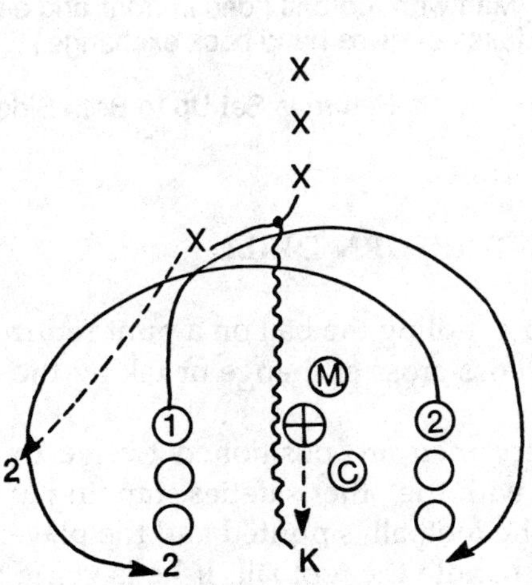

DRILL 22

The player who did not make the tag also continues to fan wide, but he must sprint hard and attempt to catch the pass that will be thrown to him by the safety man. The latter stops when he is tagged, passes the football quickly, turns and clears the area by sprinting back to the end of the line of safety men. The pass receiver returns the football to the center and goes to the end of the line opposite from where he started. In the meantime the ball has been punted again, and two more players are covering the punt.

Coaching Points: Stress hustle and hard running. Keep the downfield area clear, insisting that players fan wide after making the tag. Check the center's snap and the punter's fundamentals. A coach downfield should check the safety man handling the punt, and the players covering the kick.

23. PUNTING-CONDITIONING SQUAD DRILL

Purpose: To develop the fundamentals of the offensive and defensive punting game, and as a conditioner for the entire squad.

DRILL 23

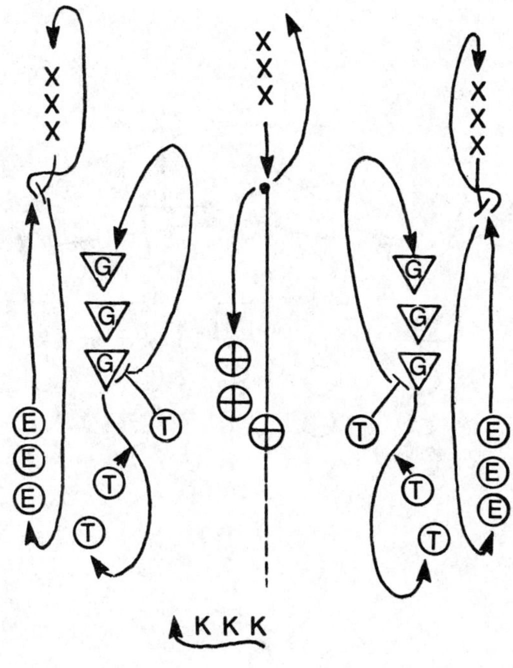

Procedure: The center snaps the ball and covers down the middle. The safety man handles the punt, sprints toward the center and gives him the football. The center carries the ball back to his position. The safety man sprints to the end of his line to wait another turn. The tackles bump the guards, who are on defense rushing the punter, and then cover on each side of the center downfield. Guards and tackles replace one another so that the guards become blockers and cover the punt downfield, and the tackles become rushers. The ends cover the punt from the outside, and will be bumped by the backs who get in position to protect and block for the safety man. The ends replace the backs, and the latter sprint foward to replace the ends. Use only the best punters, who should attempt to kick the ball straight down the middle. If the football is kicked to a (side)back, he handles the punt and the safety man bumps the covering end. Then both men return to their original positions.

Coaching Points: Stress all phases of the kicking game, with one coach working with the centers and kickers, another with the interior linemen, and a third coach with the ends and the defensive secondary.

24. PUNT COVERAGE-RETURN-TACKLE DRILL

Purpose: To develop the fundamentals of the offensive and defensive punting game, including tackling in the open field.

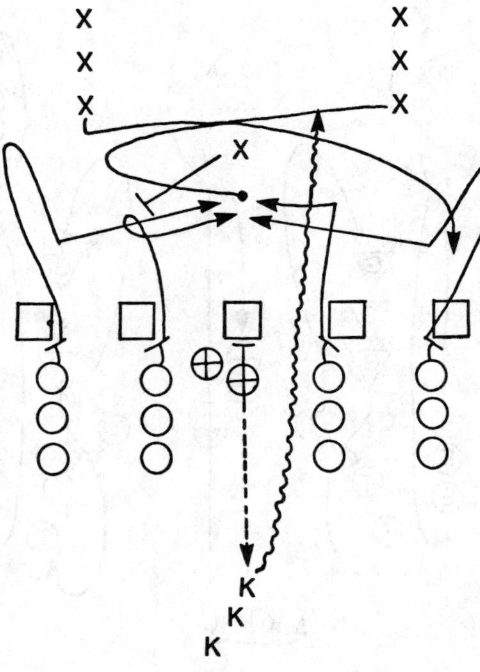

DRILL 24

Procedure: Ends (and backs if deployed on the ends of the offensive line in punt formation) cover from the outside, while the interior linemen cover the punt from the inside, after blocking upright dummies. The defensive secondary is in a 1–2 setup, with the middle man calling for and handling short high punts, and blocking for the twin safety man on kicks that go over his head. The left safety indicates which man will handle the punt, as in (21) Twin Safeties Drill, and beforehand indicates whether a criss-cross exchange will be made, faked or not executed at all. If not executed at all, then the safety not handling the punt blocks for his teammate. The covering players must take proper angles and tackle the ball carrier, who will attempt to avoid the tacklers and return the football to the line of scrimmage.

Coaching Points: The linemen should slam into the bags hard, meeting firm resistance, to give the safeties an opportunity to handle the punt. Stress proper pursuit and open-field tackling (Chapter 13). Stress all phases of the kicking game, with one coach checking the center-kicker fundamentals, and another the line blocking, coverage, pursuit and tackling. The third coach will handle the defensive secondary.

25–26. INDIVIDUALLY BLOCKING THE KICK DRILLS

25. Blocking the Punt Drill

26. Blocking the Placement Attempt Drill

Purpose: To teach selected rushers how to successfully block (25) the punt and (26) the placement attempt, without roughing the kicker and sustaining a penalty.

Procedure: Use properly marked off "lines" showing offensive punt and placement attempt (field goal and point-after-touchdown) alignment spacing, so rushers (selected personnel) will be placed in the correct lateral position to rush from the corner(s). Explain and illustrate the kicker's alley or path that must be protected offensively, and which must be penetrated by the rusher if the kick attempt is to be blocked. The rusher goes for a "spot" that is slightly in front of where the kicker's foot will meet the football. He must lay out vertically with his body, arms, and hands fully extended in an attempt to "snatch" the football off the kicker's foot. If he is coming on an inside rush, the rusher must go for a spot approximately four yards in front of where the punter lined up, not directly at him, and lay out at a 45° angle with the ground, extending the arms and hands outward (not straight up in the air).

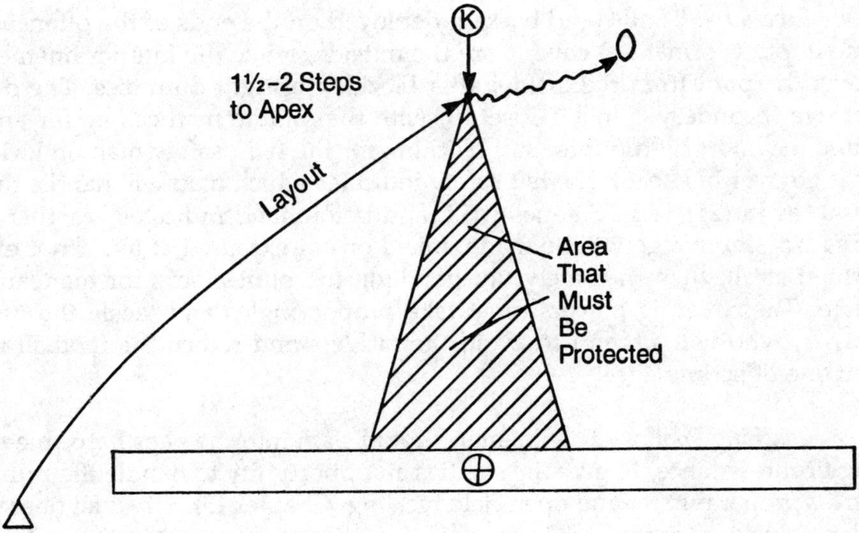

DRILL 25

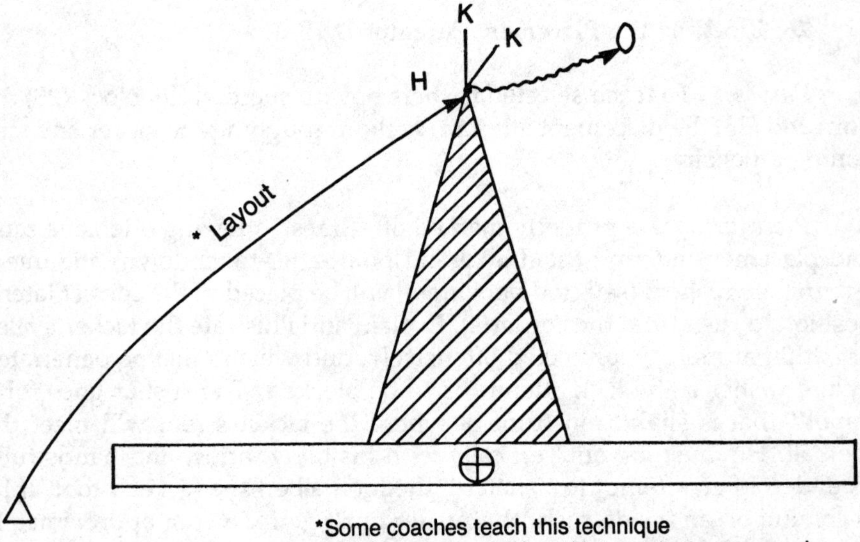

*Some coaches teach this technique utilizing a large mat in order to evaluate personnel.

DRILL 26

Coaching Points: Blocking a kick is mostly desire and determination. Work only with those who display these attributes. If the rusher does not block the kick, he should do all that is possible not to crash into the kicker (or holder). If the kick is blocked on any down except fourth down, fall on it and get possession of the football; on fourth down, scoop it up and run with it (for a score).

27–28. TEAM SCHEMES BLOCKING THE KICK DRILLS

27. Schemes for Blocking the Punt Drill

28. Schemes for Blocking the Placement Attempt Drill

Purpose: To coordinate the defensive schemes to successfully block the kick.

DRILL 27a

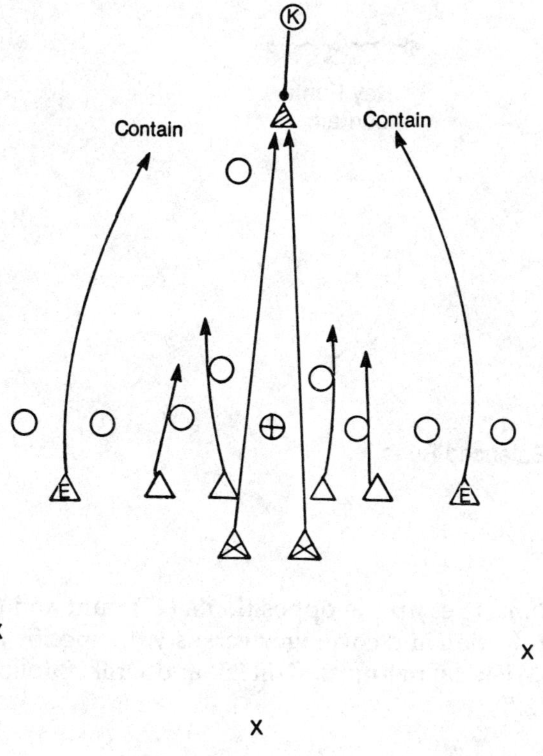

a. 8-man Balanced Rush

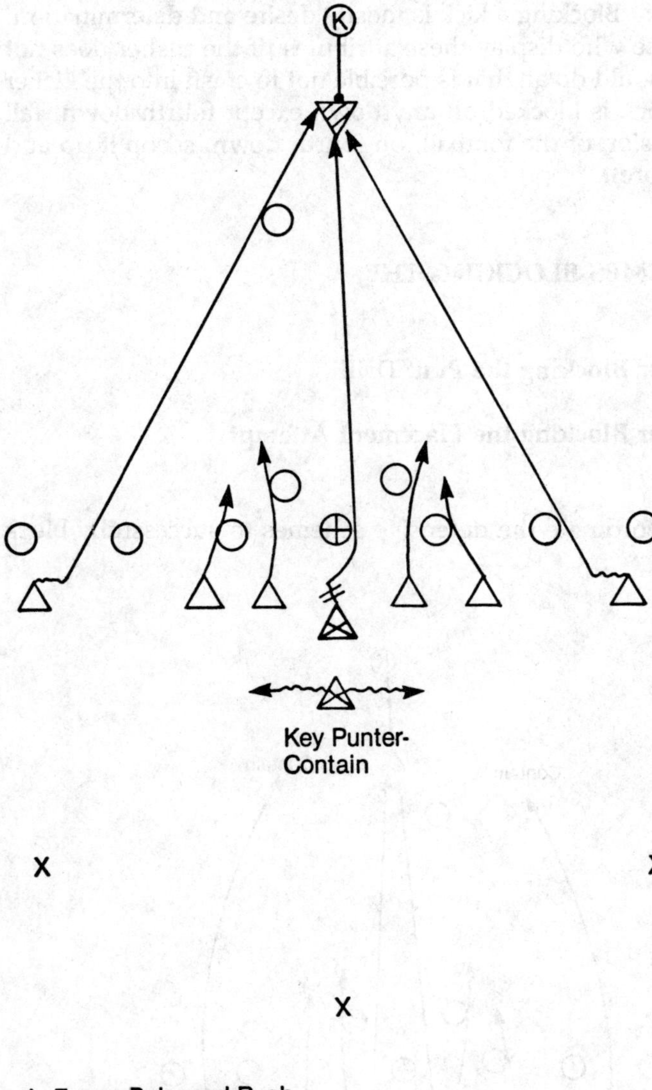

DRILL 27b

b. 7-man Balanced Rush

Procedure: Set up the opposition's (27) punt and (28) place kick formations, protection and coverages versus your specific rushes to block the kick. Drill 27 is a follow-up to Drill 25, and Drill 28 follows Drill 26. These can be "live."

Coaching Points: Same as Drills 25–26.

Drill 27c

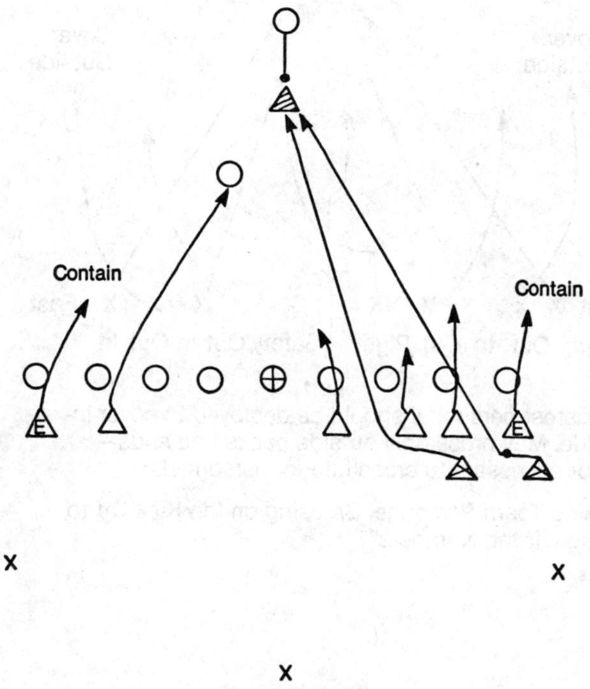

c. 8-man Rush, Overload Right

29–31. KICK-OFF ALIGNMENT AND COVERAGE DRILLS

29. Regular Kick-Off Alignment and Coverage Drills

30. Kicking-Off from the Hash Mark Drill

31. Recovering the Short (On-Side) Kick Drill

Purpose: To align properly on a kick-off (29) from the center of the field or (30) from a hash mark in order to kick deep or short, and to cover correctly to minimize the runback; (31) to attempt to recover possession of the football on the kick-off.

Procedure: In (29) regular alignment and coverage, all men are expected to sprint full speed, with the exception of the trailing safety. Their natural speed, or the lack of it, will take care of "waves" in covering kick-offs. Each man protects his own territory, and then pursues the shortest path to the ball carrier. Since the receiving team is likely to "count off"

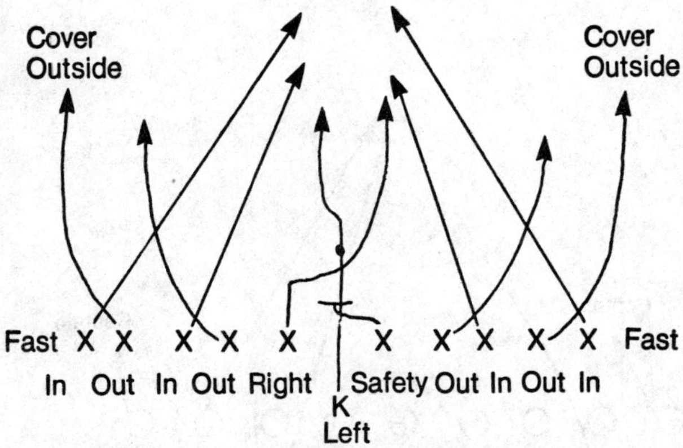

DRILL 29

Fastest personnel should be deployed to cover inside. May cross only outside backs and ends—not necessary to cross interior personnel.

Kicking Team Personnel Crossing on the Kick-Off to "Take Off the Numbers"

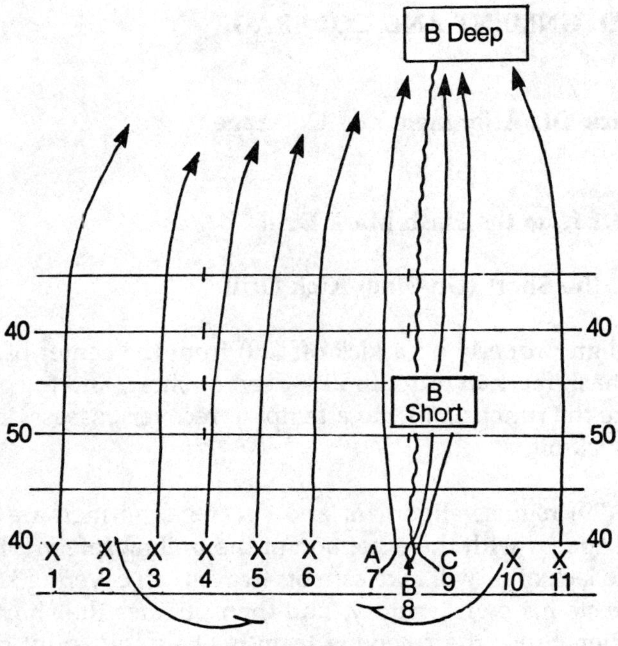

DRILL 30a

a. Kicking-Off Deep (or Short) from the Hash Mark

DRILL 30b

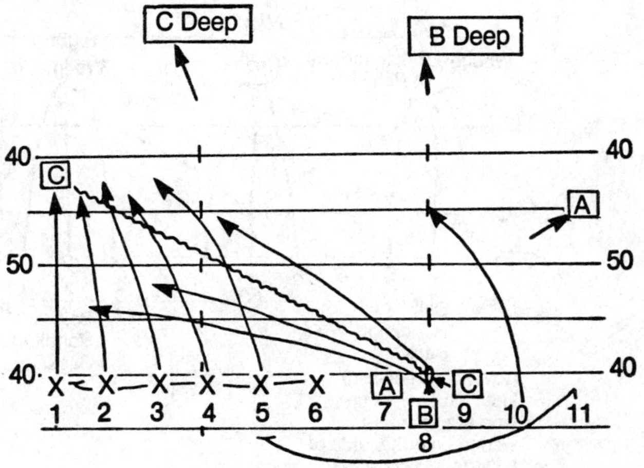

b. Attempting to Recover the Football on the Kick to the Open-Side of the Field.

DRILL 30c

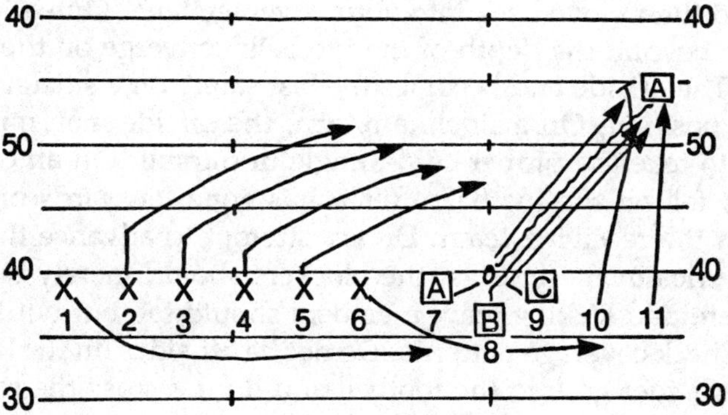

c. Attempting to Recover the Football on the Kick to the Closed-Side of the Field.

Do not allow ball to go out of bounds

the kicking team personnel as it positions itself in alignment, the illustration in (29) is an example of how the kicking team can "take off the numbers." In Drills 30–31 personnel are positioned to get faster coverage and limit the runback on the return. Drill 30 includes the possibility of regaining possession of the football, which is the primary purpose in Drill 31.

Coaching Points: Stay in covering lanes relative to the football. Sprint full speed, unless designated as a safety or trailer; break stride as a blocker approaches and then turn it on again. The depth of the ball determines

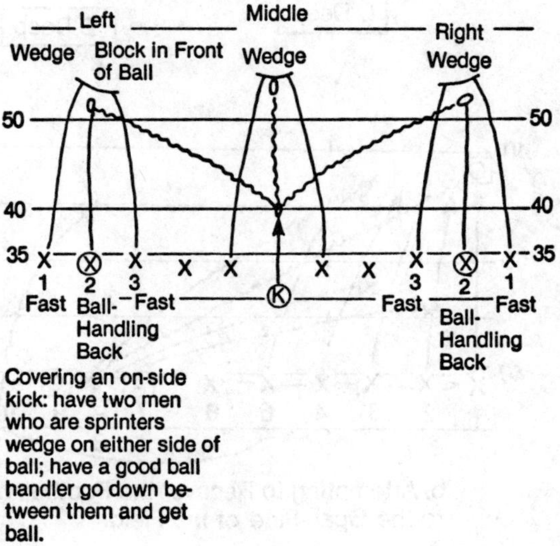

DRILL 31

whether you run through a blocker, if not designated to go into the wedge, or whether you run around the blocker (everyone always does so to the right) and then move back into your coverage lane. Out-side men should not cover beyond the depth of the football; converge on the ball from the outside. The offside end becomes the last safety on a sideline return away from his position. On a sideline return, the offside men must be taught-coached to take the proper cutoff angle in pursuit. On an on-side (short) kick (31), fall on the football after it has gone ten yards or has struck a player on the receiving team. Do *not* attempt to advance the football. To avoid injuries in these drills, the blockers should merely tag their designated men, and kicking team members should tag but not tackle the ball carrier. Check coverage patterns. Do not be off-sides on the kick-off; watch the kicker's foot go into the football and do not cross the restraining line until the kicker's foot contacts the ball.

32–34. KICK-OFF ALIGNMENTS AND RETURN DRILLS

32. Wedge (Middle) Return Drill (Usually Considered as a Middle Return)

33. Middle (Cross-Block) and Sideline Return Drills (See pp. 356–357)

34. Defensing the Short (On-Side) Kick Drill (See p. 358)

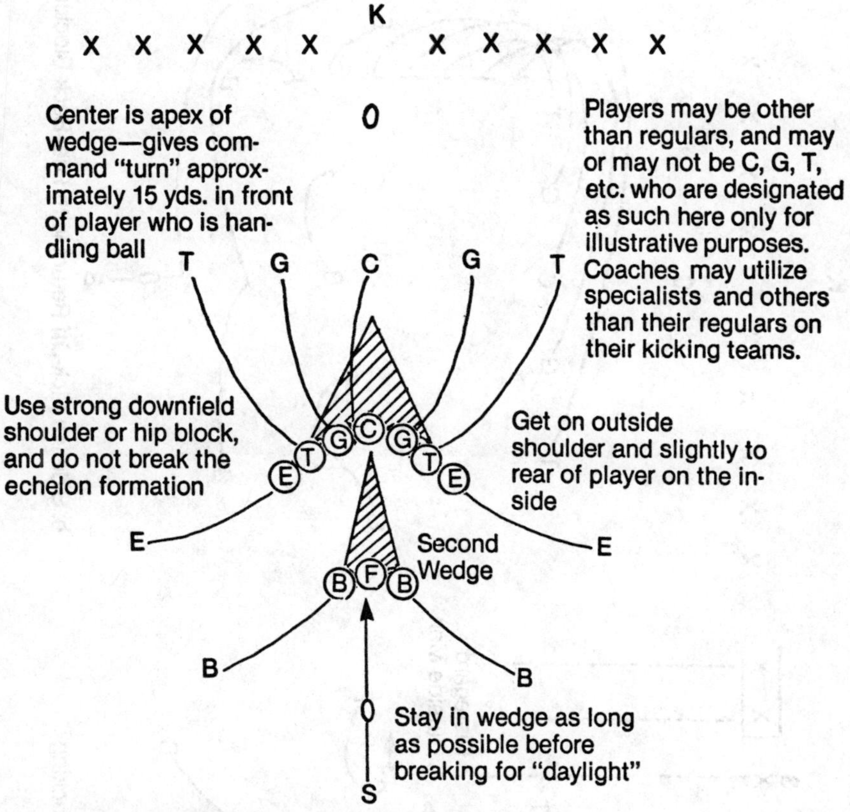

Returning the Kick-off with Wedge Blocking

DRILL 32

Purpose: To align properly, to secure possession of the football (especially in Drill 34), and to gain the maximum yardage on the return (Drills 32–33).

Procedure: Walk through the returns so your players understand the theory of what each specific return is designed to accomplish: (32) wedge in front of the football regardless of where it is handled in-bounds; (33) converging players on a middle return are cross-blocked from the inside-out, and on the sideline returns most are blocked from outside-in, with

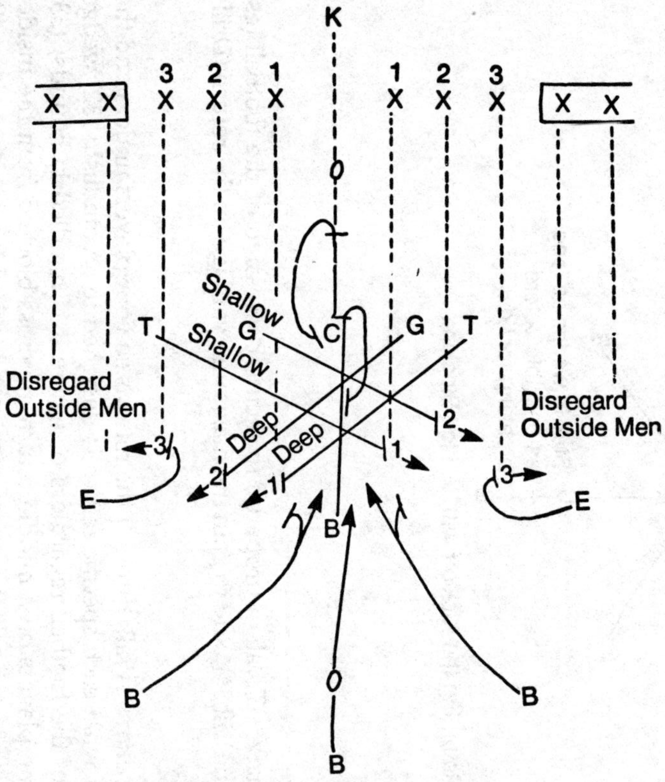

a. Kick-Off Return Using Cross-Blocking

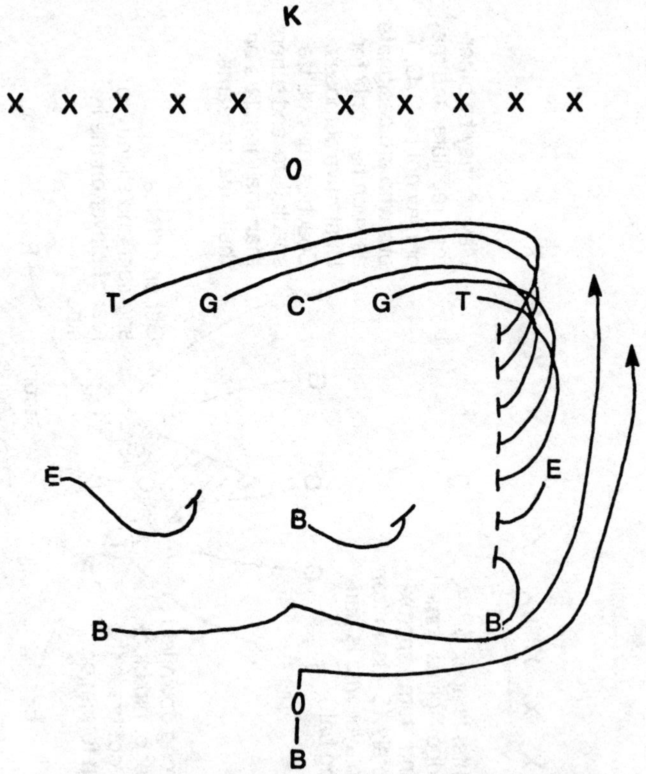

b. Sideline Kick-Off Return with Peel-Back Blocking

DRILL 33

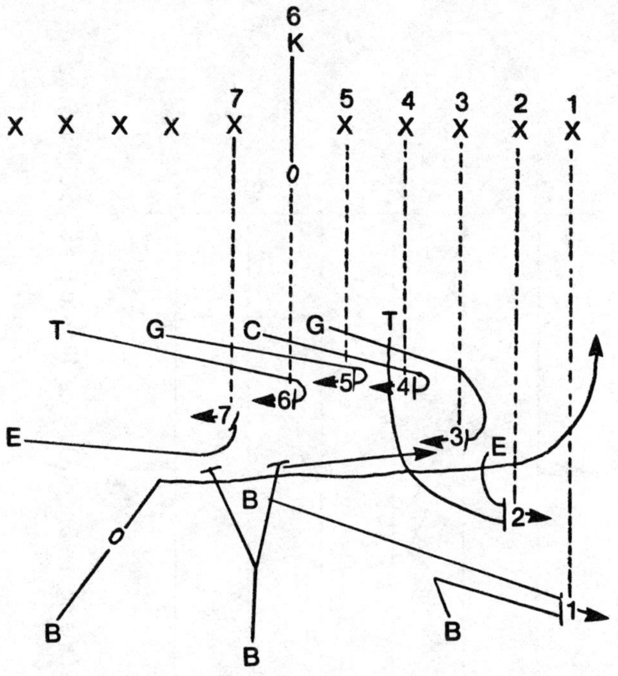

c. A Sideline Return Employing Two Double-Team Blocks

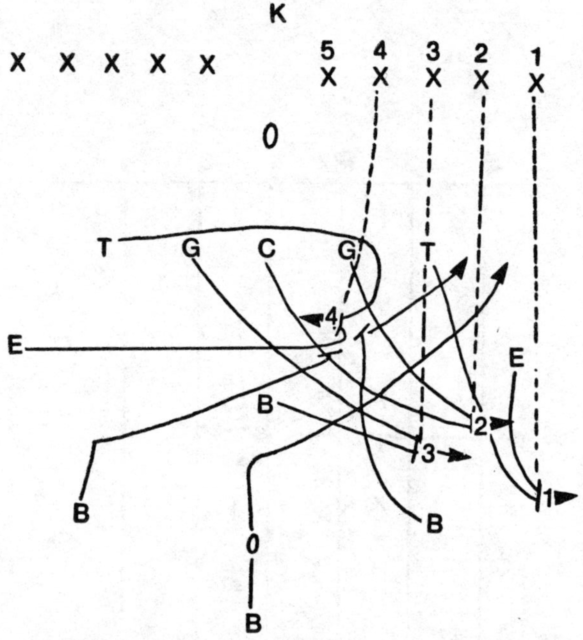

d. A Sideline Kick-Off Return Employing Four Double-Team Blocks

DRILL 33 (continued)

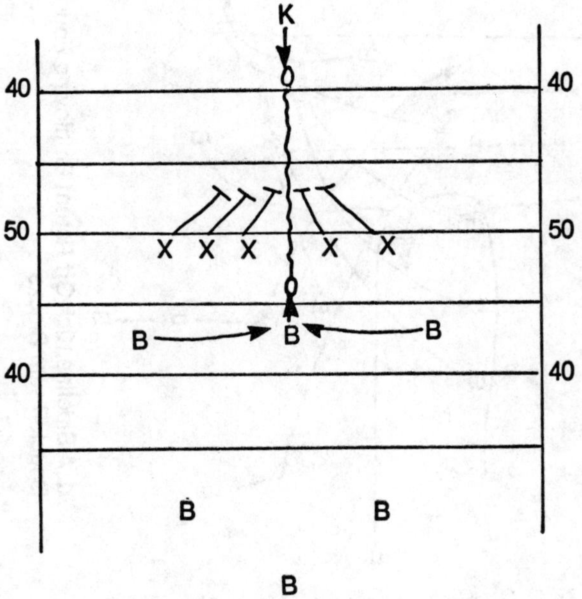

a. Defensing the Short (On-Side) Kick Down the Middle

DRILL 34

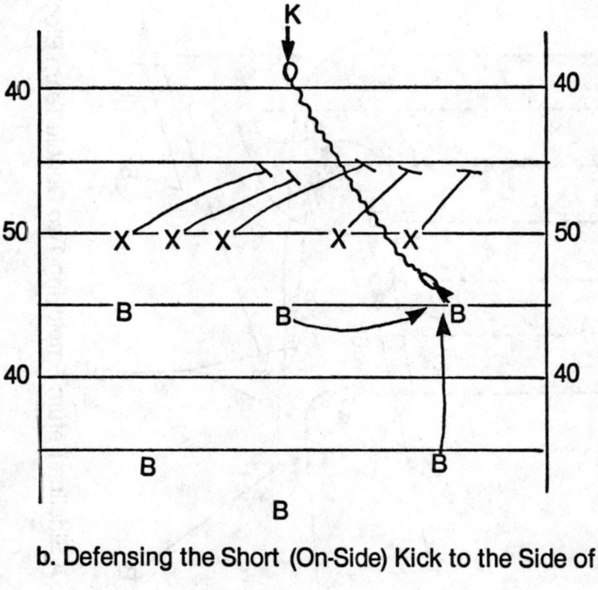

b. Defensing the Short (On-Side) Kick to the Side of the Field certain players designated to be blocked out; (34) to obtain possession of the football.

Coaching Points: Do not let the football hit the ground. One player calls for and handles the football. If cross-blocking is being employed, know the man whom you are to block. If the ball is kicked from the hash mark, locate the sixth player who is designated as the kicker and then count off locating your man. Be certain who goes shallow (deep) when crossing. If peeling for a sideline return, coaching points are the same as in Drills 19–20. Do not align incorrectly or be off-side. Do not touch or cross the restraining lines until the kicker's foot touches the football, or the receiving team will sustain a penalty. In Drill 34 fall on the football if it comes to or touches a player in the front line; *do not try to advance the football.* If the ball is kicked high and short, and has not touched the ground, fair catch the football.

DRILLS FOR THE PLACE KICKER

The success of the place kicking specialist depends primarily on his desire to be proficient, and the necessary practice to reach this goal. To gain a high degree of proficiency, the place kicker at the high school level in particular must do much of his practicing in the off-season. Drills for the place kicker are merely a matter of practicing the fundamentals and techniques of his specialty.

35. PLACE KICKING DRILLS

Purpose: To develop place kicking fundamentals and techniques.

Procedure: The center, holder, and place kicker line up in position. Retrievers return the footballs to the center. Practice the fundamentals of place kicking, including (8) Walk-Through Drill, (10) Self-Retrieving Drill, (12) Pressure Drills.

Coaching Points: Stress the correct fundamentals of place kicking, including passing and spotting the football on the tee. A well-executed place kick should take from one-and-one-tenth seconds to one-and-three-tenths seconds. The holder spots the ball on the kicking tee, which has been placed seven yards from the line of scrimmage by the kicker. An inaccurate pass from the center to the holder will not only pull the holder, who is on one knee away from the tee, but will disrupt the timing of the play.

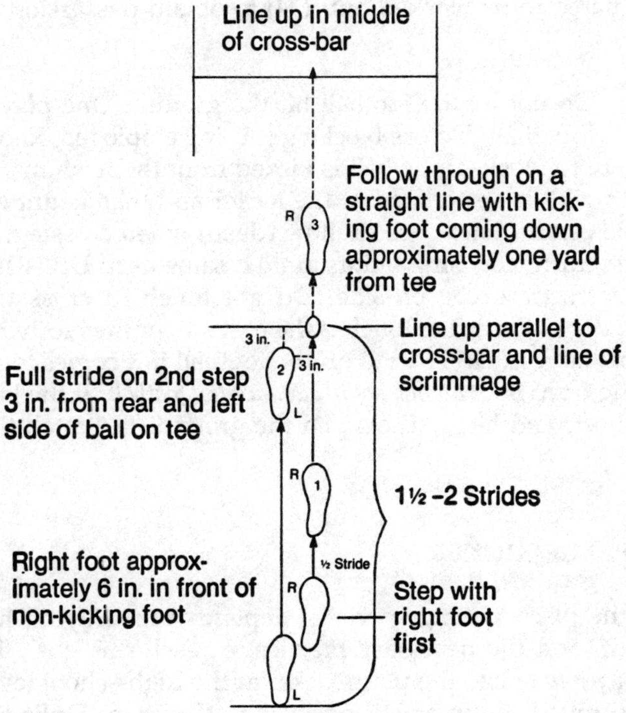

The Place Kicker's Steps
(Right-Footed Kicker)

DRILL 35

36. ALIGNMENT, PROTECTION (AND COVERAGE) PLACE KICK DRILL

Coverage on the field goal attempt would be similar to (16) Tight Punt Coverage Drill (illustrated).

Purpose: To practice the proper alignment, protection (and coverage) on the attempted place kick.

Procedure: The players in the offensive line must align themselves with the rear tip of the football. Each is responsible for the inside gap. The wingbacks are responsible for the inside gap on their side. Most coaches favor passive protection, i.e., merely wall protection permitting the defensive rushers to come to the blockers. On the snap of the ball, which is passed "at will," every blocker except the offensive center will step first with his inside foot toward his inside gap, square up, tail low, into a high pass blocking position.

DRILL 36

Protection for the Place Kick. On the field goal attempt, coverage is similar to (16) Tight Punt Coverage Drill.

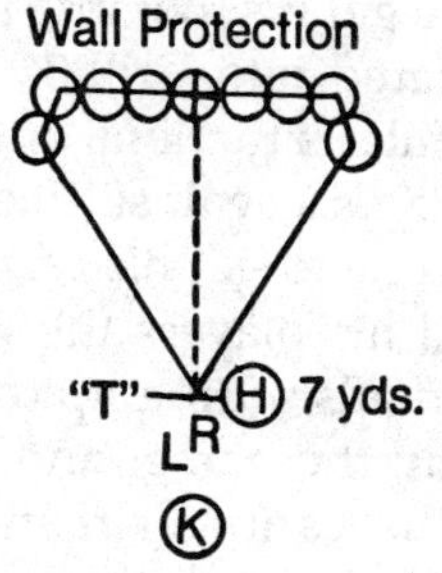

Coaching Points: Show the blockers the most vulnerable areas that must be protected, usually the inside gaps between the center and guards and those between the ends and wingbacks. Then set up standard rushes, and later load-ups and "games" attempting to block the field goal attempt. A player should never be off-side on a place kicking attempt. Emphasize and practice coverage on the field goal attempt in order to minimize a return. Stress that a place kicker is of little value if his teammates do not give him adequate protection to perform his specialty successfully.

ADDITIONAL SITUATIONAL KICKING GAME DRILLS

After the punters and place kickers have practiced their specialties individually and in combinations where several others are involved, they must practice with the team so there is a coordinated cohesive effort taking into consideration situational variables. As an example, a team may wish to include plays and passes from punt and place kick formations. A team *must* be drilled to defend against these tactics, as well as an early down (usually third down) kicking alignment when the defending team is uncertain whether the opposition is going to punt or not punt the football. (One must be in a sound alignment to defense the run and pass, and yet be able to handle the kick safely.) Also, there are situations when you cannot have an all-out rush to block the punt or place kick, but some pressure must be exerted. Conversely, there are some situations when from a defensive standpoint these must be an all-out rush to block the kick and gain possession of the football. From an offensive standpoint a team had better practice protecting and handling the ten-man rush, rather than being faced with it unexpectedly for the first time in a game.

In addition to practicing the fake field goal offensively and defending against it, a team should be drilled on making something positive happen when there is a mishandled or errant center snap, and the kicker does not have the opportunity to get his foot into the ball. Such a situational variable can easily be incorporated into Drill 36. Drills can be modified or others devised to practice similar situations offensively and defensively.

While coaching is a race against time, and probably no coach ever feels that he has sufficient time to get his team ready to play, a coach must use his time wisely to drill his players the way he wants them to perform in the game. Coaching entails setting up those situations in practice that will confront a team during the game, and then drilling players so they can react instinctively to the various situations. This not only requires time, but wise planning and adroit decision making, which usually results in effective coaching.

In conclusion, this book will have accomplished its purpose if it saves the coach time, aids him in the planning, selection and use of drills, and if it helps him coach more effectively and efficiently.